W9-DDI-596

ENEMIES OF FREEDOM

BOB ALTEMEYER

FOREWORD BY M. BREWSTER SMITH

ENEMIES OF FREEDOM

Understanding Right-Wing Authoritarianism

Jossey-Bass Publishers
San Francisco • London • 1988

ENEMIES OF FREEDOM
Understanding Right-Wing Authoritarianism
by Bob Altemeyer

Library of Congress Cataloging-in-Publication Data

Altemeyer, Bob, date.
Enemies of freedom.

(Jossey-Bass social and behavioral science series)
(Jossey-Bass public administration series)
Bibliography: p.
Includes index.
1. Authoritarianism. 2. Conservatism. I. Title.
II. Series. III. Series: Jossey-Bass public administration series.
HM271.A457 1988 303.3′6 88-42774
ISBN 1-55542-097-4 (alk. paper)

Manufactured in the United States of America

The paper in this book meets the guidelines for permanence and durability of the Committee on Production Guidelines for Book Longevity of the Council on Library Resources.

JACKET DESIGN BY WILLI BAUM

FIRST EDITION

Code 8827

A joint publication in
THE JOSSEY-BASS
SOCIAL AND BEHAVIORAL SCIENCE SERIES
and
THE JOSSEY-BASS
PUBLIC ADMINISTRATION SERIES

Contents

Foreword

It was 38 years ago that I reviewed a great, faulted, not very readable book for the old *Journal of Abnormal and Social Psychology*, then edited by my mentor Gordon Allport. The book, really a collection of semi-independent monographs, was *The Authoritarian Personality*, by T. W. Adorno, Else Frenkel-Brunswik, Daniel J. Levinson, and R. Nevitt Sanford. As I wrote at that time, "The California investigators, to put it figuratively, set out to track a jackal and found themselves at grips with behemoth. Their initial studies indicated that anti-Semitism, far from being an isolated though unrespectable psychological phenomenon, is an integral component of a general 'ethnocentric ideology.' Ethnocentrism, pursued in turn, is revealed as the expression of a distinctive 'authoritarian personality structure' whose unadmitted needs and defenses it serves. It is to the thorough empirical elucidation of this pattern of personality organization, along lines that converge strikingly with the more speculative formulations of Erich Fromm and Jean-Paul Sartre, that the volume makes its most important contribution" (*Journal of Abnormal and Social Psychology*, 1950, *45*, p. 775).

I went on to sketch the emerging portrait, developed in

terms of the broadly psychoanalytic dynamic psychology that was then at its apogee:

> What, then, is the authoritarian personality as it is here delineated? Briefly and inadequately, it characterizes the basically weak and dependent individual who has sacrificed his capacity for genuine experience of self and others in order to maintain a precarious order and safety. In the type case, he confronts with a façade of spurious strength a world in which rigidly stereotyped categories are substituted for the affectionate and individualized experience of which he is incapable. Such a person, estranged from inner values, lacks self-awareness and shuns intraception. His judgments are governed by a punitive conventional moralism, reflecting external standards in which he remains insecure since he has failed to make them really his own. His relations with others depend on considerations of power, success, and adjustment, in which people figure as means rather than as ends, and achievement is not valued for its own sake. In his world, the good, the powerful, and the in-group stand in fundamental opposition to the immoral, the weak, the out-group. For all that he seeks to align himself with the former, his underlying feelings of weakness and self-contempt commit him to a constant and embittered struggle to prove to himself and others that he really belongs to the strong and good. Prejudice against out-groups of all kinds and colors is a direct corollary of this personality structure [p. 776].

During the entire decade of the 1950s, research on the authoritarian personality dominated the social psychological literature (along with work on attitude change)—until it was displaced by the new experimental social psychology of "cognitive dissonance." So strong was the focus that the ex–Frankfurt

Institute "critical theorist" T. W. Adorno, who joined the project very late in the game at the insistence of the American Jewish Committee, which was funding the research, became one of the most frequently cited names in the psychological literature (since his name came first alphabetically: "Adorno et al.").

Unfortunately, the research of that decade dealt mainly with some serious methodological defects of only one aspect of the multifaceted work: the research developing and employing the "F Scale" of "Fascist" personal predispositions, which had the special defect, noted in my review, that all the items in the F Scale and other important pencil-and-paper measures with which it was correlated were worded in the same direction, so that agreement implied a *high* (or prejudiced, antidemocratic) score. That was most unfortunate, since the authoritarianism that the Berkeley authors intended to measure was confounded with acquiescence, the mere readiness to agree with questionnaire assertions.*

As I wrote three decades later in a disgruntled retrospective essay, "By the 1960s, interest in research on authoritarianism had flagged, and cognitive dissonance . . . carried the day. I had followed the Berkeley work with keen interest almost since its inception, so I was (and still am) deeply disappointed that the problem of authoritarianism—and more broadly, of the relation between character, social structure, and ideology—was dropped before the methodological problems that had beset the Berkeley research team had been adequately resolved, leaving the unquestionably important substantive issues hanging. This shocking failure may have helped to confirm subsequent experimental social psychology in its ahistorical, narrowly natural-science-oriented warp" ("The Shaping of American Social Psychology: A Personal Perspective from the Periphery," *Personality and Social Psychology Bulletin*, 1983, *9*, 165–180).

In that essay, I noted that Bob Altemeyer had come up

* My subsequent research with Peace Corps volunteers helped to disentangle the distinguishable psychological meanings of authoritarianism and acquiescence. See M. Brewster Smith, "An Analysis of Two Measures of 'Authoritarianism' in Peace Corps Teachers," *Journal of Personality*, 1965, *33*, 513–535.

with a better measure of authoritarianism that might "allow the topic to be revived." Indeed he had come up with such a measure. He has since revived the topic singlehanded, in this unique and important book.

Bob Altemeyer's earlier book, *Right-Wing Authoritarianism* (Winnipeg: University of Manitoba Press, 1981) gave a close critical review of the earlier literature and reported careful, psychometrically sophisticated developmental work validating his RWA Scale, a balanced scale measuring a narrower terrain, the results of which he conceptualized not within Freudian psychodynamics but in terms of Albert Bandura's social learning theory. His new scale, developed over years of thoughtful testing and experimentation, was a unidimensional measure of three attitudinal clusters:

> 1. Authoritarian submission—a high degree of submission to the authorities who are perceived to be established and legitimate in the society in which one lives.
> 2. Authoritarian aggression—a general aggressiveness, directed at various persons, which is perceived to be sanctioned by established authorities.
> 3. Conventionalism—a high degree of adherence to the social conventions which are perceived to be endorsed by society and its established authorities [p. 148].

I found the book exciting in its conceptual inventiveness and psychometric competence (a rare combination), but at best, test development is not engrossing to most people, and books published by Canadian university presses are unlikely to catch much attention south of the Canadian border. It deserved better, but *RWA* left few ripples.

Ever since *RWA* appeared, I have kept in touch with Altemeyer. I know of no one to match him in psychology. He has carried out a stunning major research program singlehanded, in a provincial university remote from the traveled highways of

United States–dominated psychology, with minimal money and maximal brains. He has not been presenting this work at meetings of the American Psychological Association or in the Journals. *RWA* described the launching and first fruits of his program. Now, seven years later, we have in this book the full mature fruits—and they are still coming in as a product of Altemeyer's industriousness and ingenuity.

The present volume stands on its own feet: we begin with a synopsis of where *RWA* left those of us who have followed his journey from the beginning. And as readers, we are carried along with much of the thrill of a good detective story—we participate vicariously in the process of exploration. Altemeyer has avoided being ruined by the atrocious conventional norms of behavioral science writing; he has a wonderful touch for informal communication.

It would be wrong, however, to put primary emphasis on the methodological and expository example that he sets. The substantive contribution of this book is spectacular. He *has* resolved the methodological problems that buried the earlier Berkeley work. He has reinstated right-wing authoritarianism as a measurable pattern of personality that today has just as major social and political consequences as the Berkeley authors believed at midcentury. He has demonstrated many of its correlates and, in an unprecedented combination of experimental and psychometric strategies, he has thrown real light on its causes and origins and on psychologically warranted approaches to dealing with the authoritarian menace.

This is an important book, its early draft richly deserving of the Prize for Behavioral Science Research of the American Association for the Advancement of Science, which it received in 1986. It should receive close attention in the social psychology programs of both psychology and sociology departments and in political psychology as an aspect of political science. Right-wing authoritarianism remains a serious threat in our political and social life. Bob Altemeyer gives us very substantial help in understanding it.

Over the years, I have used the mails to argue with Altemeyer that the Berkeley psychodynamic approach to authoritarianism fares better in his data than he has sometimes claimed. By now, I think we are reaching something of a rapprochement. Much (but not all) of the actual "syndrome" that I summarized in my early review is essentially supported. On balance, probably Bandura has the edge over Freud as to its origins in life experience—but Banduran social learning theory may be about as flexible, for better or worse, as Freudian psychodynamics. Certainly, in Altemeyer's hands, it furnishes a very workable frame for the down-to-earth understanding of the dynamics of authoritarianism.

This book deserves wide attention and a long life in print. I know of no other work to match it in the usually negatively correlated qualities of psychometric sophistication, theoretical originality, and experimental ingenuity and competence. It should, at a minimum, be read by all graduate students in social psychology for the next decade. It should attract a much broader audience.

July 1988

M. Brewster Smith
Professor of Psychology
University of California
at Santa Cruz

Preface

The struggle to understand right-wing authoritarianism has failed as surely as our society has failed to control authoritarian influences on our lives. There is hardly a front page or a news broadcast that does not carry evidence of authoritarianism's ill-doing. But if asked, "Why do people continue to support disastrous leaders?" or "Why is there still so much hate in our society toward minorities?" or "Why do seemingly sensible, progressive attempts to deal with our social problems encounter such determined resistance?" we seldom have anything to say that was not obvious to the questioner beforehand. Moreover, we have failed to realize that, to a considerable extent, there is a single answer to these three questions and to many others as well.

We have not learned the answer because we abandoned the search, in frustration, some years ago. A massive effort to come to grips with authoritarianism was ignited by the publication of *The Authoritarian Personality* in 1950. For over a decade hundreds of scientists researched far-flung fields with the Fascism Scale, and the journals fairly bulged with studies linking the "pre-Fascist personality" to almost everything imaginable. But because the underlying conceptualization was easily holed and sunk, because the F Scale was terribly flawed, and because the studies showed an uncanny knack for contradicting one another and raising impenetrable methodological thickets, virtually nothing was accomplished in the long run. And so, one by one, investigators quietly gave up. In the mid sixties and early seventies social psychology textbooks had whole chapters on authoritarianism; today they have a paragraph, or nothing at all.

But all the problems in our culture associated with the authoritarian personality have remained, and in many respects they have grown. Ironically, they were creating headlines, and enormous internal turmoil, at the very time behavioral scientists abandoned the quest. The dateline was "Saigon." And "Washington." And "My Lai." And "Kent State."

I began my research on authoritarianism at this time and in 1981 published *Right-Wing Authoritarianism*. This book laid, in two ways, a new foundation for investigating the area: by presenting an empirically based conceptualization of authoritarianism as the covariation of authoritarian submission, authoritarian aggression, and conventionalism and by producing a relatively reliable and valid instrument for measuring this syndrome, the RWA Scale. During the seven years since, I have conducted many experiments on the reason authoritarianism is organized the way it is, the way it develops in an individual, and the ways we can control it in a democratic society. I believe these investigations, reported for the first time in the present volume, give us a much clearer understanding than we have ever had before of a very serious problem in our society.

Why "very serious"? Because my research, like that of my predecessors, has been driven by the perception that there exists a vast potential for the acceptance of right-wing totalitarian rule in countries like the United States and Canada. The findings reported in the pages that follow illustrate this potential and tell us much that we need to know to safeguard our freedoms.

I have written this book, which presents a fully scientific report of my investigations, for anyone who would understandably demand a detailed proof of such a disturbing proposition. In the main such persons would be other behavioral scientists. For persons with other backgrounds, I have provided a short, nontechnical discussion of statistical matters in Appendix A as an aid in understanding the presentation.

Social psychologists and personality researchers will, I hope, find this report of direct and compelling interest. Our close associates, the developmental psychologists, might be intrigued by the evidence on how authoritarianism becomes part of adult character. Researchers who study intrapsychic phenomena and repression might also find this book rewarding, for understanding the authoritarian has required delving far beyond his own account of his behavior. Indeed, the techniques developed for these explorations might prove useful to investigators working in quite different areas.

In a broader vein, I understand that some behavioral scientists have assigned parts of my first book in their graduate methodology seminars, particularly when dealing with questionnaire construction and test administration—and the meta-issue of why we do research at all. I hope they will find sections of the present book worth sharing with students before the latter grab Test X and build rather pointless dissertations around it.

Researchers in other behavioral sciences might also find interesting reading within. Sociologists concerned with the organization of social attitudes, the role of such attitudes in thinking and behavior, and changes in the level of authoritarianism in society over time will find matters of concern here. Political scientists who study right-wing movements, or the interplay of personality and political party affiliation, or the way "liberal" and "conservative" forces in society find representation in legislatures should find material that holds their attention. Historians of Nazi Germany and Fascism in general might discover interconnections between the present and the past. Persons involved in the scientific study of religion should encounter many relevant findings.

Beyond these academic interests, other professionals who work in more applied settings may find the book profitable—psychotherapists engrossed with how the mind deceives itself, for example. Such readers should also be directed to the discoveries about authoritarians' fantasies and sexual behavior and the evidence bearing on the original psychoanalytic theory of the pre-Fascist personality.

Counselors who work with the victims of authoritarianism may find that this research can lead their clients to greater understanding of their victimization and less self-blame. Educators, in turn, may be both depressed and exhilarated by the role education plays in the development of personal authoritarianism. And professionals dedicated to social reform in general might find that this book lends insight into those most likely to oppose them and useful information on how to change these opponents' minds (or, at the minimum, avoid unnecessary backlash).

Chapter One points out how little we still know about this force that affects our lives in countless ways. It defines right-wing authoritarianism in some detail and then summarizes what we have learned so far using this new approach.

Chapter Two tells how I conducted the research to be described. It gives the latest version of the RWA Scale, along with some facts about the 20,000-plus people who have filled out this 30-item questionnaire over the past 15 years, during which time the level of authoritarianism in our society has been found to be slowly but surely rising. The importance of internal consistency in psychological tests is discussed, and the chapter closes with an account of my successes and failures at improving such consistency in typical research settings—which might prove helpful to investigators in a wide variety of fields.

Chapter Three explains how authoritarianism develops in a person. I examine the original "Berkeley theory" and develop an alternative model based on Bandura's social learning theory. Then I present research that uncovers the importance of certain experiences in an individual's life as keys to his adult authoritarianism. The chapter closes with two longitudinal studies of how higher education and experiences after university, such as parenthood, affect right-wing authoritarianism.

Chapter Four begins a two-chapter investigation of the most mysterious component of the authoritarian syndrome, authoritarian aggression. After reviewing the previous findings on the authoritarian's hostility, I turn to the issue of whether *non*authoritarians are just as aggressive, but toward different targets. Authoritarians have "enemies lists" of despised targets. Do nonauthoritarians also have groups they are ready to punish as soon as they get the chance? It appears governments would have little trouble persuading authoritarians to help hunt down and persecute Communists and homosexuals. Would nonauthoritarians respond as quickly to a call to persecute the Ku Klux Klan? Three theoretical explanations of authoritarian aggression are then considered: the classic "Berkeley" psychoanalytic model, one based on social learning theory, and that provided by the frustration-aggression hypothesis.

Chapter Five presents findings on each of the three explanations advanced in Chapter Four and then reports four pitting experiments that compared the most promising hypotheses' ability to explain various kinds of authoritarian aggression. A simple, powerful explanation emerges from these studies. The chapter ends with research on the authoritarian's awareness of his or her hostility, and on how the authoritarian maintains a righteous self-image while being prejudiced and aggressive.

Chapter Six studies the connections between religion and right-wing authoritarianism. Evidence of a mutually supporting relationship emerges, along with an explanation of why some religions produce greater levels of authoritarianism in their members than others. I then explore the authoritarian's religious beliefs and practices in depth and describe three experiments bearing on the "compartmentalized" minds of religious authoritarians.

In Chapter Seven I review evidence that authoritarianism is increasingly associated with political party preference as interest in politics rises. The chapter reports my studies of RWA Scale scores among politicians in four Canadian provincial and four American state legislatures—studies that led me to conclude that personal authoritarianism probably differentiates politicians more highly than any other ideological factor. Some very high relationships between party affiliation and authoritarianism are also described. The chapter closes by considering the implications of the accumulated research with the RWA Scale on whether there is an "authoritarian on the left."

Chapter Eight presents ways right-wing authoritarianism can be better controlled in a democratic society. I offer several proposals for steps that educators, the news media, and religious leaders might take toward moderating personal authoritarianism in our society. I also describe experiments on the use of laws to control authoritarianism, ways to limit the appeal of future demagogues, how to effect social change without raising the level of Fascist potential in society, and how to use social norms and self-insight to reduce personal authoritarianism.

A final chapter entitled "Afterthoughts" summarizes the major findings in the book and considers what they mean for the behavioral sciences. It ends with the observation that the academic community has as much at stake in the control of authoritarianism as any other group, and probably more.

Winnipeg Bob Altemeyer
July 1988

Acknowledgments

I did not anticipate the extent to which my first book, *Right-Wing Authoritarianism*, would create interest in me as a person. Many people, about three as I recall, have asked questions over the past seven years about me and my research program. I'll answer them now, once and for all.

One person, visiting our department for a job interview, asked, "How did you become interested in whatever it is you study?" The answer is, I have had a lifelong commitment to democracy. I also failed a question on my Ph.D. candidacy exams, thoughtfully asked by Daryl Bem, about response sets and the Berkeley research program – neither of which I had ever heard of. That led to a redemptive paper on the subject and a subsequent interest that would warm the cockles of Alfred Adler's heart. This book could easily be retitled *Right-Wing Authoritarianism: A Case Study in Overcompensation.*

Second, a Freudian who had heard of the RWA Scale asked me whether my middle name was William or Winfred. He suspected I had unconsciously named the test after myself, as in *R*obert *W*illiam *A*ltemeyer. I found this quite ingenious, because I have always wished my middle name were Walter. Actually, though, it is Anthony, but that explains why initially I called the test the Right-Arm Authoritarianism Scale.

The third question I recall was asked by a couple who almost became our friends. They said to me, "What do you do?" I began to review the literature on the F Scale, but my wife interrupted, "He's a professor. He teaches, and the rest doesn't matter."

A fourth question, which surprisingly no one has yet asked, is "How do you keep your research a secret in the community where you constantly collect data?" If that occurred to you, it is a very good question.

At first I thought it would be impossible. One night, for example, we attended a party and I found to my horror that a newspaper columnist was also a guest. I spent the whole night slipping out of rooms so I would never be introduced and have to answer all this person's questions about my research. At one point I pretended I needed a cigarette and slipped outside to escape, finessing the fact that it was December in Winnipeg, I was not wearing a coat, and I don't smoke.

Since then, however, my wife has become friends with a number of "media people," and as she frequently brings me along to dinner parties and the like, I have spent many evenings in the same room with a journalist and remained undetected. At first I was petrified and had memorized elaborate lies about a career in eyeblink conditioning. But I discovered that strangers' inevitable question to me, on discovering I am a university professor, is (in the summer) "Well, how long until you go back to work?" and (the rest of the year) "I guess you're back to work now, huh?"

Piqued, I began to drop hints about my research, like, "Ah, yes, Adolf Hitler. I do a lot of very interesting research on Nazi types, you know." Eyes would glaze over momentarily, and then people would say, "Oh, do you? Well, I guess you're through working until September, huh?"

One time, when we were visiting another couple, I had just steered the conversation my way when the host and hostess got into quite an argument about whether it was time for her to fix coffee or time for him to check on the kids (I later learned they were childless). Recently, we were having dinner with this same couple, and my wife said to me,

Jean: Oh, by the way, I've changed our theater tickets to October 23rd.

B.A.: October 23rd! That's the day I run my big, crucial experiment.

(Pause)

Other couple (independently but together): What are you going to see at the theater?

My first book *has* generated a lot of interest in my wife. Many of my colleagues' spouses have asked whether it is true that Jean never helped with any of the research, did none of the typing, and did not read a single word of the proofs. When I say yes, absolutely, they lick their lips a little and with shining eyes whisper, "What's her secret?"

My wife did eventually read the "Acknowledgments" in my first book, because she heard I talked about her there. It led her to ask whether I was *still* an associate professor. I replied, "If I am not a full professor in rank, I certainly am in girth." But she indicated I had misunderstood her question. Had I been demoted to assistant professor or lecturer yet, she wanted to know.

Jean tried to read the rest of *Right-Wing Authoritarianism* but lost interest at the Table of Contents. Those of you who appreciate consistency in a person will be glad to learn my wife had nothing whatsoever to do with the preparation of this manuscript either. But neither have I gone to as much avant-garde theater as she wished.

Various stout souls *did* read selected pieces of this book and made helpful suggestions: M. Brewster Smith, Fred Stambrook, Marion Aftanas, and Paul Thomas. They are responsible for all of the errors that you detect, and I am as shocked as you that these brilliant minds would have let such mistakes pass. Professor Smith has honored me with a lengthy and encouraging correspondence over the past seven years. He likes my writing style and told me not to let any editor talk me out of it. If you do not like the way this book is written, it is Brewster Smith's fault.

Fortunately, Gracia Alkema, social and behavioral sciences editor at Jossey-Bass, was willing to consider a manuscript from an obscure, remote professor sporting a publications list one line long. Most others would have quickly passed, I am sure. Jossey-Bass was the "special publisher" I was counting on finding, and Gracia surely judged the project on its own merits, not the financial rewards guaranteed by my awesome reputation. "We'll publish a book we believe in," she explained, "even though we're not sure anyone will buy it." Furthermore, Gracia never tried to change my writing style, which she said was sometimes almost as amusing as my spelling. After we became friends, she asked me why I hadn't had someone proofread the manuscript.

I also want to thank Rephah Berg, who copyedited the manuscript. She made, altogether, about 100 improvements of my spelling, grammar, wording, punctuation, sentence structure, clarity, and meaning, per paragraph.

Also, a bouquet of roses to Kate Fuller, who managed to turn my dog-eared manuscript into the smartly produced volume before you now. Kate also had the impossible task of transforming me into a respectable author aware of Jossey-Bass custom. For example, my first name ought to be "Robert," there was no precedent for tomfoolery in the Acknowledgments, and Jossey-Bass did not want authors to thank individual members of its staff in print. But like Gracia and Rephah, Kate is both very *un*authoritarian and excellent at her job. Unfortunately, Kate's contact with me may have given her pause about her choice of careers. "There is a much greater need for English teachers than I ever realized," she told her colleagues.

Thanks to various editors around the world, none of the research reported in this book has been previously published in the journals. Nor was any of it funded by any council, board, or group. The University of Manitoba provided such necessary items as subjects, computer time, a personal computer, and about $400 a year. I met other expenses as they arose by teaching extra courses. (So my answer to the strangers' question about being off work until September has been "No, I'm teaching summer school." But the truth is, I enjoy teaching as much as I love doing research; except for administrative tasks, I have never "worked" at university.)

In the spring of 1986 Brewster Smith, having just trudged his way through the manuscript of Chapters Four and Five of this book, suggested I enter them in the annual competition for the American Association for the Advancement of Science's prize for research in the behavioral sciences. "At least you'll get a more prestigious rejection letter," Brewster said. When Marge White of AAAS phoned me the news on December 17th that my paper had won, I was stunned and elated beyond words (she will confirm). I sent Brewster a basket of fruit but otherwise kept all the prize money for myself.

I have dedicated this book to the institution that plucked me up out of the blue, educated me, changed me, and sent me into the world to make some contribution. If there could be a secondary dedication, it would be to the taxpayers of Manitoba and Canada who have enabled me to pursue Daryl Bem's question so obsessively for the past 20 years. I hope I have repaid some of what has been invested in me.

B. A.

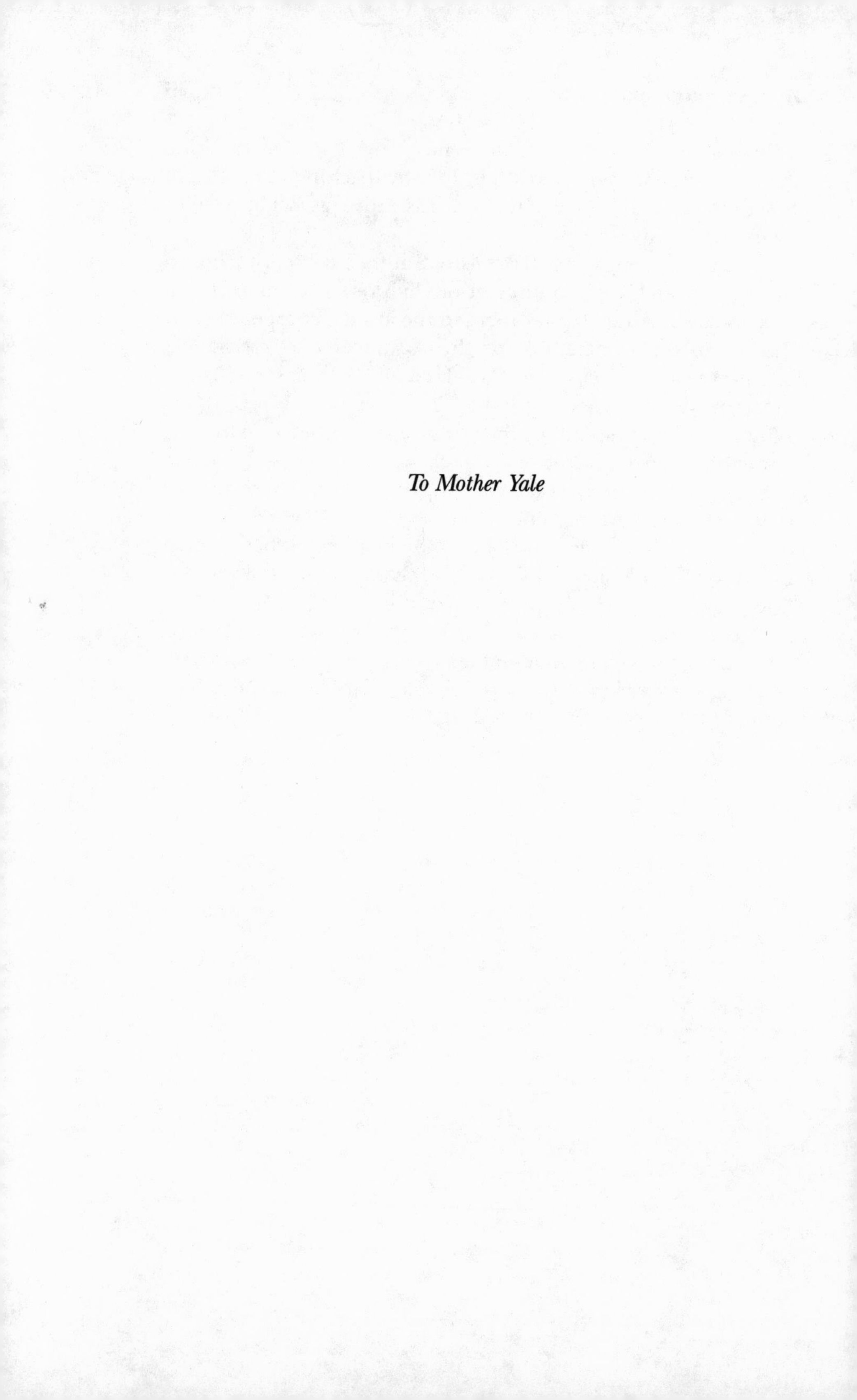

To Mother Yale

The Author

Bob Altemeyer is an associate professor of psychology at the University of Manitoba, in Winnipeg, Canada. Born in Saint Louis, he earned a B.S. at Yale University in 1962 and a Ph.D. at Carnegie-Mellon University in 1966. His first book, *Right-Wing Authoritarianism,* was published in 1981 and reports the results of 15 years of research on the "pre-Fascist personality" in North American society. This book presents his investigations since then, which won the Prize for Behavioral Science Research awarded by the American Association for the Advancement of Science in 1986.

ENEMIES OF FREEDOM

1

The Quest to Understand Right-Wing Authoritarianism

In the fall of 1981 there appeared, with a complete absence of fanfare, the first of three books I have set out to write on the subject of right-wing authoritarianism (Altemeyer, 1981). In *Right-Wing Authoritarianism*, which I shall usually refer to as "*RWA*," I reviewed the wretched scientific literature on authoritarianism, presented some research on the important psychometric topic of "response sets," and then explained how, by analyzing earlier investigations, I had developed another conceptualization of "pre-Fascist potential." Next I presented a series of studies that indicated this approach was profitable, at least compared with earlier attempts. I closed with some preliminary findings on the dynamics and personal origins of right-wing authoritarianism.

The book was, with two exceptions I shall soon discuss, well received by other scientists. (See the advertisement we placed in the November 1984 *Journal of Personality and Social Psychology* for a nonrandom sample of the reviews.) Many critics I personally admire said, "Good show!" No one was so brutal (as I probably would have been) as to say, "So what?" But the question could well have been asked. *RWA* laid a foundation for understanding authoritarianism but did not produce much. It was just a foundation that reached all the way up to ground level, no higher.

I am trying now to get us off the ground, to provide that missing understanding. Specifically, I shall try to answer the three biggest questions I see before us:

1. How does right-wing authoritarianism develop in an individual?
2. Why are authoritarians' attitudes organized as they are?
3. How can we control authoritarianism in a democratic society?

Besides pursuing the origins, dynamics, and control of authoritarianism, I shall also report a series of findings on its religious and political associations.

I hope you find all this as engrossing as I do. We are going questing after mysteries in an unexplored, if fabled, land; let us "roll" for intelligence, wisdom, and constitution.

Definitions

By "right-wing authoritarianism" I mean the combination of the following three attitudinal clusters in a person:

1. Authoritarian submission – a high degree of submission to the authorities who are perceived to be established and legitimate in the society in which one lives.
2. Authoritarian aggression – a general aggressiveness, directed against various persons, that is perceived to be sanctioned by established authorities.
3. Conventionalism – a high degree of adherence to the social conventions that are perceived to be endorsed by society and its established authorities.

By "attitudinal clusters" I mean orientations to respond in the same general way toward certain classes of stimuli (namely, established authorities, targets for sanctioned aggression, and social conventions).[1] Now, an orientation to respond is not the same thing as a response, and few social psychologists today expect attitude measures to correlate highly with more concrete behaviors in any situation. As Milgram (1974) made quite clear, most of us can rather easily be seduced by the trappings of authority and induced to commit callous, hideous deeds (*RWA*, pp. 273–276; see also Brown, 1986, pp. 1–41, and Miller, 1986). So authoritarian *behavior* results from the same interaction of individual and situational influences that governs other actions.

Right-wing authoritarian*ism* is an "individual" factor, a personality variable, a "trait" if you like, developed on the premise that some persons need very little situational pressure to (say) submit to authority, while others often require significantly more. Conceived as a set of covarying attitudes (that is, attitudes that tend to go together), it is operationally defined as the score on an attitude scale that I named (in a burst of creativity) the RWA Scale. I shall discuss this measure in the next chapter.

The central concern of my research program has been the apprehension that there may be a vast potential for the acceptance of right-wing totalitarian rule in countries such as Canada and the United States. This acceptance is essentially an attitude, a state of mind, a willingness to see democratic institutions destroyed, which in some people may even be a desire. Right-wing authoritarianism has thus been defined as an orientation, rather than a set of acts, but it is still dangerous. The mood of a populace can create a climate of public opinion that promotes totalitarian movements. It can intimidate politicians, journalists, and religious leaders who might otherwise oppose repression. It can encourage a bold, illegal grab for power, as it did in Italy in 1922. It can elect a Hitler to office, as it did in Germany in 1933. It can encourage military leaders to overthrow duly elected governments, as it has so many times since.

By "submission to established authority" I mean a general acceptance of its statements and actions and a general willingness to comply with its instructions without further inducement.

The authoritarian believes that authorities should be trusted to a relatively great extent and that they are owed obedience and respect. He believes that these are important virtues which children should be taught and that if children stray from these principles, it is the parents' duty to get them back in line. Authoritarians would ordinarily place very narrow limits on people's right to criticize authorities. They tend to believe that officials know what is best and that critics do not know what they are talking about. Criticism of authority is viewed as divisive and destructive, motivated by sinister goals and a desire to cause trouble. Authoritarians believe, to a considerable extent, that established authorities have an inherent right to decide for themselves what they may do, including breaking the laws they make for the rest of us.

By "established and legitimate authorities" I mean those people in our society who are usually considered to have a general legal or moral authority over the behavior of others. One's parents (at least through childhood), religious officials, certain civic officers (the police, judges, legislators, heads of governments), and superiors in military service are all established authorities.

The right-wing authoritarian's submission is not absolute, automatic, or blind. Like anyone else, she can be put into conflict by orders from above; she will not always accept orders, but she will accept them more often than nonauthoritarians will. Similarly, officials do not all command equal degrees of respect and submission: there are "good judges" and "bad governments," "good popes" and "poor presidents." However, the authoritarian is more likely than the nonauthoritarian to submit to established authorities she likes and to those she does not like.

By "aggressiveness" I mean a predisposition to cause harm to someone. The harm can be physical injury, psychological suffering, financial loss, social isolation, or some other negative state that people would usually avoid. Aggressiveness is authoritarian when it is accompanied by the belief that established authority approves it or that it will help preserve established authority.

The predisposition to such aggression does not mean that

the right-wing authoritarian will always act aggressively when opportunities arise. Fear of retaliation may stop him. There are also prominent legal and social prohibitions against aggression in our culture. This is why the perception of authoritative sanction is important. It disinhibits the aggressive impulse.

Right-wing authoritarians are predisposed to control the behavior of others through punishment. They advocate physical punishment in childhood and beyond. They deplore leniency in the courts and believe penal reform just encourages criminals to continue being lawless. They are strong advocates of capital punishment. All in all, there is an "Old Testament harshness" in their approach to human conduct.

The "various persons" who are the targets of authoritarian aggressiveness could be anyone, but unconventional people (including "social deviants" such as homosexuals) and people who are conventional targets of aggression (such as certain minority groups) are attacked more readily than others. Thus right-wing authoritarianism is expected to be correlated, in general, with ethnic and racial prejudice, because such prejudice is a conventional outlet of aggressive impulses. The authoritarian believes that certain authorities approve of this prejudice, and he may believe that certain groups threaten the social order. Hence the aggressiveness in prejudice can be authoritarian. But by no means is all prejudice thought to be linked to right-wing authoritarianism.

If social deviants and certain minority groups are ready targets of authoritarian aggression, others can be victims as well. The authoritarian is more likely to attack a conventional person than a nonauthoritarian is, if an established authority sanctions it. This power of authority figures to direct the hostility of authoritarians against almost any target increases the danger of authoritarian aggression to all in a society.

By "adherence to social conventions" is meant a strong acceptance of and commitment to the traditional social norms in our society. Many such norms are based on the common teachings of the Judeo-Christian religions. The right-wing authoritarian generally believes in "God's law" and thinks that the biggest reason there is so much conflict among humankind is that people are ignoring this law. Within each religion, authoritarians tend to be "fundamentalists," wishing to maintain the beliefs, teachings, and services in their traditional form and resisting change and "liberalization." Authoritarians reject the idea that people should develop their own ideas of what is moral and immoral, since this has already been determined by authorities.

Authoritarians' attitudes toward sexual behavior are strongly influenced by their religious principles. Sex outside marriage is basically sinful. Nudity is sinful. Thinking about sex is sinful. Homosexuality is sinful and is a perversion. Many sexual acts, even between married partners, are perversions.

These attitudes toward sex have their parallel in conventional attitudes toward proper behavior for men and women. Authoritarians endorse the traditional family structure in which women are subservient to their husbands. They believe women should, by and large, keep to their traditional roles in society. While a "decent, respectable appearance" is important for both sexes, it is especially important for a woman; while sexual transgression is wrong for both sexes, it is especially wrong for a woman.

There are a host of social norms that the authoritarian endorses. The flag and the national anthem should be honored, as of course the national leaders should be. There is a strong belief that "our customs and national heritage are the things that have made us great" and that everyone ought to be made to show respect for them. People should strive to be well-behaved, properly dressed, and respectable and in general stick to the "straight and narrow" course. Underlying all this is the notion that these social norms are moral as well as social imperatives. The authoritarian rejects the proposition that social customs are arbitrary and that one nation's customs may be as good as another's. Other ways of doing things are wrong.

The term *norms* is being used here in the normative, not the descriptive sense. The right-wing authoritarian's conventionalism is a code of how people ought to act, not how they do. The code is conventional because it is based on long-standing tradition and custom, not because it actually describes how most people are behaving. Thus it may be that most adults in our society engage in sexual intercourse before marriage. The authoritarian may have as well. It is nonetheless a transgression, and the fact that most people are sinning only shows the authoritarian that it is a sinful world.

This is not to say the authoritarian's adherence to traditional social norms is cast in iron and cannot be changed in his or her lifetime. But it is more resistant to change than the nonauthoritarian's, and it is more likely to be influenced by the pronouncements of authority figures than by the behavior of peers.

Two Criticisms

You have probably noticed that I use the term *authoritarian* whenever I get tired of writing out *right-wing authoritarian*. Obviously, though, modifying the noun with *right-wing* implies there might be a left-wing authoritarian, and even a flightless, unwinged authoritarian in the middle too. Eysenck (1982) believes there are authoritarians on the left and found *RWA* "odd because one would have expected a modern author to deal equally with left-wing authoritarianism" (p. 352).

I do not know whether there is an authoritarian on the left, and I offer my opinions on the matter to you at the end of Chapter Seven. But I and others have had no difficulty finding one on the right, and when I use the term *authoritarian* in this book, I mean the right-wing authoritarian who is on the road to Fascism.

Second, Ray (1985) recently concluded that the RWA Scale is "just another conservatism scale," not a measure of authoritarianism at all, because it correlated highly with a Conservatism Scale of his invention but not at all with his 14-item Directiveness Scale. (See Appendix A for a "user friendly" discussion of what *correlated* and other statistical terms used in this book mean.) The latter, consisting of questions such as "Are you the sort of person who always likes to get his own way?" and "Do you tend to boss people around?," measures what Ray (1976) means by "authoritarianism."

One can approach the subject from this perspective. Ray appears to be focusing on the leader in authoritarian systems, and if his scale measures directiveness, its scores might prove useful for understanding those who would become dictators of various groups.[2] But as Duckitt (1983, 1984) has observed, this is not the perspective that psychologists since *The Authoritarian Personality* (Adorno, Frenkel-Brunswik, Levinson, and Sanford, 1950) have usually adopted. Our focus instead has been on the submissive followers—the multitudes at the Nuremberg rallies, if you would—who have been (for us) the more amazing phenomenon and the basis for the threat that Hitlers and Mussolinis can pose.

I am not saying that researchers should use *authoritarianism* only in this sense. (Guess I'm just not that directive.) But I do not think the lack of correlation between the RWA Scale and the Directiveness Scale means the former is just another homely face.

I think this point would be so obvious to other researchers, I would not have brought it up at all except as a springboard for my second clarification: *I do not equate right-wing authoritarianism with conservatism.* I take the latter to mean a disposition to preserve the status quo, to maintain social stability, to preserve tradition. It is close to "conventionalism," *one* of the attitude clusters I use to define authoritarianism. But I know many conservative persons who do not take a hidebound view that their customs are the best for everyone. (In fact, I hope people who know me would say I am such a person.) And besides, I mean by an "authoritarian" someone who is *also* highly submissive to established authority and highly aggressive against sanctioned targets—hardly the same thing as conservatism.

Past Research Findings with the RWA Scale

Is the RWA Scale valid? That is, does it measure authoritarian submission, authoritarian aggression, and conventionalism? The answer has to be "Only to a certain extent." As is true of any "general" attitude scale that covers a lot of topics, much of the variance in its scores is item-specific; and some is "error," caused by response sets, misinterpretations, subjects' marking unintended responses, and so forth.

Still in all, the test was reported in *RWA* to have a number of significant relationships with criterion behaviors.

Acceptance of Government Injustices. Persons who scored high on the RWA Scale were found to be more accepting of illegal and highhanded acts done by government officials to harass and intimidate their opponents. Examples were illegal wiretaps, illegal letter openings, illegal searches without warrants, and blocking peaceful protests against government policies. Correlations with a ten-case version of "Government Injustices" averaged about .55. Authoritarians did not mind such activities whether they were carried out against radical leftist or radical right-wing groups, but they were somewhat concerned when more conventional, respectable groups were victimized.

In a similar vein, authoritarian American university students reported retrospectively in the fall of 1974 that it had taken them longer to become suspicious and convinced that Richard Nixon was participating in a Watergate cover-up. The overall correlations with the time it took were about .50. Eighteen percent of the sample said they still were not convinced of Nixon's wrongdoing, even though he had already resigned and accepted a pardon for his crimes.

Acceptance of Law as the Basis of Morality. Students were given a series of moral dilemmas to resolve and were asked to explain the principles they used to make their decisions. Most subjects could not be readily "typed," but among those who could, persons who scored high on the RWA Scale were found mainly to use a rationale similar to what Kohlberg (1963, 1968) called a primitive "punishment and obedience" orientation (for example, "Laws are laws and were meant to be obeyed"). Nonauthoritarians were more likely to make their decisions according to "individual principles of conscience." Eta-squared for the overall relationship was 37.8 percent, analogous to a correlation of about .60.

Punishment of Lawbreakers. Authoritarians wanted to impose relatively long prison sentences on persons convicted of various crimes, especially if the criminal was "unsavory." The correlation for a ten-trial version of the measure was usually around .45. Persons who scored high on the RWA Scale believed the crimes were more serious than nonauthoritarians did, and they believed more in the efficacy of punishment. But they also found the criminals more repulsive and disgusting and admitted to feeling satisfaction and pleasure at being able to punish such wrongdoers.

However, high RWAs did not want to punish Richard Nixon as much as nonauthoritarians did, nor were they more punitive toward some other authorities who had aggressed against unsavory targets (for example, a police officer who beat up a demonstrator, an accountant who assaulted a "hippie"). These findings appear consistent with the authoritarian's own submissiveness toward officials and/or aggressive impulses toward deviants and "troublemakers."

Punishment of Peers in a Learning Situation. When students were placed in a mock learning situation in which the subject could choose which level of electrical shock to administer to a confederate, RWA Scale scores correlated .43 with the level of punishment chosen. (Half the time the confederate was dressed to appear Jewish, a manipulation that had no detectable effect on behavior and may have been too transparent.)

Prejudice. RWA Scale scores were found to correlate about .35 with scores on an attitude scale designed to measure ethnocentric opinions about white Canadians and a variety of ethnic and racial groups (for example, Jews, blacks, Asians, North American Indians).

Religion. Authoritarians were found more accepting of their home religions than nonauthoritarians, with correlations averaging about .45. The finding held in each of the denominations studied. Among Christians, RWA scores correlated .47 with scores on a Christian Orthodoxy measure. RWA Scale scores were found to be highest among Protestant "fundamentalist" sects and lowest among atheists and agnostics.

Political Affiliation. Weak relationships, analogous to correlations of .20 to .30, were found between authoritarianism and preference for "right wing" political parties among undifferentiated samples. The relationships were about twice as strong, however, among subjects definitely interested in politics. A simulation study, in which subjects were asked to complete the RWA Scale as they thought various legislators would, suggested a much stronger relationship would be found among active politicians.

"Hitler's" Score on the RWA Scale. A group of students were asked to answer the RWA Scale as they imagined either (then) Canadian Prime Minister Pierre Trudeau, (then) President Richard Nixon, or Adolf Hitler would have answered it. "Trudeau's" average score was a little higher than the students' own, "Nixon's" was substantially higher, and "Hitler's" was very high. The overall eta-squared was 42.6 percent, the strongest relationship found by 1981 with the RWA Scale.

Demographic Relationships. RWA Scale scores correlated .30 or less with educational attainment and socioeconomic status in a number of nonstudent samples. None of the relationships reported in the paragraphs above was appreciably reduced by controlling for these variables. Scores on a standard intelligence test correlated nonsignificantly with RWA scores among a group of students. No consistent gender differences have been found on the test. And social desirability effects appear to be minimal under ordinary testing conditions.

Comparison with Other Authoritarianism Scales

The reader may rightly be unimpressed with the size of the relationships reported above. In every case, most of the variance in the criterion measure was left unexplained by RWA Scale scores. But human behavior is usually so complexly determined that single variables cannot explain much. The RWA Scale's imperfections and measurement error weigh heavily against that, and situational factors can often trump individual differences anyway.

With all its shortcomings, however, it appears to be the best measure of personal authoritarianism we have at the moment. As reported in *RWA*, I pitted the initial version of the RWA Scale in 1973 against five other tests: the California F Scale (Adorno, Frenkel-Brunswik, Levinson, and Sanford, 1950), Rokeach's (1960) Dogmatism Scale, Wilson and Patterson's (1968) Conservatism Scale, Lee and Warr's (1969) "Balanced F Scale," and Kohn's (1972) Authoritarianism-Rebellion Scale. None of these alternative measures proved as internally consistent and unidimensional as the RWA Scale. The Conservatism Scale predicted authoritarian religious behavior best, but the RWA Scale was superior at predicting five other criteria. (The Lee and Warr scale, used in the initial construction of the RWA Scale, finished second.)

Item Analyses

I have attributed the relatively good performance of the RWA Scale to a fairly unambiguous underlying conceptualization (which I did not invent but discovered in earlier data) and to my strong desire to make the test as internally consistent as possible. Because of its resulting cohesion, the test has an important ability to correlate *as a whole* with criterion behaviors. Item analyses showed, for example, that nearly all the items on the test, despite their apparent divergence, correlated significantly with the criteria used in the pitting study. Thus acceptance of government injustices was not just due to the items on the test that deal directly with trusting the government; hostility in the "Trials" situation was not just due to "crime and punishment" items; and so on. The test as a whole was predicting these various behaviors.

(By way of comparison, the Conservatism Scale's superior prediction of religious behaviors was mainly due to items on that test which tap religious and sexual conservatism. The Conservatism Scale's relationship with religious acceptance boiled down to the fact that people who continued to accept their home religions were religiously and sexually more conservative than those who did not. But how informative is that?)

The great danger of simply relating summed test scores with a criterion is that a statistically significant relationship may arise mainly because of such obvious, even tautological connections with part of the test. If a test has enough "hooks" sticking out in different directions, it can connect (weakly) with lots of different things and stir up considerable excitement among some researchers and practitioners. ("It correlates with almost everything!") But if one looked at the item analyses, one might save years of effort collecting relationships that amount, in the final analysis, to very little.

I recommended in *RWA* that researchers routinely examine the pattern of item correlations, looking for such spurious associations, and as far as I can tell not a single person has followed this advice. Journal articles still routinely report just summed-score test analyses, despite the (to me) evident danger. (I also made a plea for much more detailed reporting of experimental methodology, which also has had zippo effect. The "methodology section" of Ray's 1985 paper cited above, for example, is one sentence long.)

Replications by Other Researchers

I have naturally been interested in other researchers' experience with the RWA Scale. However, the published literature on the test consists of three papers to date, which may remind you of my success at getting item analyses and detailed methodology reports into the scientific record. Adding a few "personal communications" that have arrived in my mailbox does not greatly increase this literature review.

As for the test's *internal consistency*, Zwillenberg (1983) administered the original 24-item version of the RWA Scale to 503 students attending nine scattered American universities during the spring of 1980. She found an overall *split-half* reliability of .86 (compared with the Cronbach alpha reliability of .90 I found among a similar sample of American students in 1974).

J. Schneider (personal communication, Nov. 19, 1984) sent me a computer analysis of responses 70 West German students had made to a (translated) 30-item revision of the test. The alpha was .94, much higher than I ever obtain from my Canadian students.

J. H. Duckitt (personal communication, Sept. 24, 1984) sent me similar evidence of a .93 alpha obtained for the 30-item scale among 212 students attending the University of Natal in South Africa.

Heaven (1984) reported an alpha of .81 for the original RWA Scale among 52 Australian students and .90 among a sample of 130 more heterogeneous adults recruited (and tested) by the initial sample. (The answers were obtained on a truncated, three-category response scale.)

And finally, Ray (1985) reported an alpha of .89 for the original scale among "a random cluster sample of 84 people interviewed door-to-door" in Brisbane, Australia.

The alpha (or, more precisely, the level of interitem correlation) one obtains for a test in a study depends on several things, including the number of very high and very low scorers included in the sample. I suspect that the West German and South African students produced such high levels of internal consistency because opinions about authority may be relatively polarized among such students. But even so, the test has hung together rather well elsewhere—far better than I ever expected it to. I had no idea or hypothesis, when I began testing the notion that sentiments of authoritarian submission, authoritarian aggression, and conventionalism covary, that they would covary anywhere else than in North America. It's rather interesting, isn't it?

The vibrant literature on the RWA Scale also contains a few more empirical associations. The only nonconfirmation was by Heaven (1984), who found no correlation between persons' RWA Scale scores and a close acquaintance's rating of their aggressiveness. (But I would not call the latter a good indicator of someone's *authoritarian* aggressiveness. I also have some methodological hesitations about having undergraduates administer tests to friends, and I wonder about the range and validity of such ratings when the raters were told to chose ratees they knew well.) Zwillenberg (1983) found an overall .38 correlation between authoritarianism and sentencing in the Trials situation. But the most interesting finding, in my opinion, has been Duckitt's (personal communication, Sept. 24, 1984) discovery of RWA correlations from .53 to .69 among white subjects in South Africa with a variety of measures of antiblack prejudice. You may recall Pettigrew's (1958) famous study in which he very pointedly found *no* relationship between authoritarianism and prejudice in that country.

But these hardly constitute a "WORLDWIDE CONFIRMATION" of the RWA Scale. And even if they did, even if we found high RWA Scale alphas and sizable correlations with (say) prejudice in every nation on earth, what would that really mean? We would still not understand why the attitudes covary, or how people become authoritarians in the first place, or what we can do about it now. So—so what?

NOTES

1. The elaborations in this section on my definition of authoritarianism were originally given in *RWA*, pp. 147–155. See that source for a fuller presentation, none of which I can find reason to change seven years later.
2. Ray's 1976 *Human Relations* paper, on which his research on directiveness is based, cannot be recommended for its high scholarship. For example, he stated that the authoritative figure in Milgram's experiments was "usually a member of the Psychology Department staff" and that Milgram's subjects were students. But graver mistakes capsized Ray's own research that led him to claim the Directiveness Scale has "persuasive concurrent validity."

   He proceeded as follows. First he developed a balanced 14-item test and did some research with it. Then he gave a lecture on his conceptualization of directiveness and his findings to 250 students enrolled in a second-year sociology course. Afterward he asked the students to write items that would measure his construct. Ray does not report how many suggestions he received, but he could easily have obtained hundreds. However many he started out with, he culled eight protrait and eight contrait items from the offerings and found that summed scores on these 16 items correlated .52 with summed scores on the 14 items he directly wrote himself. This supposedly provided the persuasive evidence that the Directiveness Scale was concurrently valid.

   It is a strange use of the term, however. *Concurrent validity* classically means that a test predicts some criterion behavior measured simultaneously—as opposed to predicting a criterion behavior some time later, such as graduation or divorce. It is contemporaneous "predictive validity" (Cronbach, 1970, p. 122). But no criterion of directiveness was involved in the .52 correlation, which merely represented the relationship between the items Ray composed by himself and those he assembled with the help of others. Since Ray participated so extensively in the latter exercise, by giving the lecture and choosing among the suggestions, who can be surprised that a significant correlation was obtained? The measures were hardly independent. (The editors who thought this exercise had produced "little doubt that both scales do in fact measure what they purport to measure" should be required to find a psychological test, however crummy, that could *not* be "validated" in this way.)

   One might be surprised the correlation was not *higher* than

.52. But the alpha of the Directiveness Scale was only .64, meaning the average interitem correlation was about .10. (Adding 12 of the "students'" items raised the alpha to .74 but did not change the level of interitem correlation.) As such, the Directiveness Scale is among the most disjointed, and certainly least reliable, tests one can find—and that is saying something.

One should not, therefore, be amazed that scores on this measure were *un*correlated with various measures of prejudice, participation in antiwar or antiapartheid demonstrations, membership in conservative political clubs, religious beliefs, religious background, moralism, and attitudes toward morality. Ray, however, concluded that *these things* were therefore unrelated to authoritarianism—not that his scale was quite a poor instrument and his meaning of "authoritarianism" was fundamentally different from earlier researchers'. He has since reached the same conclusion about a number of other variables, of which "Altemeyer's Scale" (as he termed the RWA Scale in his 1985 paper) is just the latest. Interestingly, in that paper he told his readers the alpha of the RWA Scale (.89) and that of his Conservatism Scale (.82 and .79 for two different forms) but neglected to give the same information for the Directiveness Scale. If the latter were in the .65–.75 range, reporting it would make the alternative explanation, given above, obvious.

Lest I be just as selective in what I tell you, Ray (1976) *did* find a correlation of .53 between those sociology students' ratings of the directiveness of two of their acquaintances and the responses of those acquaintances to the 14-item Directiveness Scale. That is a very high correlation, in my experience, for so helter-skelter and unstable a test, but it is possible. And it is hardly fair to criticize a scale for being too unreliable to produce appreciable relationships and then refuse to believe the appreciable relationships it produces.

One would be more convinced, nevertheless, if Ray had reported his procedures in greater detail. For example, an unspecified number of questionnaires were discarded in the study; only 282 surveys of a maximum potential of 500 were "available for analysis." One also notes that Ray collected data on extremes: the students were asked to pick the most and the least directive person they knew, of their many acquaintances. And finally, these undergraduates, knowing full well Ray's hypothesis and carrying a survey they had had a hand in producing, administered the tests personally to their acquaintances and then brought the answers (*and* their ratings of their friends) back to Ray.

The construct of directiveness may or may not prove relevant to our understanding of authoritarianism (as I mean the term). But I hope the reader will understand why I presently feel we have little convincing information on the subject.

2

Studying Authoritarianism: Research Methodology and Methodology Research

I. Research Methodology

The RWA Scale

The conceptualization of right-wing authoritarianism described in Chapter One is measured by an attitude scale inventively entitled the Right-Wing Authoritarianism (or "RWA") Scale. Originally 24 items long, the test grew to its present size of 30 statements in the late 1970s. Since then I have usually appraised experimental items whenever I administered the measure, seeking to replace those statements with the lowest item-whole correlations. Either because it is hard to write good items or because I am not good at it, the RWA Scale has evolved at a Beetle's pace, averaging about one change per year.

Half the items on the test are "protraits," for which the authoritarian answer is agreement; the other half are "contraits," on which *dis*agreement indicates authoritarianism. Comparison of the test shown in Exhibit 1 (on which nearly all the research reported in this book is based) with the edition listed on pages 219–220 of *RWA* will reveal six changes—five of them involving contrait items. The latter have always had weaker item-whole relationships than the protraits. But one can cite compelling reasons for balancing authoritarianism scales with both kinds of statements (*RWA*, chap. 2).

Exhibit 1 contains as well the instructions that accompany the test. The introductory statements, presenting the cover story that the questionnaire is merely "an investigation of general public opinion concerning a variety of social issues," have not changed since the test's introduction. The last paragraph was added in 1982 to help subjects respond to items they found "double-barreled."

Subjects

Who are these persons who might find my hard-earned survey items thus flawed? Most of them have been introductory psychology students at the University of Manitoba (*RWA*, p. 316). Although there is not the remotest chance that this group is representative of the human race, of North America's population, of Canada's, or even of Manitoba's, it does at least answer my surveys in largely the same way as do samples in other places—as we saw in Chapter One. In other words, it does not seem wildly *un*representative. However confused I have been at times in my investigations, I have not had the luxury of blaming my samples for their failures to confirm my treasured notions. I would apparently have been just as confused in Birmingham, Alabama, or Brisbane, Australia.

Because Manitoba students are eager to earn a small part of their introductory psychology grade by serving in experiments, they have also been quite willing to address envelopes home and ask their parents to fill out my surveys for the same reward.[1] These parents have varied in age from the upper thirties to the low seventies but average forty-eight years in sample after sample. Their mean education has risen from 12 to nearly 13 grades over the years of my investigations, ranging from early elementary school to extensive postgraduate work. Most students' homes could be described as middle-class, but because Manitoba tuitions are low (about $900 U.S. in 1987–88), a certain number of "blue collar" offspring attend university, and hence their parents appear in my samples.[2]

Even so, these accommodating parents of university students are not representative of (say) adult Canadians. Their chief virtue, besides their self-sacrificing availability, lay in their constituting a different sample from students. If results obtained with first-year college students are also obtained with this older, more weathered and diverse population—which has proved quite the rule—we at least know that the model of behavior afoot will apply to someone besides the students. But whether the findings will hold for a whole population or are limited in countless ways remains to be determined.

If the parent samples are not representative of larger groups, are they even representative of the parent population? About 20 to 25 percent of the students who are asked to address envelopes to their folks choose not to, and a similar percentage of the parents who are mailed surveys do not return them. Are the parents who *do* participate a fair pick of all who might have?

Obviously we cannot know, since the unsolicited and the unresponsive did not participate. But I have never found a significant difference between the RWA Scale scores of the *students* for whom I have parental data and the students for whom I have none.

Curiously, this is not because there are no self-selection biases but because two small but discernible biases offset each other. Low RWA students* are a little less likely to ask that surveys be sent home. (Lows are occasionally estranged from their parents; Highs almost never are.) Parents of High RWA students, in turn, are a little less likely to return surveys sent them. (Perhaps because of wariness, but RWA Scale scores are negatively correlated with education among parents; less educated parents may be less likely to attempt the survey booklet.)

* Throughout this book, the lowest-scoring quarter of a sample will be termed "Low RWA subjects" (or simply "Lows") and the upper quartile "Highs."

Exhibit 1. The "1982" RWA Scale.

This survey is part of an investigation of general public opinion concerning a variety of social issues. You will probably find that you *agree* with some of the statements, and *disagree* with others, to varying extents. Please indicate your reaction to each of the statements by blackening a bubble in SECTION 1 of the IBM sheet, according to the following scale:

Blacken the bubble labeled – 4 if you *very strongly disagree* with the statement.
– 3 if you *strongly disagree* with the statement.
– 2 if you *moderately disagree* with the statement.
– 1 if you *slightly disagree* with the statement.

Blacken the bubble labeled + 1 if you *slightly agree* with the statement.
+ 2 if you *moderately agree* with the statement.
+ 3 if you *strongly agree* with the statement.
+ 4 if you *very strongly agree* with the statement.

If you feel exactly and precisely *neutral* about a statement, blacken the "0" bubble.

You may find that you sometimes have different reactions to different parts of a statement. For example, you might very strongly disagree ("– 4") with one idea in a statement, but slightly agree ("+ 1") with another idea in the same item. When this happens, please combine your reactions, and write down how you feel "on balance" (that is, a "– 3" in this example).[3]

1. The way things are going in this country, it's going to take a lot of "strong medicine" to straighten out the troublemakers, criminals, and perverts.
2. It is wonderful that young people today have greater freedom to protest against things they don't like and to "do their own thing."*
3. It is always better to trust the judgment of the proper authorities in government and religion than to listen to the noisy rabble-rousers in our society who are trying to create doubt in people's minds.
4. People should pay less attention to the Bible and the other old traditional forms of religious guidance and instead develop their own personal standards of what is moral and immoral.*
5. It would be best for everyone if the proper authorities censored magazines and movies to keep trashy material away from the youth.
6. It may be considered old-fashioned by some, but having a decent, respectable appearance is still the mark of a gentleman and, especially, a lady.
7. The sooner we get rid of the traditional family structure, where the father is the head of the family and the children are taught to obey authority automatically, the better. The old-fashioned way has a lot wrong with it.*
8. There is nothing wrong with premarital sexual intercourse.*
9. The facts on crime, sexual immorality, and the recent public disorders all show we have to crack down harder on deviant groups and troublemakers if we are going to save our moral standards and preserve law and order.
10. There is nothing immoral or sick in somebody's being a homosexual.*
11. It is important to protect fully the rights of radicals and deviants.*
12. Obedience and respect for authority are the most important virtues children should learn.
13. Rules about being "well-mannered" and respectable are chains from the past which we should question very thoroughly before accepting.*

14. Once our government leaders and the authorities condemn the dangerous elements in our society, it will be the duty of every patriotic citizen to help stomp out the rot that is poisoning our country from within.
15. "Free speech" means that people should even be allowed to make speeches and write books urging the overthrow of the government.*
16. Some of the worst people in our country nowadays are those who do not respect our flag, our leaders, and the normal way things are supposed to be done.
17. In these troubled times laws have to be enforced without mercy, especially when dealing with the agitators and revolutionaries who are stirring things up.
18. Atheists and others who have rebelled against the established religions are no doubt every bit as good and virtuous as those who attend church regularly.*
19. Young people sometimes get rebellious ideas, but as they grow up they ought to get over them and settle down.
20. The self-righteous "forces of law and order" threaten freedom in our country a lot more than most of the groups they claim are "radical" and "godless."*
21. The courts are right in being easy on drug users. Punishment would *not* do any good in cases like these.*
22. If a child starts becoming unconventional and disrespectful of authority, it is his parents' duty to get him back to the normal way.
23. In the final analysis the established authorities, like parents and our national leaders, generally turn out to be right about things, and all the protesters don't know what they're talking about.
24. A lot of our rules regarding modesty and sexual behavior are just customs which are not necessarily any better or holier than those which other people follow.*
25. There is absolutely nothing wrong with nudist camps.*
26. The *real* keys to the "good life" are obedience, discipline, and sticking to the straight and narrow.
27. It is best to treat dissenters with leniency and an open mind, since new ideas are the lifeblood of progressive change.*
28. The biggest threat to our freedom comes from the Communists and their kind, who are out to destroy religion, ridicule patriotism, corrupt the youth, and in general undermine our whole way of life.
29. Students in high school and university must be encouraged to challenge their parents' ways, confront established authorities, and in general criticize the customs and traditions of our society.*
30. One reason we have so many troublemakers in our society nowadays is that parents and other authorities have forgotten that good old-fashioned physical punishment is still one of the best ways to make people behave properly.

---

* Item is worded in the contrait direction; that is, the authoritarian response is to disagree.

Notes: All items are scored on a 1–9 basis. For protrait statements, "– 4" is scored as 1, and "+ 4" is scored as 9. The keying is reversed for contrait items. For both kinds of items, the neutral answer ("0") is scored as 5. The lowest possible score is 30, and the highest is 270. No one has ever answered so extremely in my studies, however.

The "1986" version of the RWA Scale substituted the following statement for Item 28: "Our country will be great if we honor the ways of our forefathers, do what the authorities tell us to do, and get rid of the 'rotten apples' who are ruining everything." And the contrait Item 21 will be replaced by "Everyone has a right to his/her own life-style, religious beliefs or disbeliefs, and sexual preferences so long as it doesn't hurt others."

These differences have seldom been statistically significant, even with fairly large samples. But I am no longer surprised to find a potential sample bias to the right as the parents' surveys go out, which then corrects itself as the booklets come in.

Cross-Sectional Changes in RWA Scale Responses over Time

Changes in Level of Authoritarianism. Has the authoritarianism of these successive Manitoba samples remained steady over time? I reported in 1981 that my student samples had grown progressively more authoritarian over the course of the 1970s. This trend was evident in the responses to 12 RWA Scale items that I had included in all my (highly standardized) autumn studies since 1973.[4] As can be seen in Figure 1, this climb has continued into the 1980s. Ten of the "Continuing Twelve" have drawn steadily more authoritarian responses over time; one ("In these troubled times . . .") has not changed; and the last ("A 'woman's place' . . .") has evoked dramatically less authoritarian answers as the years passed.

Parents' scores on these 12 items have not risen significantly over time; they averaged 71.6 in 1976 and 72.9 in 1985, representing a slight amount of authoritarianism (perfect neutrality would produce a score of $12 \times 5 = 60$).

Figure 1 supports numerous observations by educators, editorialists, and "Doonesbury" that North American undergraduates in the 1980s are more "conservative" than their predecessors of the late sixties and early seventies and more concerned with their personal futures than with broad societal issues and social injustices. The times, like Bob Dylan, have been a-changing.

In 1981 I attributed the Manitoba rise primarily to the disappearance of the Bob Dylans (that is, the radical student left), which was never prominent at my university but which scored quite low on the RWA Scale while it was around. The continuation of this trend is documented in Table 1. "Very-low-RWA students" are almost extinct on my campus now, but all the ranks of Low students have thinned as well. Thus the left wing of the distribution has withered from the tip to the center over the

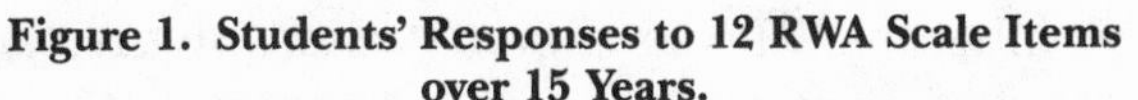

Figure 1. Students' Responses to 12 RWA Scale Items over 15 Years.

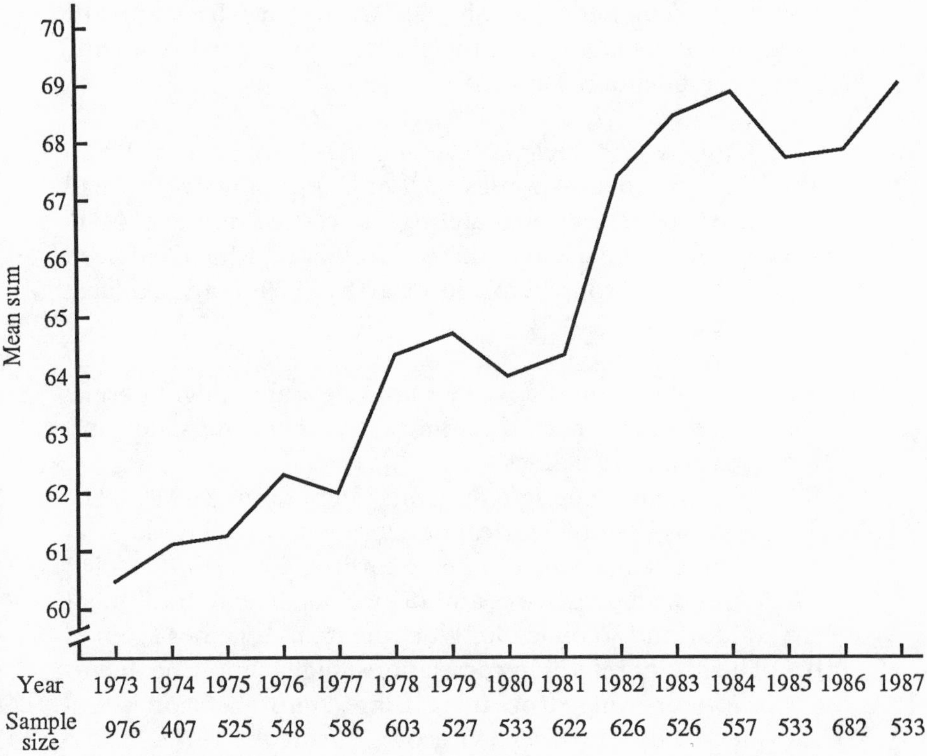

70
69
68
67
66
65
64
63
62
61
60
Mean sum
Year
1973 1974 1975 1976 1977 1978 1979 1980 1981 1982 1983 1984 1985 1986 1987
Sample size
976 407 525 548 586 603 527 533 622 626 526 557 533 682 533

Note: The RWA Scale items were answered on a –3 to +3 basis through 1979, with a neutral answer ("0") scored as a 4 on the 1–7 scale. Beginning in 1980, responses were given on a –4 to +4 basis, with a "0" scored as a 5 on the 1–9 scale. Thus a subject who said "0" to all 12 items would score 48 in 1979 but 60 afterward. To facilitate comparisons, all means above are reported on a 9-point basis. That is, 12 has been added to the values given on p. 246 of *Right-Wing Authoritarianism.*

years. (Remember the "Chicago Seven's" assertion that the "counterculture" would control the next generation?) At the other extreme, the number of "very-high-RWA students" has not really changed; but my samples are increasingly dominated by slightly high and moderately high RWA subjects.

Changes in Correlations Among RWA Scale Items. I also noted in 1981 that responses to the "Continuing Twelve" had become less intercorrelated among successive samples of Manitoba students. The mean of these correlations, which had been .25 in 1973, had dropped to almost .16 by 1979. Three explanations were offered:

I. The test (and perhaps other attitude scales) might permanently "come apart" over time as items become dated and connotations change.
II. Associations among sentiments might diminish (as in Hypothesis I), but historical developments could reestablish them at some future time; accordingly, a period of civil unrest with defiance of authority, challenges to traditional values, and so on could "glue" the items together again.
III. The loss of interitem correlations might simply be due to the depressing drop in reading comprehension documented by declining SAT scores during the 1970s.

Data collected since 1981 support the first hypothesis more than the others. As shown in Figure 2, interitem correlations among the "Continuing Twelve" have remained significantly and far below their 1973 values and appear to be dropping still. In fact, several of these items have become so unconnected they are no longer part of the test (see Note 4). I include them in my fall questionnaire merely to follow the curves in Figures 1 and 2.

The outstanding example of a dated item is "A 'woman's place' should be wherever she wants to be. The days when women are submissive to their husbands and social conventions belong strictly in the past." In 1973 the average *student* reaction to this espousal of sexual equality was to slightly disagree. By

Table 1. Distribution of Summed Scores of "Continuing Twelve" Items Among Students, 1973–1985.

		RWA Score					
Year	*N*	*Very low*	*Moderately low*	*Slightly low*	*Slightly high*	*Moderately high*	*Very high*
1973	976	3.5%	11.2%	30.9%	40.2%	13.2%	1.0%
1979	527	1.3	6.5	31.3	43.8	16.0	1.1
1985[a]	533	0.2	2.8	22.5	51.2	22.0	1.3

[a] Values obtained in 1985 are presented to match the previously reported six-year interval between 1973 and 1979 (*RWA*, pp. 245–246). The corresponding percentages in the fall 1986 study ($N = 682$) were 0.1, 4.6, 19.5, 53.1, 21.8, and 0.9, respectively; those for 1987 ($N = 533$) were 0.8, 2.2, 17.5, 51.7, 25.5, and 2.3.

Note: When RWA Scale items were answered on a −3 to +3 basis (from 1973 through 1979), "very low RWA" meant scores from 12 to 24, "moderately low" went from 25 to 36, "slightly low" ranged from 37 to 48, "slightly high" included 49–60, "moderately high" meant 61–72, and scores from 73 to 84 were called "very high RWA." When a nine-point, −4 to +4 response scale was adopted for the RWA Scale in 1980, the categories above were redefined as 12–28, 29–44, 45–60, 61–76, 77–92, and 93–108, respectively.

Figure 2. Mean Interitem Correlations Among the "Continuing Twelve" in Student Samples, 1973–1987.

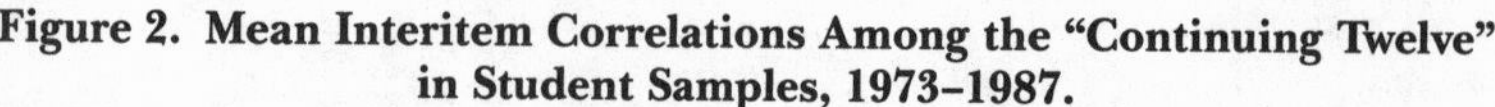

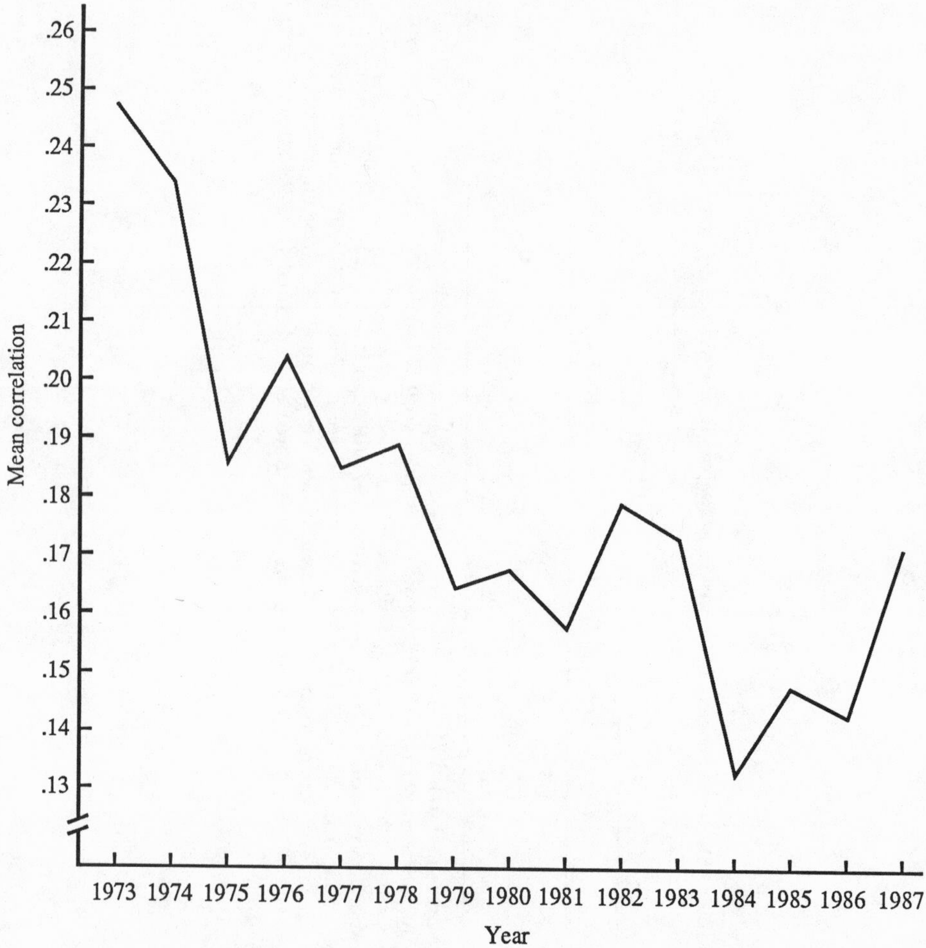

1982, however, the typical response was to strongly agree—this being the item mentioned earlier that has drawn less authoritarian reactions over time. With the item hitting its head against a ceiling of agreement, it correlated little with anything else.[5]

Part of the drop in internal consistency shown in Figure 2

undoubtedly resulted from the loss of low-scoring students discussed above. Truncated ranges reduce correlations. But clearly the "shelf life" of items on an attitude scale can be shorter than that of items on an intelligence test. Some of my creations went stale in just a few years. Yet some statements prove relatively timeless; for example, Items 12 and 19 in Exhibit 1 originally appeared on the F Scale in 1950.

The evidence to date gives no support to Hypothesis II. Yet I find it interesting that the *original* 24-item RWA Scale has had such good alphas in the 1980s elsewhere in the world (as described in Chapter One). If North America again experiences "interesting times," some regluing may occur.[6]

As for Hypothesis III, Manitoba students do not write aptitude tests on entering university, so their level of reading comprehension is unknown. However, SAT-Verbal scores in the United States bottomed out in 1979–80 and since have risen steadily—which does not exactly parallel Figure 2.

Psychometric Characteristics of the RWA Scale in This Research Program

How have the falling intercorrelations affected the RWA Scale's performance in my research? Unattended, the result would have been most depressing. But the deterioration has been controlled as weakly connected items have been replaced by statements with better "connections." The mean intercorrelation on the 30-item scale in Exhibit 1 has ranged from .15 to .21 among students, with corresponding alpha reliabilities of .85 to .89. Intercorrelations among the (more heterogeneous) parents have varied between .21 and .24, with alphas of .90 typical.

Test-retest reliabilities among students have ranged from .95 for a 1-week interval to .85 for a 28-week interval. Test-retest reliability has not been assessed for parents.

Mean student scores have varied from 148 to 157 (150, a typical average, being the midpoint of the potential range 30–270). (These scores would have been higher, with increasingly authoritarian students entering university over time, but most of the replacement items have drawn somewhat low means.) Parents' scores have been significantly higher than their children's, averaging around 175. No reliable sex differences have appeared among students or parents, although females tend to score higher on conventionalism items, and males higher on statements tapping authoritarian aggression.

Factor analyses[7] of the RWA Scale yield a variety of results, depending on what kind of analysis is chosen. The "classical factor analysis" I employed in *Right-Wing Authoritarianism* (pp. 182–188), which attempts to explain what the items on a test have in common, has always produced either a one- or a two-factor solution, accounting for about 25–30 percent of the test's total variance. The two-factor solutions have always found the protrait items loading heavily on one factor and the contrait items loading heavily on the other. These two factors correlate about .65 to .70, following Promax rotation.[8]

One can see, in conclusion, that this research program has benefited from a certain stability: partly because of item development and partly because I use large samples—but also because of a certain constancy in procedures, to which we now turn.

Studies of Manitoba Students

Other Professors' Students. Nearly all of my Manitoba student studies closely followed the standardized procedures detailed in *RWA*, pp. 176–179. In overview, equal numbers of male and female introductory psychology students were recruited in colleagues' classes for a "study of the social attitudes of Canadian students." Persons who signed up for the experiment kept their appointments by reporting to a classroom in the psychology building, where they were tested in groups of about 50 for as many minutes. Subjects typically came back a week later to answer another booklet of material, and sometimes I ran three-session experiments. Since no credits were given until the final session, return rates have always been above 90 percent. There has never been any indication that High or Low RWA students differentially miss their appointments.

At the first session subjects were reminded, through taped

instructions, that the experiment was for Canadians only. They were usually told they would be asked to give their names and booklet numbers on an attendance sheet; every one of over 10,000 students over the years has done so. Next they were told they could omit answering anything in the booklet they wished (but the solid majority of my subjects, both students and parents, have answered everything on most of my questionnaires). They were then asked to work with care and were given the instructions for the RWA Scale (see Exhibit 1). Responses were "bubbled" on a custom-made computer answer sheet (IBM Form No. 11349-9075). Subsequent material in the booklet was answered on the IBM sheet or directly in the booklet for later encoding at my dining room table.

At subsequent sessions, the students were reminded of their previous survey numbers and then provided with new booklets containing their partly filled IBM sheets. An example of the organization of material in a three-session experiment, conducted in 1984 and featured in the next chapter, is given in Appendix B.

Testing My Own Introductory Students. I have also at times involved my own introductory students in this survey research, following in general the procedures described above. However, I have administered these booklets in class, describing them as a "Psychometric Survey" composed of different professors' research instruments, routinely given at the beginning of the school year. I specifically told my classes that none of the material was my own and in general leaked a certain resentment that a whole period was being used for somebody else's benefit. (My students, however, are glad to earn experimental credits, each worth 1 percent of their final grade, during class time; over 90 percent of them show up for the "Psychometric Survey"—more than come for lectures.)

The "Secret Survey." I maintain the fiction in my classes during the academic year that the Psychometric Survey is composed of other professors' instruments, shamelessly attributing the questionnaires to real and imaginary colleagues. However, I have thrice distributed a single-sheet "Secret Survey," which I identify as my own, to these same students in January (the course runs until April). This sheet, containing highly personal questions, is attached to another giving the students a record of their test scores for the first term. Though unnumbered, the Secret Surveys were discreetly marked to indicate whether the student had been in the upper or the lower quartile of the RWA Scale distribution in the fall testing.

Subjects were asked to separate the two sheets, thus making the survey quite anonymous, and go to a place of their choice on campus to mark their answers. After folding the sheet several times, the students returned to class in about 15 minutes and placed the survey in a sealed box at the front of the room. An experimental credit was given to everyone who had picked up the grade feedback sheet. All of the surveys thus distributed have been answered and returned.

The Secret Survey has proved very useful for obtaining information about sexual behavior, family violence, deep religious feelings, cheating in class, and other sensitive matters that students do not readily reveal. Take sex, for example. In 1980 I asked students anonymously answering a booklet in my standard experiment to describe their sexual experiences. Sixteen percent of the males and 20 percent of the females did not answer the question, including a disproportionate number of High RWA students (*RWA*, p. 327, n. 29). However, at least 97 percent of both sexes have since answered this same question for me on the "Secret Survey," as we shall see in Chapter Five.

Studies of Students' Parents

When students serving in my standard experiment finished their second or third booklets, they have sometimes read that they could earn additional credits if their parents completed a similar survey "to test the generalizability of the results." Students interested in doing so addressed envelopes to their parents as they left the testing room. Booklets were mailed within a week, accompanied by a letter explaining the need to conduct "a survey on general social issues" among persons who might be more representative of the population than students. (See *RWA*, p. 308, for an example of the letters used over the years.)

I usually gave my own students the same opportunity to have booklets sent home, continuing the cover story that some of the researchers who had put together the Psychometric Survey would like to collect data from a different population.

Parents were assured that their responses would be anonymous, and their booklets were not obviously numbered. However, in some studies in which it was important to connect students' scores with their parents', the student's survey number was discreetly marked in the booklet mailed his or her parents. The parents' answers were nonetheless anonymous; either I never knew who the students were in the first place (that is, no attendance sheet was circulated), or I destroyed the attendance sheets on the day I mailed the surveys home. There was thus no way I or anyone else could learn the personal identity of subjects promised anonymity. But I did not openly write survey numbers on the parents' questionnaires, because of the obvious effect that could have on their responses.

Subject-Pool Pollution and the "Transparency" of the RWA Scale

Because I have tested most of the introductory psychology students at my university for many years, and several thousand of their parents, knowledge of my research could be widespread. Even more worrisome, perfectly naive subjects might be able to discern the purpose of the RWA Scale on their own. So a few years ago I began testing these possibilities.

In November 1982 I administered a booklet in my standard experiment in which subjects (1) completed the RWA Scale as usual, (2) next answered it as they thought their parents would like them to, and (3) then answered it as they thought they would 20 years in the future. Then, having gone through the scale three times, they were asked to write down what they thought the survey measured: "Is there anything these statements all seem to relate to? What do you think it is measuring?"

The most frequent answers reflected the cover story given

the subjects ("a variety of social opinions") or else "morals." Liberalism and conservatism had a certain popularity, and some wrote such things as "?," "Beats me," and "Nothing." Three of the 379 subjects wrote "attitudes toward authorities" or something similar.

Two months later, another group of students who also had just gone through the RWA Scale three times were asked to choose, from the list below, what they thought the scale measured. I gave them two guesses and promised them an extra experimental credit if their first choice was correct.

____ Opinions about morals and morality
____ Right-wing authoritarianism
____ Various opinions about our society
____ Liberalism versus conservatism
____ None of the above. The survey is a mixture of statements about many unrelated things.

Of 476 students, precisely 200 checked "various opinions about our society" as their first guess, and 156 guessed "morals." "Liberalism versus conservatism" came in third ($N = 67$), and 31 (or 7 percent) of the students were (quietly) awarded extra credits the following week for having chosen "right-wing authoritarianism." Twenty-two said "none of the above."

The frequency distribution of the second guesses paralleled that of the first. Forty-eight students (10 percent of the sample) made authoritarianism their second choice.

In September 1983 I asked 223 parents, who had also just waded through the RWA Scale three times, "What do you think this survey measures, if anything?" The same list of alternatives, with the order changed, was provided for two guesses. "Various opinions about our society" won by a landslide ($N = 124$), with everything else far behind. "Right-wing authoritarianism" came in last, with 9 first- and 17 second-place votes.

I have asked this same question of students (for reward) and parents every year since, changing the order of alternatives each time. The results have not varied appreciably. About 5 percent of the sample answers correctly on the first try, through either foreknowledge, insight, or luck. (In general, these subjects show a slight tendency to score low on the test.)

I have felt particularly vulnerable to my own students' pipelines to the rumor mill, but apparently they are as unaware as the rest. Only 18 of 352 credit-hungry persons in my class, promised an extra credit for a correct answer, made the right response to the question above during a survey administered at the *end* of the school year in 1985.[9]

In September 1985 I asked 533 persons to indicate what they had heard about "Experiment Survey" beforehand from friends or the "grapevine." The most common answer was "Nothing." (Some subjects indicated they had heard the experiment asked "lots of questions about homosexuals"—a theme of that particular booklet.) No one mentioned anything about authoritarianism.

If the proper conclusion is that no one cares about my research program, I am grateful, at least for the short run. I have not been extravagantly forthcoming about my investigations over the years.[10] Furthermore, the RWA Scale is not, apparently, a transparent instrument, and its cover story sells well. If subjects try to figure out what the measure measures, they seem to alight on other, rather innocuous possibilities.

I would offer two guesses of my own for this. First, the test *does* cover a lot of seemingly unrelated topics. Because I have been concentrating on authoritarianism for 20 years, I forget that many persons have never heard the word and cannot even pronounce it on the first try. So this underlying concept may not spring to mind when people are giving their opinions on the many topics that appear strewn about the RWA Scale. Second, half the statements are written in the contrait direction, making it harder, I think, for subjects to infer what the scale is "getting at." Curiously, both these features reduce the interitem correlations on the test; but they pay this back with profit by disguising the scale's purpose and protecting its summed scores from uncontrolled response sets.

II. Methodology Research

Importance of Internal Consistency for Unidimensionality

The reader may have wondered a few pages back about my concern over internal consistency. If one reduced the error in subjects' responses such that the alpha reliability of a scale rose from .80 to .90, that would more than double the test's signal-to-noise ratio (Cronbach and Gleser, 1964). But the effect on validity coefficients would be negligible; one would merely produce about a 6 percent increase in the scale's correlation with some criterion.* As Cronbach (1970, p. 171) noted, once a measure has attained a reliability of .80 or so, further increases improve validity very slowly. Many researchers are accordingly quite content to work with instruments whose alpha is .80 or less.

I argued in *Right-Wing Authoritarianism* that this practice is shortsighted because it does little good (publications aside) to correlate Measure X with some behavior if you do not know what Measure X measures. If it appreciably captures "Y" and "Z," how does one know what its relationships with other variables signify—especially if one does not perform an item analysis, which hardly anyone does? For example, the California F Scale has an alpha of about .80 and a huge literature chock full of relationships. But it is very hard to make sense of most of them, and I do not believe that anyone to this day understands what the F Scale measures (*RWA*, pp. 13–80).

Internal consistency is just as important in a psychological test as in a person. The lower the interitem correlations on a test, the less its unidimensionality, and the less useful it will prove in the long run as a research tool. Too many researchers have thrown a bunch of statements together, discarded the totally uncorrelated ones, and called the residual a measure of Something in Particular. Dozens of other investigators may publish findings with the new instrument, but if it is the kind of meter stick whose measurements reflect length, the color of your hair, and the day of the week, we should not be surprised that ultimately score upon score of research papers amount to little.

Thus my concern over the RWA Scale's interitem correlations, reflected in the item development program discussed above and in the methodological research described below, has not been dedicated to increasing the test's relationships with

* $\sqrt{.90/.80} - 1.00 = .06$, or 6 percent.

other measures. Any increase would be slight. Rather, I wanted to be able to *interpret* those relationships as cleanly as possible. Who wants dirty relationships?

As the student radical left disappeared, and changing times started to unglue the RWA Scale, I tried to slow the decline in interitem correlations by manipulating three aspects of my research methodology: the instructions that precede the test, the response format that students use to answer it, and the number of times students answer each item. It will be seen that the first approach was a failure, the second produced somewhat marginal results, and the third worked entirely too well.

I report these failures in the hope that others may profit from them.

Instructional Manipulations

I suspect that error in subjects' responses to a test such as the RWA Scale occurs largely because of language difficulties: ambiguity of terms, vagueness of referents, and the like. Compounding this inherent problem with questionnaires, however, is respondents' carelessness and lack of motivation. Subjects likely underestimate their importance in the research endeavor, especially when they serve in large groups. Their basic goal in my studies is probably to finish the booklet, not finish it well. This may contribute to nondefensive responding, but it also fattens the error term. The strong influence of response sets on authoritarianism scales (*RWA*, pp. 137, 186–188) testifies to the extent of this indifference.

Strike One. I attempted to correct this situation in the fall of 1979 by inserting special instructions in the taped introductory comments that begin my testing sessions. Four groups of 50+ subjects were told:

> First of all, I would like to emphasize to you the importance of your role as subjects in this research program. The study being conducted here today is very important to me, and it will yield valuable

> information on social attitudes in our country. Your cooperation is absolutely essential, because carelessness and sloppiness by just a few subjects can do a great deal of damage to the validity of this study.

The alpha coefficient of the 30-item RWA Scale answered by these 218 subjects was .87, which was not significantly higher than the alpha of .86 obtained for 527 other students tested in ten standard sessions ($W = 1.14$, $p < .15$; see Feldt, 1969).

Essentially the same special instructions were printed on yellow paper and attached to half the booklets mailed to a sample of parents at the same time. The RWA Scale's alpha among these respondents was .89 ($N = 203$), identical to the value obtained among 234 parents who received no such special sheet.

Strike Two. The following year I combined a modification of the special instructions above with an especially short booklet. The modification involved telling students that this was a particularly important study to me, the culmination of several years' research; I also emphasized that they had plenty of time to do a careful job on the material. The subjects did *not* appear to work slower than usual, however, but simply finished sooner. The alpha of the RWA Scale was .86 ($N = 187$), the same value obtained with 533 students who had answered longer booklets under standard instructions a few weeks earlier.

Strike Three. In the autumn of 1986 I again attempted to reduce measurement error by forewarning students about one of its principal causes. At the completion of the taped instructions in four of my testing sessions I wrote "RESPONSE SETS" on a blackboard and delivered the following memorized statement:

> I want to warn you about one thing before you begin, which is something called a response set. This is a tendency some people have to say they agree with a statement, or disagree with it, when they have read it hurriedly, and do not know what it

> really says. Thus sometimes people who quickly read an item will give the exact opposite answer from their real attitude.
>
> Such response sets can be big problems with questionnaires like mine. But they can be avoided if you simply take your time and make sure you realize the point a statement has made, the direction it has gone in, before you answer it.

The alpha of RWA Scale responses given by these 198 subjects (.87) was not, however, significantly different from that for 488 other subjects (.86) who received no such special warning.[11]

Manipulating the Number of Response Categories

The goal of a response scale is to enable subjects to make as many different answers to a question as are meaningful but no more (Guilford, 1954, Garner, 1960). Responses to the initial version of the RWA Scale were given on the widely used – 3 to + 3 basis. As the years passed, I wondered whether seven was the optimal number of alternatives for my items. Thurstone, for example, had constructed the first attitude scales by having subjects sort statements into 11 piles ranging from "strongly negative" through "neutral" to "strongly affirmative" (Thurstone and Chave, 1929). At the other extreme, Wilson and Patterson (1968) had argued that three response categories ("no," "?," and "yes") are best for getting a subject's true attitude on an issue. Where exactly had the seven-point format come from?

The RWA Scale belongs to the family of attitude measures called "Likert scales," which largely replaced Thurstone's approaches. Likert (1932) began using both the three-point system that Wilson and Patterson advocated 36 years later and a five-category format that most typically ranged from "strongly disagree" to "strongly agree." He settled on the latter because it evoked a more normal distribution of responses, but apparently he did not try anything larger. The five-point response format was widely adapted and is still used.

Osgood and Stagner (1941) employed a seven-category

response "gradient" for what eventually became the semantic differential. But the earliest report I have located of a − 3 to + 3 format wedded to a Likert-type array of statements is Levinson and Sanford's (1944) initial paper on anti-Semitism. Acknowledging "that the conventional five-point marking system was not used," Levinson and Sanford simply said they extended it to seven because "three degrees of agreement and disagreement can readily be distinguished" on each side of the neutral point (p. 353).

Thurstone and Chave's judges, of course, had been able to distinguish *five* such degrees on each side. But like so much else, the − 3 to + 3 format became standard operating procedure because of the enormous influence of *The Authoritarian Personality*. Although there really was no empirical justification for the seven-category system over others, many researchers (including me) agreeably followed along.

Wiser investigators studied the matter. Some (Remmers and Ewart, 1941; Komorita and Graham, 1965; Masters, 1974) have found that Likert measures have appreciably higher reliability when answered on five-, six-, or seven-category systems, compared with two- or three-place formats. But experimenters have also discovered instances in which no increase occurred (Bendig, 1954; Komorita, 1963; Komorita and Graham, 1965; Masters, 1974). As McKelvie (1978, p. 185) observed, "A number of authors have concluded that there is no single optimal number of categories; rather, the appropriate number is a function of the type of stimulus being rated."

What was best for the RWA Scale? In the fall of 1976 I varied the response format used to answer a 28-item version of my test. Students in three testing sessions (total $N = 150$) answered the sentences on a − 1, 0, or + 1 basis; 155 other subjects answered on a − 2 to + 2 basis; 790 students responded on the standard − 3 to + 3 format; and 153 responded on a − 4 to + 4 basis.

Subjects assigned themselves to the different conditions of the experiment according to the appointment times they chose. In all cases the test was encountered at the beginning of the survey booklet. The taped instructions were identical except for the response scale segment. Answers were placed on a custom-made computer scoring sheet (IBM Form No. 9074/9075) that had separate sections of − 1 to + 1, − 2 to + 2, − 3 to + 3, and − 4 to + 4 response bubbles. (A − 5 to + 5, 11-category response scale is decidedly impractical for computer sheet scoring.)

The alpha coefficient of the RWA Scale was .79 when answered on a three-point basis, .84 for the five-, .86 for the seven-, and back down to .84 for the nine-place format. The coefficient for three categories was significantly lower than each of the others ($W = 1.31$ to 1.50, $p < .05$ in all cases), but the five-, seven-, and nine-category coefficients were not significantly different from one another.

The following year I administered the same four versions of the RWA Scale among a new sample of Manitoba students, only in a slightly more complicated fashion. The − 3 to + 3 responses, on which other studies depended, were collected in the usual way at the beginning of their booklets from a sample of 586. The other versions, answered by other subjects, appeared in the middle of booklets where they could be distributed at random within each testing session without complicating the initial instructions. Sample sizes varied from 141 to 146 in these cases.

The results were much the same. The three-category RWA Scale had an alpha of .76; the five-place version, .82; the seven-, .87; and the nine-, .88. The figure for the three-point scale was again significantly lower than all the others, and that for the five-place format was also significantly lower than those of the larger systems.[12]

I next sent different versions of the RWA Scale to parents during the autumn of 1978. Again most parents received − 3 to + 3 versions of the scale ($N = 402$), with 98 − 1 to + 1 forms and 101 + 4 to − 4 forms also completed. (Because of previous results and other research goals, I did not distribute any − 2 to + 2 forms.)

Parents responded in much the same way as the students. The three-category version of the RWA Scale had an alpha of .80, which was significantly lower than the .87 obtained with the seven-point scale and the .89 obtained with the nine-.

Since we want to give subjects as many response alternatives as they can meaningfully use, I adopted the −4 to +4 system for the RWA Scale in 1980. The effects on the test's reliability have probably been negligible, but there is a small satisfaction in allowing respondents to make finer differentiations when they wish to. The opportunity may be lost on less educated respondents; they showed a preference for −3 and (especially) +3 responses on the original seven-point scale (*RWA*, p. 243), and they have shown the same predilections for −4 and +4 on the new nine-point scale. But more educated respondents use the intermediate categories. If we had evolved with 12 fingers and had built our computers on base 12 arithmetic, I might even be employing a −5 to +5 scale by now.

Effects of Retesting

My third approach to shoring up the internal consistency of the RWA Scale was suggested by early measurements of the instrument's test-retest reliability. The scale's internal consistency was always higher on the second administration. One can imagine several explanations. For example, (1) response sets might diminish after subjects encounter contrait items, (2) subjects might have a better idea of what the items refer to after answering the entire set once, and (3) subjects' familiarity with the test might enable them to give more consistent answers to items touching on similar content. The first two possibilities seem desirable ways of reducing experimental error; but the third is problematic, because the consistency may be artificial, based simply on a desire to *appear* consistent.

My first investigation of these possibilities (conducted during the fall 1979 student "special instructions" study described earlier) had students reanswer the RWA Scale right in the booklet at the beginning of a second testing session. They were then shown how to locate their week-old, first set of responses on the IBM sheet and asked to copy them beside the answers they had just written in the booklet. Comparing the two sets, subjects recorded their final reaction to each item on the IBM sheet.

The alpha coefficient of the final set was significantly higher than that of the initial set (.88 compared with .86 for 507 returning "regular instructions" subjects; $W = 1.25$, $p < .001$; .89 compared with .87 for 210 "special instructions" subjects; $W = 1.20$, $p < .001$; see Feldt, 1980). Most of the changes were minor—for example, from "slightly agree" to "moderately agree"—but on about three items per survey answers moved from one side of the neutral point to the other. This was especially likely on the first few items of the test. Furthermore, the amount of change correlated .47 with the length of the item, meaning that the more complicated items tended to be answered differently the second time.

These results were replicated in the fall of 1980, when the alpha rose from .86 to .89 ($N = 505$, $W = 1.31$, $p < .001$). The same tendencies for early and long items to change were noted.

Although these improvements were substantial, the process was time-consuming, and I wondered whether all the comparing allowed subjects to build more consistency into their responses than truly existed. Subjects going through a test for the third time could easily be wondering, "How did I respond to such items before?" In October 1981, therefore, I simply had students reanswer the RWA Scale on the IBM sheet at the beginning of a second session, in straight test-retest design. (Because the first RWA Scale had been preceded by six experimental items, the subjects could not locate their initial answers on the IBM sheet.)

The alpha for 401 students who served in both sessions was .86 initially and .90 one week later. (The test-retest reliability was .95.) I was troubled, however, because this increase in internal consistency did not produce *any* increase in the scale's criterion validity, when a slight increase should have been detectable. For example, the first set of RWA Scale scores correlated .50 with continued acceptance of one's home religion; the second set correlated .49 with the same responses.

I found the same thing the following year, when the alpha

rose from .87 to .90 for 584 subjects, and again there was no payoff in validity.

It appeared, then, that some of the increased consistency resulting from a second administration of the test was illegitimate and counterproductive. It is one thing to raise the alpha of a scale by giving subjects a second chance to overcome response sets and by helping them understand what you mean by the items. It is another to promote response consistency over response validity.

In 1983 and 1984 I therefore experimented with other ways to give subjects a "second chance" at the first few items on the RWA Scale. My first approach, which proved ineffective, asked subjects to review their first few answers after they had finished the entire test. Unfortunately I spotted many subjects who, eager to finish the experiment quickly, merely moved immediately to the next task in the booklet.

So I then presented the first six or so items on the test again at the end of the scale, with the following instructions:

> The items below appeared at the beginning of the survey. Just answer them again, in the spaces indicated, according to how you feel now. Don't worry if some of your answers are different from before; that's to be expected sometimes.

The second answers to such items have always correlated better with the rest of the test than the first answers did. The effect is usually strongest for the first two statements. The mean of the first item ("strong medicine," a protrait) always drops significantly, while that of the second ("do their own thing," a contrait) always rises even more. In both cases examination of subjects' responses reveals that a noticeable number of "agree" responses became "disagrees," while other "strongly agrees" became more moderate. In other words, the second administration reduces "yea-saying," especially to the first contrait item on the test.

Typically the alpha of the RWA Scale rises about .01 or .02 from this latest manipulation, and the scale's correlations with other balanced measures improve slightly, while its relationships with *un*balanced tests drop slightly—confirming the suspicion that the readministration helps overcome response sets. The effect is somewhat stronger with parents than with students.

Because of these findings, I have routinely readministered the first two to six items on the RWA Scale since 1984, using the instructions above. Most authoritarianism scores reported in later chapters employed this correction.

Summary

These methodological studies, done at very little expense while other research proceeded, have paid out about as much as they cost:

1. The only thing I have learned from my efforts to improve subjects' motivation through special instructions is that I don't know how to do it.
2. I increased the response format of the RWA Scale because it did not appear to hurt anything and would permit more discriminating subjects to "do *their* thing." (Other scales with five- and especially three-category systems might similarly improve their reliability very cheaply by adopting a more differentiated response format.)
3. The experiments with repeated test administration have led to a simple technique for reducing error in initial responses to the RWA Scale. (One might want to try this with other scales as well, especially if their internal consistency is low.)

But if someone were to say, "You are surely misguided, in a world plagued by famine, terrorism, dictatorships, and nuclear weapons, to find satisfaction in raising an alpha by .02," I am not sure I could credibly disagree. So if we now understand how, in general, this research gets done, let us move on to far more substantive matters.

NOTES

1. In the spring of 1986, after I had given feedback to several introductory classes about the studies in which they had served, I distributed an anonymous survey to them. The last question read:

   > Just as a matter of curiosity to me: One of my colleagues suggested that some of the students who turned in surveys from their parents had actually filled in one or both of the surveys themselves. Did you do so? (There's no penalty involved; I won't even know who you are. But I want to know how often this happened.)

   Of 147 students who indicated they had returned surveys from their parents, 4 said they had actually answered some or all of the questions themselves.
2. A sample of 551 parents in 1984 gave information about the occupation of the principal breadwinner in the family, which was then classified according to Blishen and McRoberts' (1976) categorization of Canadian occupational status. About a quarter of the sample was definitely "blue collar" (that is, scores less than 40 on the Blishen and McRoberts scale), and another eighth had scores in the 40s (for example, machine operators = 42, salespeople = 44, postal clerks = 48). About 20 percent had scores in the 50s (owners of small businesses = 50, bookkeepers = 51, buyers = 55). The largest number of families (fully a third) belonged in the "managerial/teacher" 60s. About 10 percent of the principal breadwinners were "professionals," scoring in the 70s.
3. When administering the scale to particularly well-educated or sophisticated groups, I have included a third introductory paragraph in the instructions:

   > Finally, it is always difficult to communicate complex ideas in a sentence or two. It is understood that a person's answers to these statements can vary quite a bit, depending on how terms are defined. But previous research indicates there is a common understanding as to what these statements are referring to, or "getting at." If you find yourself saying, "What does he mean by ______?," the answer is likely "What do you think most people mean by it?"

4. These 12 items are Numbers 4, 6, 9, 12, 13, 17, 18, 19, and 21 in Exhibit 1 and three others since replaced on the RWA Scale but still included in my large September studies: "A 'woman's place' should be wherever she wants to be. The days when women are submissive to their husbands and social conventions belong strictly in the past"; "Our customs and national heritage are the things that have made us great, and certain people should be made to show greater respect for them"; and "Our prisons are a shocking disgrace. Criminals are unfortunate people who deserve much better care, instead of so much punishment."

   Thus, of the "Continuing Twelve," only nine actually continued on the RWA Scale through 1986 and, as noted in Exhibit 1, Item 21 is about to be replaced as well.
5. If the "woman's place" item no longer discriminated among Manitoba students by the 1980s, it still evoked useful, "interconnecting" responses among parents. However, I retain items on the RWA Scale only if they have sufficient item-whole correlations among students *and* parents. So "A 'woman's place'" was dropped, as I also dropped the protrait "Women should always remember the promise they make in the marriage ceremony to obey their husbands" in the mid 1970s. (If the reader is thinking that few women make such a promise anymore, that is the point of Hypothesis I.)

   High RWA students at my university seldom say flat out, anymore, that a woman's place is in the home. But they did tend to agree with the following in a January 1987 study: "While women should have a more equal status in society, it's still right that they should do most of the child rearing when the children are young." So attitudes have changed some over the years, but Highs still resist changing the sex roles more than others do.
6. I included all the "deceased" items from the original RWA Scale in my September 1986 booklet, placing them at the end of the 30 statements shown in Exhibit 1. Combining their scores with those of surviving items permits one to look at the original 24-item test 13 years after its first use in the fall of 1973 (*RWA*, p. 181). The mean interitem correlation had dropped over time from .23 to .14, with a corresponding reduction in alpha from .88 to .79. But summed scores of the original 24 items, some 14 points higher on the average than they had been in 1973, still correlated .88 with those on the current version—aided no doubt by the many surviving items common to both tests.
7. Factor analysis is a statistical technique that can help identify what

a test really measures. The central idea is that (with a computer's help) you look at how responses to the different items on a test correlate with one another; basically, you are searching for items that seem to be tapping some common thing. Once the computer tells you what actually goes with what, you look at each set of connecting items and try to figure out what they have in common—one set at a time.

Some tests are very disjointed and will have lots of balkanized little sets of items. The RWA Scale, with just one or two sets ("factors"), is relatively unidimensional—which is good because the test is supposed to be measuring only one thing: the *covarying* of the three elements defining right-wing authoritarianism.

8. Balancing a test with equal numbers of protrait and contrait items does not prevent response sets from affecting the answers subjects give. "Yea-saying," for example, will bind the protrait items together, glue the contrait items to one another, and disassociate the two sets. Considerable evidence indicates this happens extensively on the RWA Scale and other authoritarian measures. Balancing the test will keep such acquiescence—and "nay-saying"—from affecting the *total score* a subject obtains on the measure, because the effects cancel out when half the items are scored with reversed keying. But a response set still contributes error to the answers each item receives.

9. Beginning in 1986, I summarily dropped subjects from my samples whose first "guess" was that the RWA Scale measured right-wing authoritarianism (thus I discarded data from 45 of 727 students in my usual autumn experiment and 10 of 529 of my own students tested at the same time). None of the results reported in this book would be substantially altered by the inclusion of such small numbers of possibly "aware" students.

10. A small article appeared in my university's "house organ" when *Right-Wing Authoritarianism* was published in 1981, and I was briefly interviewed on the local Canadian Broadcasting Corporation radio station. (I did not have to beg off interview requests from the rock-and-roll stations students are more likely to favor.) I was also interviewed about my research on authoritarian aggression on the CBC radio science show "Quirks and Quarks" in April 1987, and the interview was rebroadcast the following September. But again, very few students appear to have heard the programs.

    I have steadily given more feedback to subjects since 1981 than I ever gave before, but at the end of the school year, after pledging them to secrecy. Debriefed students have apparently kept their pledge to a remarkable degree.

11. Some years ago I was on a "search and destroy" committee trying to find a new head for our department. Our deliberations were naturally confidential, but during a spirited departmental meeting I blurted out a remark that clearly indicated whom we were about to recommend. It was one of the worst moments of my life, and at the next gathering of the selection committee I admitted my serious error and apologized to my colleagues. Then I discovered no one had heard my loud remark. The dean of my faculty, chairing the committee, kindly observed, "So far as we can tell, Bob, no one appears to pay any attention to anything you say"—a hypothesis that draws support from several quarters.

For yet another example, I have had little success improving subjects' *honesty* through special instructions. Even when respondents know they are anonymous, their answers may be distorted because they do not wish to admit unflattering aspects of their behavior to *themselves*. One measure on which such distortion occurs is the "Mean-Spirited Scale" (described in Chapter Five), in which subjects are asked how much they secretly chortled when misfortune befell others they did not like. In the fall of 1985, 124 students answered this survey after receiving minimal (printed) instructions, while another 125 subjects read two paragraphs of "Special Instructions" asking them essentially to tell the whole truth, even though it was unpleasant to admit such things to oneself. Both groups were answering anonymously, and the latter placed a check mark at the end of the special instructions to show they had read them. Yet there was no difference in the two groups' answers to the survey.

The "Hidden Observer" instructions described in Chapter Five, used with the "Secret Survey" testing format, have proved much more successful in this regard.

12. The 1976 and 1977 student studies were part of a series that also tested Wilson and Patterson's (1968) assertion that catchphrases such as "death penalty" make better attitude scales than the usual propositional statement.

In brief, a catchphrase version of the (then) 28-item RWA Scale was composed (for example, "Trusting authorities," "Downplaying the Bible") but was found to be significantly less reliable than the usual sentence version (alphas equaled .71 and .76, respectively, when both were answered on a −1 to +1 basis).

Sentence versions of 28 Conservatism Scale catchphrases were also invented. The 28 items chosen were the 14 protrait and 14 contrait phrases with the highest item-whole correlations in a previous administration of the test at the University of Manitoba. I simply wrote down the first thing that came into my head as I considered each phrase. For example, "death penalty" became "The death penalty is morally justified for certain crimes such as murder." I make no claim that my sentence inventions were particularly good ones; they were just *some* sentences based on the C Scale catchphrases. This sentence version of the Conservatism Scale proved to have significantly higher reliability than the original catchphrase version, however. (Alphas equaled .78 and .66, respectively, when both were answered on a −1 to +1 basis.)

I believe both results occurred because catchphrases are inherently more ambiguous, and hence produce more error, than sentences.

3

How Do People Become Authoritarians?

Every autumn since 1973, I have administered the RWA Scale to large samples of students who have been at our university for only a couple of weeks. Most of them are 18 years old, freshly graduated from high school, and look as though they had spent the summer outdoors. As mine is usually the first psychology experiment in which they serve, they frequently look a little nervous—although they understand all they are about to do is give some opinions. Once they are seated at their tables and equipped with survey booklets, pencils, and IBM "bubble sheets," I play a set of taped instructions for them. Then they are on their own, and I am at their mercy.

During the 1970s I used to feel panic creeping up my spine and perspiration filling my shoes as the students set to work—for the first task in the booklet was always the RWA Scale, and I knew that the fate of my whole research program for the coming year was largely being determined in those first few minutes. What if the test failed? What if I was inundated with unrelated answers? What if response sets largely filled the "bubbles" and burst mine? What if all the students scored the same?

They never did, of course. By now I know their scores will

be normally distributed, with a mean (most years) of about 150. The dividing line for the upper quartile will be about 20 points higher than the mean; that for the lower quartile, about 17 points less. The array is almost always a little "thick shouldered" to the left of center and strung out to the right. I have seen so many RWA Scale distributions among Manitoba students since 1973 that I can usually spot them at a glance.

But what causes this distribution? What processes have produced the Uppers and the Lowers that show up so faithfully each September? For they *arrive* at university already High and Low and (most of them) Middlin', with their answers already about as organized as those we find among adults 30 years older. How does all this occur by the time one is eighteen? What made one young man authoritarian and the young woman sitting next to him just the opposite? That is the small question we shall try to answer here.

In overview, we shall proceed by moving from the theoretical to the experimental. There exist a "classic" psychoanalytic explanation of how authoritarianism develops in a person and another explanation, based on social learning theory, that few have ever heard of. The former is largely unsupported and the latter quite untested. Most of this chapter will report research bearing on the latter, culminating in a 1984 study designed to identify the principal reasons that students distribute themselves along the RWA Scale as they so faithfully do.

The "Berkeley Theory"

The best-known explanation of personal authoritarianism, advanced by Else Frenkel-Brunswik in *The Authoritarian Personality*, traced adult "Fascist potential" to early childhood experiences. Future authoritarians were supposedly raised by threatening, forbidding, status-conscious parents who punished unconventional impulses harshly and arbitrarily. The child repressed hostility toward these distant parents and covered his or her tracks with reaction formations of abject submission and overglorification. The repressed aggression was displaced and projected onto various outgroups. Hence authoritarianism and ethnocentrism were two sides of the same coin, minted in the unconscious to avoid traumatic punishment and used to appease powerful authorities while providing a safe outlet for enormous hatred.

Although this account has spread so widely through our culture that it has become a stereotype, the scientific evidence is unconvincing. Hyman and Sheatsley (1954) identified many flaws in Frenkel-Brunswik's data-collection procedures and analyses. Subsequent research, which has often been cited as supporting her model, has mainly produced inconclusive or contradictory findings (*RWA*, pp. 33–51).

As reported in *Right-Wing Authoritarianism* (pp. 259–264), I correlated RWA Scale scores in 1978 with three retrospective measures developed to test Frenkel-Brunswik's theory of the personal origins of authoritarianism: (1) a Parental Anger Scale, which asked respondents (both university students and their parents) how angry the parents would have become over 24 youthful misdeeds, (2) a Parental Punishment Scale, which sought information on how the parents would have typically punished each of these misdeeds, and (3) a Parental Interest Scale, which asked, essentially, how close and warm the parent/child relationship had been.

Both students and parents told admirably consistent tales on these measures; alphas ranged from .87 to .92. Unfortunately, the children and their parents often seemed to be from different families, for stories within a family bore little resemblance to each other. (Would you be surprised to learn that parents described themselves as less angry, less punitive, and more interested in their children than the children recall?) But even more unfortunate, for the Berkeley theory, nobody's version of the past explained much of the students' present authoritarianism. The *largest* of 28 "validity coefficients" was .24, between students' RWA Scale scores and their accounts of mother's anger.

One cannot dismiss a theory on such questionable evidence. But the Berkeley explanation, which has great psychodynamic appeal, has proved very difficult to test. One reason is the long interval between the hypothesized cause and effect. But the explanations themselves, like many psychoanalytic concepts, are difficult to nail down. Suppose one finds that High RWA subjects gush with praise of their parents; it is the expected overglorification. If, on the other hand, they describe their parents as beasts, it is taken as proof that the parents *were* cruel and harsh. And if, on the third hand, they describe their parents' child-rearing behavior in both positive and negative terms (which is what they do), it is explained as a mixture of overglorification and accurate recollection. That may be the case, but how could we ever find out the theory is wrong, if it is wrong? It has all the angles covered.

So while some may believe that World War II got its real start in Austria in the 1890s when Adolf Hitler swallowed his hatred of a tyrannical old father, I myself know of no experimental evidence linking high RWA Scale scores to the family dynamics proposed in *The Authoritarian Personality*.

A Social Learning Explanation

Right-wing authoritarianism is here conceptualized, the reader will recall, as the covariation of three *attitudinal* clusters: authoritarian submission, authoritarian aggression, and conventionalism. The question of the origins of personal authoritarianism thus becomes, most simply, "How were these attitudes formed?" (A second question, "Why do they covary?," will occupy us in Chapters Four and Five.)

Most social psychologists would agree, I think, that we acquire our social attitudes mainly (1) from other people, through direct teaching and modeling, and (2) through our own direct and vicarious *experiences* with the objects of these attitudes. Among the various explanations of these processes presently on the shelf (Shaw and Costanzo, 1982), social learning theory (Bandura, 1977) strikes me as probably the most useful for our purposes here – although I doubt Bandura would invoke a "trait" of authoritarianism to explain authoritarian behavior in the first place.

Social learning theory, like other theories, states that attitudes are shaped by the reinforcements administered by parents and others and also by the reinforcements received while interacting with the objects of attitudes. But it also allows, indeed insists, that much is learned through imitation and vicarious reinforcement. The theory's further emphasis on our use of cognitive symbols to represent events, persons, and objects clearly accommodates an interest in attitudes. Bandura also assigns a central role to self-evaluative, self-regulatory cognitive processes, often involving abstract concepts such as fairness, goodness, and integrity ("I would not hurt someone unfairly"); but he also recognizes that people "neutralize" these processes at times—for example, by dehumanizing a victim: "Asians aren't like the rest of us" (Bandura, 1987). Finally, social learning theory acknowledges the complexity of human social behavior, stresses that people shape their environment as well as vice versa, and is supported by a considerable volume of experimental evidence.

Earlier Findings on the Origins of RWA Scale Scores

How would these broad principles apply in our case? To begin with, one's parents are naturally expected to be a primary source of attitudes toward authority, aggression, conventionality, and an enormous number of other topics.

Many of these attitudes are intentionally taught, and parents will readily use rewards and punishments to ensure that their children's verbal statements and behavior conform to their wishes. Parents also serve as powerful models (Bandura, Ross, and Ross, 1963) for their children, so that even if they do not intentionally teach certain attitudes, their offspring can still acquire them by observing the parents' behavior, from conversations around the dinner table, and so forth. And of course children can form attitudes as a result of their own direct experiences with their parents. A university student's attitude toward physical punishment, which is solicited on the RWA Scale, may mainly reflect her evaluation of how she was disciplined—a judgment that may or may not coincide with her parents' intentions or example.

A number of other people have social roles that commonly give them the right to teach attitudes directly to children: grandparents, older siblings, ministers, schoolteachers, and Scout leaders may all intentionally shape a child's opinions, though not usually in contradiction of parental teachings. These "quasi parents" can also become models whom children imitate, and experiences with them can affect children's attitudes in ways the parents may or may not wish.

Even people the child has never met, such as TV personalities, advertising executives, and comic book illustrators, can shape attitudes on certain topics and can (themselves or their creations) become models for imitation. The heroes of fairy tales and comic books are later replaced by rock-and-roll idols and the characters in novels, plays, and movies (such as *M*A*S*H*, *Missing*, *Platoon*, and even *Star Wars*), which are often written not just to make money but also to express and shape social attitudes.

Then there is the peer group, whose influence develops slowly but may eventually rival the parents'. The modes are the same: direct influence attempts, observing peers' behavior and its consequences, and the effects of one's own experience with peers. Later one acquires adult counterparts to childhood peers: spouse, friends, co-workers, and neighbors can all shape our attitudes on social issues and be shaped by us in return.

Beyond these exist the effects of the environment at large, the world beyond direct experience. People read newspapers and newsmagazines and see the day's history on television at 6, with film at 11. Whether "slanted" or not, the news can shape people's attitudes on the issues covered and affect sentiments of authoritarian submission, authoritarian aggression, and conventionalism. So can *The Reader's Digest*, *The Ladies' Home Journal*, *Playboy*, and (heaven help us) *The National Enquirer*.

The Development of Right-Wing Authoritarianism

Obviously these sources do not operate evenly over the life span. Parental influence is apt to be enormous at first, and for understandable reasons parents do not typically encourage their young children to scrutinize the dictates of authority. Thus in most families children may be taught simply to obey legitimate authority unquestioningly or from fear of punishment. The other determiners of attitudes most important to the young child (for example, teachers, extended family) usually reinforce this "reflexive" submission. We might thus expect children to believe rather uniformly that they *should* obey the authorities in their world. Conventionalism may vary more, depending on the content of the "local authorities'" teachings and life-styles; but young children, with limited cognitive abilities and experience, typically have conventional attitudes (Piaget, 1965). Authoritarian aggression, however, hostility perceived to be sanctioned by established authorities, may be relatively rare in childhood.

Right-wing authoritarianism, as I have defined it, probably does not become organized until adolescence, when cultures increasingly concentrate on preparing the child for adulthood. Children's cognitive abilities are too limited to comprehend many adult issues, much less to develop organized attitudes about them. But these attitudes can crystallize and become increasingly interconnected during adolescence—producing differentiation in young adults (such as my introductory psychology students) who ten years earlier might all have agreed that authorities should simply be obeyed.

Parents may still be the most important source of the RWA-related attitudes that develop during adolescence, not just through their teachings and expressions on an ever-widening range of subjects, but through their relationship with the emerging adult who is apt to be seeking ever-greater autonomy. But peers can also exert powerful influence, not just on clothing and music preference, but on sexual behavior, drug use, attitudes toward authority, hostility toward outgroups, and so forth. In addition, through his schoolwork, movies, TV, and the 30-second news "roundup" that hourly interrupts the drama of who's where on the Top Forty, the adolescent becomes more aware of the world he is inheriting and the issues that abound in it. But perhaps as important as all these other factors, the teenager now experiences quite a larger slice of life first-hand than ever before. By late adolescence a typical teen will have held a succession of jobs, taken trips to distant places, encountered unfairness, prejudice, and hypocrisy, met a wide range of people, and got into situations that a few years earlier he never imagined existed. (At least I did. Didn't you?)

Continuation of Earlier Trends. It appears probable that the adolescent's development will be more a continuation of earlier learnings than a radical departure. A child (let's call him "Hugh") whose parents have stressed submission to authority, who have emphasized the family religion, who have kept Hugh on a tight leash traveling in tight circles, and who have shown hostility toward various "dangerous" groups is apt to form authoritarian attitudes as an adult. The family religion itself may have stressed submission to authority, conventionalism, and (more subtly) aggression. Hugh's friends, his readings, his movies, and his travels have likely been selected by his parents to a considerable extent to reinforce the home influence; and the child who has been rewarded for submission is apt to accept this, indeed to depend on it. He does not likely hate established authorities; Hugh trusts and needs them.

At the other end of the scale, one would find a quite different teenager (let's call her Lou) whose parents rewarded independence, modeled equality within the family, emphasized no particular religious code, encouraged Lou to experience the wider world (which they did not characterize as degenerate and dangerous), had no big "enemies list," tolerated unconventional ideas and behavior, avoided self-righteousness, and in general nurtured a "question and decide" approach to life rather than "memorize and obey."

Adolescents with this sort of past are not likely to become friends with those from firmly authoritarian homes. If Hugh and Lou meet at a party, they probably will not leave together. Their experiences in life have probably been pretty different. Their reaction to common events, such as adolescent sexual impulses and highhanded teachers, will probably conflict. The books they read and the movies they see will often be different. Their interpretation of major news events may well be poles apart. And so on. They are headed toward opposite ends of the

RWA Scale distribution I was discussing at the beginning of this chapter.

Between Hugh and Lou lie hundreds of less homogeneous patterns. Most parents require submission to their authority, but in moderate amounts overall, with increasing tolerance for independence as the child grows older. Many parents may teach fear and hostility toward some groups, but the list will be short and the hostility not altogether self-righteous. Most parents want some conformity to social conventions but can live with modest deviance ("A *little* orange hair is all right, dear"). All these tendencies would head the child toward moderate levels of adult authoritarianism.

A moderate start toward authoritarianism can occur within a family in other ways. Religious parents are not necessarily highly authoritarian in their dealings with their children. A child may thus receive a thorough schooling in the Ten Commandments and learn to worship a Supreme Being; but she may also have parents who, intentionally or through neglect (or death), promote her independence from them. Likewise, atheistic parents *can* be highly domineering toward their children. The net effect in both cases is a push toward the middle of a bell-shaped distribution. Other influences in the child's home (the most important probably being different approaches to child rearing by the mother and father) can also push in opposite directions and keep the individual away from Lou's and Hugh's ends of the curve.

Effect of Personal Experiences. Even if one's early childhood has been homogeneous, other factors can modulate extreme inclinations. Ever have friends your parents did not approve of, or read verboten material under the covers with a flashlight? Or get treated unfairly by a teacher? Or, being independent, make disastrous decisions? Or fall in love with someone your folks wrung their hands over? Or enjoy a forbidden fruit? Or meet people who disconfirmed a stereotype? Or watch some monumental scandal like "Watergate" or "Iran-gate" or "Pearly-gate" unfold day after day?

How many families do you know in which the children are

"just like their mom and dad"—or even like each other? We may still shoot up in the same general direction as before, but life's experiences can bend us to the left or to the right, regressing us toward the mean—or bonking us toward the outer limits.

When Does the Development End? There is no reason to expect that a person's authoritarianism is carved in stone at the age of eighteen. Education and the greater assumption of adult status may further increase the organization of attitudes *and* change the level of RWA Scale scores. Relationships with parents can change (and eventually end), peers can change, roles can change (the shift to parenthood perhaps being the most traumatic), the world can change. People can change their minds as long as new experiences are possible, as long as new models can emerge, as long as reinforcement contingencies can be upset.

Dramatic changes may be rare, nonetheless, because for the most part life may continue in relatively stable circumstances, and we tend to interpret new experiences in terms of old learnings. But small changes are always possible, and they can accumulate over time. And large, sudden changes in the individual and a society can occur—because of economic calamity, for example, or domestic upheaval, or war.

Comparison with the "Berkeley Explanation." Aside from the fact that the psychoanalytic and social learning explanations both hold that authoritarianism is determined by experiences, the two models have little in common. The theory I have advanced, for example, holds that parental behavior is important, but it also lists many other factors that contribute to the development of right-wing authoritarianism. There is no assumption that parents will ultimately be more important than all the rest of these.

As well, the nature of the parental influence differs. I make no case for the harsh, stern, cold, distant parents. Hugh's folks could have been as close and involved with him as other parents are with their children and still could have taught him to obey authority and so forth. In short, the family origins of authoritarianism I am proposing are not nearly as dramatic or peculiar as those Frenkel-Brunswik advanced.

The explanations also differ on the age at which authoritarianism is created. Like other psychoanalytic accounts, the Berkeley model placed great emphasis on early childhood experiences. I have proposed instead that although some authoritarian attitudes are formed during early childhood, the process is hardly complete then. The most dramatic change in the organization of submissive, aggressive and conventional attitudes is expected to occur during adolescence. But I have also argued that neither the organization nor the level of authoritarianism is ever "finally established."

Important as those differences are, they are not the most fundamental distinction between the two explanations, which lies in the "mechanisms" theorized to produce authoritarianism. The psychoanalytic theory invokes powerful instinctual forces, a struggle among the id, ego, and superego, ego defense mechanisms, cathexes, and so forth. Social learning theory is based more simply on the concept of reinforcement. True, in its simplest terms it may be just as difficult to disprove as a Freudian model. But learning-theory explanations in the 1980s are not nearly as simple, or as simplistic, as they were in 1950. Today we acknowledge that reinforcements can be experienced vicariously, can be self-administered as well as encountered in the environment, and can be thoughts as well as food pellets (Bandura, 1973). Just as important, the individual's role in shaping her own behavior, directly as well as through her effect on how the environment responds to her, is accepted and employed to explain complex social behaviors. But underlying all this is still the notion of reinforcement and the fundamental laws of learning—plus a considerable amount of supporting research.

The approach advocated here has at least one major shortcoming, however. The model operates only on a very general level; it cannot predict, specifically, what the various personal, behavioral, and environmental determinants will produce when all is said and done. Take, for example, a group of eighteen-year-old students and their attitudes toward the police. Their parents, religions, and teachers have taught them to honor and obey civil authorities almost unquestioningly. But their peers make fun of the police, and they or their friends may have been (they think) treated unfairly by them. News reports cover stories of great cops and crooked cops, as do TV shows and the movies. Finally, the students want to consider themselves fair-minded, independent, rational persons with integrity.

What will their attitudes toward the police be? What formula predicts this outcome, taking all these (and other) factors into account? At present, social learning theory (and other explanations) cannot say much other than that "these factors interact" and that those which produce the greatest rewards and the least punishments will "outweigh" the others (Bandura, 1977, pp. 153–158; however, see Bandura, 1988, for a much more elaborate treatment of such issues). In short, we do not know the answers theoretically; one has to determine them empirically.

Tests of the Social Learning Explanation

Students' Attributions of Their Attitudes. If social learning theory cannot predict the "recipe" that combines various rewards and punishments to produce personal authoritarianism, it does suggest a number of "ingredients" to be considered. I gave a list of these to 437 students in 1979 who had answered the RWA Scale one week earlier. The subjects were asked to consider their earlier responses to each of the 30 items and then indicate which of eight possible origins was the basic source of each attitude. The eight alternatives were (briefly) "parents," "church," "school," "own direct personal experience," "friends' experience," "friends' opinions," "news," and "fictional works." A ninth category was provided for "other" and a tenth for "no idea" (*RWA*, p. 269).

"Parents" were named the most frequent source of RWA Scale attitudes (garnering 25 percent of all the citations), with "own direct personal experiences" (23 percent) a close second. Then came "school" and "news reports"—each receiving 12 percent of the citations. "Friends' opinions" and "friends' experiences" together were mentioned another 12 percent of the time.

The remaining four categories divided the other 16 percent of the attributions.

I found it interesting that High RWA students (the "Hughs") were significantly more likely to attribute their opinions to the influence of their parents and their religion, while Lows (the "Lous") cited "own experiences" and "peer influence" significantly more.

I asked another 585 students to make these same attributions for me in the fall of 1981, with quite similar results.

To some extent these thousand-odd students agreed with Mark Twain (1900/n.d.) that we get our opinions where we get our corn pone—at home. Mr. Clemens would not be surprised by the attributions to friends, church, schoolin', or the "news," either. But he would probably scorn these students' beliefs that they got an appreciable number of their opinions first-hand, from their own personal experiences in life. For he rather cynically wrote, "[A man] must get his opinions from other people; he must reason out none for himself; he must have no first-hand views" (p. 1400).

Tests of These Attributions: Actual Parental Influence. Since social psychologists often collect people's attributions to study their biases and errors, we cannot treat these students' opinions about their opinions optimistically. Does independent research, for example, support the corn-pone hypothesis?

It appears clear that parents are willing to furnish their children with social attitudes as well as supper. In 1976 I asked 242 parents who had just answered the RWA Scale to answer it again, the way they would want their daughter/son to answer it. Overall the parents wanted their children to be just as authoritarian as they were, and the correlation between their two sets of answers was a very robust .88 (*RWA*, p. 266).

Their children clearly "get the message." I asked seven samples of students (total $N = 3059$) between 1976 and 1983 to answer the RWA Scale as they thought their parents would want them to. In every sample the students reported that their parents wanted them to be much more authoritarian than they presently were; in fact, their average perceptions were usually about 10 points higher than the parents' own authoritarianism. The correlation between students' own RWA Scale scores and their estimates of parental wishes ranged from .42 to .57, averaging about .50.

What was the correlation between students' and parents' actual RWA Scale scores (a direct test of the corn-pone theory)? I have collected these data many times since 1976, involving altogether 2097 students and at least one parent of each. The overall correlations have varied from .27 to .51 and averaged .40. (Usually, daughters have resembled their parents more than sons have; but there has been no consistent evidence that the children represent (say) the mother more than the father or the same-sex parent more than the other parent.)

On which topics are the two generations most often in agreement? I thought the authoritarian submission items would show the highest correlations, but the conventionalism items finished ahead—especially those dealing with sex and religion ("atheists," "nudist camps," "premarital intercourse," "Bible," and "rules regarding modesty"). I also expected there to be least agreement on the aggression items. But you can more neatly classify the least similar responses under the rubric "Youth" ("young people," "unconventional child," "do own thing," "students challenge," and "obedience and respect"). The reasons for disagreements on these topics are probably self-evident.

How much of this do the parents realize? In 1983 and 1984, samples of 236 and 521 parents estimated their student-child's answers to the RWA Scale. Their responses indicated they realized their children were appreciably less authoritarian than they were; their estimates were, on the average, just 4 or 5 points off the bull's-eye. But parents also tended to see their children as scaled-down versions of themselves. Their estimates of their children's RWA Scale scores correlated significantly better with their *own* authoritarianism (.69 in 1983, .74 in 1984) than with their children's actual scores (.58, .51). (The correlation between parents' and students' actual RWA Scale scores was .42 in both studies.) Low RWA parents were about as likely to misread their children as High RWA parents were.

It is worth noting, in light of later developments, the items on the RWA Scale on which parents *expected* the greatest agreement with their children. They are mainly concerned with authoritarian aggression ("stomp out the rot," "protect radicals," "Communists," "free speech," and "good old-fashioned physical punishment"). If this surprises you, that makes two of us. Why should parents expect their grown children especially to agree with them about *these* things?

There is a simple explanation, based on a later study in which students and their parents both indicated how much the parent had tried to affect the child's attitudes on each of the 30 issues covered by the RWA Scale. Authoritarian aggression items, the ones on which parents thought there would be greatest agreement, were discussed least—in fact, hardly at all.[1] Instead the two generations discussed submission and conventionalism issues a lot more because those issues became contentious. Parents probably expected more agreement on the aggression items, and less on the others, because they had not been arguing with their kids about Communists and homosexuals for X years but, rather, about curfews and tight jeans. As we saw three paragraphs ago, parents do better on some of these contentious issues than they apparently realize, but disagreement about "youth" definitely exists.

To summarize, then, parents appear to want their university-aged children to have the same RWA Scale attitudes they do, and their children know this. Parents also know their children are not as authoritarian as they want, but they still do not realize how different their children are from them. The actual correlation between parents' and children's authoritarianism is about .40, which, though appreciable, amounts to only 16 percent of variance explained—less than 1 percent per year of supplying the corn pone.

Religious Influence on Authoritarianism. Previous research has found reliable relationships between authoritarianism and religiosity (*RWA*, pp. 240–241). Canadian and American students raised in nonreligious homes have landed rather low on the RWA Scale as a group, while those from Jewish families have scored a little higher. Among American students, Catholics placed higher still, and the Protestant mean was the highest of all. There have been no differences between Catholics and (overall) Protestants in Canadian samples, but within Protestantism both students and parents with United Church and Anglican backgrounds have always scored significantly lower than those from Mennonite and "Fundamentalist" homes. Attempts to explain these denominational differences in terms of parental education, family income, and socioeconomic status have accounted for less than 25 percent of the differences observed. The teachings and practices of different religions seemingly produce different levels of authoritarianism.

I have also found, quite regularly, that the authoritarians within any religion tend to accept the teachings of that religion more firmly than do their brethren. High RWAs tend to be the "true believers" and the most ardent practitioners among Catholics, Jews, and Protestants. So just as religious training can apparently produce authoritarianism, the latter can produce religiosity.

We shall consider these mutually supporting relationships at length in Chapter Six. For the present, we simply note that parents ordinarily choose their children's religion and shape their dedication. When one partials out the effects of parental authoritarianism from student RWA-religiosity correlations, much of the latter disappears. But religion can still have strong long-run effects. Parents quite typically raise their children in the same religion they were taught. So religions that promote submission to authority, authoritarian aggression, and conventionalism can produce authoritarianism generation after generation, through the parents, as well as through their direct instruction.

Educational Influences on Authoritarianism. Parents have more choices about which church their children will attend than they do about schools, so the educational system may have a more independent effect on their children's authoritarianism. Does it? One gets the feeling that Mel and Norma Gabler of Longview, Texas, think so. For years they have led a crusade to "cleanse U.S. schools of all materials that they consider anti-family, anti-American, and anti-God" (Kleiman, 1981, p. C1). Their principal target: textbooks. "If all the problems of our world were suddenly resolved but textbooks remained unchanged, most of these same problems would soon return because of what is being taught our children in classrooms," they say (Kleiman, 1981, p. C4). The Gablers' organization has successfully pressured school boards to withdraw textbooks that "overemphasize" Watergate and the Vietnam war. They also objected to a history text that condoned the violation of slavery laws before the Civil War, saying such texts encourage insubordination. Because publishers are reluctant to print texts that cannot be sold in Texas, Mr. and Mrs. Gabler have at times profoundly influenced what is taught in American schools.[2]

Does the educational system cause most of the problems in our world? Does it lower (or raise) the level of authoritarianism in schoolchildren? Are first-year university students, who have spent almost all their lives in school, as authoritarian or as nonauthoritarian as they are because of the earlier curricula they have completed? I have not conducted a convincing test of these hypotheses, which would require comparisons of otherwise homogeneous students instructed in different ways. But I can tell you what some students have said on the subject, which neither justifies the Gablers' concerns nor buoys my hopes in the opposite direction.

In my first study, I asked 278 of my own introductory psychology students in November 1983 to indicate the effect their high school educations were *intended* to have on their (30 RWA Scale) attitudes. "That is, what did your education in high school try to teach you?" Attributions were made on a −4 to +4 basis. "For example, if the teachers, textbooks, et cetera would want you to very strongly disagree with a statement, blacken the −4 bubble." Subjects were shown how to combine arithmetically the effects of different courses and sources and were instructed to use the "0" to indicate that no subject or teacher had dealt with a particular issue.

Overall, the students indicated their educations had made little attempt to affect their RWA Scale attitudes. Forty-two percent of the answers were 0's ("no mention"). The thrust of the remaining intended effects was, on balance, slightly pro-authoritarian. "School's Attempted RWA" was 159.6 (alpha = .82), compared with the students' own mean of 149.5 ($p < .001$). However, much of this pro-RWA orientation apparently resulted from the way the school was run, with its authority system and rules, not from the curriculum content. The items with the biggest attempted effects (all proauthoritarian) were "decent, respectable appearance," "obedience and respect," "the real keys," "young people," and "do own thing." Authoritarian aggression topics were cited least.

I also asked these students to name the particular courses in which the issues arose. Having a "decent, respectable appearance" apparently became an issue, for different students, in physical education, French, Spanish, health, home economics, law, biology, economics, commercial art, chemistry, physics, computer programming, yearbook, driver's education, shop, social studies, and every English, math, and history course on the books. Clearly the students had run into particular teachers in these diverse areas who objected to someone's appearance. I doubt the topic was discussed in many of the texts used in these classes.

Were there courses in which authoritarianism-related matters arose more often than others? Yes, English and history were cited most. But the "slant" probably depended more on the teacher than on the texts. On the item involving the limits of "free speech," for example, 61 percent of the subjects said the topic had arisen, typically in a history course. About half said the intended effect of the instruction was to make them disagree with the item; the other half said the opposite. The overall mean of the attempted effects was 5.08, where 5.00 indicates perfect neutrality. Few students said their teachers had made a determined bid to shape their opinions on the matter.

The students' own authoritarianism correlated .34 with their reports of what their education tried to teach them. Given the possibility of some projection here, it hardly appears that the school system seriously corrupted the youth—whatever one takes to be "corruption" here.

In my second study, conducted the following year, I asked

557 other students to indicate what effects their education had *actually* had on their RWA Scale opinions. The results were rather similar to those already discussed. Thirty-five percent of the responses were 0's. The school's attributed effect was an RWA of 163.7 (alpha = .86), 7.2 points higher than the students' own final opinions ($p < .001$). Education's greatest effects (in terms of fewest 0's) were on "obedience and respect," "real keys," "decent, respectable appearance," "trust proper authorities," and "young people"—and were all net proauthoritarian effects, as the "attempted" data above would lead us to expect. Least affected by the school system, also confirming the first study, were the authoritarian aggression items.

The students' own RWA Scale scores correlated .32 with their statements of how authoritarian their educations (alone) had made them—hardly the powerful effect some might expect, even if we ignore the possibility of projection and take the coefficient at face value.

Of course, the students may not realize how powerfully they have been affected, any more than most people realize how completely situational factors can control their social behavior. The true relationship may be twice as large as that obtained. But if it were, we would expect the students at least to recall topics such as civil disobedience and censorship coming up. They do not, by and large. That disturbs me, in its blandness, as much as a "humanistic indoctrination program" frightens the Gablers. Not only can't Johnny read, he seemingly isn't being asked to think very much either.

Influence of the "News" on Authoritarianism. During the mid 1980s, Senator Jesse Helms organized a right-wing attempt to gain ownership of the Columbia Broadcasting System. His central purpose was to control CBS News, to rid it of its "strong liberal bias."[3] One can speculate what the *CBS Evening News* would have become under Helms's direction—not to mention the rest of the network's programming. But no one wondered why the far right wanted to "be Dan Rather's boss," any more than anyone wonders why the Communist party in the Soviet Union finds it convenient to publish all the newspapers.

How much of the difference in authoritarianism that we find among a sample of university students is attributable to the picture of the world they get from the news media? In November 1983 I asked the same 278 students we were discussing a few paragraphs ago to indicate how the news had *attempted* to influence their opinions on the issues raised by the RWA Scale. "By 'news media' is meant the newspapers, radio and TV news programs, and newsmagazines you have read, seen, and heard. . . . [This survey] is not concerned with your attitudes on the issues, but rather with the attitudes which you think get communicated or reinforced by the news." Subjects again answered on a – 4 to + 4 basis, were told how to combine conflicting sources arithmetically, and were instructed to use "0" for no attempted effect.

The mean of these responses, 169.2 (alpha = .82), was some 20 points higher than the students' own authoritarianism level, indicating they thought the news would make them appreciably more authoritarian if they accepted it at face value. (So perhaps Canadian media are safer from Helmsian maneuvers.) Both High and Low RWA students felt this; the correlation between own RWA and perceived Media RWA was only .09. The media were, furthermore, thought to touch on more of the RWA Scale topics than their high school education had; only 21 percent of the responses were 0's.

Which items were covered most by the news? "Strong medicine," "Communists," "the facts on crime," "proper authorities censor," and "stomp out the rot"—nearly all of them authoritarian aggression items, and in every case the media's perceived orientation was, on balance, *pro*authoritarian. Least touched on (judging from the number of 0 responses) were "Bible," "atheists," "chains from the past," "nudist camps," and "traditional family"—mainly conventionalism items.

But what would students say if asked, "What effect have the news media *actually* had on your reaction to each of these 30 statements?" In January 1984 382 new subjects gave such ratings. Their mean "Media-Effect RWA," 159.2 (alpha = .80), was about halfway between their own average authoritarianism (150.4) and the 169.2 attempt we just saw. By this evidence, then, the news media had made the students more authoritarian, but not as much as they could have. On which issues? Exactly the same listed above for intended effect. And which statements were affected least? "Bible," "atheists," and so on.

It should come as no shock that these students' authoritarianism was significantly correlated with their descriptions of the media's impact on them. But the coefficient was surprisingly small, .29, and only 14 of the 30 RWA items correlated significantly with the news effects. The only item correlations larger than .20 occurred on a handful of aggression items.

Where does this leave us? Realizing that we have only subjects' attributions, not experimentally established outcomes, the data suggest the news media have their greatest effects on authoritarian aggression. One suspects the media's emphasis on violent news stories is largely responsible for this, just as violent TV programming convinces heavy viewers that the world is more dangerous, and they are personally at greater risk, than is really the case (Gerbner, Gross, Signorielli, and Morgan, 1980; Gerbner and others, 1979). Of course, the news media's impact depends on what is happening. Another "Watergate" might significantly (if only temporarily) reduce authoritarian submission. But the data speak clearly on at least one point: Jesse Helms notwithstanding, the news media do not appear to have the "liberal-izing" intent, or effect, he fears. Rather (no pun intended) (well, not at first, anyway) the opposite.[4]

Peer Influence on Student Authoritarianism. In fact, nothing so far does. Parents, religion, education, and the news all appear to push students to the right. Why don't they roll off the edge, then, instead of ending up with generally moderate scores? Does their "counterculture" peer group pull them back?

Anyone who has taken a course in adolescent psychology, or has spent much time around teenagers, or (worst of all) recalls his own youth realizes the power that peer influence can have on social attitudes. Admittedly high school corridors may not resound with intense debates about government prerogatives and free speech. But discussions of sex, dress styles, drugs, and parental authority—which may more typically be heard above the continuo of clanging lockers—can conceivably affect the moving hand of university students a few years later when they blacken bubbles in Experiment Survey. At least, some of the bubbles, some of the time.

In the fall of 1984 I invited 557 students to address envelopes to their best friends as well as to their parents, for an extra credit. Only 336 did so, compared with 422 who had surveys sent home. Of the 336 best friends, who received an explanatory letter quite similar to the one sent parents, 206 (or 61 percent) returned completed booklets (compared with 76 percent of the parents who cooperated).[5]

The mean RWA Scale score of the 206 *students* whose best friends were heard from was 155.4; the mean authoritarianism of the other 351 students was 157.2 ($t = 0.68$; $p < .50$). Thus the subjects on whom we have friends' data appear to be representative of the overall sample.

Demographically the best friends were a little older than the students who involved them in my research (20.5 years, on the average; the students averaged about 19) but comparably educated (12.3 years). They were also slightly less authoritarian ($\overline{X} = 151.4$; alpha = .89). The best friends reported having known the students for an average of eight years. Most typically they had met in school; 58 percent of the best friends were also university students.

How similar were the RWA Scale scores between these 206 pairs of good friends? They correlated .31, which is especially unimpressive when one realizes that this represents the outcome of *mutual* influence (unlike the parent-child correlations, which are more likely one-sided), plus any jointly shared influences such as attending the same school or church. So my subjects did not appear to get many of their authoritarian opinions where they got their chewing gum, cigarettes, and camaraderie.

Friends agreed most about "homosexual," "premarital intercourse," "nudist camps," "rules regarding modesty," and "Bible"—all of them involving social conventions (although the first has strong aggressive overtones). The least agreement occurred on "trust proper authorities," "established authorities right," "treat dissenters with leniency," "young people," and "free speech."

The best friends also guessed the students' answers to the RWA Scale and indicated the extent to which they had discussed each of the 30 issues involved. Their estimates were as good as the parents' discussed earlier, correlating .54 with the students' actual score, with a right-on mean of 155.5. Best friends apparently did not project their own attitudes onto the students as much as the parents had; the friends' estimates correlated only .60 with their own authoritarianism ($t = 1.03$; $p > .30$).

On which items were the friends most accurate? Exactly the same as those cited above on which agreement was closest. And why? Because those topics were discussed the most overall. Which were discussed least? Mainly authoritarian aggression items, on which estimates and agreement were subsequently poor. The data thus essentially replicate Newcomb's (1961) classic findings on the effect of acquaintanceship upon attitudes.

Then what can we say about the role that peers have had in shaping university students' answers to the RWA Scale? On a few items, mainly dealing with social customs, the friends appear to have influenced each other in an anticonventional, antiauthoritarian direction. But one finds no evidence of a *pronounced* overall pull to the left. The best friends tell us they seldom talked about most of the issues raised by the RWA Scale, and that would appear to be the case.[6]

Development of the Experiences Scale

Only a remarkably retentive reader will recall, amidst all this number crunching, that students themselves believed they got a lot of their opinions through their experiences in life. Furthermore, those who chalked up a lot of their attitudes to "experience" tended to score low on the RWA Scale; and we have had trouble finding antiauthoritarian influences. But what were the experiences, up to early adulthood at least, that affected their authoritarianism? What events, what rewards and punishments, what had been felt and witnessed, directly and vicariously, that allegedly produced these effects? It is one thing to dump the platitude "Experience is the great teacher" into our discussion, but quite another to specify what the relevant experiences are.

The September 1980 Study. I was sure I did not know. But I thought my subjects might, so I asked them. In September 1980, 483 students responded to the RWA Scale and then (one week later) reviewed their answers and indicated what had been the biggest source of each attitude (parents, news, own experiences, and so on). They were then asked to describe in detail, for seven of the items, the parental influence, news stories, experiences, or whatever that had so affected them. By asking even- and odd-numbered subjects for details of different sets of opinions and by repeating the study in September 1981 with 620 additional subjects, I covered all of the content area (and nearly all the items) on the RWA Scale.

The results of these investigations, being several thousand recollections and narratives, do not lend themselves to precise summation. But perhaps I can illustrate their usefulness with an example. The first item on the RWA Scale at the time read "Some of the worst people in our country nowadays are those who do not respect our flag, our leaders, and the normal way things are supposed to be done." About 20 percent of the relevant sample attributed their reaction to this statement to "personal experiences." (Parents, school, and the news were also cited about as often.) Students who attributed their reaction to experiences were asked to describe them. As I studied their stories, two descriptions appeared more than any others: (1) the subjects' evaluations of dissenters they had personally known, usually in high school, and (2) the competence and fairness of the authorities (for example, parents, teachers, police) whom the students had dealt with thus far.

These two themes also appeared in the explanations of responses to other items on the RWA Scale. And other experiences kept popping up here and there, such as reactions to religious teachings (and ministers and atheists), experiences with "forbidden fruits" (for example, erotic magazines, sex, marijuana), reactions to receiving physical punishment (or seeing its effects on others), encountering different ways of doing and viewing things, the consequences of ignoring parental advice, the results of doing things on their own, and so on. Naturally, not everyone had had these experiences. Furthermore, the "Lous" seemed to have had a lot more than the "Hughs"—who mainly talked about parental and religious teachings. It would take me three more studies to get it right, but I felt, as I culled, that these students were giving me insight into significant events in their lives.

The September 1982 Study. By the fall of 1982 I had compressed the most common themes from the hundreds of narratives into a 20-item survey, composed so that half the experiences described would have proauthoritarian effects and the rest the opposite (Exhibit 2). I asked 582 students, serving in the final session of a three-week experiment, to indicate on a −4 to +4 basis whether each statement was true of them. I ended the instructions by saying, "If the statement does not apply to your experience, one way or the other, if you have not had any contact with the subject of the statement, blacken the '0' bubble."

The mean intercorrelation among responses to these 20 items was .14, producing an alpha of .77. Their summed score correlated a mind-boggling .73 with the students' first-session scores on the RWA Scale.

I did not trust that correlation for a second. The subjects had answered the RWA Scale three times by then: they had given their own answers and then their perception of their parents' wishes in the first session, and then they had reanswered the scale at the beginning of the second session as part of my research on improving the test's internal consistency (see Chapter Two). Thus I realized the students could easily have seen the connection between the familiar attitude items and these "personal experiences" statements—and, in essence, given their *opinions* about authorities, physical punishment, and so forth again, rather than just indicating what their *experiences* had taught them so far.

The .14 mean intercorrelation among their responses

Exhibit 2. The Initial Version of the Experiences Scale.

1. It has been my experience that things work best when fathers are the head of their families.
2. The homosexuals I have known seemed to be normal, decent people, just like everybody else, except for their sexual orientation.*
3. The people I have known who are unpatriotic and disrespectful toward authority have seemed to me to be ignorant troublemakers.
4. My parents have always known what was right for me.
5. It has been my experience that sexual intercourse is all right for students in their last year or so of high school.*
6. I have found that breaking rules can be exciting and fun at times.*
7. It has been my experience that physical punishment is an effective way to make people behave.
8. My own experience with pornographic material indicates it is harmless and should *not* be censored.*
9. Most of the young people I know who have taken advantage of today's greater freedom have messed up their lives.
10. I have learned from my contact with lots of different kinds of people that no one group has "the truth" or knows "the one right way" to live.*
11. Whenever I did things my parents warned me against, it was usually a mistake and resulted in a bad experience.
12. I have learned from my own experience that being a decent human being has nothing to do with being religious.*
13. I have seen, both in how things have happened in history and in my own life, that many times protest is right and rebellion necessary to end injustice.*
14. It has been my experience that smoking marijuana is a big mistake.
15. My contact with nontraditional families, in which everyone is more equal than usual, has convinced me that it is basically a bad idea.
16. I have been favorably impressed by people I know who continue to have rebellious ideas and a sharply critical outlook on life.*
17. The authorities and officials I have trusted in my life, at home, in school, and so on have always treated me honestly and fairly.
18. I have found it's better to be unconventional than to be "normal."*
19. As I have gotten older, I have seen that the rebellious ideas I had earlier were really foolish.
20. The more I've thought about traditional religious beliefs, the more contradictory, irrational, and nonsensical they have seemed to me.*

* Statement is worded in the nonauthoritarian direction.

also aroused my suspicions. Why should there be that much relationship among enjoying sex, enjoying rebellious persons, not enjoying spankings, having wise parents, and all the rest? Are life's experiences that organized for us, either pro-RWA or con? The level of interitem association, *resembling that found on the RWA Scale*, reinforced my suspicion that subjects had answered the Experiences Scale as though it were an attitude measure.

I found the paucity of 0's in the students' reports, only 16 percent overall, equally troubling. Everybody had allegedly had nearly all of these experiences. Eighty-nine percent, for example, supposedly had known someone unpatriotic and disrespectful toward authority. Allegedly 51 percent knew a homosexual. And so on. But I darkly suspected I was getting *attitudes* about those who lacked patriotism, and opinions about homosexuals, whether the subject knew any or not.

In short, the possible association with the RWA Scale and the internal consistency and prevalence of the "experiences" reported made me highly skeptical of the .73 correlation. So, like some physicist who unexpectedly obtains a sensational result, I "tapped the glass on my gauges" by reanalyzing the data, and when nothing changed, I redid the experiment—only more carefully.[7]

The November 1982 Study. A large subject pool enables a careless experimenter to overcome certain inadequacies. So I quickly re-collected responses to the Experiences and RWA scales, but with some changes in procedure. Through the cooperation of several colleagues, the Experiences survey was administered to four classes of introductory psychology students in October, but by hired graduate students, cleaned and spiffied up a bit. More detailed instructions were read to the subjects, emphasizing that the measure was not an attitude scale, just a survey of what had happened to them. The students were encouraged to answer "0" when appropriate. In addition, most items had a short "jab" at the end to keep subjects on the track. Item 1, for example, read:

> It has been my experience that things work best when fathers are the head of their families. (Has that been your *experience*?)

Because of the more involved instructions, the emphasis on making careful responses, and the fact that I also included a few new items culled from the original attributions collected in September of 1980 and 1981, it took about 20 minutes of class time for my "stalking horses" to administer the revised Experiences questionnaire.[8]

Responses to the 20 items in Exhibit 2 correlated .11 among themselves on the average, a decrease that I considered a step in the right direction. The number of 0's increased a bit too, to 19 percent overall. Both changes suggested the subjects had been less attitudinal, more factual.

A month later I recruited 241 students from these classes for Experiment Survey, making (of course) no connection with the earlier in-class testing. As always, the first item of business in the Survey booklet was the RWA Scale. How far would the correlation between RWA and Experiences scores fall under the new procedures? Quite a bit, I expected. But the coefficient was .72.

To protect myself from being fooled, I had built in some checks on the students' earlier responses. At the end of the Survey booklet, subjects were asked, in disguised form, one of the questions they had answered a month earlier on the Experiences Scale. For example, a quarter of the 241 students were asked at the end of the second session whether they had known "people who might be described as 'unpatriotic and disrespectful toward authority'? Without naming names, who were they? Did they seem to be sincere, know what they were talking about, and so on? Or did they just seem to be ignorant troublemakers?" Of the 53 subjects who answered this question, only one had answered "0" on the corresponding Experiences item. But 15 others now said they too had never known such a person. So my efforts to keep subjects on the track while filling out the Experiences survey had definitely fallen short. These 15 should have said "0" then. Furthermore, of the 37 students who said on both occasions that they knew such a person, only 26 gave *consistently* positive (or negative) reactions. So the "bottom line" was that (1 + 26 =) 27 pairs of responses were consistent, and (15 + 11 =) 26 pairs were not. Although responses to single items often have low test-retest reliability, 51 percent confirmation amounts to a rather blurry bottom line.

The "experiences" checked in the other three quarters of the November sample did not fare much better: "parents warned against" showed 52 percent consistency; "nontraditional families," – 58 percent consistency; and "pornography," – 61 percent. The subjects' answers to my Experiences Scale were still tainted, and so, therefore, was its puffed-up .72 correlation with RWA Scale scores.

The January 1983 Study. A *very* large subject pool gives a persistent researcher many opportunities to rise above himself. I therefore modified the previous experiment at the beginning of the new year, using subjects from three new classes in which a hired experimenter administered a 26-item Experiences Scale.

I wrote yet more elaborate instructions, stressing the "historical," nonattitudinal nature of the task. In addition, the flow of the survey was interrupted three times by printed reminders that "this is not an attitude survey but a survey of what has happened." But the major change in procedure involved placing a large, extended "jab" (more like a good shaking) after most of the items to keep subjects' minds on the task at hand. For example, the item on homosexuals read:

> The homosexuals I have known seemed to be normal, decent people, just like everybody else, except for their sexual orientation. (First, do you know anyone who is a homosexual? If not, blacken the "0" bubble. But if you do, did that person seem like everybody else except for his or her sexual orientation?)

These four changes in procedure lengthened the survey considerably; it took three sides of legal-size paper for the instructions and the items, and some students took as long as 30 minutes to answer the scale. But this all seemed necessary to obtain more accurate information about the subjects' history. I was realizing how difficult it was for my respondents to split their experiences apart from their attitudes.

Still I made more headway. This time the Experiences

Scale items had a mean intercorrelation of .09, and the number of "0" responses rose to 23 percent of the total. The attitudinal component had apparently shrunk some more.

Several weeks later 301 of these students found themselves in one of ten runs of Experiment Survey, answering the RWA Scale. *Now* what would the correlation between the two tests be? Why, .72, naturally. I began to get intrigued.

I had again built checks into "Survey" on the students' earlier reports of their experiences in life. This time I randomly divided the sample into fifths and asked each fifth for information about two of the experiences touched on by the scale. (For example, "Have you known people who are homosexuals? Without naming names, who were they? What were they like, compared with everybody else—very different?—normal, decent?") The ten items tested for consistency of responses were the same four used in November plus Numbers 2, 5, 9, 16, 19, and 20 from Exhibit 2.

Responses to Item 9 ("messed up their lives") were least confirmed, with only 50 percent consistency between the two reports. Answers to the item about homosexuals, in contrast, were corroborated 84 percent of the time: 35/50 subjects (70 percent) said on the Experiences Scale that they had never known a homosexual (compared with 49 percent who gave the "0" answer in September 1982). Thirty of these 35 later repeated during Experiment Survey that they knew no homosexuals. The remaining 15 of the 50 students had said in class that they had at least one homosexual acquaintance; all said so again in Survey, and among their evaluations of these persons, 12 were consistent (therefore, 30 + 12 = 42; 42/50 = 84 percent consistency).

These two items represent the low- and high-water marks; the other eight checks lapped somewhere in between. The total corroboration over all ten items was 338 "hits" out of 546 match-ups, or 62 percent. All four of the items checked in November 1982 checked out better now, averaging 63 percent agreement. Furthermore, there were only 48 instances overall (or 9 percent) in which subjects said on the Experiences Scale that something had happened to them, but then indicated later it had not. I was clearly getting diminished returns, but the emphatic instructions and constant reminders had paid off.

In a sense these checks just describe the test-retest *reliability* of the ten Experiences items. The subjects' *descriptions* of their experiences at the end of Experiment Survey provide a validity test. Rebellious acquaintances were mentioned; one's encounters with erotic magazines and "skin flicks" were recalled; friends' nontraditional families were described, pro or con. High school pregnancies were cited. Times when one ignored parental advice about drinking, driving, smoking, doing drugs, choosing friends, buying cars, or quitting jobs were listed. And so on.

We do not know, of course, that the subjects actually knew rebellious students in high school, were unharmed by pornography, or knew a smooth-running nontraditional family. But the citations imply that the subjects' responses to the Experiences Scale some weeks earlier had been based on real experiences. Students apparently have them, even if professors living in their ivory towers reportedly do not.

But how do we explain that persistent correlation of .72? Maybe the students realized the connection between the two scales, whose content, after all, is too similar to be coincidental. I wondered about that after the November study, so in this January study I placed a "Postexperimental Question" at the end of the Survey booklet, which asked:

> Does the material in this survey remind you of any other experiences you have had at the university recently? That is, have you encountered these subjects before? Where?[9]

Forty-four of the 267 subjects (or 16 percent) who served in the first nine sessions indicated they had answered a similar survey in their psychology class. (More common answers were "?" and "In sociology lectures.") At the tenth and final testing session I offered the 34 students present an extra experimental credit if they correctly identified their previous encounter with this material. Eight (24 percent) did so.

These are not insignificant amounts, but they likely approximate the maximum percentages of subjects who could have noticed a connection between the two questionnaires as they served in Experiment Survey.

So what is the explanation? Over the course of these three studies, the amount of "attitudinal responding" to the Experiences Survey has seemingly dropped a fair bit. Interitem correlations have fallen satisfyingly from .14 to .09—about half the interconnecting usually found among the RWA attitudes. The number of "0" responses has risen from 16 percent to 23 percent. Cross-validating checks for response consistency have risen to more conscionable levels for single-item measures. Yet as the attitudinal responding has dropped by these three indexes, the Experiences-RWA correlation has barely been scratched—even when the two tests were administered by different experimenters weeks apart in different settings and most subjects failed to notice the similarity of material.

I have learned the hard way to be especially suspicious of gratifying results, for in the past they have blinded me to errors and led to months of "surveying up the wrong tree." I still do not believe, for reasons I shall give shortly, that personal experiences *cause* authoritarianism to the degree suggested by these recurring correlations in the .70s. But for lack of a better explanation of the findings, these experiences *do* appear to be a more powerful determinant of right-wing authoritarianism than any of the other factors we have considered so far. Even students' perceptions of their parents' wishes, taken right after the students' own answers to the very same instrument, correlate only about .50 with the students' authoritarianism.

On balance, the experiences we are discussing seem to make students less authoritarian as well. The mean score on the Experiences Scale of the 301 January 1983 subjects, for example, was 90.7, where 100 would be perfectly neutral. So here is a liberalizing "strong force," which (with the "weak force" of peer influence) counteracts the largely proauthoritarian effects of parents, religion, education, and the news. Interestingly, you will find some pages back that some "Lous" and "Hughs" indicated the direction of most of these forces in 1979.

The Fall 1984 "Origins" Study

Procedures. In September of 1984, 557 students served in a three-session run of Experiment Survey. The study was designed to answer somewhat comprehensively the question I posed at the beginning of this chapter: What causes the differences in students' level of authoritarianism by the time they enter university? My plan was simply to collect data on all the determinants we have been considering and use them in a multiple regression analysis to account for as much of the RWA Scale variance as possible. Though not as convincing (in principle) as a longitudinal study, this approach was certainly more feasible and could indicate the most promising variables to include in such a long-term investigation.

Appendix B outlines the composition of the booklets administered at the three sessions. The first booklet began with the RWA Scale ($\overline{X} = 156.5$; alpha = .86).[10] A bogus newspaper article about a fictitious political leader followed (see Chapter Eight), and several measures of authoritarian aggression (to be discussed in Chapter Five) appeared next. The session ended with standard questions about religious and political affiliations.

The second session, held one week later, began with the Experiences Scale, introduced by even more swollen instructions and now consisting of the original 20 items plus 4 others developed during the previous year's testing (Appendix C). Subjects then answered the RWA Scale twice more, first describing the effects of the news media on their RWA opinions and then attributing effects to their educations. The students were then invited, through printed instructions, to have surveys sent to their parents and best friends. I have already presented these results: 521 parents and 206 best friends responded, you may recall, giving their own RWA opinions, estimating the student's, and performing other tasks. (Appendix B also describes the composition of these booklets.)

The final session, held still another week later, was mainly devoted to measures of authoritarian aggression and need not occupy us here.

Results. The correlations among the measures are listed in Table 2. Coefficients for the entire sample are presented first, using all the students for whom data were available on each pair of measures. Next are shown the correlations for just those 178 students for whom scores on *all* measures were available.

Some of the RWA correlations were described earlier in this chapter, but the reader will note that the 24-item Experiences Scale correlated, for the third time, .72 with the students' authoritarianism. (Its mean interitem correlation was .09, and the average proportion of 0's was 25 percent.)[11]

The data were subjected to a standard multiple regression analysis, using the "Regression" program from the Statistical Package for the Social Sciences (1983). The program was told to account for students' RWA Scale scores in terms of the theoretically relevant predictor variables.[12] Both "pairwise" and "listwise" deletions of missing data, corresponding to the two halves of Table 2, were made and separately analyzed.

In the pairwise deletions analysis, which used all subjects' responses, Experiences scores naturally entered the equation first. Parents' authoritarianism entered second and raised the correlation from .72 to .75. News RWA was selected next by the program, raising the coefficient to .77. Best Friend's RWA lifted the multiple regression to .78, and the School's RWA capped the correlation at .79, thus accounting for 62 percent of the variance of students' authoritarianism.

In the listwise deletions procedure, which considered only those 178 students for whom all data were available (mean RWA = 154.6, compared with 157.4 for the rest; $t = 1.08, p < .50$), the progression was Experiences (.72 again) and Parents' RWA (.76); then News RWA, Best Friend's RWA, and School's RWA raised the multiple correlation to .78.

It obviously makes no difference which analysis one chooses, as in both cases nearly all the predictive power comes from the Experiences scores (which is why I explained the scale's

Table 2. Correlations Among the Variables in the September 1984 "Origins" Study.

	Parent's RWA[a]	*School's RWA*	*News RWA*	*Friend's RWA*	*Experiences*
			All subjects		
Student's RWA	.44 ($N = 321$)	.32 (557)	.37 (557)	.31 (206)	.72 (557)
Parent's RWA		.14 (321)	.08 (321)	.08 (178)	.35 (321)
School's RWA			.53 (557)	.01 (206)	.28 (557)
News RWA				.07 (206)	.30 (557)
Friend's RWA					.26 (206)
			Subjects for whom all data were available ($N = 178$)		
Student's RWA	.44	.20	.23	.24	.72
Parent's RWA		.14	.02	.08	.39
School's RWA			.47	−.03	.22
News RWA				.00	.26
Friend's RWA					.22

[a] Parents' RWA was averaged if scores on both parents were available; the correlation of students' and parents' authoritarianism, without averaging, was .42.

development at such length).[13] Dropping the Experiences scores from the analysis, and relying instead on all the other predictors, produces a multiple correlation of .57 in both the pairwise and listwise analyses, accounting for only 32 percent of the students' authoritarianism. But using just the Experiences Scale allows us to account for 52 percent of the variance we set out to explain. It is more powerful than all the other factors put together.[14]

Discussion. Does one's experience with authorities, radicals, sex, religion, punishment, and so on really have that powerful an effect on authoritarianism, *independent* of parents, friends, the news, and so on? I find that hard to believe. How many people meet their first "uncloseted" homosexual with a *tabula rasa*, for example? Parents and religion and friends and the media have long shaped an attitude toward gays by then. Would not these earlier influences predispose us to be frightened, or repulsed, or sympathetic, or admiring—no matter what the homosexual person was like? A great deal of research on prejudice indicates yes.

And does not the emphasis placed on the family religion color our impressions of atheists? Cannot the guilt produced by prior teachings make sex repulsive and breaking rules terrifying? Does not the acceptance of a parent's authority and judgment make a harsh spanking for misbehavior "deserved"? In other words, experiences may correlate with authoritarian attitudes, but only *because* these other factors have predisposed us to experience experiences in expected ways.

I hope you agree with me that this makes sense, because I need some company confronting a very large fact. Why do these other factors correlate so poorly, even in combination, with the students' authoritarianism if they are the true sources of "the connection"?

Were the other variables at a considerable disadvantage psychometrically? Not really. True, the student himself provided the answers to both the RWA and Experiences scales, while the parents' and best friends' input came from other folks. But these other folks were answering precisely the same items whose (student-produced) responses we were trying to predict, and both these predictors showed reasonable internal consistency. In comparison, the Experiences Scale consists of items somewhat different from the RWA Scale's, and its internal consistency is intentionally (because of our efforts to reduce attitudinal responding) a shambles.

Besides, the other predictors, News RWA and School's RWA, were also provided by the students. If there were some "set to appear consistent" that bound students' Experiences answers to their RWA Scale responses, the News and School attributions should have profited even more, being clones of the RWA Scale. (In fact, the .53 correlation between these two predictors looks highly suspect on these grounds.) But they do not begin to approach the correlation that Experiences scores had with authoritarianism. The numbers we need to back up *our* preconceptions are just not there.

Perhaps these other determinants did their determining so long ago that the student no longer remembers them, and the parents/best friends have since changed. But friends usually become more similar, not more different. And in a large number of studies in which students were asked to indicate how they thought their parents would (presently) like them to answer the RWA Scale, these projection-vulnerable estimates had correlated about .50 with the students' authoritarianism, not .70. Furthermore, the correlation between parents' and students' real authoritarianism has never risen above .51. And our efforts to produce veridical responding to the Experiences measure, plus our administering the two scales in different experiments held weeks apart, have thus far lowered the RWA-Experiences correlation from .73 to .71, tops. A correlation of .71 explains *twice* as much variance as one of .51.

I am thus led to accept the finding. Oh, I do not believe for a moment that one's experiences in life, by themselves and independent of all that has gone before, determine personal authoritarianism. But I can find no way to disbelieve that they are powerful supporters or revisers of what has previously been learned and are particularly likely to make students less authoritarian than they were originally inclined to be.

It is instructive in this regard to examine the other predictors' relationships with the Experiences Scale scores, shown in Table 2. They are rather meager overall, implying again that parents (for example) may provide us with initial attitudes and orientations, but life's direct and indirect experiences can alter these. Fathers may believe physical punishment is effective, but their children may know first-*hand* that it mainly teaches one to be careful about not getting caught. Students may meet "the sort of people your mother warned you about" and discover they are not as bad as advertised. Young people, in a timeless cycle, may become disillusioned by religion's inability to produce morality as easily as it promotes public piety.[15]

A Pragmatic Implication. Of course, life's experiences can also reinforce early learnings, and apparently they usually do for Highs. But in some instances the problem is *not* that High RWA students have had lots of encounters with proauthoritarian lessons but, rather, that they have not had the experiences at all, pro or con.

For example, 77 percent of the Highs in this 1984 study reported on the Experiences Scale that they did not know any homosexuals, compared with 54 percent of the Lows ($z = 4.18$; $p < .001$). In *both* groups most of those who did know homosexuals reported that they were "normal, decent people, just like everybody else, except for their sexual orientation" (22 to 10 subjects for Highs, 58 to 9 for Lows). Similarly, most Highs (64 percent) had never encountered a "nontraditional family, in which everyone is more equal than usual," whereas most Lows (63 percent) did know such a family—quite possibly their own ($z = 4.50$; $p < .001$). In *both* groups again, the majority of those who knew a nontraditional family did not think it was a bad idea (28–23 for Highs, 80–11 for Lows). More Highs (40 percent) than Lows (17 percent) said they had *never* done unconventional things and did not know anyone who had ($z = 4.25$; $p < .001$). But in *both* groups, most who had broken some social norms said it was better to be unconventional than "normal" (47–39 for Highs, 99–22 for Lows).

We can see, in the vastly different ways that "Hughs" and

"Lous" responded to homosexuals, nontraditional families, and unconventionality when they *did* encounter them, that other factors such as parental teachings and religious influence made acceptance more difficult for the Highs. But I found it remarkable that so many Highs, set up to disapprove, got past their expectations and were favorably impressed. My fellow cynic from the "Show Me state," Mark Twain, would have found that remarkable too. But personal experiences do shape attitudes and can sometimes even overcome "early leanings."[16] (We shall uncover, in Chapter Six, the variable that largely determines whether "Hughs'" attitudes toward homosexuals can be modified by personal experiences.)

So a large part of the reason Highs remain Highs is that, through self-selection, self-denial, and self-exclusion, they do not have the range of experiences that could have lowered their authoritarianism. Highs may have a stronger dislike for diversity and controversy than most of us do. They tend to think there is only one right way to interpret the Bible, and they immerse themselves in that particular system, shunning all others, sticking to the "straight and narrow." Schoolbooks should present a one-sided, "patriotic" view of history. The "CBS Evening News" should be like Paul Harvey's. And so on. Authoritarians do not appear to shop much in the marketplace of ideas. Indeed, many of them would like to close it down. But if we could get them into it more often. . . .

Theoretical Implications. Let's see whether we can make a two-sided evaluation of social learning theory's contributions to our discoveries. First, we should note the nature of the rewards and punishments implicitly involved in the Experiences Scale. Some are physical (sexual satisfaction, hangovers), and others are social (being accepted by peers for doing drugs—or for not doing drugs). But most seem to me to be self-evaluative cognitions: having consistent ideas, considering oneself rational and fair, having religious integrity, being wise, controlling one's own behavior, finding meaning in life, being a "good daughter" or a "good Christian" or a "good human being," promoting equality between people. These are the goals underlying most of the

Experiences items. We are a long way from rat chow and early "learning theory" models of human behavior. But one of the hallmarks of social learning theory, along with its emphasis on imitation and vicarious learning, is the stress it places on self-regulation of behavior through such cognitive evaluations.

We must recognize, however, as I said at the beginning, that social learning theory could not (I think) have predicted the importance of personal experiences, the unimportance of peer influence, and so on in shaping authoritarianism. Similarly, I doubt even a brilliant social learning theorist could have produced the Experiences Scale from an armchair, even (or especially) from one placed in a room filled with the accumulated findings on "authoritarianism." We had to find out what the most important events were (although in retrospect, as usual, the list contained in the Experiences Scale seems perfectly obvious).

Furthermore, although the theory stresses the role that cognitive self-evaluations can play in governing behavior, it does not describe (in any detail) the limits of their power. For example, we shall see that authoritarians seem to have rather "compartmentalized" minds, with notable inconsistency between their ideas and notable contradiction between what they believe and what they do. Bandura (1987, 1988) has cogently addressed the issue of "moral disengagement" recently, but we still seem some distance from being able to predict who will disengage and how.

But in the final analysis, social learning theory took us where no one had gone before. We set out to understand why university students differ in authoritarianism. The theory provided a framework of concepts and general principles readily adaptable to our interest. And after a little experimentation, we can now explain in the theory's terms *most* of what was once a mystery to us. We understand what is apparently important and what is not. We can now ask other students questions about particular events in their lives and, once we know the answers, make a good estimate of their authoritarianism. If we collect more background information, such as their parents' RWA Scale scores, our estimates become better still. The reasons behind the students' personal authoritarianism have become clear, and we can even sense (as we often do from learning-theory analyses) what needs to be done to improve the situation.

We should savor the moment. We do not often get this far.

The Spring 1986 Manitoba Alumni Studies

Having had a moment of self-congratulation, let us next wonder what will happen to these students' authoritarianism over the rest of their lives. After all, life does not end at eighteen. What will they be like when they are eighty-one?

We (or, more exactly, our successors) may find out many years from now. But in the meantime we can look at the changes that had occurred in two groups of former students who re-answered the RWA Scale in the spring of 1986. The first group had initially been tested in the fall of 1982 and was about to graduate from university. The second group had originally served in "Survey" nearly 12 years earlier, in 1974, when the RWA Scale was just a pup.

Effects of Four Years of University Education on Authoritarianism

Procedure. In May 1986 I obtained the names of students about to receive their bachelor's degrees from the University of Manitoba. Checking my own "Survey" attendance sheets from the fall of 1982, I identified 28 liberal arts majors (excluding all psychology majors, who were more likely to have heard of my research), 33 administrative studies majors, and 19 nursing majors who had answered the RWA Scale at the very beginning of their university careers. I selected these programs because incoming liberal arts majors usually score relatively low in authoritarianism, "commerce" students average about average, and nursing hopefuls score somewhat high. What, I wondered, would their RWA Scale scores be like after four uninterrupted years of university education in their chosen fields?

I sent a solicitous letter (see Appendix D), the survey, and a self-addressed stamped envelope to each of these 80 persons. I reminded them that they had completed an attitude survey for me four years earlier and asked them to answer the same survey again as part of an investigation of the ways attitudes change over time or stay the same. I also asked the subjects what they had heard about my research. (They had been given only feedback about response sets in 1982, and of course no mention was made of authoritarianism now.) Finally, I included a dollar bill with each solicitation and asked the graduates to mail it back to me if they declined to participate.

Results. I received completed forms from 77 of the 80 students (26 arts, 32 commerce, and 18 nursing majors and 1 student who removed the 1982 survey number on the questionnaire). None of the 42 females and 34 males indicated awareness of my research program. Two (commerce) respondents were nice enough to return my $1 with their answers.

The alpha reliability of the subjects' responses to the RWA Scale changed significantly over time, from .84 as first-year students to .89 as graduating seniors ($W = 1.45$, $p < .001$; see Feldt, 1980). This longitudinal change corroborates previous cross-sectional correlations between level of education and alpha (*RWA*, p. 242).[17]

The "before" and "after" levels of authoritarianism are shown in Figure 3. As expected, first-year nurses had higher RWA Scale scores than the other two groups ($\overline{X} = 167.2$) ($t = 2.15$ for the comparison with commerce, 2.02 for that with arts). But the incoming liberal arts majors were not less authoritarian than the commerce students (means of 151.2 and 151.3, respectively).[18]

These subjects cannot be considered a random sample of the original 1982 participants in "Survey." For one thing, they graduated. But they did not differ in authoritarianism. Their mean RWA Scale four years earlier had been 155.0; that of the rest of the sample was 152.3 ($p > .25$).

The reader will quickly notice from Figure 3 that authoritarianism dropped significantly over the next four years in all three programs, the drop among liberal arts students being particularly dramatic (and significantly greater than the others). Over all 76 respondents, RWA Scale scores fell an average of 17 points (or about 11 percent). This longitudinal finding also

Figure 3. Changes in RWA Scale Scores over Four Years of Education.

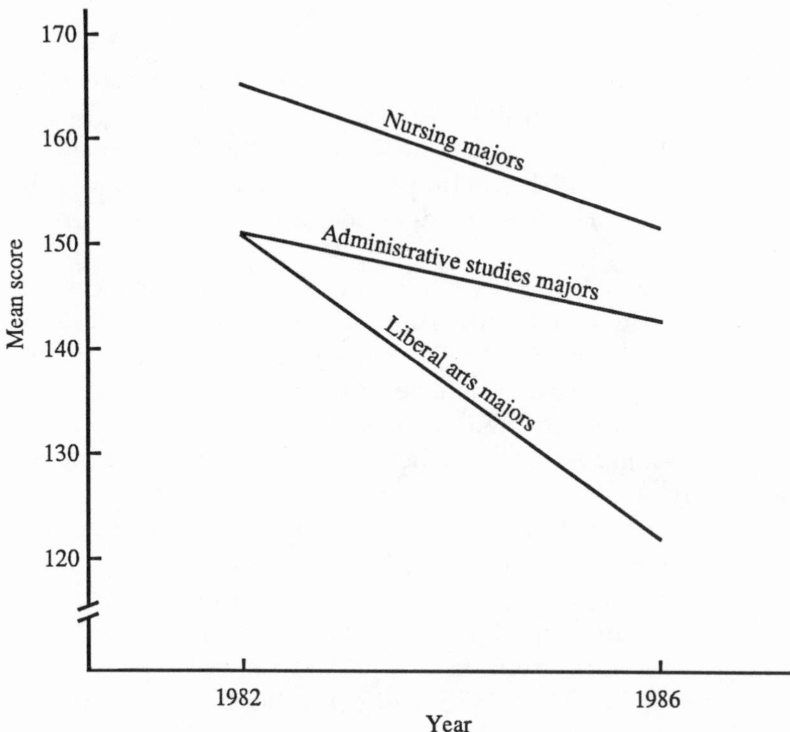

corroborates many earlier (negative) correlations between level of education and authoritarianism.

Will incoming Highs and Lows be equally affected by higher education? Not if our understanding of the way experiences can lower authoritarianism is correct. We would expect that Highs (who had presumably lived in narrower circumstances before entering university) would change more over the four years than Lows. That proved the case; freshman Highs had dropped 24.1 points by the time they graduated, compared with only a 10.0-point drop for Lows ($p < .05$). Thus getting Highs into that "marketplace of ideas" did apparently have a beneficial effect.

The correlation between pre- and postundergraduate

RWA Scale scores (that is, the scale's "four-year test-retest reliability") was .75.

Discussion. What caused the drops shown in Figure 3? Perhaps they had nothing to do with attending university; I have no control group of high school chums who followed other paths after grade 12. But many professors (myself included) will automatically assume the decline was due to their great teaching.

We can only speculate at this point. Probably course work did play a role; something certainly drove down the liberal arts scores in particular, and I doubt many educators in the humanities and social sciences would be surprised by Figure 3. But one can imagine other possibilities as well.

Play a little game with me. Look at the RWA Scale at the beginning of Chapter Two, and guess which items were most likely to be affected by university instruction. How about Item 1 ("strong medicine")? Yes, very likely if the student takes a course in criminology or encounters an "antipunishment" psychologist. Item 2 ("do their own thing")? I think not. Item 3 ("trust proper authorities")? Sure, from history, philosophy and political science courses. Item 4 ("Bible")? Quite possibly, from philosophy, religion, anthropology, and so on.

When *I* completed this exercise for the whole scale, I found I had selected nearly half the items as "most likely" to be affected by university teaching. But when I looked at the actual changes that had occurred among my 76 respondents, I found I was almost always wrong!

The greatest drops (of about 1 point each) occurred on Items 10 ("homosexual"), 18 ("atheists"), 3 ("trust proper authorities"), 12 ("obedience and respect"), 28 ("Communists"), 8 ("premarital intercourse"), and 29 ("students challenge"). Did the faculty cause these changes? Are the people on the phone-in shows who believe university professors are all gay, atheistic, fornicating Communists preaching sedition actually right?

I doubt you could staff a single tenure committee with the teachers at the University of Manitoba with half those "credentials." Instead, my guess is that these changes occurred, not just because of us professors, but also because of them students. University exposes young adults not only to the wider world of ideas, but to a wider range of people too. They may meet their first homosexual; remember, most entering freshmen said they had never known anyone gay. They may rap for the first time with a confirmed atheist. Some "rabble rousers" may come across as well informed and sincere. And I predict with great confidence that these students' experiences with premarital sex were with one another, not with the faculty.

No doubt the atmosphere of a university as a forum for open and free discussion, as well as a giant saloon, is important here. Quite probably lit, history, philosophy, psych, sosh, anthro, and so on play a liberalizing role, especially among liberal arts students, who have the greatest opportunity to take all these courses. But in retrospect I think I guessed wrong about which items would change the most because I failed to learn the lesson of this chapter: personal experiences are important. The experience of attending university is far broader than going to class and the library. Social attitudes may change as much over beers as over books.

Effects of Eight Years of Life after Graduation

The study just reviewed indicates that four years of "specialized" university education lowers authoritarianism about 8 percent on the average, while a liberal arts program drops RWA Scale scores about 18 percent. But what happens to students' authoritarianism after they graduate? We can get some idea by considering the changes in RWA Scale responses found over a 12-year period among another group of Manitoba alumni.

Procedure. Through the cooperation of our alumni office, in May 1986 I sent the same sort of solicitous letter, survey, and self-addressed stamped envelope to 160 Manitoba graduates who had served in a methodological study in the fall of 1974.[19] I also enclosed a check for $2 in (a randomly chosen) 80 of the solicitations, asking the subject to tear it up if he or she chose not to complete my questionnaire.

I doubled my solicitations from the previous study because I suspected it would prove harder to reach persons who had graduated eight or nine years before. Indeed, nine of my envelopes were returned as undeliverable by the postal service, and some others were probably discarded at the point of address. But completed surveys were returned by 90 alumni (46 females and 44 males), only 1 of whom removed the 1974 survey number from the questionnaire. Fifty of the 89 identifiable respondents had been offered $2, of whom (happily) 11 returned my personal check with their answers.

By way of academic background, 21 of the responding alumni had earned three-year arts degrees, and 2 more had a four-year B.A.; 16 had received Bachelor of Commerce diplomas, and 10 had degrees in science. There were also 4 nurses in the sample, along with a diversity of graduates from other programs (for example, education, agriculture, physical education).

The respondents, like those in the 1982–1986 study, do not constitute a random sample of those who served in the original study. They too graduated. For another thing, they were trackable; third, they responded to my request. They were also well educated, averaging 17.6 years of formal schooling; 58 had gone on to postgraduate work of some sort. Their mean age was 30.3 years, and four fifths were either married (65) or separated/divorced (6). Of these 71 subjects, 48 had children. Nearly all their children were preschoolers; the mean age of the first-borns was 3.5 years. A solid majority of the respondents lived in Winnipeg. Thus, if you consider 30 "young," the sample was mainly composed of young urban professionals.

Were my "yuppie" respondents distinguishable from the other subjects who served with them in my 1974 experiment? Not by their authoritarianism. Their mean RWA Scale score back then was 152.5.[20] The average score of the 319 other subjects who served in the 1974 experiment was 154.8 ($p > .25$).

Results. The mean interitem correlation of the subjects' responses to the RWA Scale did not change over time, producing an alpha of .87 in both 1974 and 1986. I attribute this apparent stability to two counteracting trends: (1) an increase in internal consistency due to the effects of higher education, as we saw in the previous study, and (2) the decrease in consistency caused by the "aging" of some items over the 12-year interval, as discussed in Chapter Two.

What had happened to the respondents' level of authoritarianism over the intervening years? The two sets of scores correlated only .62, so a considerable amount of personal change had occurred. One subject, originally a very high 209, had dropped to 92. Another rose from 79 to 148. In contrast to these dramatic changes, however, about half (43) of the respondents were within 16 points (half a standard deviation) of their original score.

Overall, there was a significant decrease in RWA Scale scores over time, from the 152.5 in 1974 mentioned above to 145.5 in 1986 ($t = 2.29$; $p < .01$). I would attribute this drop to the lingering effects of the six years these subjects spent (on the average) at university.

But we have reason to believe that *four* years of university education would have lowered this sample's authoritarianism *more* than 7 points. Did something cause these alumni's RWA Scale scores to bounce back up toward their preuniversity levels? Yes, parenthood.

The 41 respondents in this study who had no children showed a substantial drop in RWA Scale scores over the 12-year period, from 152.1 to 138.8 ($t = 2.78$; $p < .001$). I found this impressive. Remember "Never trust anyone over 30," which was a popular expression when these subjects were in high school and university? Well, they were 30 now, and apparently they had "kept the faith." A drop of 13 points is just about what we would expect from their educations, given the mix of their undergraduate majors. (Incidentally, 12 of these nonparents had been arts majors; the 11 other B.A.'s were parents.)

By way of comparison, the 48 parents, whose 1974 RWA Scale scores averaged 152.8, were now essentially back where they started (151.1; $p > .50$). So if education lowered most of these alumni's RWA Scale scores, parenting appears to have jacked them up again.

Discussion. Eldridge Cleaver, one-time leader of the Black Panthers and now an aspirant Republican politician, believes "everyone changes." However, Newcomb (1963) found that the women who were liberalized in a relatively "radical" environment at Bennington College during the 1930s were still liberals some 20 years later. And Myers (1983, p. 282), summarizing research on this issue, wrote, "The teens and early twenties are important formative years. The attitudes formed then tend to be stable thereafter." But consider the incredibly diverse paths taken by the "Chicago Seven," Bob Dylan, and the entire "youth counterculture" since 1970.

The results of this modest study show how paths can split. I doubt anyone would say that the University of Manitoba during the mid 1970s was a radical-leftist haven, as Bennington allegedly was in the 1930s. But undergraduate education at my school appears to lower authoritarianism by roughly 10 percent—more if one majors in the liberal arts. Does this effect last? I would say, following Newcomb, that it apparently does to a surprising extent, even after one has been out of school for six years, started a career, adopted new reference groups, and so on.

So long as one has not also started a family. Children change things. And these young parents had been young parents for only about four years.

Remember the image that began this chapter—all those students answering my survey as they entered university? How authoritarian will the 48 alumni-parents I retested in 1986 be when *their* children are completing the RWA Scale as first-year college students in about the year 2001? The well-educated parents of my student samples have usually scored about 15 points higher than their children. Will the next 15 years add 15 more points, on the average, to these 48 RWA Scale scores?[21]

Of course, the cross-sectional differences I have been finding in my usual studies may simply reflect different socialization patterns, different personal experiences, different historical circumstances, and so on (Sears, 1979). For example, we shall see in Chapter Six that certain kinds of religious training can foster authoritarianism, and today's students grew up in less religious homes than their parents did (thanks to those same parents). Similarly, higher education appears to lower RWA Scale scores, and the current generation will be better educated than their parents were, thanks again to those same parents. So today's university students may end up significantly less authoritarian in 30 years than their parents are now—other things being equal. Possibly, however, parenthood, "patriotism," and property will prove powerful in the long run.[22]

I hope we will find out some day. In the meantime, I think it is clear we should abandon the notion that personal authoritarianism is cast in stone during early childhood experiences and view it instead as typical of so many human behaviors: complexly caused and always changeable—for better or worse.

NOTES

1. Students and parents agreed the parents had made only slight to moderate efforts to shape attitudes on most of the RWA Scale issues. Emphasis was reported on a 0–4 basis for each item, and the overall item means were 1.83 by the students' reports and 1.95 by the parents', with alphas of .91 and .93, respectively. There was also substantial agreement about which issues had been emphasized most; the rank-orderings of the 30 items by the two sets of judges correlated .87.

   Incidentally, there was only a slight tendency for High RWA students to have had "emphatic" parents; the correlation between students' authoritarianism and reports of parental emphasis was .13 for both sets of reports.
2. Right-wing concern with education has extended to universities at least since the days of the "loyalty oath" crisis at the University of California. Our times have seen the emergence of "Accuracy in Academia," which places students in classes to monitor and report on courses taught by "suspect" professors ("Balance or Bias?," 1985).
3. Social judgment theory (Sherif and Hovland, 1961; Sherif, Sherif, and Nebergall, 1965) would say that left-wing radicals would see ESTABLISHMENT PROPAGANDA stamped all over the same news broadcasts that right-wing extremists find oozing with LIBERAL BIAS.
4. In the fall of 1985 I asked 571 parents, most of whom lived in the metropolitan Winnipeg area, to indicate their sources of "daily news." Authoritarians differed from Lows most noticeably in sources of radio news, Lows being four times as likely as Highs (40 to 10) to listen to the Canadian Broadcasting Corporation (CBC) news. A smaller but similar difference appeared in TV news preference, 48 Lows viewing the CBC-TV programs regularly, compared with 21 Highs. Lows were slightly more likely to read the dominant local paper, the *Winnipeg Free Press*, exclusively, than Highs: 83–66.

   It is *just* my opinion, but the CBC and the *Free Press* appear to make more determined efforts to present balanced discussions of issues than many of their competitors.
5. The implication is as clear as my children's outstretched palms before me. Students are more hesitant to ask their best friends for a favor than to ask their parents. Why? You might have to pay your

friends back! And parents, no doubt from force of long habit, come across more than friends do.

A sociobiologist would simply say that parents have more at stake in their children's survival, "genewise," than the best friends do. (They would also say that the children have no *genetic* interest whatsoever in the survival of their parents, which brings me back to my children's outstretched palms.)

6. Best friends, reporting discussions of RWA topics on the same 0–4 scale used to measure parental emphasis, averaged only 1.08, compared with the parents' 1.95.

   The reader may wonder why, if parents projected their own attitudes onto the students more than the best friends did, the parents' estimates of student RWA answers were just as accurate as the friends'. The answer is, parents influenced the students' attitudes more than the friends did. Their projection was therefore less likely to be erroneous.

7. I did not realize it at the time, but the correlation of .73 may have reminded me of the relationship the Berkeley researchers found between E and F Scale scores, which turned out to be a response-set-induced mirage. My first thought really was "What the hell went wrong?"

8. Experimental items were written with an eye on the correlations obtained between RWA items and the summed score on the Experiences measure. In other words, which statements on the authoritarianism scale was I not "capturing" in terms of personal experiences? Items were selected from among those tested largely on the basis of (high) variance among the responses. No item was chosen because it correlated with RWA Scale scores. As will be seen, altogether I added four statements (out of six tested) to the original 20 experiences listed in Exhibit 2.

9. Actually, by now these subjects had been fairly drenched in the RWA Scale, answering it three times during the session (own answers, estimating parents' wishes, and predicting their responses 20 years in the future). So they had a fair chance to be reminded of the similar "Experiences" content that had come their way in class a few weeks earlier.

10. The reader may wonder why the mean RWA Scale score was so high, compared with other runs of Experiment Survey. Some sections of our introductory psychology course have more authoritarian students in them than others because of the location of

the classroom on campus and the academic majors of the students booked into those slots. Ordinarily I am able to draw subjects equally from relatively high- and low-RWA sections, but in the fall of 1984 an eager Ph.D. candidate beat me to most of the "low" sections and signed up the students for a large dissertation experiment. (I secretly vowed revenge, but she still got her Ph.D.)

11. As will be discussed in Chapter Six, I also administered the RWA Scale (and some other materials, dealing mainly with religion) to 513 of my own introductory psychology students during class time in September 1984. Later in the booklet, the subjects answered specific questions about their encounters in life. For example, some students answered whether they had "known troublemakers or people who break the law often. If so, has it been your experience that 'cracking down hard on them' was the right, the best thing to do?" Other subjects answered questions about knowing families in which the father was not the head, or about smoking marijuana, or whether their parents always knew what was right for them.

    A month later a hired experimenter recruited 313 of these students from my classes and, in a different setting, administered a booklet that began with the Experiences Scale. The mean inter-item correlation was .09, and the proportion of 0's averaged 23 percent. The consistency of answers to the four prechecked Experiences items ranged from 55 percent ("cracking down hard") to 73 percent ("marijuana") and averaged 66 percent. The correlation between RWA Scale and Experiences scores was .71. It was nice to see a new number.

12. Using the FORWARD method, variables were entered into the equation one at a time, according to their *F* probability. The procedure was forced to include all predictors, even though the last few entered had very small effects.

13. Examination of the "residuals" left by the multiple regression analysis suggests that some kind of religion factor would raise the multiple-*R*. Most of the students whose authoritarianism was seriously underpredicted were quite religious, and most of those the equation seriously overpredicted were not religious at all.

    One approach would be to increase the number of religious items on the Experiences Scale. The three included at the moment (Items 5, 14, and 21) probably underrepresent the importance of religion as a shaper of right-wing authoritarianism, as we shall see in Chapter Six. Another approach would use the "Authoritarian Religious Background Scale" described at the beginning of that chapter.

14. As an example of the ways other experiences in life can affect authoritarianism: 43 of 274 female students completing a January 1987 Secret Survey reported they had been sexually molested at least once by an older male while they were growing up. Nineteen of these became Lows, compared with seven who became Highs ($p < .01$). Being a victim may tend to create empathy in a person, and in this case mistrust of "authorities," making it harder to be highly authoritarian.

15. Or, to toy with a *reductio ad absurdum*, my children may learn that I do not always know what is best for them, or they may sometimes feel I have treated them unjustly.

    It gives one comfort, when confronted with the stupidity of the advice you gave your offspring, to realize that at least you have probably lowered your children's authoritarianism by being wrong. I offer this rationalization to all other parents free of charge.

16. Lest we embrace the discredited "contact hypothesis" about how to reduce prejudice, I should point out that (among other things) much depends on the characteristics of the "contactee." Nearly half (47 percent) of the Highs said they did not know anyone who had "rebellious ideas and a sharply critical outlook on life." But of those Highs who did, most thought such people were real jerks, not heroes (64–11). So, incidentally, did most of the *Lows* (57–49). Contact may help break down a false stereotype in certain situations; but it can reinforce valid ones too.

    Still and all, the power of personal experience to modify preconceptions about others may be one of the best hopes a pluralistic society has. For example, Hamilton and Bishop (1976) found that opposition to black neighbors among Connecticut homeowners melted once a black family moved into their suburb, confirming a classic finding by Deutsch and Collins (1951) 25 years earlier. The importance of equal status, successful cooperation, superordinate goals, and so on in these processes is not to be minimized, however.

17. Part of the change in the students' responding over the four years, which probably helped increase the RWA Scale's alpha, was a significant decrease in the number of "+4" responses (strong yea-saying) from an average of 2.82 to 1.65 per survey. The number of "−4" responses increased nonsignificantly, from a mean of 1.89 to

2.16. Both these associations with educational attainment have appeared in cross-sectional research (*RWA*, pp. 242–243).

18. The University of Manitoba offers a three-year "general" degree in the liberal arts and several four-year degrees. The three-year degree is by far the most popular. Perhaps students who enter the four-year B.A. programs are more authoritarian as entering students than those who opt for the quicker degrees. But it may also be that Lows who are liberal arts majors are more likely to interrupt their university careers for travel or employment and hence not to be graduating in four years.
19. I would like to thank Laird Rankin and Fred Dugdale and the staff of the University of Manitoba Alumni Association for their invaluable assistance in obtaining the subjects' current addresses and also Ruby Hiebert of the student records office for her help in locating graduating students.

    The "booklet placement" study in which these subjects originally served was reported in *Right-Wing Authoritarianism* on page 326.
20. Actually, these subjects answered the original 24-item RWA Scale in the fall of 1974 (*RWA*, pp. 171–172), on a −3 to +3 basis and the same items in 1986 on the −4 to +4 scale I had by then adopted. To facilitate comparison with other results, I have rescaled the 1974 answers to the new format and multiplied the sums in both cases by 1.25 to make them equivalent to a 30-item score.
21. This is not an argument against reproduction. But anyone who has rinsed a gluppy diaper in the freezing cold toilet water can tell you reproducing has its unforeseen costs. And that is just the beginning. My children's adolescence has added at least 10 points (and counting) to my RWA Scale score. (I have told them that if they wanted a less authoritarian father, they should never have been born.)
22. As will be seen in Chapter Eight, I have often asked students to imagine how they would answer the RWA Scale in 20 years, under a variety of circumstances. I found in 1982 that such subjects, asked to imagine they had adolescent children, thought their RWA Scale scores would go up 12 points—mainly on items having to do with "the youth." In contrast, a sample in 1984, asked to simulate their responses under identical circumstances, but with no children, believed their scores would go up significantly less, 6.6 points, with no particular change on youth-oriented issues.

4

Possible Explanations of Authoritarian Aggression

As observed in Chapter One, one of the major questions left unanswered in *Right-Wing Authoritarianism* is why the three defining characteristics of authoritarianism should covary in the first place. We should recognize at the outset, however, that the covariation of authoritarian submission and conventionalism presents no mystery. Persons highly submissive to the established authorities will ordinarily be highly conventional, and vice versa. What is unclear, what is at the heart of the matter for us, is why such submissive, unconventional persons should also be so aggressive (*RWA*, p. 251).

I hope to provide the answer to this question over the next two chapters. I shall begin by reviewing what is meant by authoritarian aggression, considering how it is measured on the RWA Scale, and studying the previous findings on the subject. Then I shall develop a number of hypotheses, based on broader theories of aggression, to explain why submissive, conventional persons might also be hostile.

Chapter Five will present evidence on the merits of these hypotheses, concluding with four "pitting" experiments that directly compare the more promising explanations of the authoritarian's aggression. At the end, we may have the answer.

A Brief Review of Definitions and Elaborations

The reader will recall that authoritarian aggression was defined in Chapter One as a general aggressiveness, directed against various persons, that is perceived to be sanctioned by established authorities. By "aggressiveness" was meant a willingness or desire to cause someone harm. The harm could be physical injury, psychological suffering, financial loss, social isolation, or some other negative state that people usually avoid.

Aggression is authoritarian when it is accompanied by the belief that established authority at least tacitly approves it or that it will help preserve established authority. This "general" aggressiveness appears in numerous contexts and situations, but not in all. Fear of retaliation may stay the authoritarian's hand. There are also prominent social prohibitions against aggression in our culture which can inhibit the authoritarian's aggressiveness. Thus the perception of authoritative sanction is important because it disinhibits the hostile impulse.

I should add that the *perception* of authoritative approval, which may be accurate or mistaken, extends beyond individual authorities (such as a police chief who is believed to sanction the beating of prisoners) to vaguer and larger powers ("The government wants those demonstrators shut up" or "God wants sinners punished"). In addition, citizens who endorse police attacks on suspects and nonviolent demonstrators are being authoritarian-aggressive, even though they do nothing themselves beyond approving. They are willing to have the victims harmed.

The "various persons" who are the targets of authoritarian aggression can be anyone, but unconventional persons (for example, "deviants") and persons who are conventional targets of social hostility (such as various minority groups) are attacked more readily. Thus right-wing authoritarianism is expected to be correlated with ethnic and racial prejudice, because such prejudice is a conventional outlet for aggressive impulses, sometimes modeled by the "best people" in various subcultures. But by no means is prejudice thought to be largely linked to authoritarianism, much less caused by it, as the "Berkeley" researchers proposed. (Much prejudice is endemic to a culture, for example; some of it also originates in personal experiences.)

Assessment of Authoritarian Aggression on the RWA Scale

Because aggression is socially less acceptable than submission to authority and conventionalism, its assessment on the RWA Scale is somewhat indirect. Not many persons will agree with "I am highly aggressive against people I don't like when I think the authorities will approve." The RWA Scale comes closest to such an item with the thoroughly chilling "Once our government leaders and the authorities condemn the dangerous elements in our society, it will be the duty of every patriotic citizen to help stomp out the rot that is poisoning our country from within"—a statement with which (alarmingly) most Highs in my samples agree. Other protrait assessments of authoritarian aggression are less bald and tend to draw even higher amounts of agreement from Highs:[1]

- The way things are going in this country, it's going to take a lot of "strong medicine" to straighten out the troublemakers, criminals, and perverts.
- The facts on crime, sexual immorality, and the recent public disorders all show we have to crack down harder on deviant groups and troublemakers if we are going to save our moral standards and preserve law and order.
- Some of the worst people in our country nowadays are those who do not respect our flag, our leaders, and the normal way things are supposed to be done.
- In these troubled times laws have to be enforced without mercy, especially when dealing with the agitators and revolutionaries who are stirring things up.
- The biggest threat to our freedom comes from the Communists and their kind, who are out to destroy religion, ridicule patriotism, corrupt the youth, and in general undermine our whole way of life.

- One reason we have so many troublemakers in our society nowadays is that parents and other authorities have forgotten that good old-fashioned physical punishment is still one of the best ways to make people behave properly.

A number of *con*trait assessments of authoritarian aggression appear on the RWA Scale as well. Authoritarians do *not* agree that homosexuals are as moral or healthy as everyone else or that atheists are just as good and virtuous as those who attend church regularly. They are not in favor of protecting the rights of radicals and deviants or of treating dissenters with leniency. Nor should courts be easy on drug users. Highs tend to disagree vigorously with all these notions.

But do these *opinions* have any larger significance?

General Findings on Authoritarian Aggression

RWA Scale scores[2] have correlated, moderately, with a number of aggressive behaviors in the past. The most widely used criterion has been the prison sentence that subjects would impose in a role-playing situation on convicted criminals. Correlations of .40 to .50 have commonly been found among Manitoba students and parents with ten "Trial" cases involving unsavory criminals, and summed sentences across four such cases correlated .48 with RWA Scale scores among students at five American universities in 1974 (*RWA*, p. 233).

A 1973 laboratory study allowed Manitoba students (supposedly) to punish another student with electrical shocks for mistakes made while memorizing a list of nonsense syllables. Overall, RWA Scale scores correlated .43 with the intensity of shocks delivered. (The "victims" were sometimes attired to appear Jewish. There was no evidence that this manipulation affected the RWA correlation, but one can seriously doubt that a postexperimental interview "caught" all the subjects who were aware or highly suspicious of the deceptions involved [*RWA*, pp. 199–202].)[3]

In 1979 I found that RWA Scale scores correlated .27 with answers given by Manitoba students to a balanced 14-item prejudice scale. The relationship was .43 among a sample of their parents (*RWA*, pp. 238–239). This scale has since been expanded to 20 items, given in Exhibit 3. Correlations among the item responses have averaged about .25 among both students and parents (producing an alpha reliability of about .87). Parents usually score a little higher on the scale, and RWA Scale scores correlate higher with parents' prejudice (about .45) than with students' (about .30). (Incidentally, students' prejudice correlates about .35 with their parents'—about the same relationship we saw in Chapter Three between students' and parents' levels of authoritarianism.)

Do these accumulated findings mean anything more than that subjects who express aggressive attitudes on the RWA Scale tend to be punitive and hostile in other contexts? Yes, because in all cases the solid majority of the items on the RWA Scale (not just the statements with manifestly aggressive content) had statistically significant relationships with these criteria of authoritarian aggression. Understandably, the strongly aggressive items usually produced the highest correlations. But the statements chiefly tapping authoritarian submission and conventionalism were also related to these behaviors. Submissive, conventional people not only have hostile attitudes, they tend to act aggressively and be prejudiced as well. Again: Why?

It should be noted that High RWA subjects have not *always* been more punitive than Lows in previous research. The status of the criminal to be sentenced and the nature of the crime and the victim have sometimes tempered the authoritarian's blow. For example, High American students were less likely than Lows to want Richard Nixon punished for his Watergate crimes (*RWA*, p. 226). High Manitoba students were significantly less punitive toward a police chief who beat an accused child molester in jail than toward a prison guard who did so. (Lows sentenced the two equally.) Similarly, Highs were much less punitive toward an accountant convicted of assaulting a hippie than toward a hippie convicted of assaulting an accountant in exactly the same circumstances. (Again, Lows sentenced them equally [*RWA*, pp. 234–236].) Highs were also not particularly punitive toward a policeman who beat a protesting demonstrator while taking

Exhibit 3. The Manitoba Prejudice Scale.

1. There are entirely too many Chinese students being allowed to attend university in Canada.
2. Canadians are *not* any better than all the rest of the people in the world.*
3. The main reason certain groups like our native Indians end up in slums is because of prejudice on the part of white people.*
4. There are far too many Jews in positions of power in our country.
5. Foreign religions like Hinduism, Judaism, and Islam are not as close to God's truth as Christianity, nor do they produce as much good behavior in the world.
6. Canada should open its doors to more immigration from the West Indies.*
7. Certain races of people clearly do *not* have the natural intelligence and "get up and go" of the white race.
8. The Filipinos and other Asians who have recently moved to Canada have proven themselves to be industrious citizens, and many more should be invited in.*
9. It's good to live in a country where there are so many minority groups present, like the Indians, Chinese, and Blacks.*
10. There are entirely too many people from the wrong sorts of places being admitted into Canada now.
11. No race on this earth is as good, hardworking, and noble as the white race.
12. Jews can be trusted as much as anyone else.*
13. As a group Indians and Metis are naturally lazy, promiscuous, and irresponsible.
14. Canada should open its doors to more immigration from India and Africa.*
15. Black people as a rule are, by their nature, more violent than white people.
16. The Pakistanis and East Indians who have recently come to Canada have mainly brought disease, ignorance, and crime with them.
17. Much of the white race's accomplishments have occurred because it has continually exploited the other races.*
18. More Chinese, Arabs, and Sikhs should be recruited for our medical, pharmacy, engineering, and other professional schools.*
19. It is a waste of time to train certain races for good jobs; they simply don't have the drive and determination it takes to learn a complicated skill.
20. There is nothing wrong with intermarriage among the races.*

* Item is worded in the contrait direction; that is, the prejudiced response is to disagree.

him to jail or toward an Air Force officer who (in a disguised version of the My Lai massacre trial) ordered the bombing of Vietnamese civilians he suspected of aiding the enemy (*RWA*, p. 233).

The authoritarian may approve of attacks on such "disrespectable" targets and hence be relatively lenient toward those who commit such aggression, especially if the latter are authority figures. At the same time, high socioeconomic status in itself does not appear to inhibit the authoritarian's own punitiveness. Highs were just as hostile toward a wealthy child abuser as toward a poor one, and they sentenced a businessman convicted of bank robbery just as severely as a tramp who committed the same crime. And they were more punitive toward an industrialist convicted of defrauding the government than Lows were (*RWA*, pp. 234–237). One notes, however, that none of these criminals was a high social authority, and none of the victims (a small child, bank tellers, the government) was the sort of unsavory, unconventional person whom authoritarians more readily attack themselves.[4]

Are Highs Really More Aggressive Than Lows?

The fact that Low RWA students felt more punitive than Highs toward Richard Nixon ought to puncture immediately the oversimplification that authoritarians are always more punitive than nonauthoritarians. It also raises the interesting possibility that authoritarians are not, *overall*, any more hostile than Lows but only appear so because investigators such as I keep trooping Highs' favorite targets before samples tested in paper-and-pencil shooting galleries. Perhaps Lows would be just as hostile if we paraded a pantheon of their devils before them.

In the fall of 1983 I found that Low RWA students would take an instant dislike to another student who wore a lapel button emblazoned with a racist, sexist, or antigay slogan. The last of these three cases proved useful, because Lows' dislike for someone wearing a "Nuke Gays" button ($\overline{X} = 2.63$ on a 0–4 scale) was just as pronounced as Highs' dislike for someone wearing a "Gay Power" button ($\overline{X} = 2.88$; $p > .30$). I had hoped to use these slogans to "set up" confederate-victims in a laboratory aggression experiment. But when that proved impossible (see Note 3), I used this mirror-image dislike to study High and Low punitiveness in a pair of simulated trials focusing on the gay rights movement.

The Two Trials of William Langley. Early in 1985 I distributed two versions of a fictitious trial to 545 students. One version of the trial read as follows:

> Imagine that you are the judge presiding over the trial of Mr. William Langley. Mr. Langley is a 44-year-old civil servant who is also the founder and president of the Winnipeg chapter of Canadians for Gay Rights, a noted prohomosexual organization. A few years ago Mr. Langley was leading a demonstration on the steps of the Manitoba Legislature, supporting a proposed law which would have prohibited discrimination against homosexuals in housing and certain fields of employment. A crowd of approximately 100, mainly members of Mr. Langley's organization, had gathered around his speaker's stand. A large banner which read "GAY POWER" was tied between two columns immediately behind Mr. Langley, and some of his supporters were passing out literature to adults passing by.
>
> About half an hour after the rally began, a group of about 30 counterdemonstrators appeared and began to walk slowly and silently around the outside of Mr. Langley's audience. They carried signs which read "THE FAMILY IS SACRED" and "NO GAY RIGHTS." At first Mr. Langley did not seem to notice the counterdemonstrators, but when he did, he stopped his speech and, according to several witnesses, said, "There are some of the people who are trying to keep this bill from passing. I say we run them out of here right now. Let's show everybody we mean business."

> Upon hearing this, many members of Mr. Langley's audience turned upon the counterdemonstrators and began physically to attack them. By the time the police restored order, many of the counterdemonstrators had been injured, and one person had to be taken to hospital for overnight observation.

In the second version of this trial, distributed randomly to the students, the positions were reversed. That is, Mr. Langley was the founder and president of "Canadians Against Perversion," was leading an antigay demonstration supporting a bill allowing discrimination against homosexuals, and had a banner reading "THE FAMILY IS SACRED" displayed behind him. The counterdemonstrators carried signs reading "GAY POWER" and "RIGHTS FOR GAYS." Otherwise the narrations were exactly the same.

Following the case description, subjects (1) were told that a jury had found Mr. Langley guilty of inciting a riot, (2) were asked what sentence (from 0 to 18 months) they would impose on him, and (3) were asked how "repulsive and disgusting" they found the defendant.

The progay Langley was sentenced to 10.6 months, on the average, and the antigay Langley to 10.2 months ($t = 1.47$; $p > .20$). So overall Highs and Lows were equally punitive. But that is not the point. Our principal interest lay in the reactions of High and Low RWA subjects to the different versions of the case. Did Lows "unload" on the antigay Langley as much as Highs did on the progay version? The results are shown in Figure 4.

Highs behaved as one might expect. They sentenced the progay Langley to 12.8 months in jail and the antigay Langley to 9.2 ($t = 3.73$; $p < .001$). Lows showed the opposite tendencies, but the difference between their sentences was much smaller (11.1 compared with 9.8 months) and not statistically significant ($t = 1.28$; $p > .30$) (F-interaction = 10.4; $p < .001$).

This difference is particularly interesting because Lows thought the antigay Langley was just as "repulsive and disgust-

Figure 4. Mean Sentences Imposed on the Two "William Langleys" by Low and High RWA Subjects.

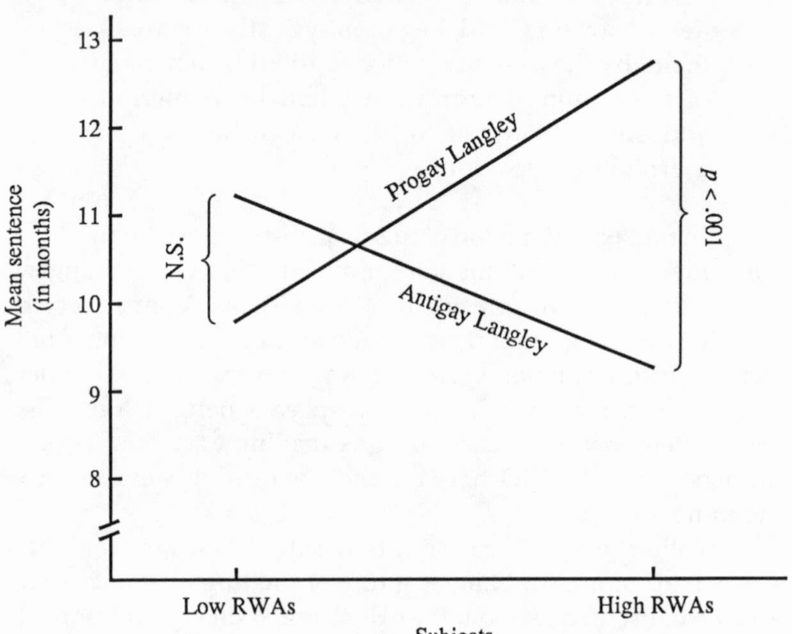

ing" as Highs considered the progay version to be (as the "button study" led us to expect; means equaled 3.42 and 3.34, respectively, on a 0–5 response scale). But Lows were much less punitive toward their strongly disliked Langley than Highs were toward theirs. Did Lows feel less of an impulse to hurt someone they disliked? Or is the explanation that authoritarians and nonauthoritarians alike felt a "positive" impulse to strike out, but the Lows experienced more inhibitions against aggressing?

Whatever the explanation, the evidence appears clear (in this case, at least) that Lows are not as prone as Highs to aggress against targets they dislike.[5]

Posse. A series of experiments on the "conative component" of attitudes leads to the same conclusion. In the fall of 1982, as I wondered how hostile authoritarians really were toward groups on their "enemies list," I asked 584 students what they would be willing to do if the government asked them to help destroy Communism in Canada:

> Suppose the Canadian government, sometime in the future, passed a law outlawing the Communist party in Canada. Government officials then stated that the law would only be effective if it were vigorously enforced at the local level and appealed to every Canadian to aid in the fight against Communism.
>
> Please respond to the following statements. . . according to the following scale:
>
> – 4 indicates the statement is extremely untrue of you. [Scored a "1"]
> – 3 indicates the statement is very untrue of you. ["2"]
> – 2 indicates the statement is moderately untrue of you. ["3"]
> – 1 indicates the statement is slightly untrue of you. ["4"]
> 0 indicates the statement is neither untrue nor true of you. ["5"]
> + 1 indicates the statement is slightly true of you. ["6"]
> + 2 indicates the statement is moderately true of you. ["7"]
> + 3 indicates the statement is very true of you. ["8"]
> + 4 indicates the statement is extremely true of you. ["9"]
>
> 1. I would tell my friends and neighbors it was a good law.
> 2. I would tell the police about any Communists I knew.
> 3. If asked by the police, I would help hunt down and arrest Communists.

4. I would participate in attacks on Communist headquarters organized by the proper authorities.
5. I would support the use of physical force to make Communists reveal the identity of other Communists.
6. I would support the execution of Communist leaders if the government insisted it was necessary to protect Canada.

For reasons I imagine are obvious, I have named this measure "Posse."

The mean intercorrelation of responses to the Posse-Communist items was .59 (alpha = .91). RWA Scale scores correlated from .32 ("support the execution of leaders") to .50 ("tell my friends and neighbors") with the six Posse items and .51 with their sum. All 30 of the RWA items correlated significantly with the Posse-Communist sum, authoritarian aggression items usually correlating highest.

Most of the students doubted they would do the acts specified; the sample mean was 20.4, on a potential range of 6 to 54. But as just seen, authoritarians said they were significantly less unlikely (that is, more likely) to help stomp out Communism on all six counts. If they are initially *un*inclined to hunt down Communists, attack their headquarters, and so on, it presumably would take less inducement to bring them around, compared with others. Besides, you could make up a pretty good-sized posse with the Highs (and others) who indicated they were already positively predisposed to persecute and execute Canadian Communists. Although I now wonder why, I was a little stunned when I first ran my fingers over these results.

I next asked the same subjects what they would do if the government asked everyone to help destroy homosexuality. The interitem correlations of Posse-Homosexual responses averaged .66, yielding a corresponding alpha of .92. RWA Scale scores correlated .42 with the summed scores, and this sum correlated significantly with all but one of the RWA Scale items. Again, aggression items correlated highest. The correlation between the two Posse scores was .67.

Overall, students appeared a little less likely (mean = 18.0) to support the persecution of homosexuals than Communists. But authoritarians were still significantly more likely to sign on for all six behaviors, RWA Scale coefficients varying from .28 ("physical force") to .47 ("tell my friends and neighbors"). Most Highs said such acts would be unlike them, but again only modestly so.[6]

I administered the same two surveys to 203 *parents* in January of 1983 and obtained quite comparable results. Alphas were .92 in both cases. RWA Scale scores correlated .49 (with 25 significant RWA item correlations) with Posse-Communist scores and .52 (with 27 significant item correlations) with Posse-Homosexual responses. The two Posse measures correlated .74.

Parents proved significantly more willing to persecute Communists than students had been ($\overline{X} = 23.1$) but in the main also doubted they would do so. The parents' Posse-Homosexual mean (18.6) was not significantly higher than the students'. In short (as usual), the parent-based findings replicated those obtained with university students.

Are There Posses for Lows Too? Often when I find a relationship between authoritarianism and some variable, I try to find a corresponding one between *un*authoritarianism and the same sort of thing. Hence I wondered, are there groups that Lows would particularly like to hunt down and destroy, and Highs not? In the fall of 1983 I asked 526 students to answer the six Posse questions for three targets: the Communist party of Canada (again), the Ku Klux Klan, and the Social Credit party.

Posse-Communist responses replicated previous results, although the overall RWA correlation (.37) was somewhat lower.

Subjects indicated a little less reluctance to go after the KKK (mean = 28.8; alpha = .89) than to hunt down Communists (24.6). But overall there was still a *positive* correlation (.19) between authoritarianism and saddling up. I rather expected this. Although the Klan is generally termed an ultraright organization, I had discovered earlier (*RWA*, pp. 228–229) that right-wing authoritarians do not like radical, "disrespectable" groups on either end of the political spectrum.

Which was why I included the "Socreds" in the experiment. The Social Credit party is often considered Canada's most conservative established political party. It had been in the headlines for several months in 1983 because it had recently been returned to power in British Columbia and, through its first budget, had significantly reduced the size of the civil service, eliminated some civil rights and regulatory commissions, and dramatically cut back on educational spending. (One columnist at the time wrote that the B.C. Socreds were keeping all of Ronald Reagan's 1980 election promises.) I thought it as likely a target of "knee-jerk liberal anger" as one could find.

Imagine my confusion, then, when RWA Scale scores still correlated *positively* (.27) with willingness to persecute Social Crediters, should someday the Canadian government deem it necessary! Overall, to be sure, there was little inclination to do so; Posse-Socred scores ($\overline{X}$ = 18.6; alpha = .90) were appreciably lower than those for Communists and the Klan. But authoritarianism was significantly related to all six Posse items, and 23 of the RWA Scale items were significantly correlated with the Posse sum (aggression items again leading the way).

Seemingly, then, the best friends Social Credit politicians would have in time of persecution, at least among these Manitoba students, would be Lows, with their "knee-jerk" defense of civil liberties. The Highs, perhaps with real reluctance, would more likely be measuring out the rope.

The fact that the data were collected in Manitoba might be important. The Social Credit party has few supporters among University of Manitoba students, and the new B.C. government did not receive a "good press" in our area. Thus the Socreds may have constituted a "flaky," disreputable group in the minds of many Manitoba authoritarians—in other words, the sort of target they attack more readily.

But I still had not found a group Lows would be more willing than Highs to persecute. I tried again the next year by asking 313 students to complete the Posse questions for a new right-wing movement in Manitoba, the Confederation of Regions party. The (few) students and parents in my samples who say they support this grass-roots movement, which advocates splitting Canada into relatively autonomous regions, have usually scored quite high on the RWA Scale.

But if the Canadian government decided to outlaw the Confederation of Regions party someday, it would be other Highs, not Lows, who would more likely hunt down its members. RWA Scale scores again correlated significantly with all six Posse items and .31 with their sum ($\overline{X} = 15.6$; alpha = .88). Twenty-one of the authoritarianism items had significant relationships with that sum, the largest again being obtained mainly by aggression items.

Of course, a political party dedicated to splitting up the country might also seem "flaky." So I took the final step of asking 248 students in the fall of 1985 how they would react if, sometime in the future, a federal government outlawed the mainstream right-wing party in Canada, the Progressive Conservatives (which, in fact, formed the Canadian government at the time). I expected a negative or null correlation with RWA Scale scores because authoritarians tend to support the PCs (*RWA*, pp. 203–204), the most respected right-wing party in the country.

But RWA Scale scores still correlated *positively* with all the Posse-PC items (though quite weakly, from .12 to .17) and .17 overall ($p < .001$). Twelve of the RWA Scale statements (a mixture of aggression and submission items) correlated with this sum, whose average (11.1; alpha = .91) was significantly lower than all the other Posse scores obtained.

Thus, although there was little indication that anyone was dying to stomp out the major conservative political organization in the country, Highs indicated they would be less reluctant than Lows to do so under the circumstances described.

Summary. One can summarize these five studies rather easily: no one is safe. While some Highs already have a foot in the stirrup when it comes to Communists and homosexuals, authoritarians in general appeared less reluctant than Lows to attack *all* the targets offered—respectable or unsavory, left wing or right. How much propaganda, persuasion, or pressure would a government have to employ to overcome Highs' modest reluctance to "name names," attack and arrest "enemies of the state," and imprison, torture, and execute them? How much has it taken in the past?

I do not propose that right-wing authoritarians want to persecute Progressive Conservatives, the way they might positively enjoy the opportunity to attack Communists, say. The Posse measure involves an element of authoritarian submission as well as authoritarian aggression, and Highs may sometimes simply be telling us that they trust the government more than Lows do (*RWA*, pp. 189–192, 227–232). As the RWA Scale item analysis indicated, they will not help persecute Tories simply because they are aggressive, but also because they are submissive. But the reasons for their violence will make little difference to their victims.

The second conclusion we can glean from these investigations concerns Lows. Although I have trotted a number of seemingly delicious targets before them, they have never appeared as ready as Highs to attack any of them. The Posse data thus confirm the results of the William Langley trials: Highs and Lows are apparently *not* equally hostile toward their respective foes. Authoritarians appear substantially more aggressive, toward a vast, bewildering array of potential victims (*RWA*, p. 251). Does this generalized hostility surpass human understanding?

Theoretical Explanations of Authoritarian Aggression

The "Berkeley Theory"

The first and best-known scientific explanation of the authoritarian's aggression appeared in *The Authoritarian Personality*. Nevitt Sanford and his colleagues proposed that the hostility manifest in highly prejudiced persons was an integral aspect of an underlying personality structure. The authoritarian was supposedly driven by repressed hatred of his or her parents and of other powerful authorities he or she later came to fear. Burying this hatred beneath a reaction formation of overt adulation and acceptance of the authorities' conventional values, the "pre-Fascist personality" displaced its hostility toward safe, unconventional targets, whose vilification endeared the authoritarian to the tyrannical figures. Prejudice and authoritarianism were thus intimately connected. And authoritarian aggression was a predictable—nay, inevitable—outcome of authoritarian submission and conventionalism, covarying with six other traits such as "anti-intraception" and "superstition and stereotypy" to make up the "high-F personality."

A generation of personality researchers and social psychologists were either fascinated by this dynamic, imaginative theory, or appalled by the evidence presented in its support, or both. But some 40 years later there is still no convincing evidence that authoritarians hated their parents, and correlations between *balanced* measures of authoritarianism and prejudice have been far too modest to support the conclusion that the two are intimately related (*RWA*, pp. 14–80). Furthermore, because of the importance that unconscious processes have in the explanation, one cannot readily imagine experimental evidence that could disprove it, if it were untrue. For these and other reasons the Berkeley theory has lost much of the appeal it once held for behavioral scientists.

Social Learning Theory

How would a social learning theorist explain the covariation of authoritarian submission, conventionalism, and authoritarian aggression? One can see numerous possibilities.[7]

General Explanations of Aggression. Bandura has written extensively on aggression in general (Bandura and Walters, 1959; Bandura, 1973, 1977, 1979, 1987, 1988). Eschewing approaches to the topic that rely on instinct (for example, Lorenz, 1966) or "drive" (for example, Berkowitz, 1962, 1965), Bandura has proposed that aggressive responses are typically learned through observation of models found in the family, subculture, and media and through practice. Like other behaviors, aggression is usually and simultaneously under (1) stimulus, (2) reinforcement, and (3) cognitive control:

1. Aversive stimuli can produce aggression; Bandura (1973) specifically discusses the effects of physical pain, verbal threats and insults, loss of rewards, and thwarting of goals (frustration).
2. Aggression is shaped not only by its instrumental, utilitarian consequences but also by self-reinforcements such as feelings of self-worth and self-criticism. Furthermore, these reinforcements can be experienced vicariously by observing the results of others' hostility.
3. Both stimulus and reinforcement effects are strongly influenced in humans by cognitive processes involving memories, beliefs, goals, expectations, problem solving, verification of beliefs, and so on. This acknowledgment of the importance of cognitions in controlling behavior is, along with the emphasis on vicarious effects, a distinctive feature of this learning theory.

How do these general principles apply to our specific question about the covariance of authoritarian submission, conventionalism, and authoritarian aggression? Why should the accepters of established power in society show such hostility? One can readily see why their victims and the disadvantaged might be aggressive. But why should the conservative forces in society, largely in control and feeling that their ideas, values, and life-styles are approved by powerful social authority—even the Almighty—be as aggressive as they are?

A Cultural Explanation. One can, at the outset, make a pretty straightforward case that any persevering culture will socialize its members (through direct instruction, modeling, use of reinforcers, and so on) to obey established authority and honor the culture's customs. To do otherwise might produce levels of confrontation and instability that would be adaptive only in times of dramatically changing circumstances. Besides, whatever persons happen to be powerful in a culture will ordinarily be motivated to promote authoritarian submission and respect for the customs of the past that promoted their rise to power—even when such hidebound subservience and traditionalism is not in the best interest of the society. Recall any tsars who stressed the importance of challenging authority?

Is it not, then, just as inevitable that a lasting society will promote punitive attitudes toward those who challenge established authority and defy customs? If it is inevitable, then the covariation of attitudes we find in responses to the RWA Scale might arise quite naturally from some of the processes whereby cultures persevere. Parents, schools, religions, the news media, and so on may inevitably promote authoritarian aggression as they teach and model authoritarian submission and conventionalism.

Is this simple "cultural Darwinism" all there is to it, then? The explanation readily accounts for most of the "Trials" findings. But why did High RWA students in my 1973 bogus shock experiment administer higher shocks to the learners? Their victims were not violating any social norms or challenging authority. Similarly, the statements making up the prejudice scale in Exhibit 3 indicate that authoritarians tend to perceive some groups as "lazy, promiscuous, and irresponsible" or "naturally violent." But the overall content of the scale (and the intercorrelation among responses to its items) makes it clear that, basically, the host of minorities mentioned are not disliked simply because of their unconventional behavior but, rather, because they are not "white."

Finally, we should recognize that societies vary considerably in the extent to which they demand submission to established authority and punish deviance. Officially, democracies such as Canada and the United States are based on such principles as equality among citizens, freedom of speech and religion, governance by the consent of the governed, and tolerance for the staggering diversity of their populations. These rank among our foremost conventions. Yet the authoritarian submits to governance and clings to her version of how everyone ought to act as though she lived in a totalitarian state. In short, her eagerness to punish those who challenge authority and violate custom will hardly preserve *our* society. Rather, the opposite.

So the cultural Darwinism hypothesis, though perhaps valid to a point, appears to fall short both empirically and theoretically in places. There would seem to be additional reasons for the authoritarian's aggression, springing perhaps from deeper wells.

Effects of Aversive Stimuli: Fear. What other wells? As we noted, Bandura believes aversive stimuli can instigate aggression. Strong fear, for example, commonly produces "flight or fight." But why would authoritarians be more fearful than others?

Persons who are very submissive to established authority and very conventional have a heavy investment in the status quo. Challenges to "our flag, our leaders, and the normal way things are supposed to be done" will probably be especially threatening to them. From their point of view, the waves of rebellion and sin might appear constantly to pound their shrinking island of respectability. If such persons feel *personally* vulnerable to attack in a disintegrating, increasingly lawless society, their level of authoritarian aggression might especially rise.[8]

Religion and Guilt. Authoritarian submission and conventionalism can make a person vulnerable to other aversive emotions. In many cultures such a person will be highly religious. Indeed, religious officials may be seen as the highest authority on certain issues, and their pronouncements on how to behave, "gospel." If the religion actively or subtly teaches hatred or shunning of others, it can directly produce authoritarian aggression by fostering the self-righteousness discussed above and by dehumanizing those with markedly different beliefs. Jews and atheists, "heathens" and "heretics" have frequently been targets of Christian hostility, for example.

But religious intensity may promote authoritarian aggression in less obvious ways. Belief in a particular religion is largely acquired from one's parents. In my Manitoba university samples, for instance, over 95 percent of the students with a religious affiliation belong to the faith in which they were raised. Few people appear to choose their religion. Most instead decide among believing all of what they were taught, some of it, or "nothing." But such fundamental principles as the existence of God cannot be demonstrated logically or empirically. Most religions therefore teach their members that these principles must be taken on faith. This faith is so important to the religious quest that the term (as I used it five sentences ago) has become synonymous with *religion.*

But faith carries risks. Suppose there is no God, no afterlife, no heaven in which rewards are being stockpiled, no hell of eternal torment for sinners. If so, then every prayer has gone into the void, every feeling of bestowed grace has been an act of self-deception, self-denial has often been a real self-abuse, and every martyrdom was an absurdity. One is staring into the abyss if there is no God, and sinners have all the laughs, including the last one.

Of course, true believers never reach this conclusion. But if they ever consider the possibility, the prospect might be enormously disconcerting.

How can this anxiety, if it exists, produce authoritarian aggression? Well, when you think about it, the punitive attitude that many religious people have toward "sinners" is curious. After all, sinners might fool their parents, the police, and juries, but can they fool the Almighty? And God's punishment will allegedly be far worse than any temporal discipline, while the righteous will receive everlasting happiness beyond any conceivable earthly pleasure.[9] Yet, as in Jesus' Palestine, the sanctimoniously religious today often seem eager to cast the first stone. And they throw hard when they get the chance. Why are they not content to leave the punishing to God? One can dissociate oneself from sin without drawing blood. Are the stones thrown "just in case"?

Besides the anxiety that might occasionally trouble one over the dangers of an inherited faith, the stones may fly for other reasons. As I suggested in *RWA* (p. 251), the earnestly righteous may be banking on a moral version of Newton's Third Law: "If I throw a stone, I shall myself be propelled away from sin." The authoritarian may truly doubt his ability to get Satan behind him; after all, he is often facing an exacting ethical code.

So condemning sin loudly and often may convince others he is righteous. Sometimes, of course, this seems cynical: Spiro Agnew, Billy James Hargis ("The Sins of Billy James," 1976), Jim Bakker, and Jimmy Swaggart come to mind. But creating the persona of virtuous sinner-stomper may also help overcome Satan's tempting voice that sounds so strangely like your own.

Guilt. If occasionally one cannot overcome temptation, there may be a heavy price to pay. Believing yourself better than others carries the obligation that you be so, and your failures may weigh more heavily than they would on someone less concerned with submission to authority and being upstanding. The resulting aversive stimuli of guilt and self-abasement might produce a general aggression as easily as pain and insults can. Bandura (1977, p. 48), for example, states, "There is no more devastating punishment than self-contempt."[10]

Envy. Submissive, conventional, self-denying individuals may also secretly envy the pleasures in which sinners so happily wallow. Let me illustrate with a personal example. When I was thirteen, my younger stepbrother became a hero to some still younger children at a family Christmas celebration by taking them upstairs and saying "cuss words" aloud. When I saw how much he was admired by my young relatives, who formerly had doted on me, I pushed him down the stairs (into the midst of a festive assembly of adults). (For some reason, telling my very embarrassed parents just why I had bounced my brother into the living room did not prevent *me* from receiving a truly memorable spanking.)

Suppose, then, in this same spirit, a High RWA student sees other students staying out all night, being sexually active, getting drunk, doing drugs, skipping church and school, using "cuss words," and so on. Such miscreance moreover seems to be popular and is lionized in movies and the Top Forty. The authoritarian will likely feel virtuous in his self-denial: "The *real* keys to the 'good life' are obedience, discipline, and sticking to the straight and narrow." But might he not also sometimes envy the fun and status that come from falling by the wayside—and hate the sinners for enjoying it so? So when the sinners suffer, won't he be glad, not only because evil deserves to be punished but also because we sometimes like to see those we envy suffer? And if the opportunity arises to help punish the sinners, won't he let fly?

Disinhibiting Effects of Self-Righteousness. Bandura believes that aggressive responses can be instigated by aversive stimuli but that they will not occur if reinforcement and cognitive controls over aggression remain sufficiently strong (for example, "It's unfair to attack someone unarmed or a child"). But if these inhibitions can be weakened, if the aggressive impulse is *disinhibited*, aggressive behavior becomes more likely.

Persons who are highly submissive to established authority and highly conventional might easily believe (because of these powerful social supports) that their attitudes and behavior are superior to others'. The authoritarian's aggressive impulses could then be disinhibited by this self-righteousness.

One of the most gruesome aspects of our times remains how sanctified various right- (and left-) wing extremists feel after murdering someone. Bandura (1977, 1987) observed that aggressors can neutralize self-punishment for aggression by justifying it in terms of higher principles: "Given sufficiently noble aims, almost any form of aggression can be justified as righteous. . . . Throughout history many have suffered at the hands of self-righteous crusaders bent on stamping out what they consider evil" (1973, p. 211). Similarly, believing that authorities sanction the aggression displaces one's personal responsibility, and accepting stereotypes about unconventional targets can dehumanize them, further disinhibiting the hostile impulse.

By this line of reasoning, then, authoritarians and nonauthoritarians may both feel hostile impulses toward those they find disgusting, such as the two "William Langleys." But Lows experience more inhibitions (such as "Who am I to punish him?") than Highs (who might think something like "I am better than he is; I have the right").

Summary. We have gleaned from social learning theory half a dozen explanations of how being highly submissive to established authority and highly conventional might also make one aggressive:

1. From adoption of the social norms (communicated by parents and other socializing agents) through which societies preserve themselves by punishing rebellious, unconventional behavior.
2. From fear that the social order is disintegrating, especially if one feels personally threatened.
3. From anxiety that one's religious beliefs and ethical code may be misguided.
4. From guilt over failures to live up to a demanding ethical code.
5. From envy of the fun that unconventional, rebellious people appear to have.
6. By creating a self-righteousness that disinhibits aggressive impulses that have arisen in the ways listed above.

These hypotheses, it should be recognized, do not flow inevitably from the principles of social learning theory, any more than they constitute the only explanations one could derive from that model. Nor, obviously, are they mutually exclusive. Submissive, conventional persons may tend to be aggressive for all, some, or none of these reasons. If all the hypotheses fail, the theory will not be particularly damaged, since it does not insist that any of these factors causes the authoritarian's aggression. If all the hypotheses succeed, it will not be such a triumph either, for the same reason. But the theory has fulfilled a worthy goal: it has generated hypotheses that can be tested.

Berkowitz's Theory of Aggression

Leonard Berkowitz has also developed a "learning theory" explanation of aggression that might account for the hostility of submissive, conventional persons. Modifying an original hypothesis of Dollard and others (1939), Berkowitz (1962, 1965) originally proposed that frustration produces a drive state, a readiness to aggress, that can then be elicited by cues in the environment which have violent associations. These cues can be weapons, toys, anything—including other people who have been the recipients of violence in the past.

Thus, if highly submissive and highly conventional persons tend to be highly frustrated as well (for example, sexually, economically), they will have high levels of a general aggressive drive. Very frustrated authoritarians would then be "an explosion looking for a place to happen"—which would explain the results of the bogus shock experiment. Furthermore, previously learned associations between violence and (1) scapegoated minority groups or (2) criminals would explain the results of the prejudice and "Trials" investigations. Thus Berkowitz's theory seems able to explain easily most of the findings in hand—*if* authoritarians are more frustrated than most.[11]

Summary

One can imagine many other factors that would probably produce authoritarian aggression, such as strong situational pressure (à la Milgram; also see *RWA*, pp. 273–276), physiological arousal (Zillman and Bryant, 1974; Bryant and Zillman, 1979), instrumental gains in property and social status obtained by attacking sanctioned targets (such as the Jews in Nazi Germany and persons of Japanese ancestry living on the west coast of North America in 1942), and revenge-stoked anger over real or imagined offenses in the past. But these factors would presumably affect almost everyone, and we are searching for reasons that persons who are submissive to authority and conventional would also be prone to authoritarian aggression.

The eight hypotheses developed above, derived from the work of the "Berkeley group," Bandura, and Berkowitz, doubtless can be supplemented—perhaps by the reader. Nevertheless, we have a fairly full plate before us. That is to the good, since the complexity of human behavior makes it unlikely that authoritarians aggress for just one reason.

But what is the evidence that any of these possibilities is a reality? Do authoritarians seethe with repressed hatred of powerful father figures? Who is not at least ambivalent toward her parents? Did they learn to hate deviants from their parents, teachers, and friends? Who is completely free of prejudice? Do they particularly fear the disintegration of society and their own victimization? Who does not? Do they have secret doubts about their fundamental religious beliefs? Don't nonbelievers as well? Are they just as immoral as those they condemn? Perhaps not. Are they envious of persons who seemingly have more fun in life than they do? Who isn't? Do they think they are morally superior to others? Doesn't nearly everyone? Are they significantly more frustrated than most? Maybe they are *less* frustrated.

Let's do some research.

NOTES

1. The reader may agree that many of these statements also tap sentiments of authoritarian submission and conventionalism. Since the RWA Scale was designed to measure the *covariation* of three traits, many of the items were written to capture two or all three of the defining elements. I am not sure one can write an authoritarian aggression item that does not imply authoritarian submission or conventionalism; I am sure there are no "pure" items on the test. The items listed in the text simply seem to me to capture sentiments of authoritarian aggression better than the rest of the statements on the test.
2. I am restricting my review to investigations that used some version of the RWA Scale to measure authoritarianism. The literature on "authoritarian aggression" is much larger; for example, the California F Scale has produced a relatively consistent set of associations with measures of hostility (see *RWA*, pp. 61–69). However, the F and other scales were based on a different conceptualization of right-wing authoritarianism than I have proposed, and enlarging our scope will gain us little, I fear (*RWA*, pp. 112–115).
3. As I wrote in 1981, it has become very difficult to study aggression in the laboratory (in my part of the world, at least) because of the fame accorded Milgram's research on obedience. In early September of that year I gave 434 introductory psychology students a paragraph-length description of the general procedures Milgram used (without revealing the deceptions involved) and asked them whether they had ever heard of such a study. Forty-eight percent said they had, compared with 28 percent who said they had heard of a classic conformity study (Asch, 1956) and 12 percent who claimed familiarity with a totally fictitious experiment involving a psychologist interviewing two students.

   The following January I gave 276 other students a similar description of the bogus shocking experiment I ran in 1973. Sixty-four percent said they had "heard of this experiment or one like it." I repeated the procedure in the fall of 1984, when 57 percent said they had heard of such a study.

   In the early fall of 1983 I designed an experiment in which students, sitting before TV monitors in individual rooms, supposedly played a game of "Battleship" with each other. The subjects were instructed to give random blasts of 100-dB noise to their opponents during the game as punishment for making wrong guesses. Supposedly, the purpose of the experiment was to study the effects of frustration and confusion on perseverance during problem solving. I do not know how many subjects "bought" this, but nearly half wrote on a postexperimental questionnaire that they thought the real purpose of the study was to see how many blasts they would give. About a third correctly guessed there was no true opponent, even though real subjects had been paired off at the beginning of the experiment.

The days of naive samples in laboratory aggression experiments seem to have slipped past, at least at my university.

4. Zwillenberg (1983) postulated that the Status of Criminal × Authoritarianism interaction sometimes found in previous research depended on the degree of extenuating circumstances that attended the crime. She accordingly administered the original 24-item RWA Scale and four versions of 16 Trials to over 500 students attending nine American colleges. The degree of extenuating circumstances and the socioeconomic status of the criminal were varied. (Unfortunately, the former manipulation was confounded by other changes in the descriptions of the crimes.) She found that the Status of Criminal × Authoritarianism interaction reached significance largely in cases with strong mitigating circumstances. High RWAs were more punitive than Lows toward both kinds of criminals. Again, Low RWA subjects were equally, and significantly less, punitive toward both kinds of targets.

   As noted in Chapter One, Zwillenberg found an overall RWA correlation of .38 with sentencing across all conditions of the study.
5. A similar pattern of results was obtained in the only other mirror-image Trial I have used, the "accountant/hippie fight" (*RWA*, p. 236, fig. 2). Zwillenberg (1983) also used both versions of this Trial in her study and obtained the same results.
6. Posse-Communist and Posse-Homosexual scores correlated .48 and .49, respectively, with scores on the Manitoba Prejudice Scale and .32 and .33 with sentences "handed down" in ten Trials by these 584 students. Understandably, the authoritarian aggression items on the RWA Scale had the highest overall correlations with all these indexes, compared with the items that more directly tap authoritarian submission or conventionalism.
7. Bandura does not speak to this issue, but he does discuss one of the kinds of aggression I have termed authoritarian: "During the process of socialization people are extensively trained to obey

orders. In the early formative years, when children cannot foresee the consequences of their actions, parents impose strict obedience demands. . . . By rewarding obedience to directives and punishing noncompliance, orders eventually acquire powerful response-controlling properties. . . . Since verbal orders quickly lose their effectiveness if they go unheeded without penalty, defiance is seldom treated lightly. . . . Given that people will obey orders, legitimate authorities can successfully command aggression from others, especially if the actions are presented as justified and necessary and the enforcing agents possess strong coercive power" (1973, pp. 174–175).

8. Whether North American societies are disintegrating is difficult to establish, but they constantly *seem* to be deteriorating to authoritarians. We may be "neck-deep in sin" in the 1980s, but the social upheavals of the late '60s and early '70s have all but vanished at this writing (knock on wood). What groups on the scene pose a serious threat to national stability? The Communists? The Weathermen? The FLQ in Quebec? Yet I have noticed that many "sixties items" on the RWA Scale have retained their psychometric usefulness over the years, even though their original referents have largely disappeared: "strong medicine," "trust proper authorities," "facts on crime," "in these troubled times," "young people," "treat dissenters," and "Communists."

   Like the religious proselytizers who have appeared on my doorstep for the last 20 years with the good news that recent earthquakes and famines indicate the world is about to end, authoritarians seem to find "recent public disorders" "in these troubled times" that call for "strong medicine" year in, year out. All the more noteworthy, since the 1980s have witnessed a strong swing to the political right, not the left, in North America—and still authoritarians feel the world is going to hell in a handbasket.

9. I found Oral Roberts's claim that God would "call him home" in March of 1987 if the faithful did not contribute $8 million to his financial operations interesting in many ways. But one of the more fascinating aspects was, he obviously didn't want to go. If he really believed in heaven, and trusted his vision in which God had declared him one of the "Elect," why didn't he just dummy up? God's threat boiled down to this: "Either you raise the dough, Oral, or I'm going to give you an eternity of happiness beyond your wildest dreams."

   Did Thorndike get the law of effect backwards?

10. I would suggest with Fest (1973, p. 41) that such self-hatred provides a more plausible explanation of Adolf Hitler's anti-Semitism than the Frommian-Berkeley hypothesis that the führer's virulent prejudice was rooted in repressed hatred of his father. Anti-Semitism was endemic in Hitler's culture, but he showed no particular hostility toward Jews during his early life. The family physician, Dr. Bloch, was a Jew. And when he was seventeen, Hitler reportedly fell madly in love (at a distance) with a well-born young woman in Linz whose surname is common among Jews (Payne, 1973, pp. 48–52). "Stephanie" was not Jewish, but the point is that Hitler did not care one way or the other. In *Mein Kampf* he maintains he had no truck with anti-Semites at the time, and that appears to be the case.

    Hitler's anti-Semitism dates quite specifically from his disreputable and desperate years in Vienna (1908–1913), after his mother had died and his pipe dream of becoming a great artist had collapsed. So depressed he did not even collect his orphan's pension, the dilettante from Linz was a tramp living in flophouses by his twentieth year.

    In *Mein Kampf* (p. 56) Hitler traces his hatred for Jews to a trip he took to the "inner city" of Vienna at the time: "I suddenly encountered an apparition in a black caftan and black side-locks. 'Is this a Jew?' was my first thought. For to be sure, they had not looked like that in Linz . . . the longer I stared at this foreign face, scrutinizing feature for feature, the more my first question assumed a new form: 'Is this a German?'"

    Whether the incident actually occurred or was invented later to suit his terrible purpose, the unconventionality of Orthodox Jews offended Hitler. But in many respects the account describes Hitler himself at the time (who might have been German*ic*, "Deutsch-osterreicher," but as a citizen of the Hapsburg empire was no more a member of the German state than the Jews he found in Vienna's ghetto). "Bohemian he certainly looked in those vagabond days in Vienna. Those who knew him remembered later his long shabby overcoat, which hung down to his ankles and resembled a caftan . . . . They remembered his greasy black derby, which he wore year round, and his matted hair . . . he rarely appeared to have had a haircut or a shave and the sides of his face and chin were usually covered with the black stubble of an incipient beard" (Shirer, 1960, p. 20).

    The parallel may not have been lost on a self-despising

Hitler, who had fallen so far short of his own mark. Whether for this reason or not, he soon distanced himself from these other disreputable Viennese, the Jews, by adopting the Aryan mythology and pan-Germanic philosophy circulating at the time.

11. Berkowitz (1978) later reformulated his theory, proposing that frustration was but one of a number of "aversive events" that could produce aggression. So could personal insult and physical pain, for example. To the extent that this approximates Bandura's (1973) position on "aversive stimuli," the possible explanations of authoritarian aggression that follow have already been discussed.

5

Solving the Mystery of Authoritarian Aggression

We shall now try to determine which of the eight hypotheses we have assembled, like suspects in the last chapter of a "whodunit," did it. At first we shall examine them one at a time, usually considering data from several lines of inquiry. Sometimes the evidence will be supportive. In other instances a familiar scene in scientific research will be reenacted, when a wonderfully plausible hypothesis expires because nature answers, "It isn't so." (Ideally, we shall have asked nature the right question.)

Once we have identified the likely candidates, we shall pit them against one another in four further experiments. Our goal: to explain as much of the relationship between authoritarianism and various indexes of aggression as possible and then to see which of the hypotheses explains the most.

EVIDENCE CONCERNING THE EIGHT HYPOTHESES

Additional Tests of the Berkeley Model

As is true of other psychoanalytic formulations, the Berkeley theory of the authoritarian personality is difficult to test because (like the model of the mind it postulates) it has so many escape hatches. Whenever its predictions come a cropper, as in the failures to find connections with early childhood experiences (see *RWA*, pp. 259–265), the explanation always *might* be that the truth has been repressed. I decided, therefore, to study repression itself, to see whether authoritarians manifest noticeable signs of repressed hostility. I did this in three ways: by collecting their spontaneous fantasies, by analyzing their reactions to prepackaged aggressive fantasies, and by studying the endings they gave a potentially violent fantasy. I also studied repression of threatening material in general, in an experiment based on Galin's (1974) theory of brain lateralization.

Authoritarianism and Aggressive Fantasies

In 1983 I offered over 500 students who had completed a survey booklet an opportunity to earn another experimental credit by recording the next three or four fantasies they had. "It will be like keeping a diary for a day," the solicitation read, "only you will be completely anonymous. If you want to serve in this study, tear the last sheet off the booklet now and take it with you."

This last sheet, which was discreetly marked with the booklet's survey number (for which no corresponding names had been collected), contained the following instructions:

> *Fantasy Study*
>
> A fantasy is an unintentional daydream. Without our realizing it, our mind "wanders off" and we begin to imagine ourselves in some situation. We usually do not realize we have been fantasizing until the "situation" has resolved itself.
>
> Fantasies are not just "idle thoughts," like "I wish I were at the beach." It usually takes a whole paragraph to describe a fantasy.
>
> It is important for the scientific value of the study you are participating in that you *do not* censor your reports. The investigator does not know you,

> and almost certainly never will. Furthermore, you are completely anonymous. So do not leave out a fantasy, or some detail of a fantasy, because it is embarrassing or "personal." Those are just as relevant as any other kind of fantasy, and it's important in all research that the sample studied be *un*biased and *un*distorted. An investigation of censored fantasies would be a waste of time and effort, and the results might mislead science for years.
>
> Finally, when you are recording your fantasies below, make them as clear and detailed as possible. For example, "I was arguing with my parents about my boyfriend" is not very detailed. A better report might be something like this:
>
> "I was in the kitchen at home. My mother asked me whom I was going out with Saturday, and I told her, 'Bill.' She said she didn't like my going out with him, because he dressed poorly and had poor manners and a 'sneaky look' all the time. I told her that Bill was much nicer than that, and besides it was my life. Then my mother began to cry, and my father came in and blamed me for speaking back to my mother. I felt very angry and ripped right out of the house. Then I realized I had just had a fantasy."
>
> So remember: Please *do not censor*, and please *give clear and detailed* reports.

Seventy-eight percent of the students tore the "report sheet" from the back of the booklet, and of these 63 percent ($N = 253$) returned forms over the next two days describing at least three fantasies. There was no difference in the RWA Scale scores of those who turned in a set of fantasies and those who (for whatever reason) did not. Two students turned in silly, obviously unfantasized "fantasies."

I read the first 50 or so sheets returned and then decided on a categorization system to capture the most common themes. I used two aggression classifications ("Physical" and "Verbal But Not Physical") and numerous other categories to arrange the great hodgepodge of stories that came my way. I was blind to the subjects' authoritarianism while I was pigeonholing their narratives.

The most common fantasies involved great accomplishments, nonsexual romance, and acquiring/spending wealth. It so happened that 62 of the subjects had scored in the bottom quartile of the RWA distribution and 65 in the upper quartile. Highs (almost always females) fantasized significantly more than Lows about marriage proposals/marriage ceremonies (14 to 5; $z = 2.13, p < .02$). Otherwise there were no significant differences between the two extreme groups.

As for aggression, nine of the Lows and ten of the Highs (almost always males) reported fantasies that involved definite physical aggression—typically fist fights. Six Lows and four Highs had Verbal But Not Physical hostility somewhere in their reports—usually "telling someone off." No one reported a fantasy in which parents were hurt in any way.

The rarity of aggressive themes may indicate that the students appreciably censored their reports, anonymity and my pleadings notwithstanding. The finding that only 23 Low and 20 High stories involved explicit sexual activity may support the same conclusion. But the subjects were asked to write down the first three or four fantasies they had; perhaps a smaller proportion of fantasies are aggressive or sexual than one might expect.

Reactions to "Prepackaged" Fantasies. I usually break into a sweat whenever I have to score something subjectively, such as these fantasies. So the following year I presented 226 male students with two aggressive fantasies of my own devising and asked for their reaction on objective rating scales. The first fantasy involved a potential rape situation and the second a male/male confrontation over a woman. *Two* versions of *each* fantasy, however, were randomly distributed among the subjects (who were serving anonymously).

The rape scenario began as follows:

> Imagine that you are making sexual advances toward an attractive woman, who indicates

> she is not interested in you. But you are persistent and even forceful, and you *demand* that she respond by holding her close and insisting she kiss you.

For *half* the men, the scene ended as it often does in movies and stag magazines:

> She seems to get caught up in your passion, so that eventually she seems just as desirous of having sexual relations as you are. The sex feels very good to you.

Subjects were then asked to say, on a 0–9 basis, how pleasant it was to think about this situation. The mean rating ($N = 114$) was 4.0 ("moderately pleasant"), and subjects' RWA Scale scores correlated $-.12$ ($p > .20$) with reports of pleasantness.

The second version of this first fantasy ended less pastorally:

> She still does not get caught up in your passion, but by now it is too late for you to try to control yourself, and against her protests you force her to have sex with you. The sex feels very good to you.

This version of the story was rated much less pleasant to contemplate ($\overline{X} = 1.1$, "very unpleasant"); the RWA correlation was but .03.

The second fantasy (which was counterbalanced with versions of the first) began as follows:

> Imagine a different fantasy. You are out with a particularly attractive woman, and another guy—somewhat bigger than you—begins to make advances toward your date. She is clearly annoyed, and you tell this other fellow to leave her alone. He says, "Beat it, jerk face, or I'll smash you into the ground." You look him straight in the eye and say, "If you want to step outside, I'll go with you."

In one version of the tale, the confrontation ended nonviolently:

> He looks at you and realizes he'll have to fight you if he's serious. He apparently decides it isn't worth the hassle, as he says, "No, I'll just wait until she gets tired of you," and walks away. You turn to your date and say, "Would you like to dance?"

This fantasy was also judged "moderately pleasant" (mean = 4.20); RWA Scale scores correlated .16 ($p < .10$) with these ratings.

In the other version, a stereotyped Hollywood ending ensued:

> Once outside, he throws a punch that you easily duck under. Then you hit him twice in the gut, really hard, and drive your fist into his face. He falls down, stunned, and says, "That's enough. I quit." You go back inside, where your date has been watching through a window, and say, "Would you like to dance?"

This fantasy was judged significantly more pleasant than the nonviolent ending ($\overline{X} = 5.0$, "moderately pleasant"; $t = 2.10$; $p < .05$), but the RWA correlation was again nonsignificant (.07). If High RWA males have powerful unconscious aggressive impulses, one would expect the correlation here to be higher than that for the nonviolent fantasy and, of course, statistically significant. But it was neither.

The same nonconfirmation of the Berkeley theory occurred among 274 females, who responded (just) to the vignette in which someone tries to steal an attractive date. In this case the confrontation took place in a powder room:

> "If he wants to go out with a sleazebag like you tomorrow, which I seriously doubt, that's his business. But tonight he's out with me, and if you come near us again tonight I'm going to tear you apart."

> Whereupon you push her up against a wall to show her you really mean it. She leaves the bathroom and does not bother you for the rest of the night.

Females rated this story less pleasant ($\overline{X} = 3.40$) than males rated their violent version. But the RWA Scale correlation was again trivial (.05). This experiment therefore provides no evidence that authoritarians enjoy aggressive fantasies more than others do.

Endings Given a Potentially Violent Fantasy. I tried once more, in January 1985, to see whether authoritarians might betray a preference for aggressive fantasies. I asked 355 students to provide an ending for a "Dirty Harry" scenario in which a very unsavory criminal is cornered and might be shot. The task was explained as follows:

> Below is the description of an imaginary situation, which does not have an ending. Your job is to assume you are the person telling the story, and then provide the ending. Do not try to be clever or witty. Just write the ending that you would most like to the story.
>
> "I am a policeman, working a late-night shift with my partner. A call comes in over the car radio—a holdup's in progress at a nearby 7-Eleven. We arrive just as a man carrying a sawed-off shotgun comes out of the store. I draw my revolver and crouch behind the car door. 'Halt! Police!' I shout. The robber turns toward me. I recognize him, he's done time before. He's a really vicious guy. 'Halt!' I repeat, 'Drop that gun!' I'm playing this strictly by the book, but I'm hoping he raises the gun in my direction. He's an animal, and I'll kill him before he gets a chance to fire, and save the taxpayers a lot of money."

Three 17-cm lines were printed on the bottom of the page for the subject's ending to the story. These endings were blindly categorized (no sweat in this case) as Violent (most typically a shoot-out in which the robber perishes), Nonviolent (for example, the robber surrenders), or Unclear (for example, "The robber tries to get away but doesn't make it").

Ninety-one of the subjects were Lows, and 93 were Highs. Violent endings were equally common in the two groups (36 percent and 39 percent, respectively), as were Nonviolent outcomes (47 percent and 51 percent). (Males in both groups and in the sample as a whole were about twice as likely to provide Violent endings as females were.)

Authoritarianism and Brain Laterality

With the psychoanalytic hypothesis batting .000, I tried to study authoritarian repression directly through an interesting hypothesis advanced by Galin (1974). Building on certain similarities between Sperry's famous research on brain laterality (Gazzaniga, 1970) and clinical experience with neurotics, Galin proposed that in most persons mental events encoded in the right cerebral hemisphere can become disconnected from the dominant left hemisphere by inhibition of neural transmission across the cerebral commissures. Thus "repressed" material may have a life of its own in the right hemisphere, unavailable to the more "logical," verbal side of the brain.

David G. Martin at the University of Manitoba has investigated this hypothesis by presenting threatening material to the brain through one ear, then the other. Subjects are then tested on their knowledge of the material, and the difference in their memories of left- and right-hemisphere-channeled material produces a measure of repression (Martin, Hawryluk, Berish, and Dushenko, 1984).

If Galin's hypothesis is correct, and if authoritarians are more likely to repress threatening material than others, then they should learn less than others of threatening material presented to the left ear (right hemisphere), compared with the left hemisphere. Accordingly, 25 Low and 24 High RWA students served in a dichotic listening experiment late in 1984 in which the first half of a 20-minute prohomosexual speech was broadcast to one side of the brain, and then the second half to the other side, over a set of earphones. (The speaker blandly recited numbers to the "other" ear at the same time; the order of presentation to the left and right ears was counterbalanced.) Subjects then answered 40 factual questions based equally on the material presented to each hemisphere.

On the average, Highs correctly answered 7.8 of the questions based on right-hemisphere input and 7.4 of those based on material sent to the left hemisphere—a nonsignificant difference in the wrong direction. (Lows did a little better on the tests, scoring 9.0 on both kinds of questions, perhaps because of greater familiarity with the prohomosexual material.)[1]

Conclusion

All the evidence from these studies indicates Lows are as likely as Highs to have and enjoy aggressive fantasies—even if they are not as aggressive in real life. The "Berkeley psychoanalytic theory" thus once again comes up empty-handed.

Freud is reported to have been insulted when someone sent him experimental evidence supporting one of his major ideas; he sent a hostile reply informing the scientist that psychoanalysis did not need outside validation (Fisher and Greenberg, 1977). Freud would probably give the studies reported here even shorter shrift, perhaps deservedly. But the Law of Effect makes one eventually weary of testing the most intriguing theory when the results are so uniformly unrewarding. If this horse is not dead, someone else is going to have to show me how to make it walk, trot, and canter.

Tests of the Social-Learning-Theory Hypotheses

Is Authoritarian Aggression Caused by Cultural Socialization?

To what extent are the aggressive attitudes that authoritarians hold simply learned from parents, educators, newspapers, and so on as they grow up? We can get some idea by examining the similarity between students' responses to the aggressive items on the RWA Scale and those of their parents. Over the years, these correlations have averaged about .20—none too impressive. Correlations between students' and parents' scores on longer, more reliable measures have been a little higher overall: .22 for "Trials" data collected in 1979, .23 for Posse-Homosexual scores obtained in 1984, and .35 across several batches of Prejudice Scale scores. Thus these students mildly resemble their parents in authoritarian hostility, but they are hardly clones.

Of course, parents are only part of the socialization process. But we saw in Chapter Three that, according to students' reports, their high school educations hardly touched on the authoritarian aggression issues raised in the RWA Scale. Nor did students and their best friends apparently discuss these matters much or hold similar attitudes (with the notable exception of attitudes toward homosexuals). The news media did apparently shape opinions on crime, Communism, and other aggression items. But the correlation between students' own opinions on these matters and their perception of the news's impact was low overall—lower than that with parents.

We are left, then, with an eminently reasonable hypothesis barely floated by a shallow sea of evidence. To be sure, we are investigating effects that presumably began some years in the past. But the data support this social learning hypothesis only marginally better than the repression data spoke for the Berkeley model.[2]

Is Authoritarian Aggression Caused by Fear?

In 1984, as part of my investigations of the cultural-socialization hypothesis discussed earlier, I tested the straightforward proposition that authoritarian students are hostile toward various groups because their parents have taught them to be. I composed a list of eight charter members in the authoritarian's closet of anxieties: radicals, Communists, atheists, homosexuals, pornographers, drug addicts, "hippies and other very unconventional people," and "members of the opposite sex with loose morals." For purposes of comparison, I intermixed these with eight other groups whom I thought parents in general would be likely to warn their children about: kidnappers, tramps, bullies, "winos," older kids with bad habits, motorcycle gangs, cult religions, and reckless drivers.

I asked the 557 students in the 1984 "Origins" study (see Chapter Three) to indicate, on a 0–5 scale, the extent to which their parents "tried to teach you, as you were growing up, that the following were *dangerous* people, whom society ought to control more through *tough discipline and punishment*."

To my certain surprise I found an appreciable intercorrelation among responses to *all* 16 items, averaging .32 and producing willy-nilly a "Dangerous Persons Scale" with an alpha reliability of .88. Moreover, RWA Scale scores correlated significantly with (taught) fear of each of the 16 groups. The correlations were not huge, the largest being .35 (with fear of homosexuals). But RWA Scale scores correlated .38 with the sum of the 16 fears, and 25 of the authoritarianism items (led mainly by the aggression statements) had significant correlations with this sum. Thus students who (said they) had been taught the world is a dangerous place ended up being more authoritarian than most.[3]

One suspects that this is one of the ways authoritarian parents produce authoritarian offspring. Fortunately I had included the same survey in the booklet answered by 521 of these students' parents, asking them the extent to which they had tried to teach their child, as he or she was growing up, that these 16 groups were dangerous. The mean interitem correlation among their answers was .46, producing an alpha of .93. The parents' RWA Scale scores correlated significantly with responses for all 16 "bad guys" and .48 with their sum. All 30 of the RWA Scale items were significantly correlated with this composite score, the aggression items understandably having the strongest relationships again. Thus the parents' data indicate that authoritarian parents see the world as a more dangerous place for their children than most parents do, and the students' evidence indicates such warnings are associated with development of their authoritarianism.

The surprising feature of these results is not that High

parents teach their children to be afraid of Communists, atheists, and homosexuals but that they teach greater fear of kidnappers, tramps, and bullies as well. The children of atheists are just as vulnerable to the appeal of religious cults as children raised in a religion by authoritarian parents—maybe more so. But the latter teach a greater fear of cults and of many other groups you would think indiscriminately threaten us all.

I have since found that both authoritarian students and parents are also more afraid of becoming the victims of terrorist attacks, automobile accidents, and contracting AIDS through blood transfusions, food preparation, drinking fountains, and so on. The correlation between authoritarianism and any of these fears is usually low, about .20. But overall, Highs perceive the world as a significantly more dangerous place than others do—which apparently was how it was explained to many of them. Such feelings of vulnerability could produce an "aggressive defense" against a hostile, dangerous world.

Is Authoritarian Aggression Caused by Guilt?

Here we are exploring the possibility that feelings of guilt and self-abasement may lead the authoritarian to aggress against others. Attacking unconventional persons in particular may assuage a guilty conscience, count as a good deed, dissociate oneself from sin, and put one firmly on the side of righteousness.

But maybe Highs *are* more moral than most and have relatively little to feel guilty about.

Cheating in the Classroom. I have tested this hypothesis from time to time through a series of field experiments conducted in the natural setting of my introductory psychology classes. As described in *Right-Wing Authoritarianism* (p. 327), I gave my 1977–78 students a "feedback sheet" midway through the course, listing their test scores to that point. I told the students to check these figures, especially the sum of their scores, since that particular number would be used to calculate their grade in a few months. I had, however, purposely given every sixth person in my grade book an extra 2 points (that is, 2 percent) through an intentional adding error. This "mistake" could conceivably turn a *C* into a *C*+, a *B* into a *B*+, and so on at the end of the course.

Only 4 of the 58 students who received this bonus reported the error, and there was no hint of a relationship with RWA Scale scores. Believing that 2 percent might be too big a gift to turn down, I repeated the experiment in 1978–79 using a 1 percent bonus, with almost identical results.

In January 1984 I modified the experiment to check the possibility (totally unsupported in my experience) that students did not care about their grades and were not checking my arithmetic. Forty randomly selected students (20 Lows and 20 Highs) were given 1 extra point, while 20 other Lows and 20 Highs were given a sum 1 point too *low*. The manipulation was carried out over two classes containing nearly 500 students. (I told the students to check my arithmetic carefully because I had computed their totals while watching football games on New Year's Day.)

Eighty-two percent of those who had been shorted brought the error to my attention, while only 15 percent (three Lows and three Highs) of those who had profited came forth.

I repeated this experiment in January 1985, making errors of 3 points in both directions. Eighty-one percent of the 36 students who received undervalued sums pointed out the error of my ways, compared with 25 percent (four Lows and five Highs) of those who thought they had received a belated Christmas present.

Thus all four of these Take-the-Grade-and-Run studies found that authoritarian students were no more likely to "do the honest thing" than Lows. Nearly all of the Highs (and Lows) did a passively dishonest thing.

Would they be just as likely to cheat actively in the classroom? My two sections of introductory psychology in 1984–85 met in a lecture hall whose 300 chairs were quite close to one another. To deter cheating on my multiple-choice exams, I usually prepare two or more versions of a test and distribute them systematically throughout the room. I was too busy running experiments during September 1984 to do so, however, and consequently I administered just one form of the first hour exam in the course. It would have been a very easy matter to copy someone else's answers, and the mean score on this test (a *B*) was rather high.

I did prepare two forms of the next exam one month later and (as I usually do) distributed them throughout the room so that, for nearly all the students, the persons sitting on each side of them and on each side of the person sitting immediately in front of them had forms of the test subtly different from their own. The mean score on this test was a *C*−; a large number of students' marks plummeted.

Although there could be additional reasons for the drop in scores, the contrasting effects of cheating on the two tests were likely part of the explanation. (Copying on the first test probably would have raised one's mark; copying on the second probably would have lowered it. Thus the more one cheated, the bigger the fall.) If Highs cheated less than Lows, their scores would have dropped less overall. In fact, though, Highs' scores on the 25-question exams dropped 4.14 questions, while Lows' dropped 3.55, although the difference was not significant ($t = 1.40$; $p > .20$).[4]

One of the questions I asked these students on the "Secret Survey" administered a few months later was "Did you cheat on any of the tests by copying other students' answers?" Overall 23 percent of the respondents said they had, including 23 of 101 Highs and 24 of 99 Lows.

Falsifying Data. In the fall of 1985, 248 students found, at the end of a booklet they had just anonymously completed, an unnumbered one-page questionnaire they could tear off and ask their best friend to complete. If their friend did so, the subjects were told, they would receive another experimental credit worth 1 percent of their introductory psychology grade. It was a small favor to ask of a buddy, but it was also a simple matter to complete the survey oneself and claim the credit by misrepresenting the responses as one's friend's.

Although 202 students tore this last page from the booklet, only 90 completed forms were returned for credit by the deadline one month later. Unbeknownst to the students, the surveys for their best friends had been discreetly coded with the original booklet number so that I could compare the handwriting on these sheets with that in the matching booklets. Being unschooled in handwriting analysis, I compared cautiously, blindly tagging altogether 25 of the "best friend's" answers as fraudulent.

It turned out that Highs had returned 27 of the 90 surveys and Lows 22. I had blindly labeled 6 of the High and 7 of the Low returns as faked. The difference in the "dishonesty rates" (22 percent versus 32 percent) was not statistically significant: chi-squared = 0.6; $p > .50$.

Prosocial Behavior. I also investigated whether Highs are more likely to perform prosocial acts. Doubtless they do more charitable work through religious organizations than Lows do. How do they respond to an appeal from a secular prosocial organization?

In 1985 I made a pitch in class for donations to a Red Cross blood drive being held on campus. Eleven Highs and ten Lows made appointments, on a sheet I circulated in the room, to give blood. The Red Cross later verified that ten of the Highs and eight of the Lows actually kept their appointments. Because this difference was statistically nonsignificant ($p > .50$), the experiment provided no evidence that Highs are more altruistic than Lows.

Summary. Compared with pillaging, rape, and murder (which my local Ethical Review Committee will not allow me to use as dependent variables in experiments), the misbehaviors I have studied are small potatoes. It may be that High RWA persons are significantly more moral than others when it comes to major immoralities. It may also be that they will behave much more morally than others in countless situations that I have not tested. Doubtless there are as well many kinds of behavior in which authoritarians are more moral, by *their* standards, than others are. For example, Highs go to church more often than most, and they are more likely, overall, to be virgins.[5]

But the significance of these little experiments lay in the fact that most people would probably agree that cheating for grades is wrong and freely donating blood is virtuous. Highs had the opportunity in these situations to behave in a morally superior way, and they did not.

Self-righteousness is an easy garment to slip into, so let me say that I can recall several instances in my undergraduate career when a prof gave me too high a mark on an exam and *I* "took the grades and ran." Not to mention lab assignments I copied, bibliographies I padded, and so forth. The point is not that authoritarians are vermin and should be stomped out but that *their* desire to crunch and crumble may be partly rooted in an inability to face their own shortcomings as readily as they find them in others.

Failure to live up to their own ethical codes may *indirectly* contribute to the authoritarians' aggression as well. Many Highs, I have discovered, believe a literal hell exists into whose real fires sinners will be cast for eternity.[6] That is a long barrel to be staring down after one has transgressed. The dramatic introductions that many Highs were given as children to the awesome suffering hellfire will bring may have raised their overall level of fear—which, we saw in the last section, may already be pumped up for other reasons. Thus when Highs sin, they may worry about hell, and that *fear* may produce aggression.

It is always possible, however, that authoritarians' consciences are "Teflon-coated" and their shortcomings are shortgoings, ignored or rationalized, making no impression whatsoever on self-images. We tend to assume, after Freud, that threatening material never truly escapes us. But maybe it can.

Is Authoritarian Aggression Caused by Secret Doubts About the Existence of God?

If you ask High RWA students whether they believe in an Almighty God who is concerned with everyone's actions and who will judge each person after death, about 90 percent will say yes. And most will answer "+ 4" on a − 4 to + 4 basis. Parents are even more emphatic than students. Belief in a judgmental God is a fundamental cornerstone in the belief system of most authoritarians I study, which is why any unresolved doubt about God's existence could trigger considerable anxiety. Such anxiety would be an aversive stimulus, which could lead to aggressive impulses, according to Bandura.

If doubts exist in the mind of the true believer, how can the researcher discover them when the person himself is reluctant to face them? A possibility came to me in November 1984 while lecturing to my introductory psychology classes on hypnosis.

It has often been reported that deeply hypnotized subjects can endure considerable amounts of pain (as in a dentist's chair or, less dramatically, in a laboratory by submerging a forearm in ice water). When asked, such persons usually say they feel no pain whatsoever. Hilgard (1973, 1977) discovered, however, that when cued, a metaphorical "Hidden Observer" in a subject will usually indicate, typically through "automatic writing," that the experience had actually hurt like hell—so to speak. Hilgard interpreted this finding as evidence that subconscious processes occur simultaneously with conscious thought, and "this concealed part knows things that are not present in the person's open consciousness." Whether that is true or not, by the time I finished reading this passage to the class, *my* conscious mind knew what to do with it.

Two months later, when over 400 of these same students received my anonymous "Secret Survey" (see Appendix E), they encountered the following proposition:

> You may recall the lecture on hypnosis dealing with Hilgard's research on the "Hidden Observer." Suppose there is a Hidden Observer in you, which knows your every thought and deed, but which only speaks when it is safe to do so, and when directly spoken to. This question is for your Hidden Observer: Does this person (that is, you) have doubts that (s)he was created by an Almighty God who will

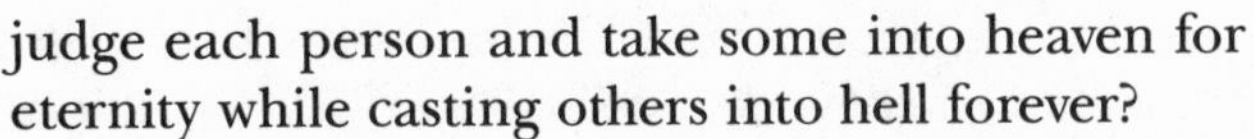

judge each person and take some into heaven for eternity while casting others into hell forever?

____ Yes, (s)he has secret doubts which (s)he has kept strictly to herself/himself that this is really true. (33) [17]

____ Yes, (s)he has such doubts, but others (such as parents or friends) know (s)he has these doubts. (20) [45]

____ No, (s)he totally believes this, and has *no doubts* whatsoever. (43) [9]

____ Yes, in fact (s)he openly says (s)he *does not believe* there is a God or an afterlife, but (s)he has some secret worries there might be. (5) [22]

____ Yes, in fact (s)he openly says (s)he *does not believe* there is a God or an afterlife, and (s)he has no doubts about this whatsoever. (0) [6]

The sample contained 101 High and 99 Low RWA students, all of whom answered this question. The distribution of the Highs' answers is given in parentheses at the end of each response alternative above. The highly contrasting distribution of Low responses follows in brackets.

It can be seen that there were 5 "off-quadrant" cases of Highs who openly did not believe in the traditional God. Of the remaining 96 authoritarian students, almost half said, through their "Hidden Observers," that they had no doubts whatsoever about such a God's existence, and about a fifth said they had some doubts, which they had shared with someone else. But about one third of the Highs said they had *secret* doubts, ones they had not shared with another soul. I still find this a remarkable admission.[7]

I argued in the last chapter that since most students simply inherit their religions and are taught to accept religious teachings on faith, they might realize what a chance they are taking. Highs do not overwhelm you with criticism of their inheritance, and the fact that so many have had to keep their doubts an absolute secret indicates the pressure they are under to believe, believe, believe. But does this pressure produce some of the explosion toward "sinners" who might be having the best of one world, not two? And do only one third have such totally secret doubts?

Is Authoritarian Aggression Caused by Envy of "Sinners"?

Our next social learning explanation of authoritarian aggression proposes that Highs have mixed feelings about being virtuous. Going to church every Sunday and forgoing sex may bring one present and future rewards, but staying in bed and fooling around are not bad ways to spend your time, either. Do authoritarians believe they are missing out on many of life's pleasures?

At the end of the 1984 "Origins" study I asked subjects to respond to the following inquiry:

> People sometimes do not have the "fun times" that others have because of their moral beliefs and principles. They do so willingly; but they also know that those who do not have the same morals or scruples are enjoying things and having good times that the first group denies itself. To what extent have your morals and your principles kept you from having a lot of the fun that others have? [Answered on a 0–9 basis.]

RWA Scale scores correlated .25 with these answers ($\overline{X} = 3.16$).

I then asked subjects to name the "fun times" they had missed. Highs mostly mentioned experiences involving sex, drugs, alcohol, partying, "showing off," disobeying parents, breaking the law, and "being popular."

Is this self-denial accompanied by envy and hostile attitudes toward those "cursed" with different ethics and weaker wills? I had discovered in 1982 that authoritarians admitted feeling that girls who got pregnant in high school "got exactly what they deserved" and that they derived a "secret pleasure" over the girls' situation. The relationships, as they often are with single-item measures, were small. But over time I developed an eight-case assessment of such mean-spirited reactions, shown in Exhibit 4, which I administered to 171 anonymous students in February 1985.

One can see that the odd-numbered items on the scale ask the subject whether transgressors of various sorts "got exactly what they deserved." The mean response across all eight cases was 4.5 ("moderately deserved") on the 0–9 response scale, and the average intercorrelation among these responses was .46, producing an alpha of .87 for what might be called a "Serves Them Right" subscale. RWA Scale correlations, ranging from .09 to .45 and statistically significant in all but one case, produced an *r* of .39 with the sum of these eight rather unsympathetic judgments.

The even-numbered items all asked the subject whether he or she felt a "secret pleasure" at acquaintances' misfortunes. Predictably, responses were lower here, averaging 2.4 ("a little pleasure"). Their mean intercorrelation was a high .51, however, producing an alpha of .91. The RWA Scale correlations ranged from .13 to .36, significant again in all but one case, and the sum of these eight "Vindictive Pleasures" correlated .36 with authoritarianism.

Summed scores of the odd and even items correlated .64, and the entire 16 items had a mean intercorrelation of .43 (alpha = .92). Their sum correlated .41 with the subjects' answers to the RWA Scale.

In short, then, the data indicate that authoritarian students are somewhat ambivalent about the "high road" they think they are taking through life. No doubt they see its advantages—advantages I have recommended to my own children. But they also have some regrets. Therefore, when they see an acquaintance on the "low road" fall farther yet, they often do not respond with sympathy, understanding, or charity. The milk of human kindness does not pulse through their veins. Instead one senses self-satisfaction: those who pursued the pleasures you passed by have been rightly punished, which is just what you hoped would

Exhibit 4. The Mean-Spirited Scale.

1. You may have known students in high school (or university) who were smoking marijuana or taking other illegal drugs who had a bad experience because of this (for example, getting caught by authorities or experiencing a "bad trip"). To what extent do you think they "got exactly what they deserved"?
2. To what extent was it satisfying, did you perhaps feel a "secret pleasure," when you found out that these students had had a bad experience because of their drug use?
3. There may have been students in your high school who broke the rules of the school fairly often (for example, smoking in unauthorized places, copying other students' work, skipping many, many classes) who may have been caught and severely punished. To what extent do you think such students "got exactly what they deserved"?
4. To what extent was it satisfying, did you perhaps feel a "secret pleasure," when you found out these students had been caught and disciplined?
5. There may have been students in your high school who often drank too much and as a result got into trouble (for example, had accidents while driving, behaved stupidly). To what extent do you think such students "got exactly what they deserved"?
6. To what extent was it satisfying, did you perhaps feel a "secret pleasure," when such students who often drank too much got into trouble because of that?
7. You may have known students in high school who rather regularly stole cosmetics, records, clothing, et cetera from stores ("shoplifting") and who were eventually caught and punished in some way. To what extent do you think such students "got exactly what they deserved"?
8. To what extent was it satisfying, did you perhaps feel a "secret pleasure," when such students were caught and punished?
9. You may have known students in high school who regularly disobeyed their parents and lied to them about where they were going, what they were going to be doing, et cetera. And as a result they had bad experiences or were caught and harshly punished. To what extent do you think these students "got exactly what they deserved"?
10. To what extent was it satisfying, did you perhaps feel a "secret pleasure," when you found out these students had suffered because of what they had been doing?
11. You may have known students in high school who ran around with the "wrong sort of kids," companions who they were warned would be a bad influence on them. And as a result, these students got into trouble with the law or made other kinds of mistakes that got them into trouble. To what extent do you think the punishment these students received was "exactly what they deserved"?
12. To what extent was it satisfying, did you perhaps feel a "secret pleasure," when such students were caught and punished?
13. There may have been girls in your high school or university who were "sexually active" with a number of guys and as a result became pregnant. To what extent do you think that such girls "got exactly what they deserved"?
14. To what extent was it satisfying, did you perhaps feel a "secret pleasure," when you found out such girls had "gotten themselves into trouble"?
15. You may have known students or other acquaintances who were sexually active and as a result contracted herpes or some other venereal disease. To what extent do you think this is "exactly what they deserved"?
16. To what extent was it satisfying, did you perhaps feel a "secret pleasure," when you found out these people had caught a venereal disease?

Note: All items were answered on a 0–9 basis.

happen to them all the while they were having such fun and you were not.[8]

Is Authoritarian Aggression Caused by Self-Righteousness?

Here we are conjecturing that authoritarians may be aggressive because they believe established authorities approve the aggression, especially against unconventional targets, making it righteous, laudatory, sometimes even holy. Such beliefs then disinhibit aggressive impulses. However, one did not have to talk with many left-wing radicals during the 1970s to realize some of them felt the same way about *their* enemies. To the extent that individuals determine their own ethical codes, which both guide and are shaped by their behavior, might not nearly everyone feel he or she is "a better person than most"?

General Perceptions of Righteousness. In 1985 I asked 354 Manitoba students, answering anonymously, "How strict would you say you are about right and wrong, how moral would you say you are, compared (say) to others your age?" Answers were given on a -4 to $+4$ scale. The mean was $+1.59$, demonstrating the well-known self-serving bias described above. However, authoritarians were *particularly* likely to pat themselves on the back; RWA Scale scores correlated .30 with self-reports of moral superiority.

Shortly thereafter 278 parents of these students, also answering anonymously, produced similar values: $\overline{X} = +1.52$; $r = .26$. Thus, while most students and parents say they are stricter about right and wrong than their peers, authoritarians believe this about themselves to a greater extent. The correlations were small again, however.

A Mirror-Image Person-Perception Experiment. In 1984 I gave over 500 students a new task involving the RWA Scale:

> I am now studying what sort of impression is formed of *another* person according to how she/he

> answers this survey. What do a person's answers to these items tell you about him or her?

The 30 items of the RWA Scale were printed on the sheet.

> Alongside each statement are the answers a subject, the same sex as you, gave to these items at the beginning of the first session. Simply read each statement, and notice the person's answers. Try to get an impression of what this person is like. Then answer the questions that follow.

Actually, *two* sets of fictitious, mirror-image "answers" were randomly distributed among the subjects (each of whom got just one version of the responses). For example, the alleged answer to the first item, concerning "strong medicine," was a +3 on one version of the responses and a −3 on the other form. The first set of answers would have produced a very high RWA Scale score of 200, the other set a very low 100. The mean RWA Scale score of the subjects themselves was 156.5.

I was interested in how Low subjects would evaluate a High RWA target person and how Highs would evaluate a Low. So all subjects were asked to indicate afterward, on 0–6 scales:

> How *carefully* do you think this student has thought about these issues? (.33; −.27)
> How *intelligent* does this student seem to be? (.40; −.36)
> How *good*, how *moral* (by your standards) would you guess this student is? (.30; −.55)
> How much *integrity* (as opposed to hypocrisy) would you say this student has? (.43; −.29)

The numbers in parentheses are the correlations between the students' own RWA Scale scores and their evaluations of the High and Low targets, respectively. It can be seen that these relationships were always positive in the former case ($N = 268$), always negative in the latter ($N = 275$).

Highs thought the authoritarian target had thought more

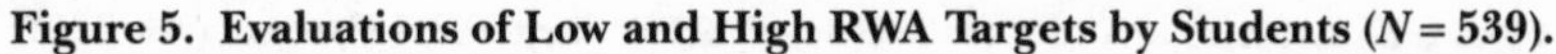

Figure 5. Evaluations of Low and High RWA Targets by Students ($N = 539$).

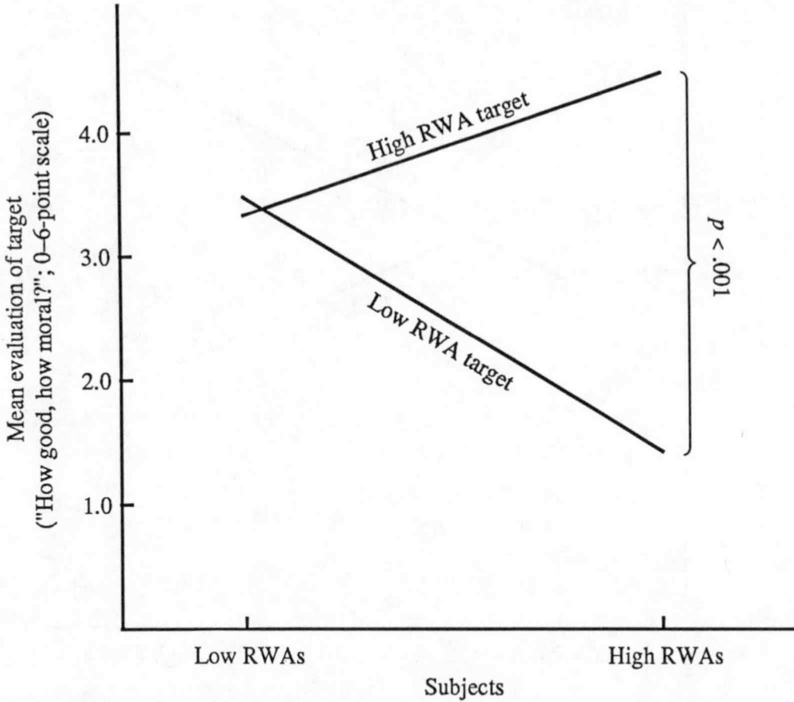

carefully about the issues than the unauthoritarian target had, was more intelligent, and had greater integrity. Low RWA subjects either rated the targets equally or rated the Low target more favorably than the High target but showed significantly less bias than the Highs did. The most dramatic difference (Figure 5), relevant to our concern here with self-righteousness, involved the judgments of "goodness" and morality (F-interaction = 54.8; $p < .001$).

I repeated this experiment with the 278 parents mentioned in the previous section, having them evaluate "another parent." Because parental RWA scores average about 175, it was impossible to mirror-image the targets' alleged responses. (If I had, the Low target's score would be much farther from the parents' mean than the High target's.) So I manufactured pseudo

Figure 6. Evaluations of Low and High RWA Targets by Parents ($N = 238$).

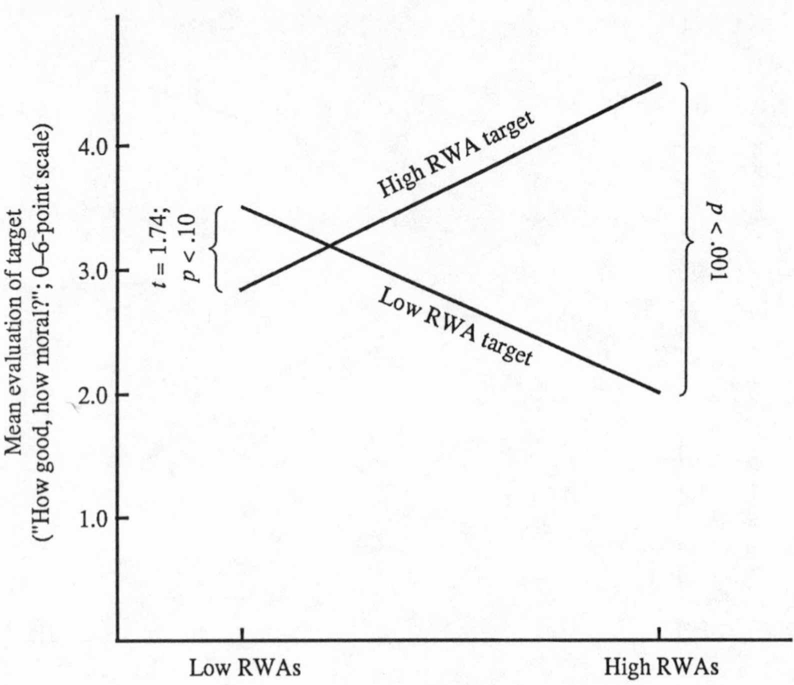

responses that produced a Low target score of 125 and a High target total of 225. (For example, the High answer to "strong medicine" was +4, while the Low response was −1.) As it happened, the mean of the parents' own RWA Scale scores was 179.4.

The parents' reactions to these targets largely replicated those obtained with students. RWA Scale scores correlated positively (.29 to .45) with all four evaluations of the High target ($N = 133$) and negatively (−.27 to −.38) with all four evaluations of the Low target ($N = 115$). Once more the biggest difference occurred on the issue of moral goodness (.42 versus −.38; *F*-interaction = 42.8, $p < .001$), and is largely attributable to the differing reactions of authoritarian subjects (see Figure 6).

Summary. Taken together, the data from these several studies indicate that authoritarians do feel themselves morally superior to others. We get a hint of this when we ask them to compare themselves with their average peer. We get a more dramatic picture of the extent of their self-righteousness when we see how they evaluate persons very different from themselves (Lows), compared with how they evaluate Highs like themselves.[9]

Lows occasionally show the opposite tendency, but to a much smaller extent. They will denigrate some targets (for example, the antigay William Langley from Chapter Four). But they do not seem nearly as self-righteous as Highs are, and they do not "unload" on their opponents the way Highs do. Bandura would probably say this is no coincidence, but cause and effect.

Tests of Berkowitz's Frustration-Aggression Hypothesis

Sexual Frustration. A finding that the authoritarian has less sexual pleasure than most would not necessarily support a frustration-based interpretation of his or her aggression. Berkowitz draws a sharp distinction between deprivation (which he says does not produce hostile impulses) and frustration (which he says does). The latter occurs only when someone is "kept from attaining the satisfactions he *expected* at the time he thought he would have them" (Berkowitz, 1978, p. 692). Authoritarian students who believe premarital sex is wrong might be deprived, but they seemingly would be among the least sexually frustrated people one could find, by this definition.[10]

Sexual behavior is not the easiest thing to study, and "Sex and the Single Authoritarian" is even more difficult because an appreciable number of Highs will not ordinarily respond, even anonymously, to questions about their sexual history (*RWA*, p. 327). However, as I mentioned in Chapter Two, the "Secret Survey" again provided a way.

In January of 1984 and 1985 I asked my introductory students, "Are you a virgin?" Although the simple answer to this question is either yes or no, I gave my subjects the six response alternatives shown below:

____ Yes, without qualification. (53) [25]
____ Yes, but I don't want to be. (7) [18]
____ Yes, but I have engaged in advanced sex acts (for example, oral-genital sex) as a way of having "sexual relations" without having intercourse. (26) [15]
____ No, but I am married/was married. (9) [14]
____ No, but it was against my will. (0) [1]
____ No, without qualification. (69) [90]
[Did not answer.] (7) [2]

The numbers in parentheses represent the answers given by 171 Highs in the combined samples; the numbers in brackets are the responses of 165 Lows. The reader can see that all but 7 of the Highs answered this question.

Not surprisingly, the distribution of responses was significantly different for the two groups (chi-squared = 22.6; $p < .001$). Most notably, Highs were over twice as likely to be "unqualified virgins" and nearly twice as likely to be "technical virgins" (who had engaged in advanced sex acts but not intercourse). Lows were more likely to be unwilling virgins and willing unvirgins.

However, these differences were largely due to the females in the sample. The distributions of responses among male Lows and Highs were *not* significantly different (chi-squared = 6.9; $p > .20$). A majority of the male Lows (56 percent) and of the male Highs (53 percent) were unqualified nonvirgins. So, indeed, were a majority of the female Lows (55 percent). But only 36 percent of the female Highs were; instead, this group was the most likely (16 percent) to be virgins who had nevertheless engaged in advanced sex acts. So there was much less difference in sexual activity between Lows and Highs than I had supposed.

In January 1984 I asked my students two more sexual questions on the Secret Survey. First, "Have you ever willingly participated in a homosexual act? How often?" Ten students, including two Lows and two Highs, said they had done so "once or twice." Three others, none of them Lows or Highs, reported more extensive homosexual activity.

Then I asked just the males, "Have you ever forced a

woman to perform sexual acts with you?" The response alternatives were:

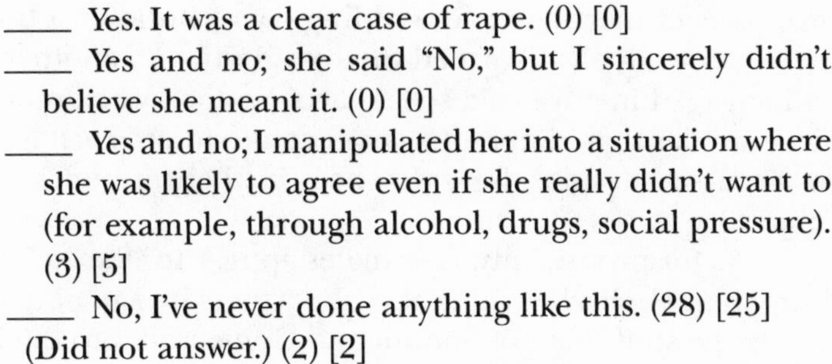

____ Yes. It was a clear case of rape. (0) [0]

____ Yes and no; she said "No," but I sincerely didn't believe she meant it. (0) [0]

____ Yes and no; I manipulated her into a situation where she was likely to agree even if she really didn't want to (for example, through alcohol, drugs, social pressure). (3) [5]

____ No, I've never done anything like this. (28) [25]

(Did not answer.) (2) [2]

The values in parentheses and brackets again depict the answers of Highs and Lows, respectively. One can see that the reports of rape were as rare as the reports of homosexual encounters, neither showing any relationship with authoritarianism.

My January 1985 students were also asked two follow-up questions about their sexual histories. First, "With how many partners have you engaged in sexual intercourse? (If you are a virgin, then the answer of course is 0.)" Then I asked, "In general, how much have you enjoyed the sexual activity you have engaged in thus far in your life?"

The sample (including virgins) had had about two intercourse partners, on the average, males reporting twice as many consorts as females. Lows had had sexual relations with significantly more persons ($\overline{X} = 2.44$) than had Highs (1.47), mainly because of Low males (3.18).

Ratings of sexual enjoyment, given on a 0–4 scale, averaged 2.85 (close to "Very much"). Females' and males' reports were equally high. Similarly, authoritarians reported enjoying sex as much as nonauthoritarians; however, about a quarter of the female Highs did not answer this question.[11]

What do these results tell us? Overall, I was surprised at how little difference there is in the sexual behavior of authoritarians and nonauthoritarians. High males were about as likely to have "lost" their virginity somewhere as Low males and females. High females were, by and large, the only ones saving themselves for their wedding night. (It will be recalled that High females were also significantly more likely to fantasize about proposals of marriage and wedding days.) But over a third of them had willingly discarded their virginity, and another sixth had engaged in advanced sexual acts. So the two extremes are more similar than different when it comes to premarital sexual intercourse—despite the differences in their attitudes on the subject.[12]

As for promiscuity, Low males appear to "tomcat" a little more than Highs, but three sexual partners by age nineteen is hardly the stuff that got Sodom and Gomorrah into the Bible. And again, Highs are not all that different. Finally, most Highs appear to enjoy sex as much as Lows do. So for all the talk, where's the payoff?

None of this, we must remind ourselves, has anything to do with Berkowitz's notion of *frustration*. We have to demonstrate that Highs are not getting as much sexual pleasure as they want and expect, compared with Lows, for the frustration-aggression hypothesis to explain the authoritarian's hostility. But the indications are hardly supportive.

Before leaving this engrossing topic, without which it appears countless magazines and "newspapers" would go unpurchased at the supermarket, we should note the implications these findings have for some of our earlier hypotheses. Do not Highs who engage in premarital intercourse feel guilty about it? Similarly, slipstreaming into oral-genital contact rather than intercourse may preserve virginity, but I doubt that the nuns who taught me catechism would call it anything less than a major-league mortal sin. And condemning acquaintances for promiscuity, being glad when they contract herpes, feeling that girls in your high school who became pregnant "got exactly what they deserved," and taking secret pleasure in their plight may all be somewhat hypocritical. Maybe authoritarians can afford so little generosity for others because they need all they have for themselves.

Economic Frustration. The reader has probably noticed that life can frustrate us in countless ways. One possibility involves our daily bread. Are authoritarians aggressive because they are economically more frustrated than others?

In 1984 I collected reports on family income from the parents of my introductory students. Total family income correlated −.18 with the parents' RWA Scale scores ($N = 508$) and −.04 with those of their children ($N = 336$). I also asked the parents to describe in detail the occupation of the principal breadwinner in the family and converted their answers to values on Blishen and McRoberts's (1976) index of the socioeconomic status of Canadian occupations (see Note 3, Chapter Two). Scores on this scale, which is based on income and educational data obtained in the national census, correlated −.29 with parents' authoritarianism and −.12 with the students'.

Thus the results uniformly support the hypothesis that Highs have somewhat lower economic and socioeconomic standing than others do. Whether this deprivation translates into frustration, however, remains to be determined.

Summary

How have our eight "suspects" fared in this review of the facts implicating them? I believe we have to release the Berkeley theory for lack of evidence. Further, there is much less of a case for the frustration-aggression hypothesis than I expected, and the cultural socialization theory seems rather weakly implicated. But there remain five prime suspects. Authoritarians appear fearful of a dangerous world. They apparently have as much to feel guilty about as the rest of us. Many of them are living with deep-seated, unexpressible doubts about their fundamental religious beliefs. And they do seem to envy, in a vindictive way, the fun that they believe "sinners" are having. All these aversive stimuli might, according to social learning theory, instigate aggressive responses. And on the disinhibitory side, Highs appear to be quite self-righteous.

As we circle the authoritarian, studying his hostility in the round, we should remember that these hypotheses are not mutually exclusive. Each of them may explain part of the authoritarian's aggression. Would that we could measure these constructs as neatly as we can name them, though! We have no indicators of guilt, for example, just the knowledge that Highs *ought* to feel guilty. Nor do we have any evidence of frustration, only of shortages. The index of fear could certainly be more direct than it is. Our measures of socializing influences, often based on cold recollections of distant events, make one squirm. We can get at hidden religious doubts only in very special testing circumstances. And so on.

So as we pit our most plausible hypotheses against one another in the following experiments, we should realize that measurement inequities may make it less than a fair contest.

FOUR PITTING STUDIES

Pit No. 1: The September 1985 Student Study

Choosing the Target Relationship

As I prepared my plots and ploddings for the fall 1985 testing season, I decided to pit, as best I could, all the hypothesized causes of authoritarian aggression except the psychoanalytic. I also chose to target, as the particular example of authoritarian aggression to be explained in the pit, hostility toward homosexuals.

People are probably hostile toward homosexuals for many reasons, some of which have little to do with right-wing authoritarianism. But the authoritarian's hostility toward gays has been evident at least since the "Berkeley" research program, and the contrait statement "There is nothing immoral or sick in somebody's being a homosexual" has been among the best-intercorrelating items on the RWA Scale for many years. Gays provide a deviant, disreputable, relatively powerless minority that one can attack with (selective) Biblical authority, the same way authoritarians in North America could openly attack Jews and blacks in past decades. Furthermore, as more homosexuals "came out of the closet" in the 1970s and pressed for equal rights in housing and employment in the '80s, they seemed to intensify the authoritarian's hatred for them the way the civil rights movement in the 1960s seemed to inflame hostility toward blacks

Exhibit 5. The Attitudes Toward Homosexuals Scale.

1. I won't associate with known homosexuals if I can help it.
2. The sight of two men kissing does not particularly bother me.*
3. Homosexuals should be locked up to protect society.
4. It would *not* be upsetting to find out that I was alone with a homosexual.*
5. I would join an organization even though I knew it had homosexuals in its membership.*
6. I find the thought of homosexual acts disgusting.
7. In many ways, the AIDS disease currently killing homosexuals is just what they deserve.
8. I would not particularly mind if my child had a homosexual teacher.*
9. Men who beat up homosexuals whom they find "hanging around" in parks, looking for "dates," in fact are committing a terrible crime.*
10. Homosexuality is "an abomination in the sight of God."
11. Homosexuals should be forced to take whatever treatments science can come up with to make them normal.
12. I wouldn't mind being seen smiling and chatting with a known homosexual.*

* Item is worded in the *con*trait direction; that is, the hostile response is to disagree.

among racist Americans. Thus homosexuals had become a prominent target for authoritarians' aggression by 1985.

By 1984 I had developed a balanced 12-item "Attitudes Toward Homosexuals Scale," shown in Exhibit 5. Inspection of these statements, which were answered on a -4 to $+4$ basis, will reveal that they assess condemning, vindictive, and punitive sentiments toward gays. The instrument proved relatively unidimensional, with average intercorrelations about .45, producing an alpha reliability of about .90. Its summed scores correlated in the .50–.60 range with answers to the RWA Scale; all the authoritarianism items had significant associations with "ATH" scores (aggression items leading the way), and all the ATH items correlated significantly with authoritarianism. Given its social relevance, then, its psychometric cohesion, and its relatively high association with authoritarianism, the ATH Scale provides a good specimen of the hostility we are trying to dissect.

Procedure

During the first month of the 1985–86 school year, 533 introductory psychology students at the University of Manitoba completed two "Survey" booklets administered one week apart. The first survey began with the RWA Scale, whose mean (152.4) and alpha (.86) were unexceptional.

The subjects then answered the Attitudes Toward Homosexuals Scale. Their mean score of 54.5 (where 60 would be perfectly "neutral") indicates a slightly nonaggressive orientation toward homosexuals overall. Responses to the 12 items intercorrelated .44, on the average, producing an alpha of .90. ATH scores correlated .54 with RWA Scale responses, indicating that the two measures shared .54 × .54, or 29 percent, of their variance. *It is this association that ultimately we shall try to explain.*

Immediately after finishing the ATH Scale, subjects indicated on a −4 to +4 basis how hostile they thought they were toward homosexuals, compared with the other students serving in the experiment. We shall take up their answers at chapter's end, when we study the authoritarian's awareness of his aggressiveness.

The "Dangerous World" Measure. Subjects next encountered six survey items, balanced against response sets, intended to assess directly the extent to which they perceived the world as dangerous and disintegrating into chaos:

1. It seems that every year there are fewer and fewer truly respectable people, and more and more persons with no morals at all who threaten everyone else.
2. Although it may *appear* that things are constantly getting more dangerous and chaotic, it really isn't so. Every era has its problems, and a person's chances of living a safe, untroubled life are better today than ever before.
3. Any day now, chaos and anarchy could erupt around us. All the signs are pointing to it.
4. Our society is *not* full of immoral and degenerate people who prey on decent people. News reports of such cases are grossly exaggerated and misleading.
5. The "end" is not near. People who think that earthquakes, wars, and famines mean God is about to destroy the world are being foolish.
6. If our society keeps degenerating the way it has been lately,

it's liable to collapse like a rotten log and everything will be chaos.

The students' mean answer (29.7) to these six items was almost exactly "neutral." These responses showed a reasonable amount of intercorrelation (.33 on the average), but with so few items (all I could think of at the time) the Dangerous World "Scale" had a very unsatisfactory alpha reliability of only .74.

Even though so handicapped, summed scores on the six items correlated .50 with the students' RWA Scale scores, confirming the hypothesis that authoritarians are particularly likely to perceive the world as threatening and falling apart around them. Dangerous World responses also correlated .32 with ATH scores.

What is our prediction here? We have hypothesized that authoritarians may be so hostile (partly) because they are afraid the world is a dangerous place. *If* this is so, then removing the mediating effects of this fear should reduce the correlation between RWA and ATH scores appreciably. And we *can* remove these theoretically mediating effects statistically through a simple partial correlation analysis. Such a procedure reveals that controlling for the relationships of RWA and ATH scores with Dangerous World scores reduces the RWA-ATH correlation from .54 to .46.

We shall produce a number of such theoretically dictated partial correlations in the next few pages and then consider their significance together.

Personal Experiences with Homosexuals. Moving to a new task in the first booklet, subjects were asked to respond to the item from the Experiences Scale dealing with homosexuals, which we discussed in Chapter Three:

> The homosexuals I have known seemed to be normal, decent people, just like everybody else, except for their sexual orientation.

Most (330 of 533) of the subjects, after the necessary reminders that the question was seeking information about experiences, not attitudes, indicated they had never known a homosexual. (As was true in the 1984 "Origins" study, High RWA students were particularly unlikely—only 30 of 132 Highs—to have had homosexual acquaintances.) Of the 203 students in the sample who said they had known persons who were gay, 80 percent agreed (to varying degrees) with the statement that these persons were normal, decent, and so on.

With the 330 "N.A." answers scored neutrally, responses to this single item correlated −.20 with RWA Scale scores and −.45 with the target ATH measure. Partialing out the effects of having personally known homosexuals lowered the RWA-ATH correlation from .54 to .51.

A Digression: Generalizing Effects of Knowing a Homosexual. Students who indicated they had had at least one homosexual acquaintance were directed to a series of questions about how they had learned the person was gay and how the acquaintanceship had affected their attitudes toward homosexuals in general. They reported that before meeting someone gay, or before discovering an acquaintance was homosexual, they had had a somewhat negative attitude toward homosexuals in general. Now their mean ATH score (46.6) was on the favorable side of the neutral point (60) and significantly lower than that of the students who had never known a homosexual. This improvement in attitude did not appear to depend on whether one had previously known the acquaintance as a "straight" or knew from the start that a new acquaintance was a homosexual.

This effect even appeared among the 30 High RWA students who said they knew a homosexual. Their mean ATH score (61.5) was significantly lower than that of the other 102 Highs (70.6) ($t = 2.44$; $p < .001$). Of course, exceptions existed. Some Highs (and a few Lows) intensely disliked the homosexuals they knew and had very high ATH scores. But in general the findings reinforce and expand on those presented in Chapter Three. Most authoritarians dislike homosexuals as an abstraction. Meeting someone gay is apt to mollify them, but most never do.

Testing the Cultural Darwinism Hypothesis. After describing their reactions to homosexual acquaintances, the students encountered a series of questions designed to assess the impact of various socializing agents on attitudes toward gays: the news media, parents, religion, school, and friends.

The first such question read, "There are occasionally stories about homosexuals in the newspapers, on the radio and TV, et cetera. Think of some that you can recall. How have these stories affected your reaction to homosexuals—*just by themselves, ignoring every other influence?*" (Answered on a −4 to +4 basis.) The responses averaged −0.38 and correlated −.18 and −.14 with RWA and ATH Scale scores, respectively. Controlling for these meager relationships left the .54 RWA-ATH correlation essentially unaffected.

Next, students were asked, "To what extent did your parents teach you, as you were growing up, that homosexuals were *dangerous* people whom society ought to control more through *tough discipline and punishment*?" (Answered on a 0–5 scale.) The mean response to this question was 0.64, and the correlations with RWA and ATH Scale scores were .16 and .20, respectively.

But are these recollections to be trusted? Not in this case, for sure, for (as will be explained later) ATH responses were also collected from 571 parents of 320 of these students. The overall correlation between parents' and children's hostility toward homosexuals was .37—significantly higher than the .20 coefficient based on the students' estimates. Controlling for *this* .37 relationship and the .35 correlation between parents' ATH and students' authoritarianism reduced the target coefficient from .54 to .47.

(Incidentally, students' authoritarianism correlated .44 with their parents'.)

Subjects then responded on a 0–5 scale to the question "To what extent did your religion teach you, as you were growing up, that homosexuals were perverted and sinful people who disgusted God?" Scores were higher ($\overline{X} = 1.25$) than attributions to parents, and they correlated .28 and .25 respectively with the students' RWA and ATH scores. The partial correlation analysis reduced the .54 correlation to .51.

Neither scale correlated significantly with answers to the question "To what extent did your teachers in school teach you, as you were growing up, that homosexuals were sick and disgusting persons in our society?" The mean of the answers, on another 0–5 scale, was but 0.41.

Finally, the students were asked, "To what extent do your closest friends think homosexuals are perverts, creeps, and disgusting?"[13] With a mean of 3.04 on a 0–5 response scale, the responses indicate that late-adolescent peer groups express more hostile, antigay sentiment than any of the other sources measured here. These ratings correlated only .18 with the students' authoritarianism, however, and .38 with their ATH scores. Controlling for best friends' opinions reduced the students' RWA-ATH correlation only from .54 to .52.

(In this case, an independent assessment of this influence supports the students' evaluation. The 206 best friends of the students who served in the earlier 1984 "Origins" experiment also completed the ATH Scale, and their scores correlated .54 with the students'. Since friends presumably influence each other's attitudes about equally, approximately half the variance explained by this correlation – that is, $.54^2/2 = .14$ – can be attributed to the best friend's influence. But a shared variance of 14 percent corresponds to a correlation of .38.)

Self-Righteousness. The second week's booklet began with the "person perception" task described earlier in which subjects were asked to evaluate the same Low RWA "student" presented in the fall 1984 "mirror-image" study. Four evaluations were solicited on the same 0–6 scales used before:

1. How carefully has this student thought about these issues?
2. How good, how moral is this student?
3. How dangerous do you think this student's ideas are to our society?
4. How sick (psychologically), how unhealthy do you think this person is?

RWA Scale scores correlated –.34, –.57, .48, and .40, respectively, with these judgments, and ATH correlations were –.25, –.39, .33, and .37. The judgments themselves intercorrelated .51, on the average (alpha = .80). Their sum ($\overline{X} = 9.40$) correlated

.55 with authoritarianism and .42 with ATH scores. Controlling for these relationships reduced the RWA-ATH coefficient to .42. (Using *just* the "how good, how moral" question also produced a partial correlation of .42.)

The Mean-Spirited Scale. Subjects then answered the 16-item Mean-Spirited Scale, whose average interitem correlation was .36 (alpha = .90). Summed scores on the measure ($\overline{X} = 47.8$) correlated .36 with RWA Scale scores and .22 with ATH responses. Partial correlation analysis reduced the .54 coefficient to .51.

The "Secret Survey"

If you are keeping track of this stream of variables flowing past, you know that so far we have collected information on nine possible explanations of the RWA-ATH relationship. Buck up. There are only seven more to go.

After answering several "Posse" surveys described elsewhere, subjects arrived at the last page of the booklet, which was entitled "Secret Survey" (see Appendix E for a similar questionnaire used with the previous year's students). Subjects were instructed to rip this sheet from the survey and respond to its questions wherever they wished, outside the testing room. They thus answered with complete anonymity, except that this last page had been discreetly coded to indicate whether the student had scored in the upper or lower quartile of the RWA and/or ATH distributions during the first session.

Sexual Behavior and Frustration. Subjects were asked their gender and whether they were virgins. The same six alternatives used in previous research were provided. All but 13 students answered this question, and the results confirmed earlier findings with regard to gender and authoritarianism. The correlation of virginity/nonvirginity with authoritarianism was fairly weak, .20 (owing mainly to the High females, as usual); that with ATH was even weaker, .14.

I chose not to ask subjects about their sexual frustration

in Berkowitz's terms (involving expectations) because I believed there would be either no relationship with authoritarianism or a negative one that could not possibly help explain hostility toward homosexuals. Instead I asked, "Regardless of your answer to the last question [about virginity], to what extent have you gotten as much sexual pleasure *as you want* in (say) the last six months or so?

Males reported experiencing significantly greater "frustration" than females (2.02 compared with 1.34 on a 0–5 scale). However, authoritarianism was negatively correlated (–.13) with these reports (owing mainly to the male Lows, who felt the most deprived), while hostility toward homosexuals was positively correlated (.12). These opposing relationships can, of course, explain none of the positive correlation between RWA and ATH scores.

Other Forms of Frustration. The students then indicated the extent to which they had obtained as much money, social esteem, or self-esteem as they had wanted during the past six months. Very modest amounts of frustration were reported, all of which were *un*correlated with authoritarianism and attitudes toward homosexuals.

Fundamental Religious Doubts. The back side of the Secret Survey began with a two-paragraph description of Hilgard's Hidden Observer research, after which the "Hidden Observer" in each subject was asked three questions. The first involved belief in a judgmental God and took the form described earlier. Only 22 of 132 Highs (17 percent) said they had secret doubts about such a God's existence, however—half the percentage obtained previously with my own students. Neither authoritarianism nor attitudes toward homosexuals were correlated with the presence or absence of such secret doubts.

Anxiety over Personal Sinfulness. The second question asked of the Hidden Observer read, "Does this person (that is, you) have some *secret* worries that his/her basic sinfulness will get out of control someday, if it is not kept under tight control?"

Highs expressed slightly more concern about this than Lows did ($r = .13$), and ATH scores were also slightly correlated (.17) with these responses. However, the coefficients are so small they explain virtually nothing of the RWA-ATH relationship.

Guilt. The last question directed at the Hidden Observer said, "Does this person have *secret* guilts about things (s)he has done wrong, which very few persons (or even no one) know about, but which trouble her/him and make her/him greatly wish (s)he had never done these things?" Most subjects admitted to having a few such guilts ($\overline{X} = 1.52$ on a 0–6 scale), but there were again no correlations with the variables of interest.

Following these rather intensive questions, which the reader may doubt (with me) evoked as much truth as could be desired, the students were asked what, if anything, they had heard about the purpose or procedures of my experiment from friends, acquaintances, or the "grapevine." The most common response, after "Nothing," was that this experiment concerned homosexuality. But no one mentioned authoritarianism or anything remotely connected with it.

The last part of the Secret Survey told the students they could earn additional credits by having questionnaires sent home and explained how to arrange for this when they returned to the testing site.

Evaluating the Results of the Experiment

We shall now use these data, with their various infirmities, to seek the underlying sources of the *authoritarian's* aggression toward homosexuals.

Table 3 presents the intercorrelations among the students' ATH scores and the variables that had relationships of at least .20 with this hostility. The number of significant ATH item correlations with each mediator is also shown in the bottom row of the table, which demonstrates that none of these variables was associated with just one aspect of the material covered in the ATH scale. The last column in Table 3 displays the partial correlations we found when we removed the effect of each vari-

Table 3. Intercorrelations Among ATH Scale Scores and Relevant Variables in the September 1985 Student Study.

	Students' RWA	*Dangerous World*	*Personal Experiences*	*Parents' ATH*[a]	*Religious influence*	*Friends influence*	*Self-Righteousness*	*Mean-Spiritedness*	*Partialed RWA-ATH correlation*
Students' ATH	.54	.32	.45	.37	.25	.38	.42	.22	–
Students' RWA		.50	.20	.35	.28	.19	.55	.36	–
Dangerous World			.16	.23	.24	.09	.33	.18	.46
Personal Experiences				.15	.00	.19	.19	.15	.51
Parents' ATH					.23	.14	.24	.14	.47
Religious influence						.21	.17	.08	.51
Friends' influence							.17	.09	.52
Self-Righteousness								.32	.42
Mean-Spiritedness									.51
Number of significant ATH item correlations	12	12	12	12	11	12	12	10	

[a] Based on the responses of 571 parents of 320 of the students. Otherwise, the sample size varies from 517 to 533.

able's mutual relationship with authoritarianism and hostility toward homosexuals. These tell us how important each variable could have been as a mediator of that hostility. The greater the importance, the bigger the drop from .54.

The largest drop in the RWA-ATH coefficient (.54 to .42) occurred when we partialed out the Self-Righteousness scores. The second-largest fall (down to .46) resulted when we controlled for fear of a dangerous world. Two "cultural factors," parents' hostility toward gays and the effects of religious instruction, produced drops to .47 and .51, respectively. Controlling for Mean-Spiritedness and partialing out the effects of personal experiences also reduced the target correlation to .51.

Why did Experiences scores and friends' influence not make more of a dent when they were removed? Because although they had sizable relationships with the students' ATH, they were relatively uncorrelated with the students' authoritarianism.

Thus they help explain why some students are hostile toward homosexuals and others are not. But they do not explain very well why *authoritarians* are hostile toward gays. And that is the understanding we are seeking.

How much of an understanding have we achieved? The correlation between RWA and ATH Scale scores (for the last time) was .54, meaning (again for the last time) that they shared 29 percent of their variance. If we *simultaneously* partial out the bonding effects of Self-Righteousness, fear of a dangerous world, parents' ATH, and the other variables shown in Table 3 (through Statistical Package for the Social Sciences program PARTIAL CORR), the target correlation drops to .33. That is, the shared variance has dropped to ($.33^2 =$) 11 percent. *We have accounted for most of the RWA-ATH relationship.*

In fact, however, we can do it much more simply. Merely partialing out simultaneously (1) Self-Righteousness and (2) fear of a dangerous world reduces the RWA-ATH coefficient to .35 (or 12 percent shared variance instead of 29 percent).

This is quite an interesting finding, given the competition, for neither of these measures mentions homosexuals. The first is based on the authoritarian's feelings of moral superiority to someone quite unauthoritarian; the second, on his or her fear of a disintegrating world and sense of personal vulnerability. We may, therefore, be onto something general here.[14]

Pit No. 2: The January 1986 Student Study

In January 1986, 395 subjects *anonymously* completed a booklet prepared to determine whether self-righteousness, fear of a dangerous world, and other variables could account for most of the relationship between RWA Scale scores and a *different* measure of authoritarian aggression: sentencing in "Trials" cases.

The booklet began with the RWA Scale and continued with an expanded, ten-item version of the Dangerous World survey.[15] Subjects then evaluated the same Low RWA target used in the last study, only on eight (instead of four) scales.[16] Next they sentenced ten unsavory criminals in the same Trials cases used in previous research (*RWA*, p. 233) and answered the 16-item Mean-Spirited survey. The last page of the booklet solicited religious affiliation information and asked the usual question about virginity. I then attempted to measure sexual frustration in precise "Berkowitzian" terms by asking, "To what extent have you gotten as much sexual pleasure *as you expected* to get, as you *anticipated* getting, in the last six months or so?" Subjects were invited to answer these questions outside the testing room and to address envelopes to their parents upon their return.

Psychometric Properties of the Measures

The various measures behaved, psychometrically, very much as expected. RWA Scales averaged 149.9, with an alpha of .88. Adding new items to the Dangerous World survey reduced the mean interitem correlation from .33 to .30 and raised the alpha of the test to .80—a doubtful trade-off. The mean of these scores was 49.5. The average intercorrelation of the eight "Low student" evaluations ($\overline{X} = 21.1$) was .44, producing an alpha of .87. Mean-spirited scores were somewhat higher under anonymous conditions than before (53.9 compared with 47.8; $p < .001$) and had an alpha of .91. Responses to the sexual frustration question averaged 1.47 on a 0–5 scale (about the same as before). The mean of the Trials sentences was 49.9 on a possible range of 0 to 90; the sentences intercorrelated .32, on the average, producing an alpha of .82.

Three hundred and forty-six parents of (a representative) 203 of these students returned completed booklets. Their mean RWA Scale score was 177.8 (alpha = .89). Parents' Trials sentences were a little heavier than their children's (51.9) and also better interconnected (alpha = .85).

Correlations with Authoritarianism and Sentencing

Students' RWA Scale scores correlated .39 with the sentences they imposed over the ten Trials. *This is the relationship we shall now try to explain.*

Dangerous World scores correlated .27 with the Trials

sentences and .53 with RWA scores. Partialing out these effects reduced the .39 correlation to .30.

(Negative) evaluations of the Low RWA "student" correlated .38 with sentences and .63 with authoritarianism. Controlling for these relationships reduced the RWA-Trials coefficient to .20.

Mean-Spirited scores correlated .36 with students' sentences and .35 with their authoritarianism. Controlling for these mutual relationships reduced the RWA-Trials coefficient to .30.[17]

Reports of sexual frustration (in Berkowitz's terms) did *not* correlate significantly with either sentencing (.04) or authoritarianism (.00).

Parents' sentencing in the Trials cases correlated .21 with their children's and .18 with their children's authoritarianism. The resulting partial was .37.

Simultaneously partialing out the effects of Self-Righteousness and Dangerous World scores reduced the .39 target correlation to .19. In other words, we have accounted for over 75 percent of the variance originally shared by authoritarianism and heavy sentencing. In fact, nearly all of this could have been done, in this case, by just the self-righteousness measure. Including the mean-spirited scores in the partialing reduces the .39 correlation still further, to .13. Berkowitzian frustration and parental attitudes had no effect.

Pit No. 3: The February 1986 Parent Study

Impressed by the success of more reliable assessments of self-righteousness and fear of a dangerous world, I decided to use just these measures to explain five types of authoritarian aggression among a sample of *parents:*

ATH scores ($\overline{X}$ = 63.1; alpha = .87)
Trials scores ($\overline{X}$ = 51.9; alpha = .85)
Posse-Cults[18] ($\overline{X}$ = 20.3; alpha = .88)
Posse-Communists ($\overline{X}$ = 23.3; alpha = .91)
Prejudice ($\overline{X}$ = 90.2; alpha = .87)

As for the "variance accountants," the eight evaluations of a Low RWA parent ($\overline{X} = 20.1$) had a mean interitem correlation of .47 and an alpha of .88. The ten Dangerous World items ($\overline{X} = 59.0$) had corresponding values of .32 and .82. As mentioned earlier, RWA Scale scores ($\overline{X} = 177.8$) intercorrelated .22 (alpha = .89).

The reader can verify, by comparing these values with earlier findings, that just as the parents were more authoritarian than their children, they were also more hostile toward homosexuals, were more prejudiced, were more willing to persecute Canadian Communists, gave slightly longer sentences, and had appreciably greater fear of a dangerous world. They were not, however, any more self-righteous when comparing themselves with a Low RWA target.

The intercorrelations among all these measures are reproduced in Table 4. The third- and second-from-last columns in the table show the effect in each case of partialing our two "accountants" from the RWA-criterion relationship. The last column reveals the result when both Self-Righteousness and fear of a dangerous world are partialed simultaneously.

The results can be stated succinctly: *in every case, most of the variance under consideration was accounted for by just these two measures.*

Pit No. 4: The September 1986 Student Study

I must confess I was pleased by the consistency and strength of the findings in these three pitting experiments. But I was also nervous about the poor job I had done collecting the more "psychodynamic" explainers of doubt and guilt in the first pitting study. So I asked to teach introductory psychology again in 1986–87 so I could ask my own students the Hidden Observer questions on the Secret Survey.

On September 16 I administered a "Psychometric Survey" (see Chapter Two) to my two classes ($N = 519$) that included the following measures of authoritarian aggression:

Table 4. Intercorrelations in the February 1986 Parent Study ($N = 346$).

	Self-Righteousness	*Dangerous World*	*ATH Scale*	*Trials sentences*	*Posse-Cults*	*Posse-Communists*	*Prejudice*	*Partial Correlations* *Self-Righteousness*	*Dangerous World*	*Both*
RWA Scale	.62	.44	.64[A]	.33[B]	.50[C]	.55[D]	.48[E]	–	–	–
Self-Righteousness		.37	.53	.26	.46	.49	.36	–	–	–
Dangerous World			.37	.35	.30	.40	.32	–	–	–
ATH Scale				.31	.54	.54	.55	.47	.57	.44[a]
Trials sentences					.28	.29	.25	.22	.21	.15[b]
Posse-Cults						.80	.51	.31	.43	.28[c]
Posse-Communists							.53	.36	.45	.30[d]
Prejudice								.36	.40	.32[e]

Note: *A-a, B-b,* and so on indicate comparisons showing the effect of partialing both Self-Righteousness and Dangerous World scores from an original authoritarian aggression relationship. In the ATH case, for example, the variance shared dropped from $.64^2$ to $.44^2$ (or from 41% to 19%).

ATH Scale ($\overline{X} = 54.9$; alpha = .90)
Posse-Radicals (such as Communists and the Ku Klux Klan) ($\overline{X} = 22.9$; alpha = .86)
Prejudice Scale ($\overline{X} = 74.5$; alpha = .88)
Trials (space limitations in the booklet permitted only the first three of my usual ten cases) ($\overline{X} = 16.3$; alpha = .50)

In addition, I collected RWA Scale scores ($\overline{X} = 151.0$; alpha = .88), the eight-item evaluation of a Low student ($\overline{X} = 21.7$; alpha = .87), a 12-item Dangerous World Scale[19] ($\overline{X} = 62.0$; alpha = .85), and the Mean-Spirited Scale ($\overline{X} = 49.9$; alpha = .88).

Thereafter classes flowed along as usual for the first term. Just before the Christmas break I covered hypnosis and Hilgard's research. Then in January I administered the Secret Survey to my classes, which included two questions for the Hidden Observer: the usual one about doubts concerning God's existence and the same question about secret guilts I had used in the first pitting experiment.

Cooperation on the Secret Survey was again excellent: all of the 108 Highs and 101 Lows in class that day answered both Hidden Observer questions. Previous findings (with my students) on the "secret doubts" question reappeared; specifically, 31 Highs said they had secret doubts, 19 said they had shared such doubts with others, and 52 said they had no doubts about God's existence at all.

My hypothesis was that such secret doubts might make Highs anxious and promote authoritarian aggression. One obvious way to test this was to compare the ATH scores, Posse scores, and so forth of Highs who kept their doubts locked up inside with the scores of other Highs who had shared such doubts and of Highs who said they had no doubts. I looked and found *no* significant difference of any sort on any of the four aggression indexes.

The students also admitted to more secret guilts than had those (from other classes) who had served in the September 1985 study. Highs confessed to a "mild amount of guilt," on average ($\overline{X} = 2.19$), and Lows admitted even more (2.76; $p < .01$). But since Highs were more aggressive than Lows, my guilt hypothesis was flatly contradicted.

In retrospect, as usual, this all makes sense. Other researchers (for example, Carlsmith and Gross, 1969; McMillan and Austin, 1971; Regan, Williams, and Sparling, 1972) have discovered that guilt has a *pro*social effect on people. (In fact, for years I have lectured on this effect in social psychology when discussing altruism; talk about compartmentalized minds!) That is, in complete contradiction to my earlier reasoning, Highs may be aggressive partly because they do *not* feel as guilty as they should—not even secretly guilty, at least so far as we can gauge by the Hidden Observer technique. Their "Teflon-coated consciences" contribute to their self-righteousness. So if we could help them admit their own failings to themselves, they might be *less* aggressive toward others they consider "sinners"—not more so, as I have been supposing.

Table 5. Intercorrelations in the September1986 Student Study ($N = 519$).

								Partial Correlations			
	Self-Righteousness	*Dangerous World*	*Mean-Spiritedness*	*ATH Scale*	*Posse-Radicals*	*Prejudice*	*Trials*	*Self-Righteousness*	*Dangerous World*	*Mean-Spiritedness*	*Self-Righteousness and Dangerous World*
RWA Scale	.60	.46	.31	.60[A]	.43[B]	.43[C]	.34[D]	—	—	—	—
Self-Righteousness		.46	.29	.40	.33	.36	.26	—	—	—	—
Dangerous World			.24	.27	.29	.26	.24	—	—	—	—
Mean-Spiritedness				.23	.25	.19	.23	—	—	—	—
ATH Scale					.33	.51	.17	.49	.55	.57	.48[a]
Posse-Radicals						.31	.16	.30	.35	.38	.27[b]
Prejudice							.17	.28	.36	.40	.26[c]
Trials								.24	.27	.29	.21[d]

Note: A-a, B-b, and so on indicate comparisons showing the effect of partialing both Self-Righteousness and Dangerous World scores from an original authoritarian aggression relationship. In the ATH case, for example, the variance shared dropped from $.60^2$ to $.48^2$ (or from 36% to 23%).

Having got seemingly definite answers to my questions about secret doubts and guilts, I shall simply report the results of the usual partial correlational analyses (Table 5). Self-Righteousness again explained most of the RWA-aggression correlation in each of the four cases, followed by fear of a dangerous world, followed by Mean-Spiritedness. Partialing Self-Righteousness and Dangerous World simultaneously explained most of the target variance in all cases except the RWA-ATH correlation. Throwing Mean-Spiritedness into the pot increased the explanations a little bit more in each case.

Conclusions and Implications

A long time ago, on a page far, far away, we set out to understand why persons who are highly submissive to established authority and highly conventional also tend to be authoritarian-aggressive. Since then we have examined over two dozen studies, involving over 8,000 different subjects, and the data have usually spoken with a clear voice. Perhaps, then, we can draw a conclusion or two.

Initially we considered three kinds of explanations of authoritarian aggression: "Berkeleyan," "Bandurian," and "Berkowitzian." We have found no support for the first or third of these, although others may in additional research. (Berkowitz's theory has proved more useful in explaining *other* kinds of aggression in our laboratory; see Josephson, 1987.) And two of the social learning hypotheses have also been disconfirmed: religious anxiety and guilt. One could make something of a case for the role of cultural socializing forces in the first pitting experiment, but not in the second. And vindictive envy may instigate aggressive behavior in some of the cases we've investigated. (It seems plausible to me that such factors may play greater or lesser roles in different examples of authoritarian aggression.) But fear of a dangerous world and self-righteousness have been definitely implicated in the authoritarian's hostility in every example in every sample studied thus far.

One can readily see how these complement one another. Believing society is falling apart, believing chaos is just around the corner, believing one is vulnerable to the bestial impulses of lawless others can certainly increase fear—and, with it, flight and fight. So one moves to the suburbs, and nourishes one's prejudices, and is a real sucker for "law and order" candidates and those who stress armaments above all. Or in extreme cases, one may slip away to remote areas, form paramilitary "Posses Comitati" and "Aryan Nations," murder one's chosen enemies, and dig in for the era of Mad Max.

The *impulse* to aggress that such fear produces does not result in hostile behavior, however, if the inhibitions against aggressing are strong enough. Lows, as we discussed earlier, apparently experience hostile impulses (and fantasies) but also greater inhibitions against acting them out. Here is where self-righteousness comes in. Social and rational inhibitions against hurting another person can be overpowered by feelings of moral superiority. And Highs tend to think of themselves as the Moral Majority, whether they are that moral or a majority or not. This feeling of superiority is accompanied, we have seen, by beliefs that they are more intelligent, more careful thinkers, the psychologically healthy "good citizens" of their country. Such persons would be quite susceptible to the flattering proposition that they are members of a master race. Once you believe that, you cock the pistol for "final solutions" to the "problem of the inferiors."

Apparently, then, the single most important thing we can do to reduce authoritarians' aggression is to reduce their self-righteousness. And after that, help them see that while society may be evolving, it is not dissolving, and the world is not really as dangerous a place as they believe.

What of the other factors we have considered? Recognizing that four studies performed in one locale do not constitute a mountain of research, we can hardly discount the other hypotheses. Besides, there remains unexplained RWA-criterion variance. A Mean-Spirited Scale for parents might have chewed up an appreciable amount of residual in the third pitting experiment. A veridical index of accumulated frustration might have helped reduce the first study's RWA-ATH correlation to nil. And so on.

I doubt, however, that any of these other factors would have proved more important than the two we have identified. We have already, in almost every case, accounted for most of the variance under discussion.

Usually, we do not explain much of anything with our research (*RWA*, pp. 112–115, 212). Occasionally we explain "a lot." But rarely do we account for most of what we do not understand. How was it done? It certainly helps to have reliable, relatively unidimensional measures. Large, cooperative, self-replenishing subject pools are also very handy. But in Kurt Lewin's famous words, "Nothing is as practical as a good theory."

I said at the end of Chapter Four that if all the social learning hypotheses were supported, it would be no great triumph for the theory, because none of the predictions was inevitable. But I also observed that the theory had a rich capacity to generate testable hypotheses; in fact, both of our data-blessed explanations (and the central notion of impulse versus inhibition) arose in a most straightforward way from Bandura's writings. In case the reader has forgotten, social learning theory also provided the framework in Chapter Three through which we explained, for the most part, how authoritarianism develops. One cannot help being impressed.

All the conclusions reported here are based on a particular interpretation of *correlational* data, however. This interpretation was hardly post hoc; it grew from theoretical expectations of why submissive, conventional persons would also be aggressive. Nevertheless, "families" of correlation coefficients, like real families, can be seen from different perspectives. Perhaps some other approach to the data will present a clearer picture still. Or maybe some other variable, not included in my studies, will prove fundamental to all these processes.[20] Time and better minds will, I hope, take us further in our understanding.[21]

IS THE AUTHORITARIAN AWARE OF HIS OR HER HOSTILITY?

This question may interest only those such as I who were betting on the guilt hypothesis. So if you are tired of all this, I shall tell you at the outset that the answer is "Yes and no"—or more precisely, "No and yes." But if you now wonder what *that* means, you'll have to read on.

In 1983 I put the proposition below to 391 (nonanonymous) Manitoba students:

> Suppose that while serving in a psychology experiment you were given a "truth drug," and that while under the influence of this drug you said, "I know I have a tendency to hurt people. I am often looking for permission, or good reasons, or excuses, to attack someone, with words or actions. And when I do it, it feels good."
>
> How would you explain this statement *to yourself* afterward?

Six response alternatives were presented, but the vast majority of subjects (Highs as well as Lows) indicated the statement would be "so completely untrue of me that even if I saw a videotape of myself saying this, I could not accept it as true."

Immediately afterward I directly asked the subjects whether they thought they had such a tendency. The sample mean on a 0–7 response scale was 1.55, and there was no correlation (–.04) with RWA Scale scores. Thus both sets of answers indicate that either Highs do not believe they are particularly aggressive, or else they know but will not admit it.

I researched this issue more extensively the following year, asking several samples how aggressive they thought they would have been (or had been) in one of my assessments of authoritarian aggression. For example, I described the circumstances of the "bogus shock" experiment to 292 students, without revealing the deception, and asked them to indicate (anonymously) on a –4 to +4 scale how much shock they thought they would deliver in that situation. Not surprisingly, a solid majority thought they would give *lower*-than-average shocks (the self-serving bias again), and the correlation with RWA Scale scores was .10—significantly less than the .43 obtained in the real study. Only 7 of 76 Highs (9 percent) said they would give stronger-than-average shocks; 57 said "less than average."

Shortly thereafter 557 other students answered my Manitoba Prejudice Scale (Exhibit 3) and then were asked, "How *prejudiced*, how *bigoted* do you think you are against the minority groups mentioned above, compared with the other students serving in this experiment?" RWA Scale scores again showed a significantly lower correlation (.17) with these social comparisons than with the actual prejudice answers (.27; $t = 2.73$; $p < .001$). Only 27 of 72 prejudiced Highs (38 percent) accurately estimated they were more prejudiced than average, compared with 73 of 84 unprejudiced Lows who correctly guessed they would prove relatively unprejudiced. The other prejudiced Highs thought they would be average (24) or less prejudiced than average (21).

In addition, 521 parents of these students (anonymously) answered the same question following the prejudice scale, with similar results. Authoritarianism correlated .20 with *estimates* of relative prejudice and .47 with actual prejudice ($t = 6.74$; $p < .001$). Only 18 of 94 prejudiced Highs (19 percent) stated they thought they would be more prejudiced than most. The other 76 thought they were average (46) or less prejudiced than average (30). By comparison, 81 of 105 unprejudiced Lows accurately estimated their standing.

The cumulative results thus indicate that most Highs either do not realize, or will not admit, how hostile they would be in a "free-style" aggression situation (the bogus shock experiment) or how relatively prejudiced they are toward ethnic and racial minorities.[22] But will their reports be as far off the mark when it comes to hostility toward a more socially acceptable target, gays?

As mentioned earlier, the 533 students who answered the ATH scale in the September 1985 pitting study were asked immediately afterward how hostile they thought they were toward homosexuals, compared with the other subjects. Authoritarianism correlated .35 with these judgments, compared with its .54 relationship with actual hostility ($t = 6.72$; $p < .001$). Again Highs made more mistakes than Lows, although they did not do as badly as earlier students had on the prejudice estimates. Of 103 relatively hostile Highs, nearly half (48 percent) thought they would be so. Forty thought their hostility would be average, and only 14 thought they would be less hostile toward homosexuals than average. (Again, though, Lows' reports were more accurate: 78 of 102 *un*hostile Lows guessed they would be.)

The 571 parents who answered the ATH Scale during October 1985 also answered the same question, with even greater insight. While RWA Scale scores correlated .69 with ATH responses, the relationship of authoritarianism with estimates of hostility toward gays was .54 ($t = 6.32$; $p < .001$). Of 111 hostile Highs, 77 (69 percent) thought they would be more hostile than average, 29 thought they would be average, and only 5 believed they would be less hostile than most. (Lows were still more accurate: 96 of 118 relatively nonhostile Lows guessed they would be.)

These same parents were also asked to estimate how hostile they were toward 11 other disreputable groups: "people with weird religions," pornographers, kidnappers, radicals, Communists, members of the opposite sex from their child with "loose morals," atheists, drug users, "hippies," "winos," and members of motorcycle gangs. (The reader will realize that previous research had indicated these were all groups that authoritarian parents, more than others, warned their children about.) *In every case* most High parents thought they would be more hostile than average, and parents' authoritarianism correlated .59 overall with self-perceptions of hostility. So in all these instances authoritarians did not make the self-serving errors in judgment found in the case of the bogus shock experiment and prejudice.

What is the difference? One can find a lot more social support for aggressing against homosexuals, religious cults, and pornographers than for shocking a helpless learner and attacking racial minorities. And the authoritarian is sensitive to what is socially permissible hostility. Thus the social acceptability of the hostility appears to mediate the authoritarian's admission, and perhaps his or her awareness, of it.

Do most Highs realize how aggressive they are in general, or are they kidding themselves as well as us when they sometimes say they have average or less-than-average amounts of socially unacceptable hostility? I have found that High students will admit a little more prejudice and mean-spiritedness when answering anonymously than when identifiable through signed attendance sheets. (Lows are largely unaffected by the manipulation.) So authoritarians may *sometimes* posture a bit to maintain their public image; privately they know better.

But to a considerable extent, they may not realize how relatively aggressive they are. After all, we make those judgments largely by comparing ourselves with others we know. And as we saw in Chapter Three, Highs travel in tighter circles than most people, limiting their contacts with persons very different from themselves. If most of your acquaintances are also highly prejudiced, you may think you are only average or even less than average.

Besides the misperceptions caused by this natural myopia, some authoritarians may also have efficient "intrapsychic" ways of dismissing the shortcomings they *do* realize—ways that explain why they did not feel as guilty about their misdeeds as Lows did in the fourth pitting study. In the Secret Survey I gave my students in January 1988, I asked, "Is there something you do to get over the guilt, to 'forgive yourself,' when you have done something morally wrong?" The next question asked "how completely forgiven" they felt, on a 0–6 scale, when they had done whatever they did to relieve their guilt.

Students indicated that they used a variety of guilt-allaying techniques, such as being nice to a third party, talking with a friend, and rationalizing the misdeed. There was only one significant difference between Highs and Lows. Of the 101 Highs, 25 said they prayed to God or went to confession for forgiveness, while only 4 of 95 Lows mentioned such a response. The fact that Highs felt significantly more forgiven for their wrongdoings than Lows did (means of 3.04 and 2.58, respectively; $p < .05$) is attributable to these 25 Highs, whose mean self-forgiveness score was a high 4.44.

It appears, in summary, that right-wing authoritarians openly admit their hostility when they perceive strong social supports for being aggressive—for example, against homosexuals. They also admit to a bit more hostility when they feel safe doing so, as when they are anonymous. But their normal social comparison processes may prevent them from learning how relatively aggressive they really are. And if they do admit to themselves that they have seriously wronged another, some of them have effective ways of disposing of the guilt, ways that could even foster the self-righteousness that will allow them to aggress again: "Yes, I am a sinner. But I am a repentant sinner, while the rest are unrepentant."

Which takes us to our next topic: authoritarianism and religion.

NOTES

1. One more "F Scale" study for the road. A friend who likes to keep me honest about the "Berkeley theory," and who enjoys playing the devil's advocate anyway, suggested that High RWAs' conventionalism might be compulsive, reflecting deeper problems. Accordingly, it was proposed, RWA Scale scores would be negatively correlated with scores on a proper measure of "good socialization"—namely, the 54-item Socialization subscale of the California Personality Inventory.

   I found, however, a weak, *positive* correlation (.22) between RWA and Socialization scores among 390 Manitoba students tested in the fall of 1983, mainly attributable to items such as "I have (not) used alcohol excessively" and "I think I am stricter about right and wrong than most people." Authoritarianism did not correlate at all with most of the Socialization items, which also did not correlate with one another. (The mean intercorrelation of .05 among the 54 items suggests, if these results are typical, that this is a "scale" in name alone.)
2. Do authoritarians come from violent homes? I asked my January 1985 "Secret Survey" sample (see Chapter Two) how many acts of physical violence had occurred in their families during the past year (not counting minor spankings for children's misbehaviors). Thirty-three of 98 Highs and 26 of 99 Lows reported various episodes of punching, slapping, kicking, angry shoving, and the like within their families. There were about twice as many parental attacks on children in homes that had produced authoritarian students: 61 to 32. (These are the total numbers of attacks; most such homes had more than one such parental attack.) There were also four times as many attacks by one parent on the other in Highs' families: 21 to 5 (in 20 of these 26 incidents the father attacked the mother). And sibling attacks upon one another were twice as common in High homes (183 to 95) and constituted the most common form of family violence.

   Such analyses can be misleading, however. Most Lows *and* Highs reported *no* violence at all at home during the previous year. Furthermore, I found the tendency reversed in a 1987 Secret Survey, in which (for example) Lows' parents reportedly attacked their children 66 times altogether, compared with 43 such attacks by Highs' parents. We should also realize that abusive parents may often make their children Lows, à la the "Experiences Scale."

3. In a later study I dropped the "tough discipline and punishment" part of the instructions and asked 372 students, "To what extent did your parents try to teach you, as you were growing up, that the following were *dangerous* people, whom you ought to be afraid of?" The results were not appreciably changed: intercorrelations among the 16 items averaged .38, producing an alpha of .91; the RWA correlation was .32.

   I also included some potential "left-wing anxieties" in this study to see whether Lows were similarly taught to be afraid of different groups: bigots, "superpatriots," corrupt authorities, the "military-industrial complex," and religious leaders. Relatively few of the subjects reported being taught to be afraid of any of these, however; the responses did not intercorrelate; nor did they correlate (negatively or positively) with RWA Scale scores.
4. The Highs' (or Lows') exam scores may have dropped for some other reason, such as lack of interest in the topics covered (sensation and perception, classical conditioning) or more earnest preparation for the first exam. But RWA Scale scores have never been significantly correlated with performance on my tests or with final grades in my course (*RWA*, p. 243).
5. Actually, a Canadian poll taken for the *Toronto Sun* in the spring of 1985 found that only 32 percent of the sample had been to church within the previous week. And the Roper Poll reported in December 1985 that 61 percent of its American sample believed premarital sex was *not* wrong.
6. Another Canadian poll, the Gallup, reported in September 1985 that 87 percent of its sample professed belief in God, but only 33 percent accepted the existence of the devil, and only 39 percent believed in hell.
7. I do not believe that I tapped subconscious processes through this approach but, rather, that the combination of several factors made it possible for these 33 Highs to reveal doubts they had consciously experienced but had kept secret. First of all, they knew they were answering anonymously, in very private circumstances chosen by themselves. Second, the description of Hilgard's research in class provided an example of "one part of the mind" telling a truth that the person ordinarily denied. Third, I use a certain amount of honest self-disclosure in my teaching, which by that point in the course may have had both a modeling and a social-exchange effect.

   As will soon be seen, I tried the "Hidden Observer" technique with a large sample of students from *other* professors' classes in the fall of 1985. They also answered anonymously, in private circumstances they had chosen. But they would not likely have heard of Hilgard's research before I told them, and I was a stranger to them. One *sixth* of the Highs admitted secret doubts about God's existence in this study.

8. Another, grittier example of this mean-spirited attitude was provided in a fall 1983 study in which I gave 526 students a recent newspaper article to read. The article described a murdered eighteen-year-old Winnipeg prostitute (who had been, in fact, a schoolmate of some of my subjects) and the risks that prostitutes take. (Speculation at the time was that the young woman had been killed by one of her "Johns.") I then asked the subjects to indicate, on a 0–9 basis, "To what extent do you think that this young woman was herself to blame for her own death?" The mean answer was 4.77 ("moderately"). RWA Scale scores correlated .30 with these judgments. Thus most Highs thought the victim was "more than moderately" to blame.
9. In September 1985 I asked 248 students to evaluate an *average* target person (whose RWA responses totaled 150). Subjects' authoritarianism ($\overline{X} = 149.3$) did not correlate with evaluations of the target's intelligence, care in thinking about the issues, or integrity. But Highs still thought the target was less "good, moral" ($\overline{X} = 2.24$ on the 0–6 scale) than Lows did ($\overline{X} = 3.42$). The overall correlation was −.31, quite similar to the value (.30) obtained earlier when 354 other students reported how strict they were about right and wrong, how moral they were compared with others their age.
10. I would define frustration as the experience resulting when a goal is blocked and would call the failure of expectations (Berkowitz's frustration) "disappointment." But who ever heard of the "disappointment-aggression theory"?
11. Morokoff (1985) found that women high in sex guilt *reported* less arousal, but *showed* greater physiological arousal while watching an erotic videotape, than others. The finding is the more impressive since a third of her potential sample (disproportionately High RWAs, one suspects) declined to serve in the study, and the difference was still found with a truncated sample.
12. In the fall of 1986 I asked 682 students to indicate, on a 0–7 scale, "How important is it to you that your husband/wife be a virgin?" The overall mean (1.70) indicated virginity was of little importance to these young adults, but Highs said they would desire it in a

bride/groom more than Lows did ($r = .43$). I was not surprised that female Highs wanted to be the first woman their husbands "knew" ($\overline{X} = 3.00$); after all, these women were usually striving to remain virgins themselves until marriage. But male Highs were equally desirous that their wives be "unsullied" ($\overline{X} = 3.16$), and as we have seen, they were already somewhat sullied themselves as a group. It is a (weak) example of the classic double standard. (Lows, males or females, were unlikely to be virgins and placed no value on it, with means less than 1.00.)

(RWA Scale scores also correlated significantly with requirements that one's spouse have the same religious beliefs [.38] and be of the same race [.31]. But Lows and Highs equally wanted well-educated partners [.06], females in both groups stressing this more than males.)

13. The students were then asked to answer several questions about the impact of learning Rock Hudson was a homosexual. (The actor died from AIDS about a month after these data were collected.) Overall the news had no effect upon attitudes toward homosexuals in general, and a slightly negative effect upon attitudes toward the actor.

Questions about religious and political affiliations ended the first booklet.

14. Inspection of Table 3 will reveal that of all the variables measured, right-wing authoritarianism had the highest relationship with hostility toward homosexuals. This is also rather remarkable because only one of the 30 RWA Scale items hits directly on this topic, and many of the other measures were concerned exclusively with homosexuality. One could argue, then, that this hostility is basically a symptom of a broader, more pervasive problem: right-wing authoritarianism.

If we apply a multiple-correlational analysis, identical to that employed in Chapter Three to explain the origins of personal authoritarianism, to the data in Table 3, we can account for 52 percent of the variance in ATH Scale scores. The RWA Scale naturally enters the equation first, then Experiences produces a multiple-R of .65. Thereafter parents' ATH, friends' influence, Self-Righteousness, and the other variables add nickels and dimes to the outcome, with a final multiple correlation of .72 ("pairwise deletion") or .73 ("listwise deletion," using just the 290 subjects for whom all scores were available).

15. The four new Dangerous World Scale items were: "There are many

dangerous people in our society who will attack someone out of pure meanness, for no reason at all." "Despite what one hears about 'crime in the street,' there probably isn't any more now than there ever has been." "If a person takes a few sensible precautions, nothing bad will likely happen to him; we do *not* live in a dangerous world." "Every day, as our society becomes more lawless and bestial, a person's chances of being robbed, assaulted, and even murdered go up and up."

16. The four additional questions used to evaluate the Low RWA target were: "How stupid, how ridiculous do you think this student's ideas are?" "How good a citizen do you think this student will be in our country?" "How much *integrity* (as opposed to hypocrisy) to you think this student has?" "Do you think your opinions on these issues are *better* than this other student's?"
17. The reader will recall that half the Mean-Spirited items involve sentiments that someone who had got into trouble "got exactly what he deserved." These reactions would obviously be related to judgments of how much punishment a criminal deserves. If one uses just the "secret pleasure" items from the Mean-Spirited Scale, its correlation with the Trials measure drops from .36 to .26, that with authoritarianism falls from .35 to .30, and the partial of the Trials-RWA correlation becomes .34, not .30.
18. This version of the "Posse" question was worded: "Suppose the Canadian government, sometime in the future, passed a law outlawing 'weird' religions and cults significantly different from our main religious traditions. Government officials stated that the law would only be effective if it were vigorously enforced at the local level and appealed to every Canadian to help destroy these religions." The usual six questions then followed.
19. The 12-item Dangerous World Scale used in this study appears below:

    1. It seems that every year there are fewer and fewer truly respectable people, and more and more persons with no morals at all who threaten everyone else.
    2. Although it may *appear* that things are constantly getting more dangerous and chaotic, it really isn't so. Every era has its problems, and a person's chances of living a safe, untroubled life are better today than ever before.
    3. If our society keeps degenerating the way it has been lately,

it's liable to collapse like a rotten log and everything will be chaos.

4. Our society is *not* full of immoral and degenerate people who prey on decent people. News reports of such cases are grossly exaggerating and misleading.
5. The "end" is *not* near. People who think that earthquakes, wars, and famines mean God might be about to destroy the world are being foolish.
6. There are many dangerous people in our society who will attack someone out of pure meanness, for no reason at all.
7. Despite what one hears about "crime in the street," there probably isn't any more now than there ever has been.
8. Any day now, chaos and anarchy could erupt around us. All the signs are pointing to it.
9. If a person takes a few sensible precautions, nothing bad will happen to him. We do *not* live in a dangerous world.
10. Every day, as our society becomes more lawless and bestial, a person's chances of being robbed, assaulted, and even murdered go up and up.
11. Things are getting so bad, even a decent law-abiding person who takes sensible precautions can still become a victim of violence and crime.
12. Our country is *not* falling apart or rotting from within.

20. Andrew Ahlgren of the American Association for the Advancement of Science kindly suggested to me in March 1987 that intellectual sophistication (as explored in William Perry's *Forms of Intellectual Development in the College Years*) might be a more fundamental distinction between Lows and Highs that could explain authoritarian aggression. The matter appears quite testable.
21. Gerry Sande and I have recently found cause-and-effect evidence of the role that fear plays in authoritarian hostility. Groups of Manitoba students, composed entirely of either High or Low RWAs, were involved in an "international simulation" in which they pretended they represented the NATO alliance in its dealings with the Warsaw Pact. The simulation opened with a report of several thoroughly ambiguous moves by Communist armed forces. If it wished to respond, the NATO team chose among a list of military and nonmilitary options, graded for threat value. In turn, the "Warsaw Pact," secretly played by the experimenters, responded in mirror-image fashion: whatever threat NATO made

was "seen and raised" an equal amount; but if NATO was non-threatening, so was the opposition. Thus a team was really playing itself. It could, entirely by its actions, keep the world at peace or increase tensions to the brink of nuclear war.

In this situation, teams of High RWAs used significantly more threat (in fact, many times as much), and thus produced much more tension, than the Lows.

But in a second version of the experiment, the subjects were told at the beginning that a recently perfected "Star Wars" defense guaranteed that if nuclear war occurred, they could not be hurt. In this situation the High RWA teams were as nonthreatening as the Lows. This surprised me. I had thought Highs would become even more aggressive, like a playground bully who knows he cannot be licked. But the data, if they are replicated, show instead that if you can allay the fears of authoritarians, they are not nearly as hostile as they are otherwise.

(Incidentally, I do not think the study shows that building "Star Wars" is the road to world peace. A nuclear umbrella may reassure the authoritarians in our government, but its deployment will probably scare the hell out of the authoritarians on the other side. How would our authoritarians react if they thought the enemy was about to deploy a shield we did not have? Remember the "mine-shaft gap" in *Dr. Strangelove*?)

22. In 1983–1984 the province of Manitoba was embroiled in a controversy over whether availability of certain French government services in French should be constitutionally guaranteed. The guarantee was advanced by the provincial government (that is, the New Democratic Party) as part of a "deal" to avoid a challenge before the Canadian Supreme Court to most of the province's laws, which for years had been passed in English only, when the province's constitution said they should also have been passed in French—but the *province's* highest court said that constitutional provision didn't really mean anything: it was only constitutional "advice," not an obligation. (Isn't this fun? You should have been here.)

    Opponents of this proposition observed that Francophones constituted only a tiny part of Manitoba's population, noted that larger minorities would not receive service in their preferred languages, objected to the cost involved, feared the consequences of entrenching such a guarantee in the Constitution, and said the Supreme Court would never rule most of Manitoba's laws unconstitutional because that would produce chaos.

Opponents of the opponents accused them of misrepresenting the reasons for the proposal and its terms, of being motivated by political opportunism, of vastly overestimating the province's chances before the Supreme Court, and in some cases of being prejudiced—there being a certain history of anti-French sentiment in the province, which had got it into this legal pickle jar in the first place. In response, opponents of the proposition insisted they were not anti-French and not at all motivated by prejudice for or against any group.

In the fall of 1984 I asked 475 Manitoba parents to indicate, on a −4 to +4 basis, whether they had supported or opposed the government's plans to expand and guarantee French-language services. The average response was 6.41 ("moderately opposed") on the resulting 1–9 scale. These answers correlated .30 ($p < .001$) with the parents' scores on my prejudice scale (Exhibit 3), so there was some justification to the charge that opponents of the plan were, in general, prejudiced persons. Furthermore, these answers also correlated .62 with responses to the item below, which immediately followed the prejudice scale:

> Canada should be an English-speaking country from shore to shore; French speakers are no more entitled to special rights than any other minority group.

I found it interesting that the answers to this statement, in turn, correlated .38 with summed scores on the prejudice scale—essentially the same as items about Jews, blacks, natives, and other groups do. In other words, the item could easily take its place on the scale; subjects who wanted an English-only Canada also tended to agree that Jews have too much power, blacks are naturally violent, Indians are naturally lazy, and so on. It seems hardly a coincidence that the Ku Klux Klan tried to infiltrate some of the opposition organizations.

Opposition to the government's plans correlated .29 with the parents' RWA Scale scores, incidentally, while answers to the "English-only Canada" item above correlated .35. Although none of these single-item relationships is large, neither is any of them surprising, is it?

(If you are dying to know how the matter was resolved, the

opposition to the proposal mounted a massive campaign, led by various dignitaries from all parts of the political spectrum. Referendums made it clear that the vast majority of Manitobans were against the proposition and wanted the Supreme Court to decide. The government modified its proposal somewhat, but opposition continued unabated. When the time came for a vote in the legislative assembly on the government's bill, the opposition party (the Progressive Conservatives) refused to take their seats. The speaker of the house ruled business could not proceed if the opposition was absent, so the parliamentary system was stymied. Eventually the government withdrew its proposal, and the matter proceeded to the Supreme Court of Canada.

The Court then declared that nearly all of Manitoba's laws *were* unconstitutional but said it would uphold them for a certain length of time until they were translated into French—dead laws as well as live ones. It was hard to find anyone who liked that decision.)

6

Authoritarianism and Religion

We shall now consider at length the association between right-wing authoritarianism and religion touched on in several previous chapters. I shall begin by reviewing past findings linking religiosity to RWA Scale scores. I shall then offer an explanation of how certain forms of religious training can increase authoritarianism. The results of several studies, designed to illuminate the role that religion plays in the lives and thinking of authoritarians, will then fill most of the pages in this chapter.

Previous Findings

In *Right-Wing Authoritarianism* (p. 240) I presented evidence that authoritarianism and religiosity often shape and reinforce each other. On the one hand, High RWA subjects usually embrace the religious teachings of their youth more tightly than others do, regardless of what the particular teachings were ($r \approx .45$). High RWAs tend to be the "true believers" in all the religions I have sampled and to practice their faith more "religiously" (in terms of church attendance, private prayer, and scriptural readings) than do less authoritarian members of the faith. So authoritarianism apparently fosters religiosity.

On the other hand, subjects raised in *any* religion generally score higher on the RWA Scale than those raised in none. So religion apparently enhances authoritarianism. But to varying degrees. Jews score lower, as a group, than Christians, who (in Canada) place evenly as Catholics or Protestants. Within Canadian Protestantism a bankable difference appears in study after study between relatively low-scoring Anglicans and United Church members and much more authoritarian Mennonites and "Fundamentalists" (mainly Baptists, Pentecostals, and Jehovah's Witnesses). Lutherans score in between, near the Catholic mean. These relationships are found across the content of the RWA Scale, incidentally, not just on those few items that directly or indirectly refer to religion.[1]

A caution: To tailor Disraeli's famous observation to the behavioral sciences, "There are lies, damnable lies, and weak generalizations." Not all the religious subjects in my samples have been High RWAs. I can pull low-scoring Baptists and high-scoring atheists from every bucket of data I have ever drawn. We are, as always, discussing differences between groups, not surefire attributes of individuals.

But such "off-quadrant" cases notwithstanding, the direction of the generalization has been clear, well established, relatively strong, and particularly ironic in the case of Christianity—for the Gospels largely portray Jesus of Nazareth as tolerant, forgiving, and preaching a message of universal love. (He was, furthermore, executed for being the kind of establishment-threatening "troublemaker" that Highs so readily pillorize on the RWA Scale.)

How Might Religious Training Foster Authoritarianism?

One can plainly deduce that authoritarians would particularly embrace the family religion, since submission to established authorities, such as parents and religious officials, is one of the three defining components of right-wing authoritarianism. But why should the relationship work in both directions?

How can religious instruction heighten authoritarian submission, authoritarian aggression, and conventionalism? And why do some religions apparently jack these things up more than others?

Authoritarian Submission. Generally speaking, Christian religions (among others) teach the child to obey a supernatural authority and, more to the point, an earthly authority system that acts in Its name. The extent to which the individual must submit to God's earthly representatives, the room that exists for disagreement, the degree to which one may decide things for oneself or must simply memorize—all these vary across religions.

But many children learn to submit to religious authority as automatically as they submit to their parents—except that religious submission does not end with adolescence but is the prescribed posture to the grave. Furthermore, the church may endorse submission to governmental authority, "rendering unto Caesar" all that does not conflict with religious principle. St. Paul even wrote to the Roman Christians, "Let everyone be subject to the higher authorities, for there exists no authority except from God, and those who exist have been appointed by God." Thus appointed or otherwise, numerous dictators have found that if they do not step directly on the bishops' toes, the church will play ball.

(There is, I hasten to add, another side to this ledger. At some times, in some places, organized religion greatly advances human freedom. At the time of this writing one finds churches confronting dictators in Poland, Haiti, the Philippines, and South Africa. The list will be different at the time of your reading, but there will be a list. Unfortunately, many counterexamples could also be cited. Like our other institutions, religion has a blemished record when it comes to promoting human liberty.)

Authoritarian Aggression. We saw in the last chapter that Highs' hostility is largely instigated by fear. But some churches are still in the "fear of the Lord" business, threatening (as we observed) eternal hellfire for lost sheep. Vindictive envy was also implicated in many examples of authoritarian aggression, and some religions draw such tight rings about their members' behavior that (secret) envy of the nonbeliever's good times may be fairly inevitable.

Just as important as these instigators, we found that self-righteousness powerfully disinhibits aggressive responses. Some religions directly teach their memberships that they are better than the rest of humanity, they are God's favorite children, they have the true religion, and they may attack others ("sinners," "heathen," "infidels") in God's name. How many wars have been "holy wars"?

Some religions thus directly teach hatred for others, for "Satan's agents." But the hottest spots in hell are reserved for those who abandon the true faith. Some religions, in fact, *order* their members to "shun" someone who has left the fold. (Those who witness the suffering such forced isolation from family and community causes will have second thoughts about questioning their religion. Hence many Highs, we saw in Chapter Five, keep their doubts entirely to themselves.)

Conventionalism. The connection between religion and conventionalism is almost tautological, it being one of religion's traditional functions to define and defend the moral norms in a culture. But faiths vary in the extent to which they tolerate deviance, assert their ethical judgment calls as absolutes, and try to influence the details of everyday life. The greater the intolerance, the certainty, and the lists of "do's and don't's," the greater the likely conventionalism.

A Test of These Observations: The Authoritarian Religious Background Scale

I tested these speculations in the fall of 1986 by asking 430 students to indicate, on a 0–6 basis, "to what extent, as you were growing up, did your *religion* and your *parents'* religious instruction"

1. teach you to obey the rules and commandments of a supreme, supernatural being?
2. teach you to obey the instructions and rules of persons in your religion (such as ministers, priests, bishops, rabbis, boards of deacons) who acted as God's representatives?
3. teach you to obey governmental authority ("rendering unto Caesar") in all matters that did not conflict with religious principles?
4. teach you to fear the wrath of God and eternal punishment for sinning?
5. label persons who broke God's laws as sinners who should be avoided and shunned?
6. draw up stricter rules about what you could and could not do than other kids had to obey?
7. teach you that your religion's rules about morality were absolutely right, not to be questioned?
8. try to influence your whole life, almost everything you did, every day?
9. teach you that persons who tried to change the meaning of Scripture and religious laws were evil and doing the devil's work?
10. teach you that you were a special group of people who were truer to God's will than others?

Responses to these ten items intercorrelated .50, on the average, producing an alpha of .91. Furthermore, subjects' RWA Scale scores were significantly related with responses to all the statements, running from .15 (Item 7) to .38 (Item 9). RWA Scale scores correlated .46 with summed scores ($\overline{X} = 15.1$) on this "Authoritarian Religious Background Scale." All but two of the RWA Scale items had significant correlations with these summed scores.

So, if we can assume the students' reports of their religious training are accurate, the ten behaviors listed above may indeed promote right-wing authoritarianism. Do some faiths stress these points more than others? Yes. Students raised as Fundamentalists and Mennonites had the highest scores on the ten items above, "No religions" (naturally) the lowest. The rank-order correlation of home religions according to their mean scores on the ten items above, and on the RWA Scale, was .88.

The 1984 Religion Study

Most of the relationships between authoritarianism and religion described so far appeared early in my research program, and over the years I have developed various measures of religiosity to probe them. These were brought together in the 1984 study of 513 of my own introductory psychology students and 549 of their parents to which reference has occasionally been made in previous chapters.

Procedure

A "Psychometric Survey" booklet, alleged to contain research instruments developed by other professors, was distributed to my two classes at our fourth meeting of the fall term. After answering the RWA Scale, evaluating "Arnold Gregson" (see Chapter Eight), and describing a few experiences, the students (who had signed a numbered attendance sheet) encountered a stream of religion questions.

The Religious Emphasis Scale. After naming the particular religion in which they had been raised, subjects answered (on a 0–5 basis) ten items reflecting how much their parents had emphasized practicing the family religion while they were growing up. The areas of emphasis were:

1. Going to church; attending religious services.
2. Attending "Sunday school"; getting systematic religious instruction regularly.
3. Reviewing the teachings of the religion at home.
4. Praying before meals.
5. Reading Scripture or other religious material.
6. Praying before bedtime.
7. Discussing moral "do's" and "don'ts" in religious terms.

8. Observing religious holidays; celebrating events like Christmas in a religious way.
9. Being a good representative of the faith; acting the way a devout member of your religion would be expected to act.
10. Taking part in religious youth groups.

The students' answers to these questions intercorrelated .55, on the average (producing an alpha of .92), supporting the sensible suspicion that parents who emphasized some of these things tended to emphasize them all. The mean response over all ten items (17.7 on a possible range of 0–50) indicates that little emphasis was placed on religion in most homes, however. The students' RWA Scale scores correlated .37 with the sum of these ten reports. Twenty-six of the 30 authoritarianism items had significant relationships with the Religious Emphasis score, and responses to all ten Religious Emphasis items correlated significantly with authoritarianism.[2]

The Religious Doubts and Religious Pressures Scales. Subjects then answered two more ten-item surveys (Exhibits 6 and 7), the first designed to measure doubts a person might have about the validity of traditional religious teachings, the other concerning pressures one might feel to remain religious in the face of such doubts. Items on both scales were again answered on a 0–5 basis.

The "Doubts" statements covered both "intellectual" and experience-based hesitations about religious commitment, and the students were asked to indicate the extent to which they had ever had such doubts. The "Pressures" items sampled both inter- and intrapersonal forces that might bind a person to his or her religion when reasons for abandoning the faith appeared. (The relatively few students raised in no religion were told to skip this scale.)

Responses to the Doubts statements intercorrelated .32, on the average (alpha = .84), while those to the Pressures Scale had a mean intercorrelation of .47 (alpha = .90). Overall, students reported relatively few doubts ($\overline{X} = 18.9$) *or* pressures ($\overline{X} = 18.1$). The whole business appears to have been played

Exhibit 6. The Religious Doubts Scale.

Below are listed reasons that people sometimes give for doubting traditional religious teachings. Please indicate the extent to which you have had these doubts.

1. Doubts that religious writings, such as the Bible, could really be the word of God, because the writings seemed contradictory, irrational, or wrong.
2. Doubts about the existence of a benevolent, good God, caused by the suffering or death of someone I knew.
3. The feeling that I had not really developed my own ideas about religion, but instead was just a copy of other people's ideas. (Or, if you were raised in no religion, that Christians, Jews, et cetera in general do not develop their own ideas, but instead are copies of other people's ideas.)
4. The feeling that religion didn't really make people better; people who went to church were still unkind, cheated others, et cetera but pretended they were better.
5. The feeling that religion exists basically because people are afraid of death and want to believe life does not end then.
6. The feeling that today's religions are based on a collection of superstitions from the past developed to "explain" things primitive people did not understand.
7. The feeling that religion makes people narrow-minded and intolerant and causes conflict between groups who believe different things.
8. A feeling that the overall religious teachings are contradictory or that they don't make very much sense.
9. Resentment or rebelliousness when someone (say, a minister, priest, or rabbi) tried to tell me how I should behave or what I should believe. (If you were raised in no religion, how resentful would you have been had this happened?)
10. The feeling that religion makes people do stupid things and give up perfectly wholesome pleasures for no good reason.

pianissimo, in general. RWA Scale scores correlated –.41 with total Doubts and .47 with the sum of the Pressures. All but one of the authoritarianism items correlated significantly with the Doubts score, and all 30 were associated at the .05 level or better with Pressures to keep the faith. Without exception, all the Doubts and Pressures items correlated significantly with RWA Scale scores.

The Christian Orthodoxy Scale. The students next encountered the 24-item Christian Orthodoxy (CO) Scale (Fullerton and Hunsberger, 1982) shown in Exhibit 8. This measure, largely

Exhibit 7. The Religious Pressures Scale.

What do you suppose it would cost you if you dropped your religion and became an agnostic or atheist? How much of the below do you think you would experience? (If you *have* dropped your religion and would now say you have "none," answer according to how you felt right at the time you decided to stop believing in that religion.)

0 = None at all
1 = Only a little bit
2 = A mild amount
3 = A moderate amount
4 = Quite a bit
5 = A great deal

1. Disappointment, disapproval of parents.
2. Disappointment, disapproval of close friends.
3. Disappointment, disapproval of ministers, priests, et cetera.
4. It would threaten a romantic love relationship.
5. I would feel lost, adrift; I'd have lost my "anchor" in life.
6. I would fear punishment from God.
7. I would fear that without my religious beliefs I would become an evil person.
8. I would be ashamed that I had not been strong enough to keep my faith.
9. I would feel I had betrayed the ultimate purpose of my life.
10. I would fear being damned and condemned to everlasting fire in hell.

based on the Nicene Creed, balanced against response sets, and answered on a −4 to +4 basis, touches on the most fundamental beliefs of the Christian faith.

Mean interitem correlation on the CO Scale was, as usual, quite high (.62), producing an alpha of .98—testimony to the thoroughness with which Christian ideology is taught in our culture. Its mean score (148.6) on a possible range of 24 to 216 indicates a general (but not overwhelming) acceptance of Christian beliefs among these students. RWA Scale scores correlated .51 with CO scores, all 30 RWA items having significant correlations with these beliefs. In turn, responses to all 24 of the CO statements correlated significantly with authoritarianism.

Allport's Intrinsic and Extrinsic Religious Orientation Scales. Taken from Allport and Ross (1967) as adapted by Batson and

Exhibit 8. The Christian Orthodoxy Scale.

---

1. God exists as Father, Son, and Holy Spirit.
2. Man is *not* a special creature made in the image of God; he is simply a recent development in the process of animal evolution.*
3. Jesus Christ was the divine Son of God.
4. The Bible is the word of God given to guide man to grace and salvation.
5. Those who feel that God answers prayers are just deceiving themselves.*
6. It is ridiculous to believe that Jesus Christ could be both human and divine.*
7. Jesus was born of a virgin.
8. The Bible may be an important book of moral teachings, but it was no more inspired by God than were many other books in the history of man.*
9. The concept of God is an old superstition that is no longer needed to explain things in the modern era.*
10. Christ will return to earth someday.
11. Most of the religions in the world have miracle stories in their traditions, but there is no reason to believe any of them are true, including those found in the Bible.*
12. God hears all our prayers.
13. Jesus Christ may have been a great ethical teacher, as other men have been in history, but he was not the divine son of God.*
14. God made man of dust in His own image and breathed life into him.
15. Through the life, death, and resurrection of Jesus, God provided a way for the forgiveness of man's sins.
16. Despite what many people believe, there is no such thing as a God who is aware of man's actions.*
17. Jesus was crucified, died, and was buried, but on the third day he arose from the dead.
18. In all likelihood there is no such thing as a God-given immortal soul in man which lives after death.*
19. If there ever was such a person as Jesus of Nazareth, he is dead now and will never walk the earth again.*
20. Jesus miraculously changed real water into real wine.
21. There is a God who is concerned with everyone's actions.
22. Jesus' death on the cross, if it actually occurred, did nothing in and of itself to save mankind.*
23. There is really no reason to hold to the idea that Jesus was born of a virgin. Jesus' life showed better than anything else that he was exceptional, so why rely on old myths that don't make any sense.*
24. The Resurrection proves beyond a doubt that Jesus was the Christ or Messiah of God.

---

* Statement is worded in the contrait direction; that is, the "Christian response" is to disagree.

Ventis (1982), these often-used religiosity scales were composed to measure the extent to which the individual values religion (1) for itself, above all else, as its own end, giving powerful meaning and joy to life, and (2) as a means to other ends, usually social or economic but also including solace and self-justification. Neither test (answered on the same −4 to +4 format used with the Christian Orthodoxy Scale) is balanced against response sets. The 9 Intrinsic items were interspersed among the 11 items measuring extrinsic orientation. Subjects with no present religion were told to answer neutrally ("0") the several statements referring to "my religion."

Answers to the Intrinsic items showed far greater cohesion (mean intercorrelation = .41, producing an alpha of .86) than answers to the Extrinsic statements (values of .11 and .56, respectively). The scale means were 42.2 and 53.6. RWA Scale scores correlated .36 with having an intrinsic orientation, attributable to 21 significant item correlations out of a possible 30. The relationship with the very unreliable Extrinsic score was but −.10. All but one of the Intrinsic items was significantly correlated with authoritarianism. The Extrinsic statements had a hodgepodge of positive and negative correlations with RWA Scale scores.

Miscellaneous Items. Eight individual items followed the Intrinsic-Extrinsic survey, as shown below:

1. "It's more important to be a good person than to believe in God or any particular religion." Answered on a −4 to +4 basis (which was, as always, converted to a 1–9 format). The mean of 6.03 indicates most students agreed with this statement. Authoritarians, however, usually did *not* ($r = -.50$).
2. "How many times would you say you ordinarily go to church in a month?" The mean of the answers was a mere 1.46, as many students said they seldom attended services. But RWA Scale scores correlated .43 with reported church attendance.
3. "How many times would you say you pray, privately, during a typical week?" This mean was also (to me) surprisingly low:

2.89, or just once every two or three days. Authoritarians reported praying more than most, however ($r = .35$).

4. "To what extent would you say you still hold the religious beliefs taught you when you were growing up?" This question was answered on a 0–5 scale, where

   0 = not at all
   1 = very slightly
   2 = mildly
   3 = moderately
   4 = nearly completely
   5 = completely

   The sample mean was 2.19, showing a considerable lack of faith corresponding to the moderate scores on the Christian Orthodoxy Scale, lack of church attendance, and infrequency of prayer we have already seen. RWA Scale scores correlated .47 with continued acceptance of the family religion, however, typical of previous results.

5. "Do you believe that Almighty God will judge each person and take some into heaven for eternity, while casting others into hell forever?" (Answered on the same 0–5 basis shown above.) The mean was 2.23, consistent with all that has preceded. Authoritarians professed greater belief in a Final Judgment than others did ($r = .44$).

6. "How important do you think your religious training has been in enabling you to control evil impulses?" (0–5) The students overall gave religion mild credit ($\overline{X} = 2.04$) in this regard; but as one would expect, authoritarians considered their religion more important for controlling evil than others did ($r = .40$).

7. "How much should one obey God's earthly representatives when they claim they are speaking for God?" (0–5) Students as a whole said they were unlikely to obey such representatives on these grounds, the sample mean being 1.54. But High RWAs appeared more obedient than the rest ($r = .38$).

8. "Do you believe there is a devil (or devils) Satan (Lucifer, Beelzebub) who actively fights God's will, tries to lead humans away from righteousness, and tempts us to sin?" (0–5) There was modest belief in Satan ($\overline{X} = 2.44$), with authori-

tarians believing in him appreciably more than other students ($r = .45$).

After answering these eight questions, students indicated their present religious affiliation and then answered a "just world" item.[3] The booklet ended with the standard invitation to earn more credits by having similar booklets mailed to their parents.

The Parent Survey. Surveys very similar to that just described were mailed to 710 parents of 406 of the students in my classes. Of these, 549 were completed (by 295 mothers and 254 fathers) and returned. There was no evidence of self-selection bias. The mean RWA Scale score of the 332 students for whom there were parental data was 150.9; that of the other 181 students was 150.0 ($p > .50$).

Averages and Alphas

Table 6 lists the psychometric properties of the parents' responses to the various measures. Those of their student-children, which we have already considered, also appear for purposes of comparison. One can see at a glance that just as the parents were more authoritarian than their children (by the usual margin), so also were they more religious on all the indexes used. (All these differences were statistically significant.) One can also verify that responses to all the scales were at least as cohesive among parents as among students.[4]

Gender and Denominational Differences. In both samples females were significantly more religious than males on several measures. Their Christian Orthodoxy scores were higher, they reported attending church and praying more often, and they had fewer doubts about the validity of their beliefs. Interestingly, they also reported that religion was stressed more to them in their youth than either fathers or sons did; one suspects at the minimum a sex-role modeling effect. Males did not appear significantly more fervent than females on any measure.

There were denominational differences as well. The impression of casual religious commitment among students in general definitely did not apply to Mennonites and Fundamentalist Protestants—nor, of course, to their parents. These two groups ranked first or second on every measure of religiosity in both samples, save "Obey religious authorities," where Catholics also scored high. Jews, United Churchers, and Anglicans consistently scored *lowest* in every category (except, naturally, for those belonging to no religion). Although the sample sizes are sometimes small (for example, 17 Mennonite students and 28 of their parents, 19 student and 16 parent Fundamentalists), all these high and low scores on all these measures replicate findings consistently obtained in previous years.

How religious are members of these most ardent denominations? Fundamentalist and Mennonite students' *mean* score on the Christian Orthodoxy Scale, whose maximum possible score is 216, was 205. As a group they had "less than slight" doubts about their religious beliefs and "almost completely" accepted the teachings of their home religion. They "strongly believed" Satan exists and tempts them and felt their religious training was "quite important" in helping them control their evil impulses. They were quite certain that a Last Judgment will occur, with damnation awaiting the wicked. They attended church at least weekly and prayed daily. They derived moderate-to-strong intrinsic (and very little extrinsic) satisfaction from their religion. They "strongly disagreed" that it is more important to be a good person than to believe in God or any particular religion. Not surprisingly, they reported feeling the greatest pressures to maintain their religious affiliations.

They were also the most authoritarian groups in the sample. Fundamentalist students averaged 189.3 on the RWA Scale, with Mennonites second at 183.8. Catholics came in a distant third ($\overline{X} = 159.3$), so these products of the Baptist and Anabaptist movements really were in a league by themselves. (By contrast, those with no religious affiliation scored lowest on the RWA Scale, 133.8.)

Such were the differences among students. Fundamentalist and Mennonite parents scored even higher on the RWA

Table 6. Psychometric Properties of the Measures Used in the 1984 Religion Study.

Measure		*N*	*No. Items*	*Item Mean*	*Scale Mean*	*Scale Variance*	*Mean Intercorrelation*	*Alpha*
RWA Scale	(Students)	513	30	5.02	150.6	964	.20	.88
	(Parents)	549		5.90	177.1	1149	.21	.89
Religious Emphasis	(S)	513	10	1.77	17.7	161	.55	.92
	(P)	549		2.50	25.0	186	.55	.92
Religious Doubts	(S)	510	10	1.89	18.9	101	.32	.84
	(P)	548		1.45	14.5	113	.39	.86
Religious Pressures	(S)	423[a]	10	1.81	18.1	154	.47	.90
	(P)	506[a]		2.11	21.1	218	.54	.92
Christian Orthodoxy	(S)	468[b]	24	6.19	148.6	2159	.62	.98
	(P)	500[b]		7.03	168.8	2185	.64	.98
Intrinsic Orientation	(S)	475	9	4.69	42.2	205	.41	.86
	(P)	519		6.04	54.4	250	.48	.89
Extrinsic Orientation	(S)	481	11	4.87	53.6	110	.11	.56
	(P)	530		4.64	51.0	179	.19	.72
Being good more important than belief?	(S)	513	1	6.03		6.45		
	(P)	549		5.12		7.56		
Church attendance	(S)	505	1	1.46		4.12		
	(P)	540		2.18		5.43		
Frequency of prayer	(S)	503	1	2.89		11.2		
	(P)	535		4.44		13.6		
Still accept home religion?	(S)	493	1	2.19		2.66		
	(P)	536		3.10		2.42		

Final Judgment?	(S)	498	1	2.23	3.02
	(P)	539		2.45	4.04
Religion for control of impulses?	(S)	488	1	2.04	2.69
	(P)	536		3.24	3.03
Obey religious authorities?	(S)	470	1	1.54	2.34
	(P)	528		2.20	2.76
Believe in Satan?	(S)	490	1	2.44	3.17
	(P)	538		2.80	4.12

[a] Of 90 nonresponding students, 57 had not been raised in a religion; of 43 nonresponding parents, 20 had not.
[b] Excludes those raised in a non-Christian religion.

Scale (means of 207.2 and 199.1, respectively). Again Catholics came in third with 184.9, and parents with no religious affiliation scored lowest (154.5).

Correlations Among the Measures. Table 7 presents the correlations among these 15 measures, first for the student sample and then for their parents. One can see that with the exception of the unstable Extrinsic Orientation Scale, most coefficients fell in the .40–.70 range. The very reliable Christian Orthodoxy Scale had the highest intercorrelations.[5]

One notes that the relationships found with students were rather faithfully replicated among the parents, albeit usually at a slightly lower level. That is, despite their different levels of authoritarianism and religiosity, the *organization* of beliefs, attitudes, and behaviors appears similar in the two generations.[6]

Table 7 also reports the number of significant RWA Scale item correlations with each of the religiosity measures, for both samples. One can verify that the authoritarianism relationships are general, not due to just a few of the RWA items.

An Unholy Alliance

What can these results tell us about the relationship between religion and authoritarianism?

First, as has been found many times before, the "true believers" within any religion tended to be authoritarians. Consider the "still accept"–RWA correlation. It was significant for every denomination, in both samples—ranging from .33 (Anglicans) to .66 (Mennonites) among students and from .44 (United Church) to .59 (Fundamentalists) among parents. So no matter what faith one was raised in, the more authoritarian one is, the more likely one is to embrace its teachings. This can be viewed simply as an example of Highs' submission to the established authorities in their lives.[7]

But are "very accepting" subjects equally authoritarian in all religions? Or do different denominations (as argued earlier) produce different levels of authoritarianism even among their strongly committed? If we examine just those subjects who answered the (0–5) "still accept" question with either a "4" or a "5" (that is, they indicated they "nearly completely" or "completely" accepted the religious beliefs taught them in childhood), who do you think were the most authoritarian of all these "true believers"? Fundamentalists (185.1) and Mennonites (185.3) among the students, Mennonites (202.1) and Fundamentalists (208.5) among the parents. The (rarer) United Church members, Anglicans, and Jews who were *just* as accepting of *their* religions scored about 25 points lower. True-believing Catholics and Lutherans lay somewhere in between.[8]

Two Cautions. The results therefore confirm the "mutually causing, mutually supporting" interpretation of the authoritarianism/religion connection offered earlier. But let us again guard against overgeneralizing. Not all authoritarians were highly religious: 18 of 129 High RWA students said they had no religion, and another 17 reported they accepted their home religion only "very slightly" or "mildly." (The corresponding frequencies for 138 High parents were less "exceptional": only 7 and 6.) Furthermore, 22 of the 129 Low RWA students were definitely religious, answering the "still accept" question with at least a "3." And among the more religious parents, 69 of 135 Lows said they still accepted the teachings of their home religion at least "moderately." So the "off quadrants" are fairly bespeckled.

Additionally, we should realize that to some extent Mennonite and Fundamentalist subjects only provide a concentrated view of a process occurring far more broadly. The student Highs also included 38 Catholics, 15 United Church members, 10 Lutherans, 7 Anglicans, and 3 Jews, besides the 18 with no religion mentioned above (representing, respectively, 31 percent, 26 percent, 34 percent, 25 percent, 20 percent, and 10 percent of their numbers in the total sample).[9] The breakdown among the parents was similar. Thus most religious Highs were not members of these relatively small Mennonite and Fundamentalist sects but belonged to the larger, "mainstream" religions. (Admittedly, though, these two denominations produced Highs at a much greater rate—12 of 17 Mennonite and 16 of 19 Fundamentalist students were Highs.)

Table 7. Correlations Among Authoritarianism and the Religiosity Measures (Students/Parents).

		Emphasis	*Doubts*	*Pressures*	*Christian Orthodoxy*	*Intrinsic Orientation*	*Extrinsic Orientation*	*Being good over belief?*	*Church attendance*	*Frequency of prayer*	*Still accept?*	*Final Judgment?*	*Control impulses?*	*Obey authorities?*	*Believe in Satan?*
RWA	(Students)	.37	–.41	.47	.51	.36	–.10	–.50	.43	.35	.47	.44	.40	.38	.45
	(Parents)	.30	–.35	.50	.43	.41	–.09	–.39	.31	.28	.41	.37	.37	.44	.41
Religious Emphasis			–.30	.59	.59	.58	–.20	–.42	.62	.55	.58	.49	.63	.36	.52
			–.23	.43	.49	.50	–.15	–.31	.44	.52	.46	.45	.53	.45	.42
Religious Doubts				–.36	–.64	–.37	.19	.37	–.39	–.38	–.50	–.45	–.38	–.32	–.45
				–.25	–.60	–.43	.35	.37	–.35	–.43	–.49	–.35	–.34	–.39	–.39
Religious Pressures					.69	.69	–.23	–.55	.60	.62	.71	.60	.68	.51	.59
					.58	.64	–.30	–.52	.57	.54	.57	.58	.47	.51	.56
Christian Orthodoxy						.63	–.24	–.59	.60	.61	.76	.71	.71	.58	.76
						.73	–.37	–.55	.53	.68	.73	.66	.48	.60	.73
Intrinsic Orientation							–.22	–.56	.65	.64	.61	.57	.66	.47	.59
							–.27	–.55	.64	.69	.61	.58	.58	.53	.60
Extrinsic Orientation								.28	–.30	–.32	–.28	–.23	–.15	–.12	–.26
								.44	–.29	–.33	–.31	–.37	–.18	–.18	–.32
Being good more important than belief?									–.46	–.45	–.49	–.52	–.44	–.42	–.54
									–.42	–.48	–.44	–.51	–.37	–.38	–.52
Church attendance										.58	.60	.51	.55	.43	.56

									.63	.53	.56	.46	.50	.54
Frequency of prayer										.61	.52	.61	.44	.55
										.57	.55	.50	.49	.62
Still accept home religion?											.60	.67	.57	.60
											.58	.58	.59	.59
Final Judgment?												.57	.49	.73
												.49	.54	.76
Religion for control of impulses?													.48	.58
													.47	.48
Obey religious authorities?														.49
														.56
Number of significant	26	29	30	30	21	12	29	30	26	30	30	30	29	30
RWA item correlations	26	25	29	30	27	12	29	23	20	28	27	29	30	29

A Closer Look at Religious Authoritarians. Although we should avoid being carried away by the data, their main drift should nonetheless move us somewhat. Seventy-three percent of the student authoritarians and 91 percent of the High parents were religious by the "still accept" criterion. How did they answer the other tests? And what can their answers tell us about authoritarianism?

As I looked over their answers, I was struck by the "tightness" of their beliefs. The mean Christian Orthodoxy score of the 89 Christian Highs whose "acceptance" answer was at least a 3 ("moderately accept") was 194.8. To score that high, these subjects had to *strongly* or *very strongly* agree (or disagree) with just about every statement in Exhibit 8. That is a remarkably consistent bit of survey answering, especially since half the items on the measure are worded in the contrait direction. High students have strongly accepted every one of the Christian beliefs surveyed. It is pointless to talk about which beliefs these subjects accepted most. They accepted all of the statements most. In fact, 15 of these 89 students scored perfect (9 × 24 =) 216s.

This ideological cohesion was even tighter among the 120 (Christian) religious High RWA parents. Ninety-two scored 192 or higher, and 38 bowled perfect CO games.

I was similarly dazzled by the religious Highs' reports that they had never seriously questioned their religious beliefs. Of the 94 religious High students (Christian and non-Christian), 73 (or 78 percent) had scores less than 20 (a "mild amount of doubt") on the Religious Doubts Scale, and 47 of them scored 10 or less. That means religious writings such as the Bible never struck them as contradictory, irrational, or wrong. The "problem of evil" had never created a serious doubt in their minds. They never felt *their* religious beliefs were "just a copy of other people's ideas." And so on. Parents reported even lower levels of doubts.

You will recall we have reasons for some doubts of our own here. A few months later, fully one third of these authoritarian students said they had misgivings about whether God actually exists (see Chapter Five). But these were *secret* doubts, so dangerous that the student had never revealed them to anyone. Instead the authoritarian's normal, "most available" answer, which we obtained in the present study, is that he believes: fervently, completely, easily. Whatever doubts exist, they are isolated, suppressed, and well contained under considerable pressure.[10]

The pressure comes from without and within. Forty-eight of the 94 religious student Highs had scores of at least 30 on the Religious Pressures Scale. What do you suppose is the greatest pressure they feel? What can we imagine would be the first thing these students would think of if they found themselves wondering whether God really exists?

The greatest pressure to "keep the faith" that religious Highs reported was fear of parental disappointment and disapproval (*mean* = 4.27, where the highest possible answer was 5.00). Additionally, they had a pronounced fear of disappointing religious authorities ($\overline{X} = 4.15$). But they were also afraid they "would feel lost, adrift, having lost their anchor in life" (3.29) and ashamed that they had not been strong enough to keep their faith (3.12). They also feared punishment from God (2.95) if they ceased to believe. One recalls, in reviewing these anxieties, the role that fear plays in the authoritarian's aggression.

High religious parents felt similar pressures, the strongest also being interpersonal: disappointment/disapproval by ministers ($\overline{X} = 4.34$), their children (4.22), and their spouses (3.97). But these parents also said they would feel "adrift" ($\overline{X} = 4.21$) and "ashamed" (3.77), and would feel they had betrayed the ultimate purpose of their lives (3.72).

Whatever doubts occasionally arise in the thoughts of Highs, their answers to Allport's Intrinsic Orientation Scale indicate that most of them derive great satisfaction from their faith. It answers questions "about the meaning of life." It lies behind their "whole approach to life." At times they have even "been keenly aware of the presence of God" in their midst.

Highs also rely on their religion to control their evil impulses (means of 3.60 and 4.26 among students and parents, respectively) and to resist Satan ($\overline{X} = 3.93$ and 4.07). But they believe that they are evil, that Satan exists, and that God will send them to hell for all eternity unless they are saved, because their religion teaches it.[11]

So the religion of authoritarians is all of a piece: a self-serving belief system, acquired in childhood and strongly reinforced thereafter, which requires no external confirmation and which can probably survive intact in the face of considerable *dis*confirmation.

Thus the High students stated, by more than two to one, that it is less important to be a good person than to believe in God and the right religion. High parents endorsed this view, which seems to get "means" and "ends" all mixed up, even more.[12]

Explorations in Compartmentalized Minds

Contradictions with Jesus' Teachings. I commented at the beginning of this chapter that the authoritarian aggression of Christian Highs is particularly ironic, given the main themes of Jesus' life. How do authoritarians reconcile their attitudes with Christ's example? Or do they see the contradiction?

Many of my introductory psychology students still needed experimental credits at the end of the 1984–85 school year, so I allegedly scrounged around among my colleagues and put together another (nonanonymous) in-class survey. The booklet began with the RWA Scale, and then subjects were asked what they thought this test measured (see Chapter Two), with a promise of an extra credit if they answered correctly. Sixteen of 309 students checked the "right-wing authoritarianism" alternative and were dropped from subsequent analyses. Subjects proceeded to several exploratory (but nonreligious) surveys and then indicated the extent to which they still accepted the teachings of their home religion. (The mean was 2.28, not significantly different from their answers six months earlier, with which the March answers correlated .75.) The booklet ended with several intensive questions about religion.

The first "intensive" question read as follows:

> In the New Testament, Jesus seems to make it very clear that we should not judge, or find fault with, or

> punish others for sinning. For example, in the Sermon on the Mount he says, "Do not judge, that you may not be judged. For with what judgment you judge, you shall be judged" (Matthew 7:1). And when the scribes and Pharisees brought an adulteress to him and pointed out that, by law, she should be stoned, he answered, "Let he who is without sin among you be the first to cast a stone at her" (John 8:7). But who among us is without sin?
>
> Is it not wrong, then, for a Christian to find fault with others and to punish someone who has acted immorally? If not, why not?

Of 71 Highs in the sample (so classified by their September scores), 60 were religious Christians. Twenty said we should take Jesus' words literally. Twenty-seven others wrote it was still all right to punish (10 because it was necessary to protect society, 6 because wickedness deserved to be punished, 7 because punishment would help sinners change their ways, and 4 said it was all right to punish provided you remembered you were a sinner too). None of these 27 subjects really addressed the contradiction of their beliefs with Jesus' teaching, however. Six additional subjects gave confusing, off-the-point responses worthy of a politician seeking office—for example, "Yes. If we are a democratic society we should allow non-Christian beliefs as long as they are practiced inside the law." (At least I find that off the point, given the question.) And seven of these Christian Highs did not put down any answer at all.

Because I had collected responses to my Attitudes Toward Homosexuals, Posse-Homosexuals, and Manitoba Prejudice scales from these same subjects at other times during the year (in various disguising circumstances), I was able to compare the "stone throwing" behavior of the 20 "true followers of Christ" who said we should not judge or punish others with that of the 27 Christian Highs who essentially ignored Jesus' words. To make a long story short, there was no difference. For example, 12 of the 20 and 15 of the 27 placed in the upper quartile of the ATH distribution—typical values for Highs. (Two from each group scored in the lowest quartile.) So some authoritarian Christians said we should heed Jesus' words, and others quietly stole past a "hard teaching." But it really made no difference what they *said*. Their behavior in other situations made it clear their hearts were with the scribes and Pharisees.

Which is all rather interesting. I am sure that many of these students could have told me, in the wink of an eye, the chapter-and-verse locations of the Sermon on the Mount and the story of the adulteress about to be stoned. They would have known as well that Paul's famous statement that faith which can move mountains is nothing without charity is found in I Corinthians 13:2. They know all these passages by heart. They have filled boxes in their minds with them. But tragically, the meanings do not seem to be connected with the rest of their lives.

Imagining Reactions to a Very Threatening Discovery. The last task in the booklet asked subjects to imagine what they would do if some future event cast the gravest doubts on Jesus' existence.

> Suppose that next month a group of archeologists working in the Near East announce the discovery of a group of ancient parchments, very similar to the famous Dead Sea Scrolls, in a Syrian cave. Except these scrolls are somewhat older. Radiocarbon dating establishes that the inscriptions were made on the parchments about 200 B.C. ± 100 years. The inscriptions are in ancient Greek and contain many of the myths and teachings of the "mystery religions" which arose in Asia Minor at the time. But what is astounding about these scrolls is that they also contain much of the story of "Jesus" as well.
>
> Specifically, the scrolls tell the story of Attis, a carpenter's son raised in a Greek settlement in what is now Lebanon. Attis was born of a virgin, though in this myth his father was a Zeus-like god. He began a three-year public ministry at the age of 30,

> drawing a multitude of followers and eventually coming into conflict with the established religion in his region. Attis was put to death but arose three days later and eventually rose into the heavens. Furthermore, most of the parables, miracle stories, and teachings of the Gospels are found in these scrolls, which clearly predate the reform movement that arose in Judaism during the First Century A.D. and which eventually became Christianity.
>
> Other scholars examine the scrolls and eventually pronounce them genuine. Scholars of Near East religions generally conclude that the long-forgotten myth of Attis was adapted and embellished by a group of Jewish reformers during the Roman occupation of Palestine to suit their own purposes—just as much of the book of Genesis has long been traced to earlier Sumerian myths. In short, there never was a Jesus of Nazareth.
>
> Now, this story is *not* true. It is entirely hypothetical. But imagine for the sake of the following question that the discovery and conclusions described above actually occurred. What effect would this have upon your religious beliefs?

Of the 60 religious Christian Highs, 3 said something in their open-ended responses I simply could not make heads or tails of. Seven said such new evidence would definitely change their beliefs in at least some way. Five others said the scrolls would raise doubts, and they did not know how they would react. Seven more said such evidence would raise questions in their minds, but they probably would not change. Ten did not answer the question. And the remaining 28 said, flat out, that such a discovery would have no effect on their beliefs. The most common explanation went along the lines of "My faith in the Lord is based on personal experience and could never be shaken by such things." Others said things like "I know it would be a test of my faith by God" and "It would simply be one of the devil's tricks." I was given lots of Biblical citations proving the story could not be true.

Thus, of the 60, only 7 said that pretty firm evidence of Jesus' nonexistence would definitely affect their faith. Of course, the students were only guessing, without time for reflection, how they would react to such a momentous development. But if that story of Attis does lie buried in some Levantine cave, its discovery may not change many High RWA minds.[13]

Let me see whether I can make a self-serving point without reeking of self-righteousness. We all have our faiths, our firmest convictions. I hope, for example, you will not be astonished to learn that I believe one can discover some useful things about human behavior through the scientific method. It is also probable that I would have abandoned this notion years ago if my own experiments had led nowhere.

Similarly, I do not believe in extrasensory perception.[14] I take quite a stand on that in my introductory psychology classes. But I like to think it will take only one sound, replicable demonstration of such powers to change my mind—and if one comes along, I will eat the crow and then, probably like you, get very excited at the changed perspective on human behavior. And suitable evidence would make me change my mind about everything I have said in this book about authoritarianism.

But there may be no conceivable evidence that will change the mind of the religious authoritarian about his religion. If he is wrong, he appears to have been inoculated against catching the truth. Unfortunately, though, his religious beliefs appear to contribute to his submission, aggression, and conventionalism.

An Experimental Attempt to Reduce Hostility Toward Homosexuals

For example, one more experiment using these same introductory psychology students is relevant here.

Procedure. In early January of 1985, as described in Chapter Five, I gave my classes a "Secret Survey" soliciting highly personal information (see Appendix E). The sheets were answered anonymously, outside class, except that I had discreetly coded the questionnaires to indicate whether the recipient had scored in the top or bottom quartile of the RWA Scale distribution four months earlier.

The second to last set of questions on the Secret Survey solicited the sexual information described in Chapter Five. The last set contained, for *half* the students, a somewhat unusual "admission":

> You probably have not guessed this, but I, Dr. Altemeyer, am a practicing homosexual and have been active in the Gays for Equality group in Winnipeg for many years. I believe I became a homosexual because of various factors in my early life, but whatever the reason I am comfortable with the fact of my homosexuality and do not mind telling others about it. But I have wondered how people react to this "news" about me and thought this would be a good time to get some honest, anonymous answers. So would you use the scales below to rate me, on an overall basis, using all the information and all the impressions you have about me.

Three seven-point semantic differential scales followed, anchored with the descriptions "PSYCHOLOGICALLY UNHEALTHY–PSYCHOLOGICALLY HEALTHY," "ATTRACTIVE AS A PERSON–UNATTRACTIVE AS A PERSON," and "DISGUSTING–ADMIRABLE."

After rating their beloved-if-gay teacher, the students were asked to rate "homosexuals in general" on another set of these scales.

The other (randomly selected) half of my students, serving as a control group, encountered a much duller ending to their survey and wondered what the whispering was about when they returned to the classroom. They were simply told:

> I, Dr. Altemeyer, have wondered at times how people react to me and thought this would be a good

> time to get some honest, anonymous answers. So would you use the scales below to rate me, on an overall basis, using all the information and all the impressions you have about me.

These students rated me on the same three scales described above. Then all students read that another professor (the one who conducted the brain laterality experiment described in Chapter Five) was interested in people's ratings of "homosexuals in general," which they were invited to give on another set of the same semantic differential scales.

Results. I am, on balance, pleased to report that the control subjects rated me as slightly healthy, neither attractive nor unattractive as a person, and slightly admirable—far higher than my in-laws, my department heads, and other researchers whose work I have slammed would place me, I am sure. The mean of the summed ratings, by the controls, was exactly 15.0 (where 12.0 would be "neutral" and 21.0 is the tops). These subjects rated "homosexuals in general" significantly lower, 9.92 on the average.

What happened in the experimental group? Osgood, Suci, and Tannenbaum (1957) would predict that the "positive object" (ahem, I) will lose favor but the negative object (homosexuals in general) will be seen more positively if the two become associated. And they were proved right. My rating "fell" to 13.5 ($t = 4.58$, $p < .001$), while that of homosexuals "rose" to 10.8 ($t = 2.62$, $p < .001$).

While I was happy for Osgood et al., I was disappointed to see that I had fallen farther than homosexuals in general had improved. I had hoped that when a generally respectable person such as a university professor "came out of the closet," it would help gays in general more than it would hurt the individual and would prove a useful technique for reducing this prejudice.[15] Where had this hypothesis gone wrong?

Among the authoritarians, that's where. I fell farthest among the Highs, from 14.4 (control Highs) to 11.7 (experimental Highs). The experimental Lows liked me just as much after I "decloseted" (15.6) as the control Lows unwittingly had (15.2).

At the next class meeting I dehoaxed my students, explained the experiment as a congruency-theory attitude change study, and presented the basic results. Then, without mentioning authoritarianism in the least, I concluded by saying something rather Lewinian:

> You know, I expected that attitudes toward homosexuals in general would change a lot more than attitudes toward me, because you know me and ought to have lots of feelings about me already. When I looked over the surveys, it was pretty clear why I dropped so much in general. A small number of experimental subjects gave me very low ratings across the board, far worse than I got among the controls. These same people also gave homosexuals in general very negative evaluations.
>
> It's clear what happened, isn't it? There are people who dislike homosexuals so much that if they think someone is gay, they will ignore all the good things about that person and badmouth him completely. And that is really very sad, because they're being blinded to the complexities of life, of a person, by a mean and unreasonable prejudice.

I then picked up my chalk and began to lecture on the limbic system, in a very quiet theater.

Now here is why this story is ending a chapter on authoritarianism and religion. You will recall from a few pages ago that a few months later 309 of these students answered the RWA Scale at the beginning of a survey booklet. The contrait Item 10 on the scale reads, "There is nothing immoral or sick in somebody's being a homosexual." But these students had responded to the same item 28 weeks earlier. So I could look at the authoritarians and see whose attitudes toward homosexuals had softened during the year and whose had not.

Of the 71 Highs in the March sample, 17 had been very

hostile in September (their mean response was 8.7 on a 1–9 scale), and they *still* "strongly" or "very strongly" disagreed with Item 10. Sixteen others had been just as hostile earlier ($\overline{X} = 8.6$) but had since moved at least three places down on the nine-category response scale. The rest either (1) had not been so unfavorable toward homosexuals earlier or (2) had been hostile but had moved smaller amounts.

What was the difference between the 16 very antigay Highs who changed (and who give us hope) and the 17 who were unmoved by my experiment, by my remonstration afterward, or by anything else that had happened to them during that school year? Not authoritarianism. Not gender. Not grades in my course. Not academic major. Not age. Not anything I could find, except one thing: religion. The mean Christian Orthodoxy score of the 16 modifiable High homophobes was 126.4; that of the 17 *un*modifiable High homophobes was 197.0 ($t = 4.97$; $p < .001$). If it says somewhere in the Bible that homosexuality is an abomination in the sight of God, it is going to take more than a 60-second sermonette from me to change minds steeped in the Old Testament.

Summary

I am not sure I have dispassionately discussed religion; but I have tried to base the presentation on experimental, replicable studies. The findings are really rather simple. Authoritarians in my samples tend to be religious persons, and vice versa. High RWAs usually have tightly wound religious ideologies. They appear to be under appreciable pressure to believe truly, and they keep doubts to themselves, split off and tucked away.[16]

One finds other evidence of balkanizing. Vast, complicated religious material such as the Bible is "lined up" to support authoritarian submission, aggression, and conventionalism. Contradictory material exists alongside the selected interpretation but is disconnected. Or Highs may say they agree with Jesus' admonition not to judge and condemn others, but this "agreement" has no apparent effect on their behavior. Their belief system appears self-confirming, enduring, and closed. Really, the beliefs could be anything, and hostilities based on them appear highly resistant to change.

I do not want to characterize the authoritarian as being closed-minded, rigid, or compartmentalized in all things or as being so "anti-intraceptive" as the Berkeley researchers believed. I can recall several studies in which a surprising number of Highs have, in the right circumstances, admitted threatening material they could have denied. For example, fundamental doubts about God's existence. For another, the cheating on my exams. For a third, admitting "secret pleasure" at the misfortune of others on the Mean-Spirited Scale; and fourthly, pleasure at punishing criminals on Trial (*RWA*, p. 234). For a fifth, acknowledging extra strong hostilities toward various (socially disreputable) targets. The trick is to provide circumstances in which such admissions become "available."

But it does appear that, relative to others, High RWAs keep their shortcomings from themselves even when circumstances favor self-honesty. In my January 1988 Secret Survey I reminded my students of Hilgard's Hidden Observer research and then asked their "Observers" to "name two or three things which your person is very reluctant to admit about herself/himself, and maybe would never admit to herself/himself, but which are still true." Highs named significantly fewer than Lows (means of 1.29 and 1.87; $p < .01$). This was almost entirely due to the large number of Highs (42 of 101) who wrote down nothing, compared with 19 of 95 Lows.

I had expected that some students would find it difficult to admit, even through the Hidden Observer, even one dark secret about themselves, and I wondered whether they really could think of nothing or were simply too embarrassed or frightened to write down what they could think of. So a few questions later in the survey I asked these nonresponders to indicate which it was. Nearly all the silent Highs (36 of 42) checked "I cannot think of anything to say." So did nearly all the nonresponding Lows (15 of 19). But the point is, there were twice as many Highs who were that closed off to themselves. This "amnesia" promotes the self-righteousness that disinhibits their aggressive impulses, as can the religious routes to self-forgiveness discussed at the end of Chapter Five.[17]

In closing, let me speak once again to the exceptions to my larger generalization. Some people appear intensely religious in beliefs and behavior but are not highly authoritarian. Atheists, in turn, can be High RWAs. If we were to try to guess an individual's authoritarianism from his or her Christian Orthodoxy score, we could *easily* be wrong.

We should also remember that the data reported here were all collected in one region, and it is likely other denominational patterns exist elsewhere. (For example, I found that Protestant students on five American campuses scored significantly higher than Catholics on the RWA Scale, and I could not locate a low-scoring Protestant sect: *RWA*, p. 240.) But in the region where I hunt data, these findings have been as steady as the Rock of Ages, year after year.

A last thought: I wonder whether any of this surprises anyone. If not, then we have confirmed a stereotype, and that ought to make us uneasy.

NOTES

1. The findings are all correlational, but the failure of intelligence, education, and socioeconomic status to account for more than a slice of these relationships has thus far discouraged "third factor" explanations of the associations.
2. Although subjects' retrospective reports of their childhoods are often unsupported by others' recollections, previous research has reasonably verified students' reports of the religious circumstances of their youth. For example, students' and parents' accounts of the emphasis placed on religion in the home correlated .70 and .73 in two previous studies (*RWA*, p. 267).
3. The "just world" question centered on a recent incident in Winnipeg that tragically presented the "problem of evil." A mother took her two children to a downtown movie as a reward for earning good grades in school. While they were waiting for a bus home, a large underground electrical transformer exploded and shot burning oil up through the sidewalk grate on which the three happened to be standing. All were horribly burned, and one of the children later died.

   I asked the subjects how they explained such a tragedy to themselves, providing eight possible answers. The strongest correlations with authoritarianism occurred with "It really is a just world and everything does happen for some underlying reason, but it is not possible for Man to understand God's purpose in everything. Such suffering is a mystery" (.35 among students, .34 among parents); "Part of God's plan is that things happen randomly on earth, but in the end the just will be rewarded and the wicked punished" (.31 and .37); "God allows evil to exist as a way to test mankind's faith" (.38 and .29). Highs thus appear to have a *religious* "just world" outlook. Perhaps this belief facilitates their aggression; that is, they are so punitive toward "transgressors" because they feel it is their right, as part of their self-righteousness, to balance the books for God.
4. We can speculate that the students are "going through a phase" and will be just as religious in 30 years as their parents are now. However, these same parents apparently did not emphasize religion to their children as much as the grandparents emphasized it to them ($t=9.03$; $p<.001$). So the children may be permanently less religious than their parents—a self-inflicted generation gap.

   Incidentally, the 76 graduating students tested in May 1986

(see the end of Chapter Three) answered the "still accept" question, as they had four years earlier. The level of religious acceptance had dropped slightly (from a mean of 2.95 to one of 2.71) but not significantly ($p > .25$). This longitudinal finding that religiosity does not change over the undergraduate years at the University of Manitoba replicates Hunsberger (1973).

The 89 "12-year" alumni (also described at the end of Chapter Three) did not answer the "still accept" question in 1974. But their level of acceptance in 1986 was relatively low ($\overline{X} = 2.31$), suggesting that any "religious rebound" had yet to begin—and might not.

5. In 1982 I administered Batson and Ventis's (1982) six-item Interaction Scale to a sample of 584 students. This survey is used with other instruments to compute a "quest orientation" in religious matters. It had a mean interitem correlation of .18, producing (with its short length) an alpha of only .57. Its only significant correlations with a variety of other religious measures were .15 with frequency of prayer and .11 with Christian Orthodoxy.
6. Correlations between students' and parents' scores on the religious scales were as follows: Religious Emphasis during youth, .43; Religious Doubts, .15 (clearly students do not get their religious doubts from their parents); Religious Pressures, .53; Christian Orthodoxy, .43; and Intrinsic Orientation, .39.
7. The association of authoritarianism with continued religious acceptance has almost always been lowest in "liberal" Protestant denominations and highest among the Mennonites and Fundamentalists, presumably because religion is more salient in the latter homes, and the child's submission to (or independence from) parents will more likely involve religious issues.
8. It may be that certain religions promote authoritarianism, not just by the content of their teachings, but also by the intensity of religious activity they promote among their members. Mennonites and Fundamentalists, after all, reported greater emphasis on religion in their homes than any other group. However, when one compares all the students who went to church a lot, prayed a lot, and so on during their youths (that is, when one looks at the upper quartile of the Religious Emphasis distribution), Fundamentalists and Mennonites still had the highest RWA Scale scores (186.6 and 186.3), compared with Lutherans (165.2), Catholics (162.6), United Church members (160.6), and Anglicans (158.9). Thus

content, rather than activity level, appears to be the more important shaper.

9. There were also ten High students who were Greek Orthodox, Moslem, or Hindu or who simply called themselves "Christians."

10. These secret doubts, which we failed to implicate in the authoritarian's aggression in Chapter Five, might still have psychodynamic implications. They could produce more intense religiosity or proselytizing, which Festinger might call "dissonance reduction."

    Incidentally, the vast majority of the apostates among my students reported that very little emphasis was placed on religion as they were growing up, so their initial commitment was probably rather shallow. But there were 15 more interesting apostates who apparently grew up in very religious homes (that is, their Emphasis scores were in the top quartile and averaged 37.6). What led them to stray? They simply became overwhelmed with doubts ($\bar{X} = 26.8$). What was the biggest cause for doubt among these "lost sheep"? See Item 8 in Exhibit 6.

11. My 1984 question about the Final Judgment did not touch on the drama of hellfire, so the following year I asked 533 students, "Do you believe that God will judge each person after he dies and that the wicked will be sent into a hell of everlasting fire and unbearable pain?" The mean (on a 0–6 response scale) was 2.33 ("mildly believe"), but RWA Scale scores correlated .46 with these judgments. Forty-seven of 132 Highs said they "completely believed" this statement.

12. I phrased the question about "being good versus having the right faith" in the opposite direction for samples of 354 students and 278 parents in the spring of 1985: "It is more important to believe in God and the right religion than to be a good person." This time most authoritarians agreed, the RWA correlations being .49 for students and .31 for parents.

13. Are atheistic Lows just as resistant to change as true-believing Christian Highs? In October 1986 I asked 430 students to indicate, on a −4 to +4 basis, whether they believed Jesus of Nazareth was divine, the Son of God. Then I gave them, in counterbalanced order, both the "scrolls finding" story about Attis *and* another archeological-discovery story *backing up* the New Testament:

    > Suppose that next month a group of archeologists working in the Near East announce the discovery of a

group of ancient parchments very similar to the famous Dead Sea Scrolls in a Syrian cave. Except these scrolls are somewhat older. Radiocarbon dating establishes that the inscriptions were made on parchment between 25 and 50 A.D.; the language is plainly classical Latin, and the scrolls are quite clearly the "file" that the Romans compiled on Jesus of Nazareth. They establish that Jesus, a carpenter's son from Nazareth, the only child of Joseph and Mary, began to preach in Palestine when he was 30, claiming to be the Messiah. Witnesses, including spies sent by the occupying Romans, confirm the miracles reported in the New Testament. Specifically, Jesus turned ordinary water to wine, walked upon water, multiplied loaves and fishes, raised Lazarus to life, and cured scores of people of many serious illnesses. The Roman officials, it is clear from the file, were plainly skeptical of these stories, but painstaking and detailed examination of the evidence could not discredit it and left them very worried and puzzled.

They decided, therefore, to put Jesus to death, fearing he was the Messiah who would overthrow their rule. After the crucifixion, Pontius Pilate made sure Jesus was dead, according to the records, and posted soldiers at the tomb to make sure the body stayed inside. The guards testified that they periodically rolled aside the stone to make sure Jesus' body was exactly as it should be, and the body was unquestionably dead. Then, the guards said, after several days a very bright light suddenly burst from the tomb, the rock fell away, and a very alive and radiant Jesus emerged and spoke to them. The file then contains many reports that Jesus was seen for several weeks thereafter in various parts of Palestine and then disappeared. Pontius Pilate, fearing for his position if the story ever reached home, ordered the file destroyed and the followers of Jesus persecuted. But instead the file was apparently hidden, then lost until now.

Other scholars examine the scrolls and eventually pronounce them genuine and unaltered in any way. In short, there apparently was a Jesus of Nazareth, and the story of the Gospels is confirmed by records kept by the government at the time.

At the end of each hypothetical case, subjects were asked to reanswer the question about Jesus' divinity according to what they would believe *if* such a discovery were to occur.

Eighty of the 100 responding Highs had answered the original question about Jesus being the Son of God with either a "+4" or a "+3." Of these, 43 (54 percent) indicated they were completely unmoved by the story of Attis and gave exactly the same response as before (or one higher). By way of contrast, only 21 of 107 Lows said "−4" or "−3" to the initial question. Of these, seven (33 percent) said they would be completely unaffected by the hypothetical discovery above.

Thus nonbelieving Lows appear, as a group, more persuadable by such scientific/historical evidence ($z = 3.45$; $p < .001$). The persuadable Lows also changed their opinions slightly more (3.78 compared with 3.37 units, on the average) than the persuadable Highs.

14. I have developed a modest, balanced 20-item "Superstition Scale" tapping beliefs in ESP, astrology, "Bigfoot," "ancient cosmonauts," witches, dowsing rods, and so forth. In a sample of 372 students tested in January 1985, responses to the items intercorrelated .26, on the average, producing an alpha of .88. Curiously, and contrary to the Adorno et al. theory of the (superstitious) authoritarian personality, RWA Scale scores correlated −.12 with total superstition ($p < .05$). (I have dubbed this the "Shirley MacLaine coefficient.")

15. Although if evaluations of "all homosexuals" went up even a small amount, that would be a large cumulative effect, if one of little practical consequence.

    Incidentally, I am not gay. If you know someone who stopped reading this book at page 227 because he discovered it was written by a homosexual, tell him it is all right to read on.

16. I wondered whether this tendency to see religious (and other) issues in closed, "black and white" terms meant authoritarians would dislike two-sided arguments in general and prefer one-sided approaches to an issue. So in the fall of 1986 I presented 519 of my own students with one of three "letters to the editor" about the merits of using automobile seat belts—an issue I knew was uncorrelated with RWA Scale scores. One of the letters was very one-sided in favor of "buckling up," another was quite opposed to the practice, and a third presented both sides of these arguments

and concluded, "Each person has to make up his own mind." I thought Highs might like, and be convinced most by, one-sided arguments (either pro or con), while Lows would differentially prefer a two-sided presentation. But RWA Scale scores were *un*correlated with reactions to all three letters.

17. At the next class meeting after the Secret Survey, I asked my students to rip off a piece of scrap paper and tell me how they felt about having admitted any "dark secrets" on the Hidden Observer question. I explained that they might feel worse for having done so, realizing "I'm not as good as I tell myself I am." Or they might feel better because "I have at least been honest with myself." Or they might feel unchanged. I asked them to answer in terms of a five-category, "double minus" to "double plus" scale I placed on the blackboard.

    Fifty-six percent of the students said they felt no different. Two percent wrote down a "– –" and eight percent a "–." Thirty percent marked a single "+," and four percent wrote down a "+ +." On balance, then, the self-admissions through the Hidden Observer appear to have been good for the students, although most felt nothing and a few felt quite bad afterward. One wonders how this compares with the effects of developing "clinical insight" through psychotherapy.

7

Authoritarianism and Politics

The question "What kind of political party do right-wing authoritarians prefer?" may remind one of Groucho Marx's famous "Who's buried in Grant's tomb?" The answer seems self-evident. Except that President Grant *is* buried in his tomb (I gather), but right-wing authoritarians show little preference in general for any political party.[1]

In Canada the three major parties arrange themselves in a somewhat orderly manner along the political spectrum. The New Democratic party (NDP), with its socialist roots, anchors the left. The Liberal party tries to stay astride the political center, which sometimes swings to the more right-wing Progressive Conservatives. Federally, Canadians take turns electing, and then becoming disgusted with, the Liberals and the Tories. The NDP has occasionally formed provincial governments but until recently has never been a power on the national scene.

In every sample of Canadian students and parents I have asked over the last 15 years, Progressive Conservative (PC) supporters have scored significantly higher (as a group) on the RWA Scale than Liberal and NDP backers. The latter usually end up relatively close to each other; occasionally NDP partisans score significantly lower than Liberal enthusiasts. Independents usually place close to the NDP mean (see *Right-Wing Authoritarianism*, pp. 204, 221–222).

Why do I say, then, that authoritarians show little preference for any party? Because there has always been tremendous overlap in the distributions of these group scores. One could easily find PC supporters who were less authoritarian than most NDP advocates. So the generalization "Conservatives are all authoritarians" would be one of those lies that are worse than "damnable lies" and even worse than cooked "statistics."

In terms of variance shared, eta-squared for undifferentiated samples of students and their parents has varied from 4 to 9 percent, analogous to correlations in the .20 to .30 range, which most behavioral scientists would call "weak relationships," I think.

In the United States, with its two-party system and different political culture (see, for example, Gibbons and Nevitte, 1985), the Republicans are usually considered "right of center" and the Democrats "left." But enormous regional differences allegedly exist. Eastern Republicans are expected to be more liberal than Southern Democrats. As well, each party necessarily harbors a considerable range of opinion, reminding one of Will Rogers's classic remark "I'm not a member of an organized political party. I'm a Democrat." Depending on which faction wins the nomination, a party platform during presidential elections may swing considerably. But to gain the White House, one must win the political center, and so Republican and Democratic national positions often coincide appreciably.

Nevertheless, I found that Republican supporters scored significantly higher on the RWA Scale than Democrats at each of six state universities I visited in the mid 1970s: Alabama, Indiana, North Dakota, Pennsylvania, Virginia, and Wyoming. The same strong caveat about distribution overlap applies, however; overall eta-squared = .09 (*RWA*, p. 221).

Importance of Political Interest

It became clear early in my research program that subjects' interest in politics affected the relationship between RWA and party preference. Most university students (and their parents) had either a "slight interest" in politics or "no interest at all." Students' party preferences were based largely on parental inclinations, even though both parents and students said politics was seldom discussed at home. Not surprisingly, such subjects' understanding of what each party stood for was even vaguer than the parties deliberately made it. There was almost no relationship between personal authoritarianism and party preference among such uninterested subjects.

If, however, one looked at those in my samples who were "moderately interested" in politics, and especially if one studied the 15 percent or so who said they were "quite interested," the relationship grew much stronger (*RWA*, p. 221). That is, when one examined "real NDPers," "real Liberals," and so on (among both students and parents), the overlap in distributions decreased considerably. Low RWA Conservative supporters became rarer, as did High RWA NDP enthusiasts. Many could still be found; but usually eta-squared came in about twice as large among interested subjects as in the undifferentiated sample.[2] That is, the relationship between authoritarianism and party preference was twice as strong among politically interested persons as among subjects in general.

If the relationship between authoritarianism and party association grows stronger as interest rises, then authoritarianism should best differentiate those most involved with the political process—namely, active politicians. A simulation study in 1979 supported this prediction. Manitoba students were asked to guess the typical responses to the RWA Scale items among *either* the NDP, Liberal, or Progressive Conservative caucus in the Canadian House of Commons (*RWA*, pp. 222-224).[3] The means of the simulated scores were all significantly different from one another in the expected way. According to the students, the NDP caucus would have the lowest RWA Scale scores and the Tories the highest. The differentiation was particularly strong among those students "quite interested" in politics (who would presumably know better what sort of beliefs would be found in each caucus). Eta-squared among these judges was 39 percent, the second-strongest relationship ever found with the

RWA Scale to that point (behind the similar "Trudeau/Nixon/Hitler" finding described in Chapter One).

Provocative as this result was, the study was unquestionably flawed in that it was only a simulation. I hesitated to send the RWA Scale to the real members of Parliament, however, because I doubted many would be returned, I feared that those few that did come back would have been filled out by legislative aides, and I even worried that some assistant might discover the purpose of the RWA Scale and organize a major distortion of the results. But my curiosity nattered and nagged.

Right-Wing Authoritarianism and Political Party Membership Among Canadian Legislators

Manitoba Lawmakers

Provincial legislators in Canada might be less busy than federal lawmakers and are less likely to have legislative aides. Yet, because of the division of powers in Canadian confederation, they are at least as important in the day-to-day lives of Canadians as their federal counterparts.

Procedure. So in November 1983 I sent solicitous letters, surveys, and self-addressed stamped envelopes to the members of the NDP and PC caucuses of the Manitoba Legislative Assembly. (There were no Liberals at the time; Manitoba politics were "polarized" from 1969 until 1988, with the NDP being in power for all but four of those years.) The letter, similar to that shown in Appendix F, presented the standard cover story that the RWA Scale surveyed "a variety of social issues" and said the results would probably be published in an academic journal someday, along with many other findings. The members of the assembly were promised personal confidentiality.[4]

At the time the NDP held a 32–23 majority, with two independents, in the Manitoba legislature. Over the next few weeks surveys drifted in one at a time until I had received 11 returns. I sent a second letter to each legislator, which reported the return rate thus far, extended thanks if the legislator had participated, but included another survey and stamped envelope if he or she had not. Five more questionnaires eventually arrived, giving me a sample of ten New Democratic and six Conservative respondents. Small returns, to be sure, but I was grateful for each one.[5]

Results. The mean interitem correlation on the RWA Scale for the sample of 16 was .41, far higher than anything I had ever seen before—indicating these responses were much more organized in the minds of these lawmakers than they have been in any of my previous samples.[6] One could easily call them ideologies, despite the seemingly disjointed topics. The index of internal consistency among the responses was .95, the highest RWA Scale alpha I had ever found.

The ten New Democratic scores on the RWA Scale ranged from 52 to 158 and averaged 95.7. The Conservative scores ranged from 173 to 210 and averaged 190.7, nearly twice the NDP mean. Just as interesting, there was no overlap in the scores, as the reader can see. The least authoritarian Conservative respondent scored 15 points higher than the most authoritarian New Democrat. With variances* of 1092 and 251 respectively, $F = 59.8$, $p < .0001$, and eta-squared = .82, this was about

* This chapter is chock full of statistics, and since it may be of particular interest to persons who do not speak "statistics," here are a few translations:

"Variance" refers to how spread out scores are in a sample. The major goal of research is to explain variance—that is, to explain the differences among people. The symbol for variance is s^2.

"Eta-squared" is a statistic that tells us how much variance we have explained with a factor such as RWA Scale scores. Usually we explain very little with a single variable. The eta-squared of .82 indicates the relationship described above is stronger than almost all the findings in psychology and sociology textbooks.

You can safely ignore statements such as "$F = 59.8$" and "$t = 2.31$." They are just stepping stones to the letter p—which graduate students in the social sciences learn to worship. Essentially, p means the probability that some finding is due to chance, that it is an illusion created by a lucky choice of subjects. We don't want to be lucky, we want to be right, so we want that probability to be *small*. When p is less than 5 out of 100 ("$p < .05$"), we say the finding is "statistically significant."

There's a fuller user-friendly explanation of statistics in Appendix A.

the strongest relationship I had ever seen in the behavioral sciences.[7]

As one would expect by the values above, New Democratic lawmakers scored significantly lower than Tory respondents on all 30 items on the RWA Scale, except Numbers 5, 8, 15, and 24 ("proper authorities censor," "premarital intercourse," "free speech," and "rules regarding modesty")—and even then the differences were in the expected direction and were nonsignificant only because of the small samples. Thus the huge gap between the two parties' authoritarianism was not simply due to a predictable difference in conventionalism. Conservatives also scored higher on nearly all the authoritarian submission and authoritarian aggression items. In fact, the largest differences occurred on Items 30 ("good old-fashioned physical punishment"), 28 ("Communists"), 16 ("some of the worst people"), 20 ("the self-righteous 'forces of law and order'"), and 12 ("obedience and respect")—all of them aggression or submission, not conventionalism, items.

Discussion. I was amazed. I had undertaken the study to test the hypothesis that the relationship between authoritarianism and political party association was strongest among active politicians. I expected a modestly strong relationship, perhaps an eta-squared of .30 if the hypothesis was valid, but I was not sure it was. Instead I found so strong an association that one could say these NDP and PC politicians probably differed more, as people, in the level of their authoritarianism than in anything else. And the unprecedented consistency of their individual responses reminded me more of how people answer an ideological measure, such as the Christian Orthodoxy Scale, than give "a variety of social attitudes."

There were several hesitations, however. First, were the samples representative of the whole caucuses? I had data from fewer than a third of the government members and about a quarter of the opposition. These politicians were *self*-selected. Perhaps I had heard from the least authoritarian NDP members and the most authoritarian Conservatives. We shall make an educated guess about this in a few pages, but there is no way to evaluate this possibility conclusively, since we obviously have no information about the nonrespondents.

Second, being a social psychologist, I immediately suspected I had been outdeceived. The Tories' scores are rather high, especially given their levels of education. (My parent samples average about 175, for example, and those with university educations would have a mean score in the 160s.) But the truly extraordinary feature of the study has to be the very low scores produced by the NDP respondents. About 3 percent of my parent samples score under 100 on the RWA Scale, but seven out of ten government members did. Are these politicians among the very least authoritarian persons in our society, or did they know what the "diverse attitudes" were tapping?

Arguing against this possibility, however, were the way the responses came in (one at a time over five weeks), their eventual number (why stop with 10 out of 32?), and the high variance of the NDP scores (four times that of the Tories) – hardly the signs of a leftist conspiracy.[8]

Assuming the NDP answers were genuine, they were remarkable in other respects. After all, these lawmakers who strongly agreed that citizens should not trust their governments, should not submit blindly, should be ready to protest against injustice, and so on *were* the government in Manitoba and had been for 10 of the past 14 years. But the Conservative politicians, out of power for the same period, and with the Liberals controlling the federal government at the time, said one *should* in general trust one's government, and so on.[9] (So much for the "role theory" of attitudes – for example, Lieberman, 1956.)

I also found the item analyses provocative. Again, it would be inaccurate to describe the Conservatives as "highly aggressive" and "very submissive." Overall they were *modestly* high in both respects. But that contrasted sharply with the NDP respondents, who can only be described as incredibly low in both regards.[10]

Ontario Lawmakers

As these findings "sank in," I realized the importance of collecting more data for comparison. Would the same results appear with other, larger samples? Was the very strong relationship between authoritarianism and party membership peculiar to "polarized Manitoba"? Would the Conservative mean be as high elsewhere? How would a Liberal caucus score? And would the NDP mean be so extraordinarily low in another legislature?

The ideal place to test next was Ontario, Canada's most populous province, with the largest legislature. At the time, the Conservatives controlled the Ontario Provincial Parliament with 69 seats, compared with 33 for the Liberals and 22 for the New Democrats. I sent off my first solicitation in June 1984 and over the next month received 32 responses in dribbles and drabbles. A second request in July brought in 13 more for a total of 45, nearly three times as large as my Manitoba sample, from 18 Tory lawmakers, 14 Liberals, and 13 New Democrats.

The mean interitem correlation of the responses was .40, again producing a very high alpha reliability of .95.

Tory scores showed much greater variability than in Manitoba, ranging from 118 to 212 and averaging 167.7 ($s^2 = 1024$). The Liberals showed even greater range, from a low low of 68 to a high high of 214; their mean was 136.5 (s^2 = an astounding 2057). The NDP scores ranged from 64 to 132, averaging 98.5 ($s^2 = 400$).

One can thus see similarities to the Manitoba data—and differences. The most striking difference, for my money, involves the Liberal party's ability to harbor such a wide range of opinion. Many of these Liberal lawmakers were Lows. Five of them scored under 100, and another four placed lower than 160, the average score of college-educated parents. But the Liberal sample also included several Highs. The Tories, in turn, had a few Lows, not found in the (small) Manitoba sample. Four Conservative members of the Ontario Provincial Parliament scored between 118 and 122 and were largely responsible for the fact that the Ontario PC mean was significantly lower than the Manitoba PC mean ($t = 2.31, p < .001$). These four Tories scored lower than one of the New Democrats, so one finds a slight overlap in these distributions in Ontario. The NDP mean, one observes, was quite comparable to that found in Manitoba.

As for the strength of the relationship between authoritarianism and party membership, eta-squared for the whole sample was .43 ($F = 15.6$). Thus RWA Scale scores were less related to party membership in the Ontario Provincial Parliament than they were in Manitoba, largely because of the spread of scores found within the Liberal sample. The relationship was still substantial, however, greater than any other ever obtained with the instrument save the previous study. If one looks only at the NDP/PC data (to make a direct comparison with the Manitoba results), $F = 54.8$ and eta-squared = .66.

As one would expect, the parties arranged themselves from left to right on almost all the RWA Scale items, with significant differences on all but Numbers 4, 8, 18, and 24. The largest differences between NDP and PC lawmakers occurred on Items 28 ("Communists"), 12 ("obedience and respect"), 9 ("the facts on crime"), 20 ("the self-righteous 'forces of law and order'"), and 30 ("good old-fashioned physical punishment")—basically the same items that most differentiated the Manitoba factions.[11]

British Columbia Legislators

Having sampled legislatures in the middle of the country, I next sent surveys off to the west and east coasts. British Columbia promised to be another "polarized" province, with the Social Credit party (34 seats) representing the right wing of the political spectrum, in lieu of a dormant Progressive Conservative party, and the New Democrats (23 seats) the left. I sent my first solicitation in January of 1985, and after 13 replies came back in a month, I sent a second request, which brought back only 2 more. The sample was thus almost identical to that in Manitoba: nine NDPers and six Social Crediters.

The mean interitem correlation was .50, indicating an *even tighter* ideological organization of attitudes than that found before, producing an alpha of .97 (a new record).

The NDP scores ranged from 44 to 119 and averaged an even more incredible 81.7 ($s^2 = 552$). Social Credit scores went from 122 to 198, with a mean of 168.5 and a variance of 971. Eta-squared was .72 ($F = 33.8$). All item means were significantly different except for Numbers 5, 13, 14, and 24. The largest differences occurred on Items 28 ("Communists"), 1 ("strong medicine"), 17 ("in these troubled times"), 9 ("the facts on crime"), and 21 ("the courts are right")—all of them authoritarian aggression items.

The reader may agree that the results essentially replicate the Manitoba findings. True, the half-dozen Social Credit respondents scored considerably lower on the RWA Scale than the half-dozen Manitoba Tories and are by no means "highly authoritarian" as a group. But the British Columbia NDPers' mean is lower than their prairie counterparts' too. So the Social Credit scores were still twice as large as the NDP's, and there was no overlap. Most psychologists, I believe, would call the relationship between authoritarianism and party membership among these B.C. legislators a "very strong" one. And the very high interitem correlations suggest that the RWA Scale taps a fundamental dimension of these politicians' social thinking.

New Brunswick Legislators

The Conservatives had such large majorities in the Maritime provinces in the spring of 1985 that I had little choice about which Atlantic legislature to sample. In New Brunswick the Tory majority was "only" 38 to 17 over the Liberals, with 2 NDP members. I sent my first appeal in May, and after 14 answers came back sent out a second appeal the following month, which netted another 10 completed surveys. The final sample consisted of 16 Conservatives, 6 Liberals, and both NDP legislators. (Legislators in *un*polarized provinces seem more willing to answer attitude surveys.)

The interitem correlations averaged only .18, producing an alpha of .88. Tory scores on the RWA Scale ranged from 131 to 217 and averaged 179.6 ($s^2 = 650$). Liberals' responses went from 105 to 220, with a mean of 170.5 ($s^2 = 1460$). The NDP mean was 117.0.[12] As in Ontario, Liberal scores overlapped those of the Conservatives and the NDP. In contrast to Ontario, but as in Manitoba and British Columbia (if we consider the

Social Credit party the equivalent of the Conservatives), the NDP and PC distributions did not overlap. The NDP mean was significantly lower than the other two parties', which did not differ statistically ($t = 0.5, p > .50$). Eta-squared for all 24 legislators was .29 ($F = 4.3$); that for just the NDP versus the Conservatives was a compelling .81 ($F = 69.2$).

NDP answers to the 30 items were always lower, on the average, than the Conservative responses; but with such a small sample size, only 15 of the differences were statistically significant. The largest differences occurred on the usual items.[13]

Discussion

Hesitations. Before proceeding, we should recall that we have no direct knowledge that any of the 100 surveys under discussion was actually completed by a Canadian legislator. Maybe an assistant or a secretary wrote in the " – 4's" and " + 2's." Furthermore, we have no knowledge that the questionnaires that were completed by a lawmaker were filled out seriously, candidly, and without consultation with colleagues. All we can say is that this approach probably tells us more about who these politicians are, and what they truly believe, than the manufactured images presented during election campaigns. Nor do we know that these elected officials were blind to the instrument's purpose. Research indicates almost all ordinary persons are, but these are extraordinary, not ordinary, subjects.

As for our earlier concern whether these self-selected samples are representative of their larger groups, we are now able to make an educated guess. Inspection of Table 8 will reveal that in every case the response rate was higher among the least authoritarian party than among the most authoritarian. One might, then, conclude that Low RWA politicians were more likely to answer the RWA Scale than Highs, just as parents of Low RWA students have always been more likely over the years to answer the survey than parents of Highs.

If this is true, then it means that we have got a somewhat biased picture of the authoritarianism within each party. The *true* level of RWA Scale scores in each caucus is probably some-

Table 8. Results of the Canadian Legislator Study.

Province	*Party*	*Total No. of Legislators*	*No. of Replies*	*Response Rate*	*Range*	*Mean*	*Variance*	*Alpha*	*Eta² — All*	*Eta² — Left versus Right*
Manitoba	NDP	32	10	31%	52–158	95.7	1092	.95	.82	.82
	PC	23	6	26	173–210	190.7	251			
Ontario	NDP	22	13	59	64–132	98.5	400			
	Liberal	33	14	42	68–214	136.5	2057	.95	.43	.66
	PC	69	18	26	118–212	167.7	1024			
British Columbia	NDP	23	9	39	44–119	81.7	552	.97	.72	.72
	Soc. Cr.	34	6	18	122–198	168.5	971			
New Brunswick	NDP	2	2	100	N.A.[a]	117.0	N.A.[a]			
	Liberal	17	6	35	105–220	170.5	1460	.88	.29	.81
	PC	38	16	42	131–217	179.6	650			

[a] Not available for ethical reasons. See Note 12.

what higher than our returns indicate. But the distortion is not equal in all parties, because where the response rates were highest (among the NDP in all four cases), there is accordingly less room for distortion. Distortion will be greatest among the underresponding right-wing parties, whose high Highs particularly tended, we infer, not to answer the survey.

In other words, the very large differences we have found between left-wing and right-wing Canadian provincial legislators probably still *underestimate* the difference that exists. The true NDP means are probably higher than we found, but the true Tory or Social Credit averages would jump even more, it appears, if we obtained responses from the entire caucus.

Conclusions. Assuming our hesitations are unjustified, and bearing in mind the implications of the self-selection bias, some conclusions seem unavoidable.

1. The content of the RWA Scale is highly organized in the minds of these lawmakers. Sentiments of authoritarian submission, authoritarian aggression, and conventionalism *covary more strongly among these legislators than in any other group I have tested.* The legislators may or may not realize they have ideologies about the social issues raised on the RWA Scale, but these underlying ideologies probably differentiate them more strongly, within their legislature, than anything else save party label.

2. There are very large—nay, enormous—differences in the levels of right-wing authoritarianism found in the left-wing and right-wing legislative caucuses we have sampled. The eta-squared values in the last column of Table 8 average .75, which is a stronger relationship than one finds between height and weight, race and income, gender and aggression, or almost anything else you can think of that has been discovered in the behavioral sciences. The difference obviously extends over the whole content of the RWA Scale. It is not simply that right-wing politicians in these studies are more conventional than leftists. Indeed, the largest differences occur on items tapping authoritarian aggression and authoritarian submission.

3. The range of scores in a "centrist" party such as the Liberals tends to be very large.

4. The overall relationship between authoritarianism and caucus membership depends on whether there is a centrist party. Such parties, when successful at the polls, send both "High RWA" and "Low RWA" politicians to the legislature. If the province is politically polarized, however (to reinforce the obvious with some empirical data), the legislature is apt to contain two camps of lawmakers with virtually no common ground.

Fallacies to Be Avoided. All these conclusions concern *relative* differences. Let me repeat an earlier observation that the data do not indicate that conservative politicians are "extremely authoritarian"—for two reasons. First, with one exception (Manitoba), their provincial averages were rather ordinary for persons of their age and educational attainment. (According to some theories of leadership, they would best represent the citizenry.)[14] The maximum score possible on the RWA Scale is (30 × 9 =) 270. The highest Tory score obtained was 217. I am not saying that a lawmaker with a score that high is not alarming; Hitler's score, according to one group of judges, would have been about 230 or 240 (*RWA*, p. 210). But most of the 46 conservative lawmakers in these samples scored well within normal ranges, and some scored lower.

And that is the second point: there *were* low-scoring conservatives. Lawmaker X may be a conservative and one of the staunchest defenders of democratic freedoms in history—as many have been.

Finally, I think it would be a mistake to think that because low RWA Scale scores were most concentrated on the political left in these studies, so necessarily is wisdom. Or to believe that any politician is immune to "political realities" and governed just by attitudes or principles. Or that some politicians will not do or say almost anything to get elected or reelected. Or that because all the NDP respondents were Lows, a leftist government could never infringe on democratic freedoms—or a right-wing government probably would.

Right-Wing Authoritarianism and Political Party Membership Among American Legislators

As I mulled over the Canadian results, I wondered whether the same strong relationships would be found in the United States, with its different political system, its political culture, regional differences, and two "centrist" parties. I therefore sent off surveys to four state legislatures during the spring of 1986, following the procedures described above.

Because there are so many lawmakers in the bicameral state legislatures (and since I was buying all those American postage stamps with weakling 71-cent Canadian dollars), I usually sent my requests to just the "upper house" of each capitol, reasoning that these legislators were more comparable to the Canadian lawmakers I had already tested.

Since the United States has not only a political East and West but also a North and South, I tried to get responses from the four points of the compass by sending surveys to the Minnesota, California, Mississippi, and Connecticut senates, plus a few other places I shall describe.

Minnesota Senators. The 67-seat Minnesota Senate was composed of 42 members of the Democratic Farm Labor party, and 25 Independent Republicans at the time. I eventually received completed surveys from 16 Democrats and 9 Republicans, a relatively good return rate that struck me as quite neighborly.

The mean intercorrelation of these 25 senators' responses to the RWA Scale was .39, producing an alpha of .95.

Democrats' scores ranged from a very low 47 to an incredibly high 248, averaging 146.3, with a huge variance of 2526. The nine Republicans ranged from 128 to 199, with a mean of 160.7 and variance of 408. With their considerable overlap (nine Democrats scored higher than the lowest Republican, and one scored higher than any Republican) and the enormous variance of the Democratic scores, there was no way this difference could approach statistical significance. Apparently authoritarianism, though definitely present, is quite *un*related to party affiliation in the Minnesota Senate.

So much for universal truths.

California Legislators. Because California is the most populous state in the Union, and because it has one of the smallest legislatures, I reasoned these lawmakers would be busier than any others I sampled. I decided, therefore, to send surveys to both chambers of the California legislature in order to obtain usable numbers.

At the time, the Democrats controlled the California Senate by a 25–15 margin and the Assembly by 47–33 seats. (Each member of the California Assembly thus represents about three times as many persons as a Canadian member of Parliament; each senator, about six times as many. One hopes that these folks have, not just aides, but staffs of them.)

I eventually received, after two solicitations, completed forms from nine Democratic and six Republican members of the Assembly and four Democratic and two Republican senators. It was clear from handwritten notes that some of the 21 forms were completed by legislators, but the possibility that some were answered by assistants cannot be dismissed.

The mean interitem correlation of responses to the RWA Scale was .52 (surpassing the record set by the British Columbia legislators), producing an alpha reliability of .97.

The 13 Democrats ranged from an absolutely astonishing 33 to 189, averaging 115.3, with another mammoth variance of 2285. (As one can judge from the mean, most of the Democrats were low Lows, reminding one of the Canadian New Democrats. Six scored 100 or lower; there was a minority "wing" of 178, 186, and 189 among them.) The Republicans, in turn, ranged from 137 to 232, with a mean of 175.5 ($s^2 = 894$). Thus there was overlap between the parties' scores, though much less than in Minnesota. The Republican mean was significantly higher than the Democrats', with $F = 10.1$. Eta-squared for the sample was .35, a sizable relationship in the behavioral sciences but still not nearly so strong as that found in Canadian "two party" legislatures.

Republicans scored higher than Democrats on all 30 of the RWA Scale items, significantly so in 20 instances. The *non*-significant differences occurred on Items 1, 3, 4, 8, 11, 12, 15, 16, 17, and 21. The largest differences occurred on statements 20 ("The self-righteous 'forces of law and order'"), 30 ("good old-fashioned physical punishment"), 28 ("Communists"), 18 ("atheists"), and 19 ("young people sometimes get rebellious ideas")—mainly authoritarian aggression and authoritarian submission items again.

Mississippi Legislators. The Mississippi Senate in the spring of 1986 consisted of 49 Democrats and 4 Republicans. Thirteen of the former and one of the latter were kind enough to complete the survey I sent them. To supplement the possible Republican sample, I also sent requests off to the (few) Republican senators in the Louisiana, Alabama, and Georgia senates. One Republican from each of the last two states responded.

The correlations among responses to the RWA items averaged .34 among these 16 legislators, producing an alpha of .94. The Mississippi Democrats' authoritarianism scores ranged from 146 to 245, averaging a high 210.1 with a variance of 892. For what it is worth, the three Republicans (from three different states) ranged precisely 100 points, from 112 to 212. Their average was 175.0, with a hefty variance of 3003. The difference between the two parties was, with such small *N*'s, not statistically significant.

Connecticut Legislators. I received six replies from the relatively small Connecticut Senate, all from Republicans, who controlled the upper chamber 24 to 12. The mean intercorrelation among responses to the RWA Scale was .48, with a corresponding alpha of .97. The six scores ranged from 108 to 209, with a mean of 138.0 ($s^2 = 1313$). With no Democrats for comparison, we can only observe that this (small sample) "eastern Republican" mean was noticeably lower than that obtained from Republicans in Minnesota, California, and the South.

Conclusions. For my money, the most interesting finding among these 68 American state legislators was the consistency of their responses to the RWA Scale. The average of their inter-item correlations (following *Z*-transformation) was .47, exceeding the .41 found among their Canadian counterparts, which itself was about *twice* that found among my usual parent samples. This consistency was most notable, obviously, among the very low-scoring lawmakers, such as we found in Canada, and among the very high-scoring ones as well, who did not appear as often up north. A number of the returned surveys had the " + 4's" and " – 4's" marked on the sheet just as if the lawmaker were reciting his catechism.

So although one would never realize this to look at it, the RWA Scale apparently taps a basic ideological dimension among these politicians. It may be more fundamental than the "liberal/conservative" dimension typically invoked to explain political philosophies. Or, alternatively, it appears to be a more precise, and certainly more operational, definition of what the basic "left/right" dimension really is.

Which has been discovered quite accidentally. Do you remember where the RWA Scale came from? Studies of Manitoba university students in the early 1970s indicated that three traits (authoritarian submission, authoritarian aggression, and conventionalism) tended to covary. And they have since covaried in every study I know of, studies done in Canada, the United States, West Germany, South Africa, and Australia. But these traits *especially* covary in the North American legislators we have been discussing. Is it not interesting?

In the American samples, however, the only justified generalization one can draw about party membership and authoritarianism is that no generalization is justified. This contrasts sharply with the Canadian data, where several patterns were discernible. Perhaps the small sample sizes are to blame; American legislators were probably less motivated to help a Canadian researcher, and they were undoubtedly busier to boot. But the lack of overriding structure was not entirely unexpected. There appear to be strong regional differences, and in their local contexts both Democrats and Republicans appear to select a wide diversity of candidates. Only the California legislature (of the four studied) appears to be divided along *relatively* sharp unauthoritarian/authoritarian lines.

I do not know that this general lack of association would be found everywhere in the United States. I recall that *students* at all six of the scattered state universities where I tested in the 1970s showed significant (if small) Democrat/Republican differences. But if you want a thumbnail summary of the overall lack of association between authoritarianism and party affiliation among the American lawmakers who completed my survey, consider the following. The "33" produced by a member of the California Assembly was the lowest RWA Scale score I have ever collected—and I have collected a few. And the "248" obtained from the Minnesota senator was one of the highest I have ever seen. And both were produced by Democrats.

We should remember that although we did not find a consistent RWA-party relationship among these American legislators, we did discover a considerable amount of right-wing authoritarianism. Some (successful!) politicians in both these democracies appear strongly committed to an authoritarian ideology akin to fascism. Others are strongly opposed to this ideology; still other lawmakers hold it moderately or indifferently. In Canada this ideology has been found to be associated with party affiliation. In the United States there appears to be little connection to party labels, but the authoritarian predisposition is nevertheless definitely present.

In closing, we should note the simple model of the relationship between North American politicians' personalities and their party affiliation that emerges from these data. Persons who are interested in entering politics will naturally vary in their degree of right-wing authoritarianism. In Canada, which has a generally identifiable "left to right" political spectrum, Lows will tend to be attracted to (and presumably welcomed by) the New Democratic party, while Highs will tend to have the same inclinations toward the Progressive Conservatives. Of course, other factors affect this plighting, not the least of which will be the party's prospects at the polls, the "availability" of the nomination, family traditions, and "connections."

But the "centrist" party, the Liberals, hosts a larger array of Lows, Moderates, and Highs than either of the other two; it may be the hallmark of a party intent on dominating the political center. Similarly, in the United States, where both parties strive to capture the middle ground, both the Republicans and Democrats attract (and present to the voters) quite a range of RWA Scale scores in their candidates. An aspirant politician's choice will probably be more affected by regional factors, family ties, personal opportunism, and so on than by ideology, compared with Canada, since *each* American party is a marked coalition, with identifiable left and right wings.

It would be interesting to see whether the RWA Scale scores of lawmakers in Western Europe, with their many diverse political parties, show the "Canadian" pattern described above.

Is There an Authoritarian on the Left?

We shall end this chapter on politics by asking a question that is nearly as old as research on authoritarianism itself: Is there an "authoritarian on the left"? I shall say at the outset that, except in a trivial sense, I do not know the answer. But I believe the accumulated findings with the RWA Scale do place some constraints on the possibilities.

A Little Background

Shortly after *The Authoritarian Personality* was published, Shils (1954) noted that Fascist governments were quite "left wing" in their regulation of the economy and that Communist governments were quite fascist in their suppression of individual freedom and demands for submission to the party's authority. He argued that the Berkeley researchers had misjudged political reality by expecting "the complete democrat" at one end of the F Scale, with the fascist at the other end. At the left end of the political spectrum, Shils argued, reposed an authoritarian impressively like the authoritarian on the right.

At a minimal, semantic level, I think Shils is holding all the aces. Dictionaries tend to give, as their first definition of *authoritarian*, something like "favorable to the principle of authority, as opposed to that of individual liberty" (*The Oxford English Dictionary*) or "favoring a principle of often blind submission to authority as opposed to individual freedom of thought and action" (*Webster's Third New International Dictionary*). Communists certainly have their authorities and seem to want us all to obey them, at great cost to individual liberty. So if you will settle for a generic, "no brand" answer wrapped in yellow (or black and white) paper, there are authoritarians on the left and right and probably in the middle too.

Behavioral scientists, however, have usually meant something more involved, more dynamic, and psychologically more powerful by *authoritarian* than simple submission to *an* authority. And so the real issue has been "Does the same kind of *personality* become a Communist *or* a Fascist, or both (like Mussolini), but not a 'democrat'?" We can clearly label some leftist extremists as violent, dogmatic, and hell-bent on imposing their dictatorship. Can we also call them "authoritarian" in the same sense and with the same empirical justification we can muster when applying the term to various right-wing extremists?

The Possibilities

Roger Brown (1965, p. 529) observed cogently, as usual, that in its first stab at the truth the human mind tries to dichotomize the world of political ideologies. We who cherish democracy would thus prefer to have all our enemies in one camp, at the opposite pole from us on some "good guy"/"bad guy" dimension.

I. It would therefore be cognitively satisfying to find a factor on which Fascist and Communist types both scored very high when "democrats" are low. This is what Shils had in mind, and Rokeach (1960) after him. A good and proper "authoritarianism" scale, according to this model, would range from democrat to Fascist/Communist.

II. An alternative model has us clustered about the golden mean of some dimension, halfway between enemies at each extreme. This more complicated model is inherently less satisfying because it seems analogous to saying that a moderate amount of virtue is better than a lot. The "Berkeley researchers," who were accused of a leftist bias, seemed to build along these lines and thought Communists would be extremely "unauthoritarian."

(A third possibility proposes a dimension that ranges from democrat to authoritarian, as Model I states, but also proposes that in different countries different kinds of people join the Communist party. Communists in countries such as Canada and the United States will be very *un*submissive to the established authorities; they will favor free speech, the right to dissent, and so on, and thus they will be "democrats." In places such as the Soviet Union and Poland, however, Communists will be opposed to these things and so be highly authoritarian.)

Examples of Models I and II

Are there plausible examples of Model I differences between democracies and Fascist and Communist states? Certainly: the importance of the individual versus the dominance of the state; personal liberty versus totalitarianism; rule by elected representatives versus dictatorship. On a more psychological level, Eysenck (1954) proposed that Fascists and Communists are both tough-minded, compared with tender-minded democrats. The evidence he provided was anything but convincing, however (*RWA*, pp. 80–89). Rokeach (1960), in turn, suggested Fascists and Communists are both dogmatic, while the rest of us are more open-minded. I am quite prepared to believe this. But Communists (in Western countries) have usually scored low, not high, on Rokeach's Dogmatism Scale, a finding that indicts either the theory, the scale, the research methodology, or the sample (as noted above, Fascists and Communists in democracies may be very different kinds of people from party members in Fascist and Communist countries).

The outstanding example of Model II is the frequently used "liberal/conservative" dimension, at one end of which sit the Communists favoring a revolutionary restructuring of economic systems, wealth, conventions, and so on, while at the other end sit right-wing extremists determined to preserve traditional systems, customs, institutions, and so on at all costs. Some writers have called this the most basic factor underlying social attitudes (Wilson, 1973) and even the only ideological factor present in the attitude field (Eysenck, 1954). Whether or not it is that fundamental, no one can deny its common use by the news media, behavioral scientists, and politicians themselves to conceptualize political positions.

Recent Developments

Controversy over the existence of the left-wing authoritarian continues to the present. In 1980 Stone concluded the left-wing authoritarian was a myth. He cited Dogmatism Scale findings in several studies: that by Rokeach (1960) with British university students, that by Barker (1963) with American university students, an impressive study by DiRenzo (1967) involving 124 members of the Italian House of Deputies, and a compelling investigation by Knutson (1974) of the governing bodies of six American political parties (ranging from the Communist party to the neo-Nazi American Socialist White People's party). In all these investigations, "left-wingers" scored the same as or significantly lower than "moderates" or "right-wingers." If we only knew what the Dogmatism Scale measures (its interitem correlations average .10 or less, even with unidirectional wording), these findings might convince us there is at least no dogmatic authoritarian on the left in these countries.

Eysenck (1981) took Stone's paper to task on several points, some of which may be appropriate (Communists show prejudice, such as Soviet anti-Semitism) but most of which seem off the mark (more unconvincing data about "tough-mindedness"; saying Stone would have reached a different conclusion if he had considered European evidence). Much of the argument concerns whose biases are leading whom down the garden path. But the only data Eysenck cited that purportedly show Communists score high on a measure of *authoritarianism* were obtained by Coulter (1953, cited in Eysenck and Coulter, 1972), who found that her sample of Communists scored significantly higher on the F Scale than a (controversial) control group but significantly *lower* than a group of fascists (*RWA*, pp. 70–71). The results thus did *not* support Eysenck's position in the 1950s, but he has cited them for over 30 years as if they did.[15]

What Can the RWA Scale Tell Us?

The RWA Scale, as its name makes clear, was invented to measure fascist authoritarianism. Thus, for example, "authoritarian submission" was defined as submission to *established* authority (not, say, to a "preferred authority," which could include Karl Marx and Chairman Mao). I had no preconception about what the other end of the dimension would be, and I have simply characterized low scorers as "unauthoritarians" or "Lows" (not "left-wing authoritarians," "Communists," or "democrats").

But we now know quite a bit about Lows—as much, in fact, as we know about Highs, from whom they differ so much. Lows strike me as being fair-minded, evenhanded, tolerant, nonaggressive persons. Time and again they have indicated outrage at government injustices, regardless of the government's political stripes or the identity of its victims. They do not maintain the double standards we find among Highs. Similarly, Lows have shown greater fairness in punishing criminals, being less swayed by who the criminal was than Highs are. They are more likely to make moral judgments on the basis of "individual principles of conscience" in Kohlberg-style situations (*RWA*, pp. 192–196). They were less aggressive than others in my bogus "effects of shock on learning" experiment. Lows seem extremely disinclined to join "posses," whether the quarry is a left-winger or a right-. They score low on my prejudice scale. They are not self-righteous; they do not feel superior to persons with opposing opinions. They are not mean-spirited.

They probably make awful soldiers and terrible housewives and rebellious clergy. But they do not remind me at all of doctrinaire Communists who think they have a full nelson on the truth and an armlock on history and who want to close down churches, make us all memorize their particular ideology, control the news media, and punish those who deviate from the party line. Low RWAs strike me instead as good democratic citizens. They would probably be just as opposed to Communist totalitarianism as Fascist totalitarianism.

So empirically the RWA Scale appears to run from "democrat" to "Fascist." I do not think "an authoritarian impressively like the authoritarian on the right" reposes on the left end of the RWA Scale. Rather the contrary.

So Is There an Authoritarian on the Left?

In the generic, no-brand, no-personality sense, the answer is almost certainly yes. Communists have authorities they would insist everyone obey, just as Fascists do, just as many others do. But this has not been the issue among behavioral scientists.

Going beyond that initial treatment of the issue, what is the evidence for Model I? Are Communists and Fascists in a democracy both high in the same personality trait of authoritarianism, while democrats are low? *If* such Communists score high on the RWA Scale, then yes. But I doubt Communists (in Western democracies) will ever score high on a scale that measures *right-wing* authoritarianism. Who would expect Canadian Communists to say we should obey the established authorities, crush dissenters, and reshape unconventional people?

Accordingly, over the years I have captured about 20 students in my Survey net who said they were "Communists." They have usually scored low on the RWA Scale (though not extremely low).

To prove Shils's position, which, of course, may be correct, we need a firm, clear conceptualization of "general authoritarianism," a valid technique for its measurement, and convincing data. Presently we have none of these. I therefore think Shils's proposal lacks empirical support. I do not see why anyone should presently accept it.

What about Model II? Are Communists and Fascists on opposite poles of an authoritarianism spectrum, with democrats in the middle? Apparently not. If staunch democrats had scored middlin' on the RWA Scale, and some suitable sample of Communists much lower, Model II would have been confirmed. But this has not been my experience. Most *really* low RWA subjects I have encountered in Canada have been politically independent, or NDP supporters, or Liberals. But in the final analysis, it all may depend on what nation we are discussing and whom we call a Communist.

So we are left with a disconfirmed Model I and an unsubstantiated Model II. At the moment, the only empirically anchored "authoritarianism" dimension I know of, the RWA Scale, appears to run from democrat to Fascist, not democrat to Fascist/Communist, not Communist to democrat to Fascist. The "third possibility" mentioned a few pages ago may prove the best.

Accordingly, I would suggest in closing that the clearest case of an "authoritarian on the left" today might be found in the Soviet Union. But it is a right-wing authoritarian, only figuratively "on the left." That is, I rather expect that dissidents within the Soviet Union would score low on the RWA Scale, and hard-line, un-"glasnosted" Soviet Communists would end up on the *Animal Farm*, with Hitler and Joe McCarthy right next door. If this turned out to be true, the "third" model proposed a few pages back would seem to explain most of the observations. But the necessary study has not yet been done.

NOTES

1. Some readers might assume that because I am so concerned about right-wing authoritarianism, I must be a left-winger myself. But (if you will tolerate some self-revelation) I would characterize myself as a moderate, very independent, and cynical. I find *some* merit in most sides of a controversy, and I have been wrong too many times in my life to be enthralled by the dogmatic certainties of the far left. I also remember the late 1960s and early '70s, when sanctimonious leftist revolutionaries were destroying professors' lifetime research as they saw fit. (It was the only time I feared for my own data archives, which, of course, could only have been accumulated in a stable, supportive, and protective organization.)

   But just for the record, I have never been a member of the Communist party or any other revolutionary (or nonrevolutionary) political party/group. I did know a Communist once and spent an evening listening to his ideas. And mightily bored I was.

   I don't even score particularly low on the RWA Scale, for someone who went to school for 20 years. My major psychometric abnormality shows up on the Edwards Personal Preference Schedule, where I ring the bell at the top of the pole on the "need Autonomy" subscale. Which has something to do with my being an independent, I suspect, and may even explain the field I have chosen to plow for the past 20 years.

   As for cynicism, if science (among other disciplines) is dedicated to discovering the truth, and religion is devoted to finding God, politics is the art of acquiring and using power—toward which truth and godliness are very often irrelevant.
2. As a group Lows are slightly more interested in politics than Highs ($r \approx -.10$). Lows are also a *little* better informed about "current affairs" and politics. For example, 59 percent of 167 student Lows knew in September 1986 that Canada was a member of both the British Commonwealth and NATO, compared with 50 percent of 165 Highs ($z = 1.65$; $p < .10$). Lows also scored higher on the other three questions asked, knowing better the current party composition of the House of Commons (58 percent to 43 percent), that of the Manitoba Legislative Assembly (58 percent to 51 percent), and the name of the premier of British Columbia (27 percent to 21 percent). Lows' average score (50 percent) was significantly (if quite modestly) higher than Highs' (41 percent) ($z = 3.38$; $p < .001$).

3. The reader may wonder about the political preferences of these students. During the early 1970s Manitoba students preferred the Liberal party by a wide margin over its federal rivals. By the late '70s, however, the Conservatives gained the lead, and as late as 1986 they drew more support than the Liberals and NDP combined. So there were more Tory supporters in this "House of Commons" experiment than any other kind.
4. In this study the name of each legislator was typed at the top of the survey, and he or she was asked to tear it off if anonymity was desired. Most did, so no names were placed on the questionnaires in subsequent surveys of lawmakers. But each form was discreetly marked to indicate the caucus to which the recipient belonged. This proved unnecessary, however, as all respondents marked their party affiliation (accurately) in the place requested—except one Canadian legislator who said he belonged to "all caucuses."
5. These were tumultuous times in the Manitoba legislature. The two parties were engaged in a very acrimonious debate over French-language rights, which reached unprecedented dimensions a few months later (see Note 22 of Chapter Five). Moreover, the Conservatives were in the process of selecting a new leader. Either factor could have made the legislators hesitant to answer an "attitude survey" from a local professor.
6. The first two items on the survey were "throwaways" designed to help respondents avoid response sets by making a strongly positive and a strongly negative answer at the beginning. Item 1 read, "The number of nuclear weapons in the world should be reduced," and Item 2 went, "The rest of Canada, as a whole, would be better off if Quebec became an independent country."

   The precaution was probably unnecessary. As the very high internal consistency of their responses indicates, legislators do not seem susceptible to "yea-saying" or "nay-saying." They appear to read things quite carefully. Whenever I made a typograpical error on a survey, a number of the returns would come back with the error corrected, usually in black ink from a fine-tipped pen. It was very impressive.

   Did you notice I misspelled *typographical* above? Your elected representative probably would have.
7. I recently obtained, through the kindness of Professor William F. Stone of the University of Maine at Orono, an unpublished study by the late Jeanne Knutson (1974) that reports a relationship nearly as strong; and interestingly, it concerns virtually the same issue.

Knutson managed to get active members of six political parties in Los Angeles County to complete a very long battery of psychological tests. The parties were (from left to right) Communist ($N=11$), Peace and Freedom ($N=40$), Democratic ($N=21$), Republican ($N=11$), American Independent ($N=11$), and Nazi ($N=13$). This rank-order alignment of the parties correlated most highly (.83) with members' scores on the California F Scale. The party (item) means were 1.49, 1.62, 1.99, 3.23, 4.29, and 4.76 respectively. As noted later, Rokeach's Dogmatism Scale also systematically differentiated the parties, but not nearly so strongly ($r=.50$).

8. In February 1984 I sent each member of the legislature a general summary of the results, indicating the average response *to each item* for the whole sample of 16. No one asked me anything about the results, such as "What does this mean?" or "Did the two parties answer the survey differently?" I take this as further evidence that no one answered for political gain. I think if the NDP had known what the scale measures and had orchestrated the results, they might have asked for the data when they were fighting for their lives during the French-language debate a few months later or during the next election.
9. The Conservatives present a classic example of the fallibility of general attitude measures such as the RWA Scale (Fishbein and Ajzen, 1975). At the same time that they were agreeing *in general* on my survey that citizens should support their government, they were encouraging a massive public protest against the NDP's French-language proposals.
10. Besides the RWA Scale, the legislators answered several items included as part of my efforts to improve the instrument. They also answered, as Item 40, the following: "French speakers should be entitled to all the language rights outside Quebec that English speakers want within Quebec." All the NDP respondents either "strongly agreed" or "very strongly agreed" with this statement. Only one of the six Conservatives agreed at all, however, and only "moderately" at that.

    Following the RWA Scale and its associated items, I asked the legislators to give their opinions about "university professors in our province" along ten dimensions—for example, "How many professors do very little work for the salaries they receive?" In general their opinions were modestly positive, with little difference between the parties. However, the Tory legislators thought that about *half* the Manitoba professors "have definite Socialist or

Communist leanings"; the NDP mean was "20 percent." And NDP politicians thought, on the average, that about 50 percent of the faculty should have tenure, compared with a mean of 6 percent among Tory respondents.

11. Some months later Ontario voters went to the polls and gave the Liberals a plurality but not a majority of seats. With the third-place NDP holding the balance of power, which coalition would you suspect was politically and attitudinally most comfortable?

    Similarly, the *federal* Liberals have occasionally formed minority governments with the aid of the NDP, who have never made a similar arrangement with the Tories.

12. Since there were only two NDP members of the New Brunswick legislature, who, like everyone else, were promised personal confidentiality, I cannot give the range or variance of their scores. (The only value given, the mean, could have occurred in many, many ways.)

13. The legislators in Ontario, British Columbia, and New Brunswick also answered my item on "French-language rights" described in Note 10. All the Ontario lawmakers except five Tories and three Liberals agreed that French speakers should have all the language rights outside Quebec that English speakers want within Quebec. Two Social Credit members and one NDPer in British Columbia also did not agree. Seven (of 16) New Brunswick Tories and one Liberal also disagreed to one extent or another.

14. Although this may be analogous to saying we should elect people whose IQs are 100. Another theory of leadership says the persons who best represent the *ideals* of an organization will make the best leaders. The NDP might prefer this line of reasoning in the present circumstances. The Liberals, on the third hand, would probably argue that leadership which takes into account the widest range of opinions and positions will serve the democratic process best.

    Ah, theories that are almost impossible to test! Like some politicians, they are enough to make one very independently inclined.

15. Offering a different point of view, Ray (1983) argued that since his measure of Directiveness is uncorrelated with liberalism/conservatism, and since F Scale scores show little correlation with voting preference, half the authoritarians in society are on the left. The reader can probably see several alternative interpretations of these facts, however; if not, see Note 2 of Chapter One. (And actually, one of the few things the F Scale *did* do with some regularity was correlate with political conservatism: *RWA*, pp. 70–79, and also Note 7 above.)

8

Protecting Ourselves from Authoritarianism

You may not be surprised to learn that I find little that is commendable in right-wing authoritarianism. Oh, I am far too "straight" myself to be bothered much by conventionalism; and society functions smoothly because people follow norms. I also agree that in situations such as World War II, unusual submission to authority benefits a democracy in the long run, and aggression in the name of that authority is certainly necessary. But social psychologists have long realized the power that situations have over individuals. I am not worried that "the Rooskies will be dictating terms in the Rose Garden" if the highest High in the United States scores only 200 on the RWA Scale. Democracies have a pretty good record at defending themselves against attacks from without.

The larger danger, inherently, comes from within, where extremists on the left and extremists on the right will use the freedoms guaranteed to all to take liberty from everyone but themselves. The research reported in this book is concerned with the threat from the right, which I consider the greater in our present circumstances.[1] It deals with the large segment of our populations who do not require special situations to act in authoritarian ways but who do so every day. I see them as a threat to my freedom, to yours, and to our children's.

Susceptibility to Antidemocratic Appeals

Let me give you one more example of this threat. If you ask North American authoritarians whether they believe in democracy, individual liberty, and justice for all, they will usually insist they do, strongly. But it appears to be a superficial, reflexive endorsement, based on thousands of oaths and salutes that have substituted ritual for understanding and commitment. So unexamined is this endorsement, one is inevitably reminded of McGuire's (1964) finding that "cultural truisms" are surprisingly vulnerable to sudden, unexpected attack. So in 1986 I asked 519 Manitoba students to react to a (bogus) letter to the editor attacking Canada's "Bill of Rights":

> One of the biggest mistakes Canada ever made was to adopt the Charter of Rights and Freedoms in 1981. This document has set more criminals free, encouraged more perversion, and in general caused more trouble than anyone could have imagined. For example, the Charter says everyone should have freedom of speech; so every nut in the land is mouthing off now, and no one can shut them up. It says there should be freedom of the press, and so raw pornography is on sale in every neighborhood across Canada. It says everyone should be entitled to a fair trial, and so lawbreakers in every province are getting off scot-free thanks to lawyers paid for by you and me through the legal-aid system. It says everyone should be able to pursue happiness, and so homosexuals demand the "right" to get married to each other. It says there should be freedom of religion, and so "Moonies" and Scientologists and all sorts of other cults are popping up all over the place. In short, every freedom given by the Charter has led to abuse and trouble.

> The biggest problem with the Charter is that it gives rights to everyone, no matter who he is or what he does. But we learned back in school, when schools still taught you things, that rights carry with them responsibilities. The responsible people do not need the Charter; it just gives privileges to those who haven't earned them. We had freedom of speech, et cetera, in Canada before 1981, and most people used it properly, not like today. Now it's part of the Constitution, and any judge anywhere can say it's a person's right to be a drug addict or to have an abortion, and the rest of us have to pay that person's hospital bills as well.
>
> The Charter was made up by politicians making deals in back rooms, not by the people of Canada. You and I never voted for it; it was railroaded through. It should be repealed immediately.

After subjects had read this thinly veiled attack on democratic guarantees, full of oversimplifications, distortions, and outright lies, they indicated on a 0–6 basis how much sense the letter made to them. You may be glad to learn that, overall, the letter appeared only *mildly* sensible to the students ($\overline{X} = 2.46$). But RWA Scale scores correlated .42 with positive reactions to the attack on the Charter, and most of the 129 responding Highs rated the arguments "moderately" ($N = 32$), "definitely" (26), "quite" (26), or "extremely sensible" (9). RWA Scale scores also correlated .45 with agreement that the Charter should be repealed, most Highs at least "moderately" agreeing.

Thus commitment to democracy appears very shallow among right-wing authoritarians, their often showy patriotism notwithstanding. Think of all the times American segregationists said the Pledge of Allegiance, with their hands over their hearts, and never thought for a second what the words "with liberty and justice for all" meant.

Right-wing authoritarians are ready for the next Hitler. And there will always be a supply of would-be fascist dictators available, I am afraid—twisted, ruthless demagogues, but clever as well. You and I both know the appeals the next Hitler will make to rally, organize, and mobilize the authoritarians in our society—the kind of lies he will tell, the fears he will fan, the dark impulses he will call upon.

Lest I become exactly the kind of alarmist I am speaking of, let me quickly add that I think we are in no immediate danger, for North Americans are presently protected by splintering among the right-wing extremists, the effectiveness of our judicial systems when these extremists become violent, and the stability of our economic and political systems. I passionately desire that these fortunate circumstances prevail forever and that all my research turns out to be just "academic." But in case they do not, my hope is to thin the ranks of the ready followers. And that calls for some applied science, some "behavioral engineering" in the real world.

Some clarifications are necessary here. Many people understandably fear the psychologist's ability to turn us into automatons. Actually, if the general public understood how hard it is for psychologists to help people do what they *want* to do, as in cases of neuroses, cigarette smoking, eating habits, and even studying, it would see how far we still are from Aldous Huxley's *Brave New World*. I want "mind control" even less than a fascist state, so I am not going to advocate anything as controversial as electrode implants, drug control, sleep learning, or subliminal stimulation.

But I want to shape the upper quartile of the RWA Scale distribution away from authoritarianism, and I believe the techniques I openly advocate here are consistent with the practices of a democratic society. I shall avoid the "fight fire with fire" and the "end justifies the means" mentality that can destroy freedom. But if shaping seems unethical to you in any form—well, I would have agreed with you 20 years ago, until I became a teacher and learned that "no shaping" was not only impossible but also one of the worst kinds of manipulation.

Further, I do not wish to shape or control *conservatism* within a democratic society, any more than I would want to limit liberal activity. These are the two necessary forces among a free people, and we must always have a viable choice between the two. I am enough of a liberal to realize there are many, many things wrong, cruel, and unfair in the status quo; and enough of a conservative to appreciate that there are also many things very right and that some of the liberal "cures" will prove ineffective or worse than the disease.

What, then, is the difference between a conservative and a right-wing authoritarian? As I said in Chapter One, the conservative wishes to preserve what is established, social stability, tradition. But among the established traditions and rights of a democratic society are freedom of speech, freedom of opportunity, the right to due process, the principle that no one is above the law, tolerance of others, blind and impartial justice, and so on. A conservative who embraces these is not going to score high on the RWA Scale. Conservatism may naturally be associated with right-wing authoritarianism (as we saw in Chapter Seven), but the two are still distinguishable and not isomorphic.

To cite a concrete example, Richard Nixon's Watergate crisis was largely brought on by a conservative, Republican-appointed federal judge (John Sirica), a conservative senator from North Carolina (Sam Ervin), a conservative special prosecutor from Texas (Leon Jaworski), the conservative members of the Supreme Court who ruled unanimously with the rest of the justices that Nixon had to release subpoenaed evidence, and (at critical junctures in the impeachment process) Senator James Buckley of New York and "Mr. Conservative," Barry Goldwater.

Finally, I do not expect Highs to be pleased at being considered dangerous persons who need to be controlled. After all, they think they are the "good people" in our society, and it is others who are the threat. Well, there are different kinds of threats, but highly submissive, highly aggressive folks who are waiting for the government to point the finger at various groups so they can saddle up and "stomp out the rot" are hardly a blessing to freedom. I am not going to advocate stomping out the authoritarians. But I would like to lessen their fear, lower their self-righteousness, raise their independence, broaden their outlook, increase their charity and acceptance of others, heighten their self-awareness, and do other things to protect them and us from their present inclinations.

Overview

First of all, I shall offer some general observations of ways the educational systems, news media, and religions in our society can help control authoritarianism, based on data we have already considered. Then I shall describe five additional approaches I have also researched:

1. The usefulness of laws for controlling authoritarian behavior.
2. Limiting the appeal of future Hitlers.
3. Keeping national crises from stimulating authoritarianism.
4. The effects of social norms on authoritarians.
5. The results of giving Highs accurate feedback about their authoritarianism.

We shall see that most of these approaches produce modest effects at best; none will bring water from rocks at one stroke. But they might have significant cumulative effects.

Educational, Media, and Religious Contributions

Our model of the personal origins of authoritarianism states that adult RWA Scale scores are shaped during adolescence. I have suggested that most young children have relatively authoritarian attitudes, but these can change appreciably during the teen years. The major reasons for change, ones that basically lower RWA Scale scores, involve certain *experiences* the individual has as he or she progresses toward adulthood. Lows have lots of these experiences (listed in Appendix C). Highs (among entering university students) have had relatively few, apparently because they travel in rather tight circles of similar-minded persons, which keeps them from encountering life's diverse persons and philosophies.

I do not propose that we force Highs to meet gays, dissenters, nontraditional families, and so on. But when authoritarians move out of their normal orbits—when they receive public educations, for example—we should take advantage of the opportunity to modify their extremism. For example, I think we should be creating a greater understanding, love, and appreciation of democracy during secondary education. A publicly educated citizenry ought to be a bulwark against tyranny in a free society. I also would have high school students learn of instances (for example, Watergate, Vietnam, Iran-gate) when public officials proved deceitful, incompetent, and untrustworthy. The next generation deserves more than "patriotic history" if we want it to learn from our mistakes.

You will recall we found that higher education in a public institution had particularly beneficial effects on Highs, so we would seem wise to make such education as available in our country as possible. The data also indicated that courses in the liberal arts seem to have particularly lowered authoritarianism. Perhaps the trend toward highly specialized *under*graduate educations should be reversed somewhat on these grounds.

The media could make a contribution toward safeguarding freedom in our society. Perceptions of a "dangerous world," which are a major instigator of authoritarian aggression, are probably reinforced by accounts of violence among us. These are quite often distorted, and I think we all know why. But as well as selling theater tickets and increasing market share, portraying our society as a highly dangerous place may unnecessarily increase a threat to our basic freedoms—including freedom of speech and freedom of the press.[2]

Finally, religion has also been implicated as a potential source of authoritarianism. It is not for me to say what any religion should teach or practice. But we can point to certain religious behaviors (see the beginning of Chapter Six) that appear to foster fascism. We can ask women and men of good will, "Is this what you wish to do?" And "Can you help us *lower* self-righteousness?"—which, we have seen, is the main releaser of authoritarian aggression. Freedom of religion may someday be at stake if we do not.

Usefulness of Laws for Controlling Authoritarian Behavior

I have no doubt that vigorously enforced laws have powerful effects on behavior. If such laws can make Lows act in discriminatory ways, as they did in Nazi Germany and South Africa, for example, they can also make Highs behave nondiscriminatorily. In fact, authoritarians' everyday hostile impulses toward hated groups are probably greatly inhibited by fear of legal punishment. So in this direct sense, enforced laws protecting minorities and dissenters are quite useful means of controlling authoritarian aggression.

Beyond this obvious coercive power of the law, does it also have a normative, moral impact? That is, does it do any good to pass laws promoting minority rights? Can you legislate brotherhood? Some doubt that you can, and certainly few are going to obey a law they know was passed for "window dressing." But after all, Highs believe they are *the* law-abiding citizens. Can this feature of authoritarians' self-image become a means of controlling their hostility and eventually lessening their prejudices?

The September 1981 Study. I first investigated these issues in a fall 1981 experiment in which 622 students were asked to imagine 20 years had passed and they were in charge of hiring teachers for the Winnipeg School Division. "As you are investigating the background of the best-qualified candidate for a position in a junior high school, you discover by accident that he is a homosexual." *Half* the students were told the government had just passed a law prohibiting discrimination against homosexuals. "In other words, the law requires you to offer the teaching position to the homosexual candidate." They were then asked to indicate, on the checklist below, what they would most probably do in that situation:

____ I would gladly offer him the job, since I agree with such a law. (16) [61]

____ I would offer him the job, though I would hate doing so, because laws are laws and must be obeyed whether one thinks they are right or not. (24) [7]

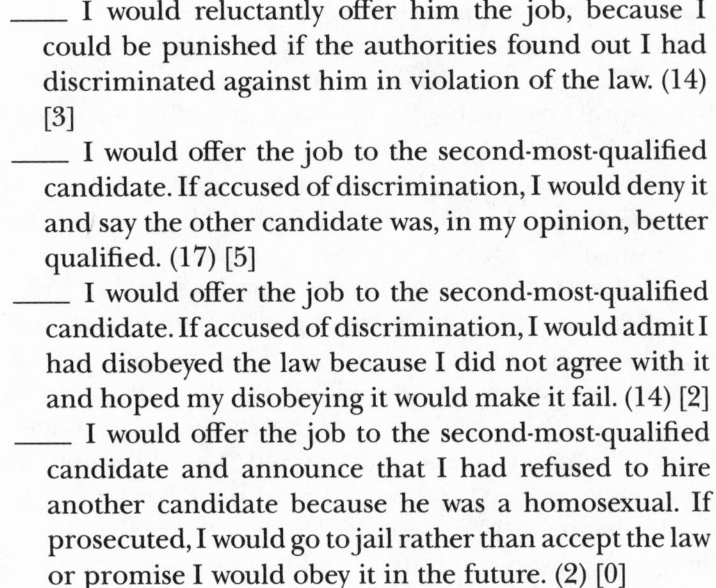

____ I would reluctantly offer him the job, because I could be punished if the authorities found out I had discriminated against him in violation of the law. (14) [3]

____ I would offer the job to the second-most-qualified candidate. If accused of discrimination, I would deny it and say the other candidate was, in my opinion, better qualified. (17) [5]

____ I would offer the job to the second-most-qualified candidate. If accused of discrimination, I would admit I had disobeyed the law because I did not agree with it and hoped my disobeying it would make it fail. (14) [2]

____ I would offer the job to the second-most-qualified candidate and announce that I had refused to hire another candidate because he was a homosexual. If prosecuted, I would go to jail rather than accept the law or promise I would obey it in the future. (2) [0]

Following our usual practice, the numbers in parentheses show how the 87 Highs in the sample responded, and the figures in brackets display the distribution of the 78 Lows. The patterns of responses within the two groups were significantly different (chi-squared = 61.2; $p < .001$).

The reader will not be surprised that most of the Lows (61 of 78 = 78 percent) said they would gladly obey this law since they agree with it. But 71 of the 87 Highs said they would dislike it. What, then, would these Highs do, faced with a personally objectionable law? Their modal response ($N = 24$) was that they would obey it, although they would hate doing so, "because laws are laws and must be obeyed whether one thinks they are right or not." Another 14 said they would obey because of fear of punishment.[3] Seventeen Highs said they would disobey the law but pragmatically cover their tracks by lying about the teacher's qualifications. Only 16 said they would openly disobey the law, through either passive resistance (14) or open civil disobedience (2).

The long and the short of it is, most of the Highs (supposedly) would comply with this law, because they feel laws have a moral imperative or from fear of punishment.

This pattern of High compliance can be contrasted to the behavior of Lows facing the mirror-image situation, as the other half of the sample was told the government had passed a law *prohibiting* the hiring of homosexuals as schoolteachers. Ninety-four percent of the Lows (72 of 77) said they would find such a law repugnant. Only 2 of these 72 repugged Lows said they would obey such a law "because laws are laws. . . ," and 12 others said they would obey out of fear of punishment. Twenty-one Lows said they would hire the homosexual and lie that they had not known about his homosexuality if caught. But the modal response among Lows ($N = 36$) was passive resistance. They would hire the homosexual and, if discovered, "I would admit doing so knowingly because I did not agree with the law and hoped my disobeying it would make it fail." So in a nutshell, only 14 of 72 disagreeing Lows (said they) would comply with the law. Many more indicated they would disobey and resist the government's plans. The overall chi-squared was 53.0 ($p < .001$).

Now, one can seriously doubt that these subjects' check marks represent how they would actually behave in these situations. Highs, we know, tend to portray themselves as the good, morally superior folks and yet have failed in many experiments to act more morally than others. Lows, in turn, may gravely underestimate the power that authorities, group pressure, and self-interest can have over behavior, à la Milgram, à la McCarthyism. Very likely I was collecting "poses" here, statements of how the subjects believed they should act. It would not be too surprising if many Highs quietly disobeyed a progay law. Similarly, many Lows might comply with an antigay law more than they anticipate, rather than go to jail for someone they did not even know. But whether all differences between the two groups would disappear in the "real world" is another matter and is subject to various factors we shall consider later.

The January 1982 Study. I wondered how far the authoritarian's statement that he would obey the law, no matter what, would extend. As we have seen, Highs tend to be very religious, and if the law dictates morality to some authoritarians, so especially does their religion. How would they react to an anti-religion law?

I asked 308 students to imagine they were elementary schoolteachers facing a new education act. Half the students were told the new law completely eliminated all religious instruction in public schools. God could be mentioned only in the context of discussing superstitions. Saying the Lord's Prayer and Bible readings (common practice in Manitoba public schools) were now forbidden. Morality could not be taught in religious terms. Jesus could be described only as a man some people believe lived 2000 years ago. The appearance of life and the human species on earth could be explained only in terms of the theory of evolution.

Students were asked to indicate how they would react to this law, using essentially the same checklist of options provided in the "homosexual teacher" case:

____ I would gladly refrain from giving any religious instruction, because I would agree with such a law. (0) [12]

____ I would reluctantly refrain from giving any religious instruction, though I would hate doing so, because laws are laws and must be obeyed whether one thinks they are right or not. (7) [3]

____ I would reluctantly refrain from giving any religious instruction rather than take the chance of getting caught and punished for breaking the law. (4) [5]

____ I would give religious instruction and take the chance of getting caught. If the authorities accused me of breaking the law, I would say I had made an honest mistake in misinterpreting the curriculum guidelines. (3) [3]

____ I would give religious instruction quietly as a form of "passive resistance." If caught, I would admit I had disobeyed the law because I did not agree with it and hoped my disobeying it would help make it fail. I would be willing to go to jail for my disobedience. (10) [12]

> ____ I would give religious instruction openly as an act of "civil disobedience" of what I consider a bad law. I would join with others and fight the law in the courts. I would go to jail rather than comply with the law. (6) [3]

It can be seen that most of the 30 Highs who faced this dilemma said they would break this law, usually through passive resistance. Clearly I evoked a stronger reaction here than in the case of the homosexual teacher. Still, about a quarter of the Highs said they would hatefully obey the antireligion act because "laws must be obeyed whether one thinks they are right or not."

Most Lows also disagreed with the law (chi-squared = 15.6, $p < .02$). (As we saw in Chapter Six, many Lows are also religious, although few are as intense as most Highs.) Their characteristic reaction to the law was also to resist passively. But only 3 of 38 Lows said they would obey because "laws are laws."

The other half of the sample was told a very *proreligion* law had been passed,

> requiring the strenuous teaching of religion in public schools. Beginning in kindergarten, all children would be taught to believe in God, pray together in school several times each day, memorize the Ten Commandments and other parts of the Bible, learn the principles of "Christian morality," and eventually be encouraged to accept Jesus Christ as their personal savior. The teaching of evolution, among other things, would be downplayed and a religious "creation science" emphasized instead.

As you might guess, right-wing authoritarians liked this law (which would force a particular religious orientation on all children attending public school) much more than Lows did. Nearly half the Highs (20 of 43) said they "would gladly teach this material, because I would agree with such a law," compared with 2 of 38 Lows.[4] The characteristic reaction of Low objectors was passive disobedience (45 percent) or civil disobedience (37 percent). Only one said he would obey because all laws must be obeyed (chi-squared = 38.3; $p < .001$).

Discussion. The data, taken together, offer some hope that we can control authoritarian behavior through laws. High RWA subjects, as one would expect, are more likely than Lows to say they are inclined to obey disagreeable laws. We are talking only about "inclinations" here, not actual compliance (Carlsmith, Ellsworth, and Aronson, 1976). But provided laws are benign, the authoritarian is leaning in the direction we would choose.

What factors determine whether this inclination to obey will prevail or be trumped? Clearly the nature of the law itself matters. Although authoritarians may believe one should obey laws in general, it was not hard to devise an act most Highs said they would disobey. A second factor that might prove particularly important for authoritarians' compliance is the perceived social support for disobedience. When one's neighbors, co-workers, and "drinking buddies" oppose a law, Highs may receive a boost to disobey that Lows do not need as much. Third, the public opposition of acknowledged authorities (such as state governors in civil rights matters and church leaders on sex education and birth control) may also particularly encourage the authoritarian to resist.

A fourth factor, mentioned earlier, is the perception of enforcement. One can think of many antidiscrimination laws that did diddly-squat about racist behavior as long as they were just passed for appearances. One can also cite numerous murders and other acts of authoritarian aggression that occurred because their perpetrators believed the law would never be enforced in their case. All too frequently, they were proved right.

But enforced laws can make the authoritarian behave more humanely, especially since Highs seem to fear punishment more than Lows do. And that can have payoffs beyond the immediate benefits to the black family who can buy a house, the Hispanic who gets hired, and the woman who gets promoted. As we have noted before, one reason Highs are Highs is that they travel in tighter self-confirming circles than most of us do. When they meet someone gay, for example, some authoritarians learn from their *personal experiences* to discard their stereotypes. I do not mean they would want their sister to marry one; but laws that put minorities on an equal footing with the majority, especially in situations rife with superordinate goals, can be beneficial in several ways (Allport, 1954; Sherif, 1966; Cook, 1978).

Enforced antidiscrimination laws also give the passively prejudiced person, the individual who discriminates in conformity to local custom, a social excuse for acting fairly: "I don't want to sell them the house, but the law says I have to. Which of you will go to jail for me if I don't?"

I hope the reader can tell from this discussion that I am not in favor of laws outlawing authoritarians—even though Highs might be the first to volunteer for posse duty to hunt themselves down. Instead I am saying that the authoritarian's penchant for obeying the law, whatever it is, can cut two ways. It endangers everyone if malevolent forces make the laws, but it also offers some hope if fair and humane laws protecting democratic rights can be passed. Highs may not like them, but they may also be particularly likely to obey them—and, obeying them, be changed for the better.

For example, let me propose a law that might someday protect our freedoms. This law would require all soldiers, who presently take just an oath of allegiance to their government/constitution, to be specifically instructed that they are *ordered in advance to disobey* any command that would lead to the overthrow of the government. Scheming generals and ambitious colonels do not produce coups by themselves. At the moment, however, we train our soldiers to follow blindly, and there is disturbing evidence that our troops would obey orders from a military commander to overthrow our governments (*RWA*, pp. 274–275). Let's use that obedience, and the authoritarian's submission to the law in general, to protect the highest laws of the land, not endanger them.

Limiting the Appeal of Future Hitlers

I said at the beginning of this chapter that we "enjoy" a constant supply of Hitlers. I did not mean, of course, that there are 94 "Boys from Brazil" stored in warehouses around the world but, rather, that we can always find demagogues on the far right, twisted by prejudice, craving adoration, often thirsting for revenge, who will ruthlessly try to rally the right-wing authoritarians in our society to their terrible cause, while disguising their true purposes with noble phrases and pious appearances. They may not have Hitler's oratorical skills, his extraordinary political acumen, or his devastated historical circumstances to exploit. But these men exist, toiling tirelessly on the radical right, hoping for the social devastation that will give them their big chance.

What can we do to limit their appeal when they emerge from the wings and begin to catch the spotlight? It will not do much good, I fear, to point out to authoritarians that the aspirant leader is a potential dictator who will demand submission to his authority. Nor are future Hitlers likely to lose support among Highs if they are labeled aggressive and belligerent. Highs believe in "strong medicine." But what would happen if the *unconventionality* of such a person were publicized as his movement began to grow?

The January 1983 Study: *Procedure.* I investigated this possibility in a January 1983 experiment involving 474 Manitoba students who, halfway through a booklet, came upon a fake newspaper article. The two-column story was headlined "Is Arnold Gregson to be the first PM of Western Canada?" and described the fictitious leader of a fictitious Western separatist movement. Superimposed on a page from a Winnipeg paper and set in the same type as the surrounding text, the article was accompanied by a photograph of a pleasant-looking middle-aged man wearing a golf cap, giving a "thumbs up" signal.[5] Actually, three versions of the newspaper story were randomly distributed in each testing session. A *control* story described Gregson in socially respectable terms as the leader of the "Western Alienation Alliance." The second version described him as socially *disrespectable*. The third returned his *respectability* and gave him *High RWA* attitudes.

The control story ran as follows.

CALGARY (CP)—If you can't judge a book by its cover, you certainly couldn't tell by looking at him that Arnold Gregson will be the founding father of a new country, Western Canada. But that is precisely what the 53-year-old Alberta businessman is aiming at, and people who know him well say it could all come true someday.

Gregson is the founder of the Western Alienation Alliance, an "umbrella" organization which hopes to unite the many groups which currently are championing Western separatism in Canada. "There are lots of good folks who have the same basic idea," Gregson explains, "and if somebody can get them all together, they'll become the new power in Western Canada." Gregson is not too modest to say that he is just the man to consolidate this movement and drive it forward.

"I am first and foremost my own man," Gregson explains. "I've never belonged to any political party, and I don't owe a thing to any politician . . . except distrust. I was talking about how Ottawa was cheating the West 20 years ago, and now, at last, everybody's beginning to see I was right."

Gregson's struggle to organize the separatist groups from Manitoba to British Columbia contrasts sharply with his own personal background. Born to a prominent family in Calgary and educated for the most part in private schools, he admits he has little to complain about personally. "I know I've had it good. I've been successful in business. I've got a lot of friends in my community, and I've been married to a good woman for nearly 30 years."

Many people in his home town consider Gregson to be one of the pillars of the community, long active in civic affairs and charities. The most common descriptions of Gregson among people who know him seem to be "reliable," "decent," and "respectable."

> Gregson will need considerable skill if he is to unite the separatist movement and fulfill its dream of carving a new country out of Western Canada. The odds against him seem overwhelming, but he does not agree. "Look at what happened when Gord Kesler was elected to the Alberta legislature last year. All the old-style politicians were absolutely stunned. Nobody realized how many thousands of people there are out here who are mad as can be at Ottawa. The farmers are going to be driven under when the Crow rates are changed, the small businessman is already being crushed by incredibly high interest rates, and the federal government has almost destroyed the oil and gas industries in the West with its national energy policies. But most of all, what works folks up is the sense that nobody in Ottawa will ever listen to us. The West is a foreign colony of Ontario, growing its food and sending raw materials to its factories. But they make all the decisions about our lives. And the system that's set up now will never treat us any better."
>
> (SEE "GREGSON"—P. 30)

The "disrespectable" version of the article was exactly the same except that the following was substituted for the fourth and fifth paragraphs.

> Gregson's struggle to organize separatist groups from Manitoba to British Columbia is not the first time he has championed a radical idea. In 1968 he chained himself to the front of Calgary's city hall to protest the taxes levied against his property in the city. He soaked his 1971 income tax return in blood before delivering it to the Revenue Canada office. Through the mid 1970s Gregson was a member of an extremist group which urged Albertans not to pay their mortgages so as "to make

> the big Eastern banks fail." While he now disavows illegal tactics, he has been called a "radical weirdo" and a "degenerate" by his opponents. Many city officials cannot believe that "this nut," as they call him, is being taken seriously.

Finally, the "respectable and High RWA" story ran exactly like the control version, except for the last paragraph, which stated:

> Gregson views the Western separatist movement as a grand opportunity to create a new country with rich natural resources and none of the problems which plague Canada in the 1980s. "We aren't going to make any of the mistakes that muddle-headed liberals have passed into law in Ottawa. Western Canada is going to be an English-speaking, free-enterprising, God-fearing, law-abiding country. People who want to speak French, or measure things in kilograms, or live on welfare, or take drugs and live promiscuously will all be sent back East, where most of them came from in the first place. Criminals can expect a swift punishment, and if somebody gets out of jail and goes back to crime, we're going to lock him up and throw away the key. And we're not going to have a lot of Asians, Africans, and Hottentots moving in either. This rich, beautiful land was put here for us to develop and use. We're the ones who have made it great, and we don't want all the poor people in the world coming over here to sponge off our efforts. We'll take care of ourselves just fine." (SEE "GREGSON"—P. 30)

After reading the article, each subject was asked to rate Arnold Gregson on five −4 to +4 rating scales anchored by the phrases "Quite a bad person–Quite a good person," "Quite worthwhile–Quite worthless," "Quite irrational–Quite rational,"

"Quite admirable–Quite despicable" and "Quite untrustworthy–Quite trustworthy." Summed scores could range from 5 to 45, with 25 perfectly neutral.

Results. An ANOVA of the summed ratings (with appropriate reversals of keying) found a significant main effect for Version ($F = 16.9, p < .001$), no main effect for subjects' Authoritarianism, but the expected significant interaction between the two ($F = 17.2, p < .001$). In other words, the different stories affected subjects' ratings of Arnold Gregson, and the authoritarianism of the subjects determined how they reacted to the particular story they read.

Arnold Gregson's average rating in the control condition was 29.4 ($N = 156$), significantly higher than that obtained when he was disrespectable (24.6; $N = 159$) or respectable and High RWA (26.4; $N = 159$). The latter mean was also significantly higher than the former ($t = 2.49; p < .001$).

The tale of the Version × Authoritarianism interaction is told in Figure 7. One can quickly see that Low and High RWA students evaluated the control Gregson evenly and somewhat positively. The correlation between RWA Scale scores and these ratings for all 156 subjects was .00. But when Gregson had a disrespectable past, Highs' evaluations were significantly lower; his rating also dropped a little among the Lows, but not significantly. The overall correlation was $-.24$ ($p < .01$). When Gregson was respectable and authoritarian, Highs liked him more than they had in the control condition ($t = 1.93; p < .03$ by a one-tailed test), whereas Lows disliked him much more.[6] The correlation between RWA Scale scores and evaluations of this Arnold Gregson for the 159 subjects involved was .48.

Our interest lies in the significant drop in Highs' evaluations when Gregson was given an eccentric past, a change that did not affect Lows very much. Authoritarians do not like "radical, extremist, degenerate weirdos." Relating abnormal behaviors from his past, reporting that he once advocated illegal acts, having officials call him a "nut" all probably cost him points in the minds of authoritarians a real Arnold Gregson would try to attract.

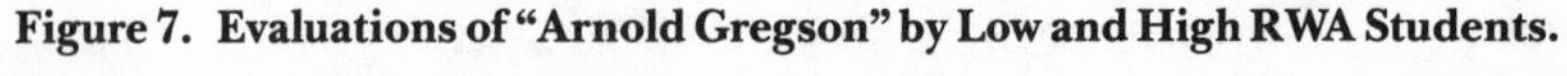

Figure 7. Evaluations of "Arnold Gregson" by Low and High RWA Students.

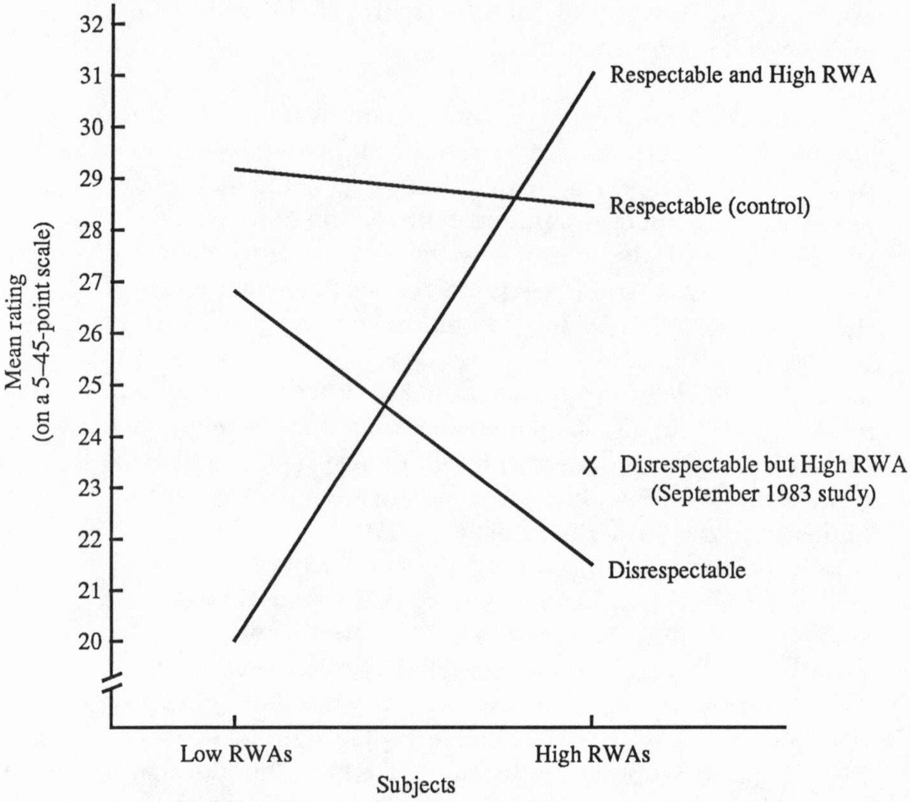

How damaging was this characterization for Highs? Suppose we give another batch of students a "disrespectable but High RWA" Arnold Gregson to evaluate, by substituting the appropriate paragraphs in the control version. How should Highs react? Will they be swayed more by the High RWA platform or the disreputable background? The previous study suggests lack of respectability will count a lot, and that is what I found when I gave this description to 133 Manitoba students the following September. Gregson's mean score among the Highs was 23.4 (*X* marks the spot in Figure 7), significantly lower than the "respectable but High RWA" mean among the January Highs (31.1) but not significantly higher than the earlier Highs' ratings of the "disrespectable" Gregson (21.6). Unconventionality apparently weighs heavily in the judgments authoritarians make.[7]

Discussion. Let me inject a few cautions and hesitations. First, we are talking about relatively small shifts here. Even making Arnold Gregson into a real screwball dropped his appeal to Highs only about 7 points, or about 25 percent of his total evaluation in the control condition.

Second, Arnold could not fight back in my experiment; all the subjects knew was what I told them. In real life political leaders can lie, obfuscate, counterattack in kind, cry "character assassination," blame others, present contradictory evidence, portray themselves as David fighting Goliath, focus attention on other subjects, say they have seen the error of their earlier ways, and use all the other tricks of a trickster's trade. Hitler had a terribly disrespectable past to overcome while seeking election, including a prison term for leading an armed rebellion against the constitution he now promised to uphold. And he succeeded.

Third, I am not recommending distorting someone's past to make him appear unconventional when he is not—although my hesitation may strike "hardball" political strategists as gutless, absurdly goody-goody, and stupid when the wolf is at the door.

But until I see confounding or complicating data, I *would* recommend informing the public about disrespectable, unconventional, and deviant details of a dangerous demagogue's past. Presenting such facts, according to our laws and fulfilling the electorate's fundamental right to know the relevant truths about those who would lead us, would probably make some authoritarians hesitate to join the grass roots that could someday sprout a tyrant.

Keeping National Crises from Stimulating Authoritarianism

We saw in Chapter Three that authoritarianism dropped over the course of undergraduate education, but becoming a parent apparently raised it again. What other factors might raise or reduce adult authoritarianism?

I have several times in this book repeated the common observation that various national crises primed the German people for Hitler's appeals: the loss of World War I, the crippling Versailles treaty, the rampant inflation in the 1920s that wiped out the savings of the middle class, and the Great Depression. But many historians have proposed that Hitler owed his sweeping gains in popularity during the early Thirties to the equally sudden growth of the Communist movement in Germany during the first years of the Depression. The emergence of a threatening, radical left supposedly drove many moderates and conservatives to the swastika.

I had reason to recall this explanation during the late 1960s, when both the protest against the Vietnam war and the civil rights movement began to grow violent fringes. As the American effort in Southeast Asia constantly intensified, and when Martin Luther King and Robert Kennedy were assassinated, violent radical leftist groups began to capture the headlines. I thought I could feel the whole continent vibrate as tens of millions of Americans moved toward Richard Nixon and Spiro Agnew. As I watched the riots inside and outside the Democratic National Convention in 1968, I agreed with the TV commentators that only Nixon could win those fights. But I thought the big losers were not just Hubert Humphrey, the Democratic party, and the Chicago police force but also the peace movement.

The November 1982 Student Study

Procedure. I tested this hunch about the effects of leftist violence in the fall of 1982, when 379 students answered the RWA Scale as they thought they would under hypothetical circumstances set 20 years in the future. Three scenarios were randomly distributed among the subjects: a *control* condition in which the students were told simply to imagine they were 20 years older, personally well off, and the parents of teenage children; a *violent left-wing threat* condition in which Canadian cities had become dangerous ghettoes, the economy was in a turmoil, bloody demonstrations were erupting in many cities, and leftist "urban guerrillas" had appeared on the scene; and a *violent right-wing threat* condition in which grave economic problems produced a new prime minister, who used his power to begin violently destroying Canadian democracy.

The *control* instructions ran as follows:

> Suppose it is 20 years from now. Imagine that you are married and have children who are in junior high school and high school. You have a good-paying job that you've held for a number of years, and you've recently bought a house. You are in reasonably good health.
>
> Imagine also that Canada is basically the same 20 years from now that it is today. That is, there are moderate but not overwhelming economic problems. Inflation has continued at 8–10 percent per year, and about 8–10 percent of the work force has usually been unemployed. Energy costs continue to run high, but Canada still has about the cheapest oil, gas, and electricity prices in the world because of its abundant natural resources. The federal and provincial governments continue to argue over their powers, and the various political parties continue to blame one another for anything that's wrong. But basically the country is at peace internally, and one of the most prosperous in the world.
>
> Things have not changed very much internationally either. Canada remains militarily and politically allied with the Commonwealth and the United States. The Soviet Union continues to be the most likely foe; the arms race continues. But after a long, painful involvement in Afghanistan and a brief shooting war with China, Russia does not seem to pose any immediate threat, at least, to Canada and its allies.

The *violent left-wing threat* condition, based on recent American and European history, began with the same paragraph used in the control group describing parenthood and fortunate personal circumstances. It then went on to say:

> Internationally things are basically as they were in 1982, but it is a time of great unrest and civil disturbance *within* Canada. Problems which appeared small in the 1980s have become very large indeed now. In Winnipeg and other cities the migration of native peoples into urban areas has reached massive proportions. The entire cores of cities have become vast ghettoes, where poverty, drug usage, crime, and violence have become widespread. No sensible white person, for example, would go downtown in Winnipeg after dark. It seems that every day the newspapers contain stories of ordinary people being mugged, brutally beaten, raped, and even murdered in and around the spreading core of the city's ghetto. Most other Canadian cities face the same problems.
>
> As well, the country is in very bad economic shape. The high price of foreign oil, competition from Asian manufacturers, and gross economic mismanagement have given the country both record-high inflation and an ever-deepening depression. Although your job is quite secure, millions upon millions of Canadians are suddenly becoming unemployed. Welfare and unemployment insurance costs are straining the government, with subsequent pressure upon the country's banks and other financial institutions.
>
> Furthermore, there have been angry and increasingly violent demonstrations against these conditions across Canada in the last year or so. Riots have broken out in Calgary and Regina, with widespread looting, fires, and destruction. Indian leaders warn that the same thing will happen in Winnipeg if their demands are not met. Angry groups of unemployed laborers have taken to the

> streets, fighting with the police and military and calling for a general strike which would paralyze the country. Finally, small but deadly groups of leftist "urban guerrillas" have appeared across the country, assassinating political leaders and municipal officials, planting terrorist bombs in public buildings and department stores, and calling for the violent overthrow of the government.

The *violent right-wing threat* condition, which was patterned in some respects on Hitler's path to power, also began with the same paragraph used in the control group to describe the subject's personal situation. It then continued:

> Internationally things are basically as they were in 1982, but there are grave disturbances within Canada. Problems which seemed manageable in the 1980s have become very large now. Prices have been going up over 15 percent annually, year after year, and on several occasions inflation seemed about to completely destroy the value of the Canadian dollar. Interest rates over 30 percent have virtually wiped out home construction, plant expansion, et cetera. Several million consumers have gone into serious debt and even bankruptcy. Many businesses have failed or been taken over by foreign investors using cheap Canadian dollars. In short, the economy is nearly in ruins.
>
> The government has changed several times through elections in the past few years, but each new government has failed to cure the nation's economic woes. Six months ago a revolt within the ruling majority party, led by an obscure backbencher from Alberta, produced a new prime minister who has taken the country on a dramatically new course. Promising "strong action" against the labor unions which he said were causing the inflation, the new prime minister invoked the War Mea-

> sures Act to deal with the economic problems. He then had many union leaders arrested, and he closed down several prounion newspapers. With the backing of powerful business groups, the government used the armed forces to break up strikes in the steel and auto industries. Nearly 40 strikers were killed in Windsor, Ontario, when troops opened fire on picketers. The RCMP has since arrested all known strike organizers and is holding them in jail indefinitely without trial.
>
> Union meetings may only be held with government approval. Several leftist groups have been outlawed by the government, and in some cases their leaders have mysteriously disappeared—reportedly having been executed by "death squads" operating semiofficially within the military and the RCMP. As the clamor over these and other events has risen in Parliament, the prime minister has threatened to outlaw the New Democratic party if its leaders do not cooperate with the government's "plan to save Canada from economic ruin."

After reading whichever scenario they received, the subjects were asked to indicate, on a six-point scale, "How serious, how grave would you say the situation described would be for Canada?" They then were asked to respond to the RWA Scale, according to how they imagined they would feel under the circumstances described.

Results. Understandably, the 126 control subjects did not think their Canada was in very dire straits. Their mean "How serious" rating was only 1.41 on a 0–5 scale. However, the 128 students who read about the violent left-wing threat and the 125 who encountered a violent right-wing threat thought Canada would be in very serious difficulty. Their mean answers were 4.57 and 4.54, respectively. Obviously, these means were not significantly different, a point to keep in mind: both violent threats were seen as being very, and equally, serious.

What happened to subjects' projected answers to the RWA Scale in the different conditions? Interestingly, the control mean rose from the subjects' present 151.6 (obtained at the beginning of the booklet) to 163.6—a gain of 12.0 points. Seventeen items showed significant increases, led by submission and conventionalism items dealing with "young people," "the youth," "premarital intercourse," "proper authorities censor," and "the real keys." These control subjects were thus telling us that they expected to become more authority-oriented and conventional when they grew older, became parents, and enjoyed personal prosperity. As we saw in Chapter Three, they were right at least about the effects of parenthood.[8]

Those students facing a violent left-wing crisis 20 years in the future thought their RWA Scale scores would rise (a significantly greater) 31.2 points, from 151.1 to 182.3. The increase was spread across the content of the scale, with 28 of 30 items showing significant rises. But the items with the largest increases tapped authoritarian aggression: "enforce laws without mercy," "treat dissenters," "some of the worst people," "strong medicine," and "good old-fashioned physical punishment." This surge in hostile sentiments was largely responsible for the 19.2-point increase beyond the mean increase among controls.

So what will happen to subjects who are told that an emerging dictator in the prime minister's office is pulling out the cornerstones of democracy one after the other, while ruthlessly using the military and the police to crush any opposition? Will this violent right-wing threat lower RWA Scale scores (after correcting for the "20-year control shift") as much as the equally serious left-wing crisis raised them? If so, then the second set of answers should be about (+ 12 – 19 =) 7 points *lower* than the first set of scores. But they were not lower; instead they went *up* 4.4 points, from 150.4 to 154.8. Thus, as can be seen in the upper diagram in Figure 8, the violent right-wing threat had *less than half* the effect that the violent left-wing threat had. This difference in results was significant beyond the .001 level.

The January 1983 Parents Study

I replicated this study a few months later when 203 parents of Manitoba students responded to the same three futures.

Figure 8. Effects of Violent Left- and Right-Wing Threats on Projected RWA Scale Responses.

A. Students

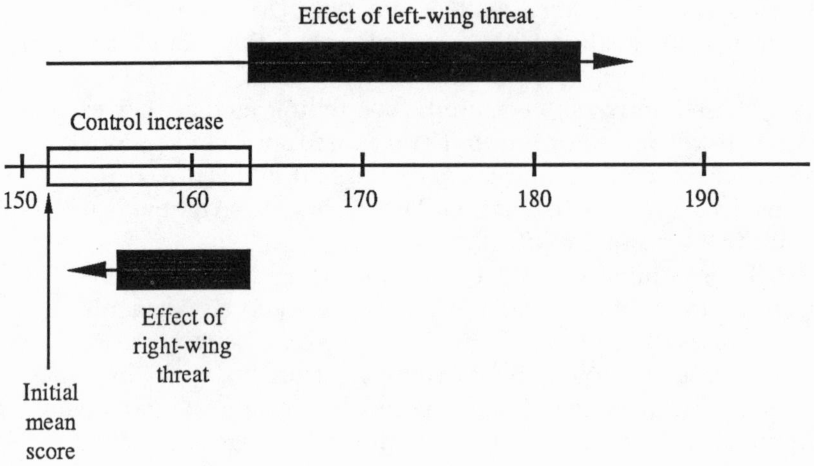

B. Parents

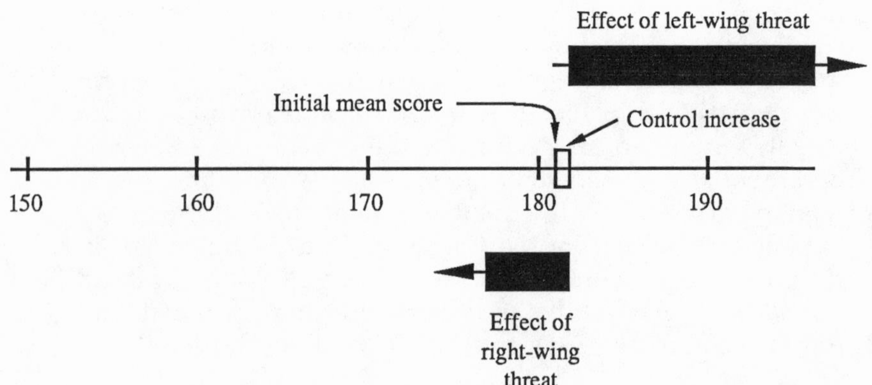

Only one change was made: the parents were asked to imagine that in 20 years they would be grandparents, near or past retirement age, living off their pensions and savings, but still reasonably well off and secure.

Results. The 61 control parents, like the control students before them, thought Canada would be in good shape in the circumstances they were given; their mean "How serious" score was 1.54. In contrast, both the 73 left-wing-threat and 69 right-wing threat parents thought their situations would be grave, with means of 4.26 and 4.51, respectively. The right-wing rating was almost significantly higher than the left ($t = 1.76$; $p < .08$).

Parents in the *control* group hardly changed their answers to the RWA Scale. The mean increased only 0.6 points, from 180.8 to 181.4, and the two sets of scores correlated .92. Clearly these parents were saying that if everything was basically the same 20 years hence, except that they would be about sixty-eight instead of forty-eight, they expected their attitudes to be the same.

Parents facing the violent left-wing threat in the future showed a 12.8 point increase in their RWA Scale scores, however, from 169.4 to 182.2 ($p < .001$)—a milder version of the net 19.2-point rise shown by the students. Thirteen items received significant increases, the largest gains again being shown by statements tapping authoritarian aggression: "enforce laws without mercy," "stomp out the rot," "treat dissenters," "strong medicine," and "some of the worst people."

By contrast, the parents facing a very serious right-wing threat showed only a 4.0 point drop in RWA Scale scores, from 172.3 to 168.3, which was *not* significantly different from the negligible rise found in the control group. So again, the left-wing threat provoked a much stronger reaction than an equally grave right-wing threat (Figure 8).

Discussion. We have no difficulty explaining the backlash from the violent leftist threat. As we saw in Chapter Five, authoritarian aggression appears to be triggered primarily by fear of a dangerous world, a fear that the world is about to disintegrate into chaos. A left-wing reformist group will almost inevitably challenge custom, the government, and the status quo, evoking a certain amount of that anxiety. A *violent* left-wing movement will probably produce far greater fear. Hence the increase in authoritarian aggression and (to lesser extents) the desire that everyone submit to authority and preserve conventions during a crisis. Interestingly, the greatest rise in RWA Scale scores did not occur among the High RWA students or parents (who believed all along we were on the road to ruin) but among the "moderates," who suddenly had their fear of a dangerous, disintegrating world raised to "authoritarian levels."[9]

That much interconnects and seems clear. But why does the violent right-wing threat not produce just as strong a backlash to the left? Perhaps the RWA Scale is unresponsive to such a shift. But it ought to be quite easy for subjects faced with a malevolent, violent national leader to say that authorities should not be trusted so much, that force is not the answer, and so on, if that is what they feel. There certainly can be no "basement effect" here either—that is, a truncated movement because there is so little room to the left to move. And the right-wing threat was viewed as just as serious as the left.

One difference is that the left-wing threat arose in the streets, while the right-wing threat arose in government. People may not react against a government as they would against "extremist hooligans." So would a violent *fascist* street movement drop RWA Scale scores as much as the urban rioters and guerrillas raised them?

The January 1984 Student Study

I administered two different scenarios to 373 students in January 1984. In one treatment, which I shall call the "Brownshirts condition," 190 subjects were given the same two-paragraph introduction used in the violent right-wing threat. However, after the sentence "In short, the economy is nearly in ruins," the narration continued:

> As the economy has spiraled downwards, the government has changed several times. But none of

> the traditional political parties has been able to straighten things out. Numerous new parties have thus been formed across the country, some more radical than others, all espousing different solutions to the country's problems. By far the biggest is an extremist group which has advocated outlawing the labor unions, which it blames for the inflation, using the military to break up strikes and crush leftist groups, and giving great power to "one strong leader" (that is, the party president) to run the country until the emergency is over.
>
> Supporters of this movement have been involved in numerous street brawls with other groups over the past year and in several cities have fought with police who tried to break up their demonstrations or keep them from attacking their political opponents. Many members of the middle class, however—their life savings destroyed by the inflation and their jobs gravely threatened—have joined the movement. Large marches and demonstrations in support of the party's program have recently taken place in Toronto, Ottawa, Winnipeg, Calgary, and Vancouver. While the party's leader has pledged to seek power legally, through elections, some observers believe the group would violently overthrow the Canadian government if it thought it could.

Readers will recognize the similarity of this description to Hitler's use of his "storm troopers" during his rise to power.[10]

This situation was judged significantly less serious than the first crises ($\overline{X} = 4.24$), although naturally it was still considered quite grave. What happened to the authoritarianism of these subjects asked to imagine that a violent group of right-wing thugs was roaming the streets trying to attack their opponents and fighting the police? If you guessed that they would become *less* authoritarian, as I did, you're in for a surprise. For their scores went *up* 17.4 points, from 151.4 to 168.8, significantly more than our "12.0 control group." Which items led the increase? "Strong medicine," "enforce laws without mercy," "some of the worst people," "the real keys," and "treat dissenters."

So apparently when violent mobs roam the streets, people want law and order restored no matter who is causing the trouble. They want authorities to crack down on the troublemakers. People should submit to the government more. Unconventional people should be straightened out or punished. In short, civil disorder may make people more right-wing authoritarian, even when the right-wingers are causing the trouble. If the radical left join in battle, so much the better for the fascist cause. Left-wing violence really drives RWA Scale scores up and makes your cause noble.

You say, people would see right through this sham. I sincerely hope they can. But Hitler ran on a "law and order" platform in 1932 while his storm troopers were doing most of the beating and killing in the streets. And the populace elected the Nazis to power, not the Communists. It appears Hitler could hardly lose, once the Weimar authorities lost control over the situation in the streets.

The January 1983 Student Study

My "Brownshirts" scenario had clearly failed to evoke a strong backlash to the left. Would everything? At the beginning of 1983 I presented 160 students with an even stronger version of the violent right-wing threat used in the first study. The description was the same as that given earlier, to the point where an obscure back-bencher from Alberta had become prime minister and invoked the War Measures Act. It then ran:

> He has arrested all the top union leaders in the country. With the backing of powerful business groups, the government used the armed forces to break up strikes in the steel and auto industries. Over 200 strikers have been killed in Halifax, Windsor and Sudbury when troops opened fire on picketers. The RCMP has arrested all local strike

> organizers, holding them without trial along with several thousand others judged to be "subversives" or "Communists." Union meetings are forbidden.
>
> Numerous leftist groups have been outlawed by the government, and their leaders have vanished in the night. "Death squads" operating semi-officially within the military and the police forces have been kidnapping and executing "state enemies" on an ever-increasing scale. Newspapers which protested the arrests or blamed the government for the executions have been shut down. All remaining newspapers, TV news, et cetera are now heavily censored by the state authorities.
>
> Most recently, the prime minister declared Parliament "closed until further notice," had the leaders of the opposition parties arrested, and announced he would rule by decree until "the emergency passes." A crowd of protesters, including many members of Parliament, gathered at the foot of Parliament Hill and marched toward the House, carrying signs saying the prime minister had no legal right to do all he had done. Soldiers were ordered to fire into the crowd, which they did, killing over 30 and wounding many more.

Students judged this the most serious crisis of all ($\overline{X} = 4.71$), significantly graver than any used earlier. And the subjects' RWA Scale scores *dropped* significantly, from 152.1 to 145.9, a loss of 6.2 points. Recalling that their new status as parents and so forth would have raised their scores about 12 points, the net effect of the right-wing coup d'etat was a shift to the left of (12 + 6.2 =) 18.2 points, very nearly the 19-point shift to the right obtained in the (less serious) violent left-wing threat condition. Fourteen items on the RWA Scale received significantly lower scores the second time around, led by "trust the judgment of the proper authorities," "self-righteous 'forces of law and order,'" "obedience and respect," "the facts on crime," and "students confront established authorities." Most of these, I believe, tap authoritarian submission more than anything else; such a drop in authoritarian submission seems understandable in the circumstances.

So we can invent a situation that would produce a "full blown" backlash against a right-wing threat—or, rather, to a fascist *fait accompli*. For in the present case it would be too late, with democracy destroyed and a dictator firmly in control, for the backlash to affect anything.

Comparing Violent and Nonviolent Left-Wing Protests

If these data are to be trusted, they raise the question "What can one do to correct serious wrongs in our society without driving the populace toward the demagogues on the right?" I explored this question with 316 other students who served with the 160 subjects just described.

These 316 students received either a violent or a *nonviolent* left-wing threat. Both versions began with the first three paragraphs used in the earlier violent left-wing threat. The subject was a parent, well off as usual, and the international scene was stable and nonthreatening. But the cores of many Canadian cities had become violent ghettoes, and both runaway inflation and widespread unemployment were causing severe economic problems.

The violent left-wing threat, which was based on my perception of how the Vietnam protest movement changed over time, proceeded as follows:

> Furthermore, there have been widespread and increasingly violent demonstrations against these conditions across Canada in the past year. These have become more frequent and grown in size, such that the news now seems full of them. Poorly controlled protest marches of at least a hundred thousand persons were held recently in Ottawa, Montreal, Toronto, and Vancouver. Speakers at these rallies ridiculed the government's economic policies, made personal attacks on the

> prime minister, and threatened violence in the streets if job creation programs and massive aid for the inner cities were not forthcoming. Speakers for the government, on the other hand, were loudly booed and shouted down. Some participants in these "marches for justice" then went on looting and vandalism sprees after the meetings ended, resulting in many injuries when the police moved in to restore order. This situation has spread to Winnipeg, where unemployed and Native demonstrators recently went on a window-smashing and looting spree along North Main Street. Seventeen persons, including six policemen, were injured then.
>
> More recently a bomb exploded in the middle of the night in a national taxation center, killing an employee who was working late. National leaders of the protest movement have blamed these outbreaks of violence on "militants" and "outsiders" who join their demonstrations but warn the militants will gain control of the movement if the government does not act soon. Finally, some labor leaders have begun calling for a national strike which, if carried out, would paralyze the country.

The nonviolent threat also described a large, determined protest movement, but it was portrayed as peaceful, well disciplined, and civil, if also civil-disobedient:

> Furthermore, there have been widespread but peaceful demonstrations against these conditions across Canada in the past year. These have become more frequent and have grown in size, such that the news now seems full of them. Well-controlled protest marches of at least a hundred thousand persons were held recently in Ottawa, Montreal, Toronto, and Vancouver. Speakers at these rallies severely criticized the government's

> economic policies and demanded job creation programs and massive aid for the inner cities. Government spokesmen at these meetings were listened to politely but not applauded. Many participants in these "marches for justice" then committed peaceful acts of civil disobedience after the meetings ended, refusing to move from Parliament Hill, et cetera, forcing the authorities to arrest them. This tactic has spread to Winnipeg, where unemployed and Native demonstrators by the hundreds have "squatted" in Manpower Offices and other government buildings, until police had to carry them away.
>
> Finally, some labor leaders have begun calling for a national strike which, if carried out, would paralyze the country.

The 159 students who read about the violent left-wing threat rated the situation as quite serious ($\overline{X} = 4.43$, not significantly different from the November 1982 students' 4.57 rating of the first violent left-wing threat). The 157 students who encountered the *non*violent leftist threat also thought the situation was serious (4.12), but significantly less so than the violent threat.

Estimated RWA Scale scores in the violent threat condition rose 29.3 points, from 145.4 to 174.7—quite similar to the 31.2-point increase found the previous November. Twenty-eight of the 30 items showed increases, led (for reasons we think we understand) by the usual authoritarian aggression statements.

By way of contrast, scores in the *non*violent threat condition rose significantly less, 17.2 points, from 152.5 to 169.7. Making our usual 12-point allowance for the first paragraph, the nonviolent leftist threat raised authoritarianism by only 5.2 points, compared with a 17.3-point increase caused by the violent protest movement. The nonviolent effect was nevertheless significantly greater than that obtained in the November control group. Twenty-three items showed significant increases, the aggression items again showing the greatest gains—but much smaller than those produced in the violent condition.

We must recognize that the "nonviolent" leftist scenario still began with the description of crime-ridden urban ghettoes, which would alarm many subjects.[11] But clearly the difference in the protest movements that arose to challenge the government's policies produced an appreciable difference in authoritarian backlash.

Effects of Government Repression on Nonviolent Protests

What happens when a repressive government uses force to suppress nonviolent protest? I pursued this question in the autumn of 1986, when 224 students responded to an addended version of the nonviolent left-wing threat. The scenario was exactly the same as that used in January 1983 except that the following paragraph (based loosely on Martin Luther King's march on Selma, Alabama, in 1965) was added.

> The authorities have reacted brutally to these nonviolent protests, at first firing fire hoses at the demonstrators, but then turning attack dogs loose upon them, and finally charging into the unarmed "squatters," assaulting them with truncheons and clubs. Several demonstrators across the nation have been killed by these attacks, and hundreds hospitalized with serious injuries. The government says the demonstrators are bringing this suffering upon themselves, but the protest leaders say their nonviolent protests will continue, saying their cause is just and does not need violence to prevail.

This crisis was judged a little more serious (4.25; $t = 2.15$; $p < .05$) than the original nonviolent protest. More interesting was the difference in projected authoritarianism scores. Instead of boosting RWA Scale responses 17.2 points, as the original nonviolent protest crisis had, the new scenario raised mean authoritarianism only 2.7 points, from 148.9 to 151.6 ($p > .20$). Since we expect a noticeable shift to the right owing to the changes in the subjects' personal status, the nonchange suggests that governments that attempt brutal repression of nonviolent protests produce a backlash against themselves, a significant shift to the left—as many civil rights leaders have realized and counted on (see, for example, Manchester, 1974, p. 1059).

What would happen if, after years of consistent repression by a morally bankrupt government, a nonviolent movement turned violent? I tested this in the same study by presenting 222 other students with a Canadianized version of the turmoil in South Africa. This crisis began with the usual first paragraph and then continued:

> Internationally things are basically as they were in 1986, but it is a time of great unrest and civil disturbance *within* Canada. Problems which appeared small in the 1980s have become very large indeed now. In Winnipeg and other cities the entire cores of cities have become vast ghettoes, where poverty, unemployment, and drug usage have become widespread. The "Native Question" has become Canada's No. 1 problem.
>
> Beginning about 1988, militant native leaders began to point out that Canada once belonged just to Indian peoples. But then the English, French, and other groups invaded the New World and took the land and its wealth for themselves, destroying the Indians' way of life. Indian leaders began to take their cases for compensation to the Canadian courts and often won. But when a judge, and even the Supreme Court, decided in the Indians' favor, the federal government refused to obey the ruling.
>
> As a result of its refusal to compensate Native peoples, to take steps to end discrimination against them, and to eliminate corruption in the Department of Indian Affairs, the Canadian government has been condemned by many nations around the world.

> The Native community reacted nonviolently to the unyielding attitude of the Canadian government, staging sit-ins, holding demonstrations, and refusing to allow federal officials on the reserves. The government reacted to these protests, however, by arresting Indian leaders (several of whom died "mysteriously" while in custody), by placing tight restrictions on Indians living off the reserves, and forcibly moving Treaty Indians from Canadian cities to their designated reserves. As a result, the Native movement, after many years of nonviolent protest, has recently become increasingly violent. Riots have broken out in Winnipeg, Calgary, and other centers. No sensible white person would go into the Native community in Winnipeg after dark now. The government has beefed up its police and army units, imposed still tighter restrictions upon Indians' movements, and said the Indians' lawlessness shows its policy was right all along.

This situation was also judged "very serious" ($\overline{X} = 4.02$), but mean RWA Scale scores rose only slightly, from 150.5 to 154.6. This again represents a net backlash against the government, though slightly less than that produced immediately above when the nonviolent movement remained nonviolent.

Although the philosophy of nonviolent protest hardly needs experimental support of this kind, the data reinforce Mohandas Gandhi's and Martin Luther King's strategy for producing significant social reforms. Violent protests may well frighten a populace and drive it to the right, *away* from accommodation with those who seek change. Indeed, violent demonstrations themselves can become *the* crisis, replacing in the public's mind the problems that caused the protest in the first place. (Remember the Students for a Democratic Society's "Days of Rage"?) But appeals to the consciences of a people, to their sense of fairness and justice, especially when contrasted with the brutal repression of a Dharasana or a Selma or an assassinated Benigno Aquino, may work where force will fail.

Cautions and Summary

All these studies,[12] summarized in Figure 9, involve subjects' *predictions* of how they would react in the circumstances described, and our earlier warning about subjects' imagined responses and "poses" certainly applies. It is quite possible that people will behave differently in a real crisis than they imagine beforehand. My own guess is that we tend to underestimate how strongly we will react when we are truly frightened and disturbed. And we should recall that in all cases the subjects were told they were personally well off and financially secure, which would hardly be true for everyone. Personal economic peril would likely produce much stronger reactions. Nevertheless, all of us might behave completely differently in a real crisis than we would guess beforehand.

I hope my country and yours will continue to develop peacefully, in stable circumstances, in "uninteresting times," so we shall never see these models put to the test. But nations have undergone crises in the *past*, and as I have pointed out as we poked along, these students and their parents have reacted rather like the populaces of Germany and the United States during periods of domestic upheaval. That rather impresses me, because as each subject faced his one situation in the experiment, he did not know the other variations that existed and what was to be compared. That is, the data at least have an internal validity among themselves. We can compare how people *think* they will react to this kind of threat and that kind of threat.

Here is the gist of what they have said:

1. Violent left-wing threats will drive people considerably to the right, making them more authoritarian-aggressive in particular. The less violent the protest movement, the less backlash.
2. Violent right-wing threats do not produce nearly the backlash that violent left-wing threats do. In fact, a violent fascist "street movement" makes people more right-wing authoritarian, not less so. It takes an extremely serious right-wing threat to lower RWA Scale scores.

Figure 9. Effects of Various Threats on Authoritarianism, Compared with Control Groups.

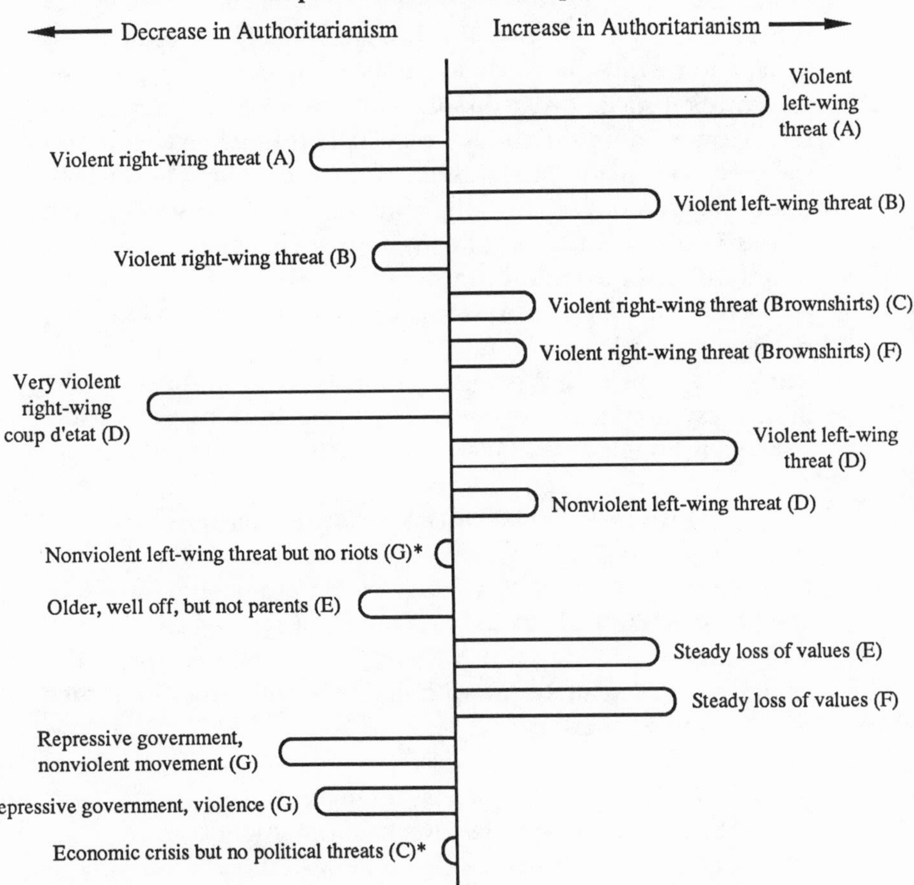

A = November 1982 student study
B = January 1983 parent study
C = January 1984 student study
D = January 1983 student study
E = January 1985 student study (see Notes 7 and 8)
F = March 1985 parent study (see Note 11)
G = September 1986 student study

* See Notes 9 and 10.

As a rule of thumb, differences in horizontal bars as wide as your little finger are statistically significant. See text for details of important comparisons.

In short, then, we have an asymmetrical system of reactions. Freedom can be crushed from either side, but it seems my subjects reacted more to the breakdown of law than to its usurpation. And the cards are stacked in favor of right-wing extremists if social order dissolves and organized violence and terrorism erupt in the street—especially if the demagogues on the right can blame their excesses on the radical left, which would happen quite naturally. Thus leftists who resort to such tactics would seem to be playing into their enemies' hands. I would call this the "Nixon trap."

But nonviolent protest may be the trump card of left-wing reformers, which we can most earnestly recommend to right-wing activists as well. When governments try to suppress peaceful protest movements with force, they appear to trigger a backlash against themselves. This might be called the "Gandhi trap."

Effects of Social Norms on Authoritarians

In the fall of 1983 a batch of Manitoba students completed the RWA Scale at the beginning of a two-session study. When they returned to finish the experiment a week later, the second booklet again began with the RWA Scale, but with rather peculiar instructions:

> Below is the social issues survey you answered at the beginning of last week. Many students wonder how their attitudes compare with those of others. Next to each statement is printed the *average response* (rounded off to the nearest response category) of the 532 students who answered the survey last week.
>
> You are asked to indicate your opinion on these matters again today. You may take into account the average response printed alongside each statement, or you may ignore it completely.

Each statement then appeared, with the response (for example, " – 1") nearest the mean of the first week's answers printed alongside. Because students' answers to nearly all the items average between 3.5 and 6.4 on the 1–9 response scale, nearly all the printed norms were – 1's, 0's, or + 1's. These answers added to a 154 total, naturally close to the first week's mean of 154.3. The veridical feedback therefore allowed Low and High RWA students to see how different their opinions were from the average and consciously or unconsciously to make social comparisons (Festinger, 1954).

The mean of the second week's answers ($N = 495$) was 152.8, not significantly different from the first week's average. Scores from the two administrations correlated .90, significantly below the usual one-week test-retest reliability of about .95 ($t = 5.86$; $p < .001$). So the printed norms had affected the second answers, and you will probably not be surprised to learn that Lows and Highs changed their answers more than moderates.

But not equally. First-session Lows increased their scores 5.7 points, from an average of 114.7 to 120.4. First-session Highs, in turn, decreased their scores more than twice as much, 12.5 points, from 192.0 to 179.5. The difference in the magnitude of the two shifts was statistically significant ($t = 3.43$; $p < .001$).

Was this simply regression toward the mean? If so, perhaps Highs just regress more. But the previous autumn 584 students had answered the RWA Scale at the beginning of two sessions held one week apart (as part of the research reported in Chapter Two on improving the internal consistency of responses to the test). Lows' scores went up 0.2 points, while Highs' also increased minutely, 0.5 points. Neither change was significant in any sense. So it appears that the shifts of 5.7 and 12.5 points reported above can be attributed to differential effects of the printed norms: Highs were more affected than Lows. The implication is that authoritarians may, in general, be particularly influenced more than most of us by the social comparisons we all make.

This possibility was buttressed by two later studies of personal values. In February 1985 I asked 168 students to rank-order ten traits "according to how important they are to you." The traits were open-mindedness, determination, compassion, integrity, self-understanding, being normal, independence, will power, tolerance, and stability. Compassion and open-mindedness were ranked highest overall, while "being normal" was rated dead last.

This last result is apt to make a social psychologist snort, because desires to appear "normal" have proved very powerful in many people in many situations. Lows uniformly dumped on the notion of pursuing normality; its mean ranking was 9.62, where "10" (unlike a "10" in gymnastics and heterosexual evaluations) is the pits. Highs gave "being normal" a mean ranking of 7.00 – still low but not so uniformly scorned. The correlation for all 168 students between their RWA Scale scores and valuing normality was .35 ($p < .001$).[13]

I repeated the experiment the following month with 270 parents. Again "being normal" was ranked lowest, but while Lows gave it an average ranking of 9.16, Highs' mean ranking was 6.53. The correlation between these ratings and parents' authoritarianism was .30 ($p < .001$).[14]

Results of Giving Authoritarians Accurate Feedback About Their Authoritarianism

The implication of these findings appears obvious: we might be able to reduce Highs' authoritarianism by simply explaining to them what right-wing authoritarianism is and then letting them discover they score unusually high on the RWA Scale. Since Highs have a certain desire to be "normal," and since authoritarianism can be rather easily shown (in itself and through its covariates of prejudice, mean-spiritedness, hypocrisy, and so on) to be socially undesirable, the information itself might motivate many Highs to want to change. Which is not the same thing as actually changing, but probably a nice step in the right direction.

I tested this premise one day at the end of the 1985–86 school year, by taking the introductory psychology classes of two colleagues whose students had earlier served in "Survey" (specifically, the first "pitting experiment" described in Chapter Five). I announced I was there to give promised feedback about the purpose and results of my study and proceeded to deliver a 45-

minute lecture giving the definition of right-wing authoritarianism and some findings involving government injustices, Watergate, Trials, and my laboratory aggression study. The last half of the lecture focused on the authoritarian aggression experiment in which the students themselves had served, including the findings that such aggression appears to be caused mainly by fear of a dangerous world and the disinhibiting effects of self-righteousness.

In one class I made a particularly emotional presentation, beginning with readings about the Nazi concentration camps from Shirer's *Rise and Fall of the Third Reich*. In the other class I instead presented evidence from four studies showing Highs' tendencies to maintain double standards in opinions and judgments. Students in the first class later wrote that the concentration camp reading had been very dramatic and effective; however, I found no difference in subsequent behavior of the two classes, so their results are presented here as one combined sample of 226.

These particular class periods ran for 75 minutes, and at the end of my presentation I told the students I had come prepared to give them individual feedback about their scores the previous fall on the RWA Scale. (The reader may realize that this was entirely unethical.) I placed a sheaf of papers in alphabetical piles at the front of the room and asked all the students who had served in "Survey" to come up and claim the sheet with their name on it. Actually, each student found *two* sheets stapled together, the first of which simply had the name printed at the top.

When they had returned to their seats, I asked my recaptured subjects to separate the two sheets, discard the first, and look at the second, which was obviously a questionnaire. I said I was going to collect the second sheets in a few minutes (and would give whoever needed it another experimental credit) and that with the first sheet removed, their answers would be completely anonymous.

A frequency distribution graph was printed on the *front* of the second sheet, illustrating every one of the 533 RWA Scale scores obtained the previous autumn. These scores ranged from

65 to 234 (pp. 138–139 in *RWA* present similar graphs). The mean score (152) was highlighted on the graph, and both the lower and upper quartiles were labeled. The reader should note that the upper quartile ("Highs," whom I had just spent 45 minutes talking about) ran from 172 to 234; I made this boundary clear as I explained the graph to the class.

My first question was printed under the graph:

> If you had to guess (say you'd get a million dollars if you were right), where on the scale above would you guess *your* score is? Draw a circle *in ink* around the column you think contains your score.
>
> (Please don't do this if you can't do it seriously.)

After the students had guessed their score (and all did so), I explained it was unusual to give personal feedback in a class, and they should take care that no one else discovered their actual score. I then asked them to retrieve the "first sheet," which they had just discarded, and turn it over. If they looked very closely, they would find a number printed in the upper left corner. ("For almost all of you, it will be a '1.' That is the first digit in your score.") The students were then told to go counterclockwise to the next two corners, at the bottom of the sheet. "They contain the last two digits in your score. Don't let anyone else see your numbers." I illustrated the process on the blackboard with the score "152," to make sure everyone knew how to do it.

Any psychology professor who has ever demonstrated the "universal attribute" or "Barnum" effect in class (for example, Snyder, Shenkel, and Lowery, 1977) has probably guessed from my repeated warnings about "keeping your score secret" what was going on. I told all the students their score was either 178, 179, 180, or 181—smack dab in the "High" range. (Thus, with subsequent dehoaxing, I was *not* telling anyone his score on the RWA Scale, so far as he could ever tell, a point my local Ethical Review Committee took some months to appreciate.)

I saw some students blink their eyes in amazement. A few

whistled and some quietly laughed, but when I asked, "Would anyone like to read his score aloud?," it got very quiet.

Having now "privately" told each of the students in the class he or she had scored quite high on the RWA Scale (which was the truth for the real Highs but false for everyone else), I asked the students to answer a series of questions on the back of the second sheet. I then collected these surveys (which I had discreetly premarked for real Highs and Lows) and revealed the ruse. When the laughter died down, I explained my real purpose, which was (truthfully, at last) to give different kinds of presentations in different classes and see how people responded to "news" that they were authoritarian, searching for the best way to motivate real Highs to change. I then used the class's experience to highlight the danger of giving individuals detailed feedback about psychological test scores, commenting that all "psychological tests are error-prone, but even persons who know that still take them too seriously. Didn't you?"

Estimating Own RWA Scale Score. My little show found 62 Lows and 56 Highs (according to their responses six months earlier) in attendance that day. When asked to guess their own RWA Scale scores, the Lows' average estimate was 136.0, very close to the "Low/Moderate border" of 134. None thought he would have been a High, and 23 (37 percent) correctly guessed they would be Lows.

What did the Highs estimate? As we would expect from the "self-awareness" data presented at the end of Chapter Five, and realizing that authoritarianism (like prejudice) would be a socially *un*desirable trait for most Highs, their estimates were markedly inaccurate. Five (9 percent) thought they would be Lows, and 42 (75 percent) thought they would be Moderates. Only 9 (16 percent) correctly guessed they were Highs. The mean of their estimates was 157.1 – rather far from the Moderate/High border of 171. The chi-squared for accuracy/inaccuracy by Lows and Highs was 9.5 ($p < .001$).

So authoritarians once again showed a pronounced tendency to think they are more normal than they really are. The lesson was clear: if you describe right-wing authoritarianism to a group of people, most of the Highs in the group will think you are talking about somebody else.

Wishing for an RWA Scale Score. After all the subjects had been told they were Highs, I asked them to write down the score they would *like* to have instead. The Low mean was 130.3, not too far from their actual mean of 120. Most Lows wanted to be Lows.[15] Highs wished their scores would be, on the average, 146.4, quite a distance from their real mean of about 185. Only 11 Highs, after hearing of research on authoritarianism, said they wanted to be Highs. Sixteen said they would rather have a score in the lowest quartile. But most Highs (29), consistent with the findings we examined a few pages ago, said they wanted to be not high, not low, but average.

How Much Would You Like to Change? I next asked subjects, "How much would you like to change your attitudes, so as to be less authoritarian?" Answering on a 0–6 basis (for this and all subsequent questions), most subjects said "moderately" ("3"). Only 74 of 226 wanted to change their supposedly high scores "a lot" ("4") or more, and most of these were Lows (23) or Moderates (38). Highs were significantly less interested in changing than Lows were (means of 2.36 and 3.31, respectively; $t = 3.27$, $p < .001$). So, though arousing a general desire Highs have to be normal, my presentations did not light any great fires under them. While a better talk could have done more, it may take more than a simple lecture to motivate most Highs to change.

How Serious Is Authoritarianism? The next question inquired, "How serious a danger do you think right-wing authoritarianism poses to freedom in our society?" Most subjects said either "a lot" or "moderately." Predictably, Lows were more concerned about right-wing authoritarianism ($\overline{X} = 4.06$) than Highs (3.40) ($t = 2.38$; $p < .01$).

Conative Opinions. I next asked for reactions to three concrete proposals for safeguarding society from authoritarianism, similar to ones readers encountered earlier in this chapter:

(1) emphasizing in high school courses freedom of speech and the right to protest against the government, (2) passing laws protecting homosexuals, racial groups, and religious minorities from discrimination in housing and employment, and (3) urging religions to stress tolerance, acceptance of others, and other democratic values. In all cases, Lows were significantly more in favor of these proposals than Highs, but the latter showed more support for these ideas than usual. They were least willing to stress democratic freedoms to high school students ($\overline{X} = 2.82$) and most in favor of having religions stress democratic values ($\overline{X} = 3.35$).[16]

Summary. Although the results are subject to several interpretations (I may have fooled no one; Highs may simply have been responding to "demand characteristics" in the situation), they do offer a little additional hope. High RWAs may be truly upset to find out they are as authoritarian as they are, compared with others. Just as with their self-perceptions of how prejudiced they are against racial minorities, they may seriously misperceive how different they are from others—an easy thing to get wrong if they associate mainly with other Highs. They do not think authoritarianism poses a very serious threat to society, but when they are told the truth about their attitudes, they show a (modest) desire to change—not to become Lows, usually, but to be at least average. This motivation appears, on the surface, to translate into an increased (if still modest) willingness to protect freedom in our society.

These were the general trends, to which exceptions existed. About a fifth of the Highs told me to stick it in my ear. They guessed they would score high on the RWA Scale, they were glad when I told them they had, they thought authoritarianism was just what our society needed, and so on. But there was another, larger group of Highs who thought they were Moderates or Lows but who, when they discovered they were Highs, appeared concerned, said they saw the danger authoritarianism posed, wished they were Lows, and seemed more willing to promote the teaching of democratic rights in school, and so forth.

Perhaps these persons never were as authoritarian as they

appeared to be on the RWA Scale the previous autumn. Psychological tests *do* make grievous errors. Or perhaps they had changed over time. Or perhaps the feedback they received did cause some shifts in attitudes, but these shifts evaporated overnight. But also, perhaps part of the way to protect society from the threat on the far right is to disseminate the findings on right-wing authoritarianism, to teach our populations what we have discovered about authoritarians, and to find ways that Highs can learn about themselves.

Summary

The situation regarding right-wing authoritarianism in North America appears neither desperate nor hopeless. If there is no simple button we can push to make authoritarianism disappear, there *are* quite a number of things we can do that will apparently lower RWA Scale scores in a population and reduce the worst authoritarian behaviors.

For example, our educational systems should be teaching a greater love and appreciation of freedom. And higher education should remain accessible to as many qualified persons as possible. Furthermore, university students should be encouraged to do as much course work in the liberal arts as feasible. The media can be more responsible in carrying news of crime and violence to the public; they have as much at stake in protecting freedom as anyone. So do religions; anything they can do to lower self-righteousness and curtail the aspects of religious training that (we saw in Chapter Six) apparently promote authoritarianism will help ensure freedom of religion.

Since authoritarians tend to have a "punishment and obedience" orientation to the law, one of the best ways to change their behavior is to have established authority promote the change. Behavioral scientists have known for some time that benevolent laws redressing wrongs and protecting minorities can have several positive effects. In the right circumstances, changes in behavior required by law can lead to unrequired but enlightened changes in attitudes. Authoritarians have had limited contact with a cross-section of humanity. Many apparently have an encouraging capacity to grow when their lives are broadened.[17]

When society will not easily change "from the top," people can try to institute reforms through protest movements. Our data strongly imply that violent left-wing protest will often be self-defeating. Even *right*-wing violence in the streets may make the population more right-wing authoritarian. But nonviolent protest movements produce little backlash (and may have their chances for success increased if they are violently repressed). However, people appear slow to react against the threat of a right-wing coup.

Authoritarians have a relatively strong desire to be "normal." Unconventionality and lack of respectability disturb them. Consequently, demagogues trying to attract Highs to their banner (such as Arnold Gregson) may be checked to some extent by pointing out the eccentricity of their behavior and the radical nature of their cause.

Finally, it appears that even though authoritarians do not typically realize they are unusually submissive to authority, unusually hostile, and unusually conventional, most of them want to become less so when they are made more self-aware. So we are not necessarily fighting an uphill battle in attempting to help Highs change. If our society learns more about the authoritarian syndrome and the threat it poses to our freedoms, highly authoritarian behavior may have The Flag unwrapped from about it—and diminish accordingly.

NOTES

1. It is hard for me, living in North America during the 1980s, to be very worried about left-wing extremism. I imagine though that if I lived in certain other places in the world, I would find it much easier.
2. As this book was going to press I discovered another, rather obvious way the media can help control authoritarianism: allow information about it to reach the public.

   In March 1988, as I began making my findings available, I offered a 1,200 word account of Chapter Seven's Canadian legislator study to the *Winnipeg Free Press*. The editor of the "op-ed" page declined the essay however because a (sudden) provincial election was underway, and he thought it unfair to print the article then. When I subsequently offered the piece to Canada's "national newspaper," the *Toronto Globe and Mail*, the *Globe* reporter in Winnipeg wrote a news story about the study which appeared on the front page of his paper's April 4th edition. However, an editor in Toronto deleted all the connections between authoritarianism and political party affiliation, so the gist of the story ran, "Did you know that *some* of our lawmakers are pretty authoritarian?"

   The *Globe* story led the Winnipeg representative of the Canadian Press, a national news wire service, to send a fuller account of the research across the country. This story was printed, complete with party scores, by our local tabloid, the *Winnipeg Sun*, on the morning of April 5th, and then later that day by the *Free Press*.

   These several reports of the study led radio stations in Toronto, Ottawa, and Montreal to arrange telephone interviews, and I appeared on the local Canadian Broadcasting Corporation (radio) morning news program on April 6th. A week later a *Free Press* columnist, alarmed by the implications of the research, wrote an insightful essay based on the study. Then the story, like most reports of research, understandably evaporated from the public view.

   As pleased as I was to have the "15 minutes of fame" Andy Warhol promised us all, and as displeased as my "phone-mate" at the University of Manitoba was on April 5th, there were still many large gaps in the coverage. None of the national CBC news/ analysis programs (radio or TV) touched the story. Nor did any other network to my knowledge. Nor were any of the other radio and TV stations in my home town, including several which have extensive interview formats, interested in pursuing the matter. Furthermore, I eventually discovered that many communities in Canada had no chance to learn of the findings; only 5 of 12 out-of-town Canadian newspapers available in my university's library printed the Canadian Press item.

It is quite possible that the story was passed over because various editors and producers decided it had little news value. I realize I am the person least able to judge objectively the significance of my research. But every interviewer I spoke with audibly gasped when I reported the differences in the parties' scores on the RWA Scale. And it does seem to me that discovering huge differences in the levels of authoritarianism in different legislative caucuses is worthy of some mention.

Perhaps, instead, some editors decided that I was a "kook," or that I had ulterior partisan motives, or that the findings simply could not be true. Perhaps. But *no one* has ever said, "This can't be true" or "Do you belong to a political party?" or "What are your scientific credentials?" In fact, no one has questioned the findings in any way, not even the leaders of the right-wing parties—who along with the other caucus leaders had received a write-up of the results in January 1988. (This, of course, suggested a study for the fall of 1988 on the willingness of Lows and Highs to learn more about "bad traits" they supposedly have.)

I suppose a third possibility is that some decision makers in the media rejected the study, not because they found it bland, or unbelievable, but because they did not want their public to learn of the results. One has no way of gauging this possibility, but I have been told that such things happen. Which I suppose underscores the necessity of having a free, and competitive, press.

3. These responses are similar to those given by Highs in a 1973 Kohlberg-style moral reasoning experiment, mentioned in Chapter One, that found authoritarians were likely to use the most primitive "Stage 1: punishment-and-obedience orientation" in resolving moral dilemmas (*RWA*, pp. 192–196).
4. We should note in passing the attitude that many Highs have toward freedom of religion. As is often the case, it is not a freedom they would share with others. The "proreligion" law described in the text would have forced a particular religious orientation (one that many Highs favor) on all children attending public school. So while many Highs would mightily protest the teaching of some

other religion in the schools or the exclusion of all religious teaching, they would be happy for the opportunity to make everyone learn what they believe.

Recall also that in the February 1986 pitting study (see Table 4, in Chapter Five) RWA Scale scores correlated .50 with willingness among parents to join a posse hunting down "weird religions and cults significantly different from our main religious traditions." Authoritarians are no more friends of religious freedom than were the Romans who threw the early Christians to the lions.

5. The photo was actually of James Brady, Ronald Reagan's former press secretary, from an April 1982 *Washington Post* article describing his recovery from head wounds suffered during the 1981 assassination attempt on President Reagan. Only one subject ever indicated to me he knew the photo was not of the fictitious Arnold Gregson.

6. I wondered why the "respectable and High RWA" version of Arnold Gregson did not draw more support from Highs and hypothesized that the reason might be the overt racism at the end of Gregson's statement. As we saw in Chapter Five, few Highs (say they) think they are prejudiced, and Highs might be repelled by an unmistakably racist appeal. So in September 1983 I gave two versions of a very prejudiced Arnold Gregson to 258 students (serving with the same subjects who evaluated a disrespectable but High RWA Gregson, to be described). One version described a "respectable but racist" Arnold, the other a "disrespectable and racist" one. The results were instructive. Both Lows and Highs evaluated the strongly racist Gregson negatively, whether he had a respectable past or not, with means of about 17 and 14, respectively.

   As many North American politicians have shown, appeals to prejudice work best when disguised as other issues. Overt racism can alienate even prejudiced voters.

7. Being worried about comparing "September 1983" students with "January 1983" ones, I repeated the entire experiment in September 1984 with 557 new students. The subjects received one of the *four* versions of Arnold Gregson described in the text and evaluated him as before. The ANOVA found significant main effects for both Version and Authoritarianism (Lows liked the four Gregsons less overall than Highs did), and the Version × Authoritarianism interaction was again significant. The shapes in Figure 7 were rather faithfully reproduced. The mean reactions of

Highs and Lows to the different depictions of Gregson were: control (28.8) [29.2]; disrespectable (21.9) [25.6]; respectable and High RWA (28.8) [20.2]; disrespectable but High RWA (24.9) [18.3]. The overall correlations between subjects' RWA Scale scores and their likings for these versions of Arnold Gregson were .06, −.24, .44, and .44, respectively, compared with .00, −.24, .48, and .36 in the initial studies.

8. In January 1985 I administered the control scenario to 186 students, except the subjects were told they were married but *childless* 20 years in the future. Their RWA Scale scores went up 6.6 points (from 149.2 to 155.8), significantly less than the jump of 12.0 points among the November 1982 controls.

9. Fear of revolution in the street is not the only anxiety that will raise authoritarianism. An additional 187 students served in the January 1985 experiment described in Note 8. They were given the usual introductory paragraph and then told, "There is a significant problem within Canada. As many social observers and religious leaders have put it, the traditional values our society has been based upon, such as the importance of the family, reverence for God, respect for human life and the law—these values are being discredited and overturned.

> All in all, this has not happened overnight, but gradually. For example, the divorce rate has risen year after year, such that now *most* marriages fail. Fewer and fewer families attend church, such that most children receive little if any religious instruction. The abortion rate is more than twice what it was in 1985. Child abuse, including sexual molestation, is increasingly widespread.
>
> As more children have been raised by single parents or brought up in "mix and match marriages," vandalism and juvenile delinquency have increased. There are very few working telephones on the streets; most buses have mutilated seats and broken windows. Crime rates have, in general, risen substantially. The inability of society to maintain normal public services and protect private property has reinforced the growing feeling that the "social bond" is disintegrating and the "law of the jungle is just around the corner."

This "loss of values" scenario was judged nearly as serious as many of the violent futures used in other studies ($\overline{X}=4.05$). Furthermore,

RWA Scale scores rose 23.9 points (or 11.9 points after controlling for the "first-paragraph effects"). There were 26 significant item increases, led mainly by the authoritarian aggression items. Thus the sense that society is slowly decaying, that values are being forgotten, that the social fabric is steadily pulling apart can apparently frighten many persons and produce a significant rise in authoritarianism. The increase was significantly less than that produced in the violent left-wing threat scenario answered by other students, however.

10. The other 183 subjects responded to a new *control* description, which was identical to that used in the "Brownshirts condition" but ended with the sentence "The government has changed several times . . . but each new government has failed to cure the nation's economic woes." Therefore these subjects were simply told they were 20 years older, parents, and well off, but the economy was in a mess because of severe inflation. There was no description of any group posing any kind of threat to the country. In short, I was trying to see how much of my earlier effects were attributable to the sense of an economic crisis, in itself, without any political threat.

    This situation was judged very serious ($\overline{X}=4.23$), but the students' RWA Scale scores rose only 11.9 points, on the average, from 149.5 to 161.4. This, of course, is attributable to the "first paragraph." Recalling that the subjects were told they were in no personal economic danger, news of an economic crisis affecting many others did not appear to change their authoritarianism.

11. In the autumn of 1986, 230 students responded to the nonviolent left-wing protest scenario, only with references to "crime and violence" in the urban ghettoes removed from the second paragraph. The overall situation in Canada was still judged very serious ($\overline{X}=4.13$), but RWA Scale scores rose only 11.1 points (from 152.3 to 163.4)—significantly less than the 17.3-point rise found for the equally serious threat tested in the January 1983 study. In other words, this *totally nonviolent* movement produced no backlash at all, when we recall that RWA Scale scores will go up about 12 points as a result of the changed personal status of the subjects.

12. In March 1985 I administered the "Brownshirts" and "slow loss of values" scenarios to 131 and 145 *parents*, respectively. The results replicated student-based findings. The "Brownshirts situation" was judged very serious ($\overline{X}=4.29$) and raised RWA Scale scores 5.2 points. The loss-of-values situation was judged a little less serious (4.10) but raised authoritarianism 13.1 points (comparable to the

12.2-point increase shown by parents who responded to the violent left-wing threat condition in January 1983). Both increases were statistically significant. (Recall that there is apparently no "first-paragraph effect" with parents.)

13. The only other significant correlations between RWA Scale scores and trait evaluations were −.33 for "open-mindedness," .27 for "will power," .23 for "stability," −.22 for "tolerance," and −.20 for "self-understanding." But all these small relationships reflect modest differences in Lows' and Highs' preferences. Interestingly, Highs' most valued traits were compassion, determination, open-mindedness, and integrity—on most of which they do not score very high.

14. I wondered whether these "normality seeking" Highs might be more susceptible to social embarrassment than others. So in January 1985 I asked 353 students how upset they would be, on a 0–5 basis, in a dozen different embarrassing situations. RWA Scale scores correlated positively with estimates of being upset in all instances, significantly so in 11 cases. Some of these relationships were quite predictable (for example, "Suppose someone saw you looking at magazines in a drugstore in front of the place where *Playboy, Playgirl,* et cetera are kept"). Others seem as though they would be embarrassing to almost anyone: belching in a restaurant; finding you had just given a speech with your blouse unbuttoned or your fly down (a professor's nightmare). Correlations among responses to the 12 items averaged .29 (alpha = .83); RWA Scale scores correlated .33 with their sum.

    I have the feeling a lot of Highs were often warned in their youth to keep their behavior circumspect, so as not to "scandalize" others. For example, the item from the Religious Emphasis Scale (Chapter Six) with the highest RWA Scale correlation over the years has consistently been (that emphasis was placed on) "Being a good representative of the faith; acting the way a devout member of your religion would be expected to act." An unintended consequence of this emphasis may have been to make Highs rather vulnerable to their own social comparison processes in some situations.

15. In fact, six Lows (but no Highs) wrote on the survey sheet that they could not believe they had scored so high. Two even accused me of fabricating their alleged scores. Imagine!

16. At the very end of this anonymous survey I asked the question

about students' filling out "parents' surveys" that is reproduced in Note 2 of Chapter Two.

17. An interesting example of this effect may have occurred in Manitoba in 1987 when the ruling New Democratic Party introduced legislation which specified that (among other things) persons could not be denied housing, employment, and other basic civil rights because of their sexual orientation. Many persons, including me, expected the opposition Tories to raise as much political Cain over this proposal as possible.

    There was an intense citizens' protest in public hearings, but the Progressive Conservatives did not appear nearly as interested in harnessing this energy as they had been a few years earlier during the language rights debate (see Note 22 of Chapter Five), and the debate in the House was relatively subdued. The Tories' opposition *may* have been lessened by a series of unpublicized, frank meetings that leaders of the gay community organized with Manitoba lawmakers. According to a Canadian Broadcasting Corporation report, legislators who considered homosexuals degenerates and repulsive deviants had difficulty matching these attitudes to the people they met, and some found their personal opinions about gays changed as a result.

    We, of course, have seen evidence for that effect at several points in this book.

Afterthoughts

Where Have We Got?

Social scientists have been studying "authoritarianism" in democracies for over 40 years. If you agree that right-wing authoritarianism can be usefully conceived as the covariation of authoritarian submission, authoritarian aggression, and conventionalism, then we have seemingly traveled farther in the past eight chapters than we did in the past four decades. Specifically:

- We saw that these defining attitudes go together in a number of places in the world, not just in North America, where the covariation was discovered.
- We have reviewed evidence that authoritarianism has increased in society during the 1970s and 1980s. Fully 80 percent of the incoming Manitoba students in 1987 scored at least "slightly authoritarian" on the "Continuing Twelve" items of the original RWA Scale, compared with 54 percent in 1973.
- We have developed an understanding of the personal origins of right-wing authoritarianism in adults. Certain experiences in life appear to shape these attitudes more than parental influence, the peer group, and so on. If we know

whether a university student has had these experiences and how much they affected her one way or the other, we can usually make a pretty accurate prediction of her RWA Scale score.

- We also saw that higher education, particularly in the liberal arts, tends to lower authoritarianism and that parenthood apparently increases it. Various changes in society, such as violence in the streets, also appear likely to raise adult RWA Scale scores.
- We now understand why authoritarian submission, authoritarian aggression, and conventionalism covary. Highly submissive, conventional persons seem unusually fearful that the world is personally dangerous and that society is collapsing into lawlessness. This fear, along with other factors, instigates aggressive impulses. Submissive, conventional persons also tend to be highly self-righteous (although they have failed numerous times to prove more moral than others). This self-righteousness disinhibits the aggressive impulse. Highs accordingly have a considerable capacity for hostile behavior toward a bewildering array of victims. Other people, especially Lows, are markedly less fearful, less self-righteous, and hence much less authoritarian-aggressive.

  The combination of fear and self-righteousness can account for most of the authoritarian aggression we have uncovered in our various measures.
- We have turned up a wealth of evidence that certain religious training and experiences are liable to foster authoritarianism. Although one can find Highs among the "true believers" of any religious category or sect, they have been most concentrated in my samples among "Fundamentalist Protestants." Authoritarians tend to have highly organized religious ideologies, which are often, however, unconnected with other aspects of their behavior. Though professing great religious certainty, many Highs have hidden, unexpressible doubts about the tenets of their faith.
- The RWA Scale seems to tap a fundamental ideological dimension among North American lawmakers. In Canada

we found very powerful differences in authoritarianism among the politicians in different political parties. RWA Scale scores also varied greatly among American legislators but were not reliably related to party label.

- We found no evidence for "the authoritarian on the left." One can call left-wing extremists many things, but there appears to be no psychological basis thus far for labeling them "authoritarian."
- We saw that authoritarianism may be controllable within our societies in many ways. Various contributions that the educational system, the media, and religions could make were outlined. Laws promoting civil liberties appear beneficial in several respects. A technique for undercutting the popular appeal of right-wing demagogues was found promising. We discovered how social reform movements can apparently best avoid creating a backlash against their causes. And we considered evidence that many authoritarians might be willing to moderate their attitudes and behavior, if they can be brought to realize they are Highs.

To summarize this summary, I believe we have provided experimental, data-blessed answers to most of the important questions we have about the "pre-Fascist personality"—and discovered a number of other very interesting things as well, about both Lows and Highs. We can surely expect these answers to be refined by further research. But I think we have now, for the first time, a valid and useful scientific understanding of right-wing authoritarianism—which is what this book promised in its title. We are hardly at square one, as we were at the end of Chapter One when we asked, "So what?" Indeed, I think we are most of the way across the board now.

I find little mystery in how we have made such progress. First, others led the way some years ago and by their successes and failures pointed to a workable conceptualization of right-wing authoritarianism. Second, this research program has embodied a certain dedication to psychometric integrity that made interpretations relatively straightforward and "confounding results" rare. And third, people kept reproducing, so I could correct my mistakes of previous years through the never-ending batches of fresh subjects who appeared each September. It was science by groping and grinding. But grinders can make useful contributions in science.

Theoretical Implications

If you are familiar with the "Berkeley theory" of the authoritarian personality, you may feel that my research confirms much that was first published in 1950. That is to be expected, I think, since these two efforts were spawned by the same terrifying historical events, and they looked at the same kinds of people. The two undertakings would naturally see many of the same behaviors and covariates.

In at least one respect Nevitt Sanford's theory has been stunningly supported. If you look on page 228 of *The Authoritarian Personality*, you will find listed as the first three traits of the authoritarian personality (characterizing a "strong superego") "conventionalism, authoritarian submission, and authoritarian aggression." The things that Sanford may have noticed first about authoritarians seemingly turn out to be their most enduring and distinctive characteristics.

However, I have found only spotty support for the rest of the Berkeley model. Take the signs of a "weak ego," for example. Highs do appear relatively anti-intraceptive, but they still seem to know a fair bit about themselves; it's often just a matter of creating the right conditions for them to admit what they realize. What they do not realize (for example, how *relatively* prejudiced they are) may be attributable to limited social experiences, not repressed anxiety. Then, are Highs particularly superstitious, believing in "mystical determinants of the individual's fate"? No. (See Note 14 of Chapter Six.) But do they tend to think in rigid categories, "stereotypy"? Yes, guilty; and the association between RWA Scale scores and prejudice supports the central conclusion of the Berkeley researchers, who started out to explain anti-Semitism. But the association has been much weaker than the response-set-soaked correlations reported in 1950.

So some of the findings reported in *The Authoritarian*

Personality have been replicated and some of its insights confirmed. But not all, by any means, and not to the extent thought in 1950.

Besides these indications of support and disconfirmation of the Berkeley findings, we have to acknowledge the profound difference between the two *theoretical* explanations of authoritarianism advanced. The psychoanalytic model has virtually no evidence to support its most distinctive feature: the importance of certain early childhood experiences in a special home environment. And its array of unconscious mechanisms has proved difficult to verify and ultimately discouraging even to pursue.

All of this was true by 1954 (Christie and Jahoda), but since then the question has been "If you don't like the Berkeley theory, how *do* you explain authoritarianism?" I think we have a very sound answer to that now. Bandura's social learning theory has produced models for the personal origin and dynamics of right-wing authoritarianism that not only explain *more* of these things than other theories can, they explain *most* of these things, period. And explain them in terms of principles well established in psychology by the 1980s.

A good friend of mine, M. Brewster Smith, without whose help this book might never have been published, once observed that I have used social learning theory as a convenient semantic framework, whose flexible principles I could turn to my purposes without ever getting down to some nitty-gritty. That is undoubtedly true to some extent, and Bandura would almost certainly approach the subject of authoritarian behavior differently, and use his theory in different (probably better) ways, than I have. But it is something of a tribute to a theory that, even when misused by others, it takes us much further in our understanding than we have ever been before.

A Final, Personal Observation

I have written this book primarily for my academic colleagues in North America, and in closing I would like to point out something we might naturally fail to appreciate in the details of our lives. We are about the freest people in the world.

To start with, we have all the freedoms promised any citizen in our countries: freedom of speech, freedom of religion, the right to personal liberty, the right to protest, freedom of association, freedom of information, the right to vote and stand for office, freedom of movement and residence, the right to pursue the career of our choice, the right of *habeas corpus* when we run afoul of the law, the right to a fair trial, and a long list of other rights that we quite take for granted.

Beyond these, however, we have additional enormous freedoms as professors. I do not mean that with our "light" teaching responsibilities we enjoy enormous leisure. But we do lead relatively self-controlled lives; few of us *have* to be somewhere doing a certain thing 40 hours a week. Beyond that, we have a gift almost no one else has, a gift of immense value to a species characterized by its extraordinary curiosity. We have the opportunity to spend our lives studying whatever interests us. Our societies realize it is in their best interest to let some of their members do so, and we have been selected.

This right to investigate whatever we want is part of academic freedom. The other part is the right to teach whatever we consider to be the truth on a subject. I have been a professor for 20 years and during that time have taught in a small church-related college in the American Midwest and a large public Canadian university. I have worried plenty about whether I was adequately prepared for class but never about whether I would get into trouble for what I was going to say.

Similarly, all the while I have been researching authoritarianism (of all things), even in the halls of power (of all places), and writing up my findings, I have never worried for a second about the possible reaction of the "authorities." And I'll bet you never worry about that either, as you prepare your lectures, your studies, and your writings. Our sacred trust with society is to learn the truth and teach it, whatever it may be. And in our countries, we do both without fear or hesitation.

It is not so everywhere. One of the first targets of dictators, whether on the left or the right, is the academic community. We have many, many colleagues in Latin American, Eastern European, Asian, and African universities who must worry constantly whether the authorities will approve of their research and their speeches. We have colleagues, as a reading of *Amnesty International* reports will reveal, who have lost their jobs and lost their freedom and lost their lives for doing things that we do without pause because they are so integral to freely searching and freely professing. The kinds of freedoms we take for granted are antithetical to totalitarianism. We will probably never experience Big Brother, but can you imagine what it would be like to work under such surveillance and fear? Ask someone who was thrown into the crucible of McCarthyism (for example, Smith, 1986).

All our freedoms are guaranteed in our democracy, but democracy is not guaranteed in our society. Presently I feel safe, but I do not feel safeguarded, for reasons given in the previous pages. I sense a latent vulnerability to our lives, partly because we do not really appreciate the blessings of liberty—especially those we especially enjoy. You and I do not have as much at stake in freedom as others do. We have more. And we owe it to the democracies that have given us so much, and to our quest for the truth, to preserve the blessings of liberty for ourselves and our posterity.

Appendix A: A Brief Discussion of Statistical Matters

A behavioral scientist usually does research by drawing a random sample of some group and measuring something about the individuals chosen. Once we have collected our measurements, we turn to analyzing them, usually with some kind of statistical technique. The particular technique used depends on what we are trying to discover.

Let us say we are interested in how tall people are, specifically what causes adult height. We suspect that people "get their height" from their parents, so we measure a lot of university students and their parents to see whether this is true. Do tall mothers and tall fathers have tall offspring? How much correspondence is there?

We can tell mathematically by computing the *correlation* coefficient between parents' height and that of their adult children. This statistic can theoretically vary from 0.00 (for no relationship at all) to 1.00 (for a perfect relationship, which is as rare in the behavioral sciences as it is in love). The more children resemble their parents, the higher the correlation will be. In fact, the correlation between parent/child height is about .50. Some people resemble their parents, but if you look at a family reunion photo, you will probably see others who do not. (Incidentally, correlations do not prove one thing is *causing* another. But in this case we are pretty sure, for genetic reasons, that parents' height does affect their children's.)

When the scores of two variables go up together, such as height and weight, we say they are "positively" correlated. But sometimes as scores on one variable go up, the scores on the other variable go down, as with amount of exercise and weight. Then we say the two variables are "negatively" correlated.

Actually, each of us comes from two different families. As we look at pictures of our two family trees, we may notice that one seems to have taller members than the other. For example, I am the result of a tree of Altemeyers and a tree of Fiesers, and I have always thought that while the branches on both trees tend to be stout, the Fiesers were a little taller overall.

I could test this hypothesis by measuring my aunts and uncles and calculating the average height in each family by dividing the sum of their heights by the number of persons I measured. Researchers call this kind of an average the *mean*, and we could see whether the Fieser mean was actually larger than the Altemeyer mean. Similarly, I could look, as I sometimes have, to see whether the mean score of Republicans on the RWA Scale is higher than the mean score of Democrats.

But won't that depend on the particular Republicans and Democrats I happened to ask? Certainly. A researcher will try to draw as random a sample as possible, but if you have ever been dealt a great poker hand, you know that a random sample can still be pretty extraordinary sometimes. So how can we tell, when we have compared the mean RWA Scale scores of Republicans and Democrats, that we have not just happened to draw, purely by accident, an extraordinary sample of Republicans, or Democrats, or both?

The answer is that we cannot, at least not directly, unless we give the RWA Scale to all Republicans and Democrats. That would be a little tedious. But there are mathematical models that enable us to calculate the *probability* that any particular difference in means, or any particular correlation, could have been obtained by such sampling luck. So after we calculate the means of some samples of Republicans and Democrats on the RWA Scale, we calculate a little more to find out what the chances are that we got those results because we tested a nonrepresentative group of people.

Researchers usually want to be very sure their results are not due to luck, so we typically do not pay attention to a finding if the chances are greater than five out of a hundred that it could have occurred because of sampling error. That may strike you as quite conservative. It would be like a poker player who bets only on a full house or better. It means we will ignore a lot of true things; but it also means we can be pretty sure that what we *do* consider the Truth really is true. We call a finding that can pass this 5/100 test "statistically significant." Some results are even more impressive; calculations reveal they could have happened by chance only 1 in 100 or 1 in 1000 times. But if we are *at least* 95 percent sure that a correlation is trustworthy or that the difference between two means really exists in the population, we say the finding is statistically significant.

Unless I indicate otherwise, all the findings reported in this book are statistically significant.

Ready for some abbreviations for all this?

r means a correlation coefficient.
$\overline{X}$ is a mean.
N is the number of persons in a sample.
t, z, F, and W all stand for a test of the difference between averages of some kind.
p means the probability that some correlation or some difference between averages was due to sampling error. Thus "$p < .05$" means the result was statistically significant. And "$p < .001$" means the result was even more trustworthy—there is only 1 chance in 1000 that it was due to sampling error.

Researchers usually design experiments in such a way that nature has to send a pretty definite signal before we will accept it. That's the thinking behind "$p < .05$." But sometimes the logic of a situation makes you want p to be *greater* than .05—you want a nonsignificant difference. For example, you might want to show that two samples are basically equal in IQ before you use them in an experiment involving intelligence. If you found a statistically significant difference in IQ *before* you started the experiment, you would have to begin again from scratch. So a p greater than .05 is not always a bad thing. It depends on what you are trying to do.

You will find strange statements in this book such as "$t = 2.31$," "$z = 1.06$," "$F = 64.5$," "$W = 1.72$," and (as if all this were not bad enough) "chi-squared = 6.7." Here is the good news—far better news than I got in my statistics courses: you do not have to know what these mean. They are merely stepping stones in the calculations that lead to the value of p. The value of p is important; it tells us whether the result should be trusted. But you can skip happily over the stepping stones and not miss a thing.

The only other bit of statistical jargon that pops up regularly in this book is *internal consistency*. Psychological tests usually contain many items, and *if* all the items basically measure the same thing, then responses to them ought to be intercorrelated. Putting together the two kinds of statistics described above, we can calculate the mean of the correlations between all the pairs of items on a test. The higher this average intercorrelation is, the more internally consistent, the more unidimensional, the more reliable, the purer a test is. "*Alpha*" is the statistic that reflects a test's overall internal consistency. Theoretically alpha can vary, like the correlations it represents, from 0.00 to 1.00. The higher the alpha, the better the test usually is. The best IQ tests have alphas of .90 or even higher. Many other psychological tests have much poorer levels of internal consistency. In Chapter One you will run into a scale whose alpha is so low (about .70), its measurements contain a large amount of unconnected "noise."

Here are some other "translations" that might be helpful from time to time.

"Variance accounted for"—The whole point to behavioral research is to be able to explain the differences among people. These differences are called variance. How much do people vary in height? Some, but they vary even more in weight and even more than that in sexual appetite. Scientists try to explain such differences, and the "bottom line" of the scientific quest is how much variance we can explain ("account for") in terms of other variables such as gender or age.

You can tell how much one variable explains about another by *squaring the correlation* between them. Thus, if parents' height correlates .50 with their children's, you can explain only .50 times .50, or 25 percent, of the latter in terms of the former. That means your predictions of how tall children will eventually be, based on their parents' height, will be only about 25 percent accurate. Why so little? Mainly because of recombination of the mothers' and fathers' genes. But disease, nutrition, and other factors can play a role in determining height too. (Human beings are the most complicated things we know of in the universe. Our behavior is very complexly determined, and we seldom find we can explain much with just one factor.)

"Eta-squared" is a similar statistic that tells us how much of the differences among subjects in a study, like the height of the Altemeyers and the Fiesers, can be explained by a certain factor, such as which family one belongs to. Eta-squared can vary from 0 percent to 100 percent and is usually very low (less than 10 percent) for one-factor explanations.

In Chapter Three I perform a "multiple regression analysis" on students' RWA Scale scores. It sounds like a group adventure into reincarnation, but all it really does is let us try to explain behavior with more than one factor, such as using gender as well as family background to explain height. In Chapter Three we see how much of the difference in the students' authoritarianism we can explain with our most powerful predictor. Then we see how much more we can explain by adding in a second predictor, and so on. (It may seem that by simply using enough predictors, we should be able to explain everything. But you are working with diminishing returns, and you quickly reach the point where using more predictors adds practically nothing to what you already know.)

Finally, in Chapter Five I use a "partial correlational analysis" to uncover the roots of authoritarian aggression. This is simply a technique that enables us to pry apart two correlated variables to see whether some third factor accounts for the connection between them. The more highly such a third favor is correlated with the first two, the more it can potentially explain about the connection between them.

Appendix B: Organization of Surveys in the 1984 "Origins" Experiment

Students

First session	*Second session*	*Third session*
RWA Scale	Experiences Scale	Rate High/Low student
"Arnold Gregson"	RWA – effect of news media	"William Langley"
"Dangerous People"	RWA – effect of education	Prejudice Scale
Attitudes Toward Homosexuals Scale		How prejudiced are you?
Religious and political affiliations		Fantasies; various questions

Parents

RWA Scale
Estimate child's RWA
"Emphasize" RWA
"Dangerous People"
Attitudes Toward Homosexuals Scale
Prejudice Scale
French-language Issue
How prejudiced are you?
Demographics: gender, age, education, socioeconomic status, political affiliation
Manitoba language debate

Best Friends

RWA Scale
Estimate friend's RWA
Discuss RWA
Attitudes Toward Homosexuals Scale
Demographics: gender, age, education, how met friend, occupation

Appendix C: Final Version of the Experiences Scale, Including Instructions

[This survey is quite different from most of the questionnaires you answer in experiments. It is NOT an *opinion* survey. Instead it seeks information about the *experiences* you have had in life. It is like a "personal history" survey, designed to find out what sorts of things have happened to people by the time they become university students.

This questionnaire covers a lot of different topics, and you may *not* have encountered some of the situations described. *The first question you should ask yourself in each case is, "Have I ever had the experience involved?"* If the answer is "No," then blacken the "0" bubble on the IBM sheet, no matter what your opinion on the subject may be.

Take, for example, the following statement:

> "It has been my experience that physical punishment is an effective way to make people behave."

Maybe you never received any physical punishment yourself and never saw anyone else you knew receive it. If so, since you never had any such direct experience with the effects of physical punishment, you would blacken the "0" bubble for this item.

−4	−3	−2	−1	0	+1	+2	+3	+4
○	○	○	○	●	○	○	○	○

If, on the other hand, you or someone you knew *did* receive physical punishment, then your job is to indicate whether it had the intended effect, or did it make things worse.

If, in your direct experience, physical punishment almost always had the desired effect, if it made you or the persons you knew change your behavior and act the way the punisher intended, you would blacken the "+ 3" or "+ 4" bubble.

But if, in your own experience, physical punishment has almost always "backfired," if it didn't change behavior and instead caused resentment and made things worse, then you would blacken the "− 3" or "− 4" bubble.

The intermediate bubbles, "− 2," "− 1," "+ 1," and "+ 2" are for more qualified responses. For example, maybe *sometimes* physical punishment, in your experience, has made things better, but *usually* it has made things worse—then you would do a sort of arithmetic and end up blackening the "− 1" or "− 2" bubble. *On balance,* that would be what your experiences have shown.

. . . .

The important thing to remember is, this is *not* an attitude survey, but a report of your own personal experiences.

- It is not a survey of what your parents have taught you,
- It is not a survey of what your teachers have taught you,
- It is not a survey of what your friends have taught you,
- It is not a survey of what the news has taught you.

It is a survey of what *your experience* has taught you.*

* The survey was printed on legal-size paper (21.5 × 36.0 cm). The instructions to this point covered the first side of the first sheet. Other page breaks occurred after items 9 and 20.

EXPERIENCES SURVEY

A. First, decide if the statement concerns something you have experienced. *If it does not, blacken the "0" bubble.*

B. If the statement *does* refer to an experience you've had, to things that *have* happened to you, or to people you *do* know, then answer according to the following scale:

Blacken the – 4 bubble if the statement is *very untrue* of your experiences.
– 3 bubble if the statement is *pretty untrue* of your experiences.
– 2 bubble if the statement is *moderately untrue* of your experiences.
– 1 bubble if the statement is *slightly untrue* of your experiences.

Blacken the + 1 bubble if the statement is *slightly true* of your experiences.
+ 2 bubble if the statement is *moderately true* of your experiences.
+ 3 bubble if the statement is *pretty true* of your experiences.
+ 4 bubble if the statement is *very true* of your experiences.]

1. It has been my experience that physical punishment is an effective way to make people behave. (Have you received physical punishment or known others who did? If not, blacken the "0" bubble. If so, to what extent did it make you and/or others behave as intended?)
2. I have known people with "poor manners" who really did not care whether people thought they were respectable or not, and they seemed basically as good and pleasant as everybody else. (Have you personally known persons with poor manners, who did not care if they were behaving respectably or not? If *not*, blacken the "0" bubble. If so, did they seem basically as good and pleasant as everybody else?)

3. The homosexuals I have known seemed to be normal, decent people, just like everybody else, except for their sexual orientation. (First, do you know any homosexuals, are you acquainted with someone who is a homosexual? If not, blacken the "0" bubble. If so, do they seem like everybody else except for their sexual orientation?)
4. The people I know who are disrespectful toward authority and unpatriotic have seemed to me to be ignorant troublemakers. (Again, do you know people who could be described as disrespectful toward authority and unpatriotic? If not, blacken the "0" bubble. If so, has it been your experience that they are "ignorant troublemakers"?)

   Remember, the question is not what have you learned from your parents, your teachers, your friends, your church, or the news. It is, instead, what have you learned from your own personal experience?
5. I have learned from my own experience that being a decent human being has nothing to do with being religious. (Do you know religious *and* nonreligious people, and do you have an impression of how good and decent they are? If not, blacken the "0" bubble. If so, is it your experience that being a decent human being has nothing to do with being religious?)
6. It has been my experience that things work best when fathers are the head of their families. (Do you know families in which the father is "the head" and others in which he is not? If not, blacken the "0" bubble. But if so, is it your experience that things work best when fathers are the head of their families?)
7. It has been my experience that sexual intercourse is all right for students in their last year or so of high school. (Do you know people who were engaging in sexual intercourse in, say, Grade 11 or Grade 12? If not, blacken the "0" bubble. If so, did it seem to be a positive experience for them, with positive outcomes?)
8. My parents have always known what was right for me. (Has it been your experience that they have?)
9. My own experience with pornographic material indicates

it is harmless and should *not* be censored. (Have you, or persons you know, encountered material that might be considered pornographic? If not, blacken the "0" bubble. But if so, has it been your experience that it is harmless and should not be censored?)

It is natural, as you go through these statements, to begin responding in terms of what others have taught you is right, or a fact, or the truth. For example, with regard to the last question you answered, people have ideas about what scientific research has shown on the effects of pornography; and your church may have told you what the effects are. But that is not what this survey is about. Instead it is saying, "Forget all these other things. What has YOUR EXPERIENCE in life shown you?"

10. Most of the young people I know who have taken advantage of today's greater freedom have messed up their lives. (Have you, or have young people you personally know, taken advantage of today's greater freedoms? If you know no one like that, blacken the "0" bubble. But if you know of such persons, did taking advantage of today's greater freedom lead to messed-up lives?)
11. I have learned from my contact with lots of different kinds of people that no one group has "the truth" or knows "the one right way to live." (Have you met lots of different kinds of people thus far in your life? If not, blacken the "0" bubble. If you have, did this contact lead you to conclude that no one group has "the truth" or knows "the one right way to live"?)
12. I have found that breaking rules can be exciting and fun at times. (Have you broken rules at times? If not, blacken the "0" bubble. But if you have, did it prove exciting and fun?)
13. I have seen, both in how things have happened in history and in my own life, that many times protest is right and rebellion necessary to end injustice. (Have you studied rebellions in history, engaged in protests yourself, or know others who did? If not, blacken the "0" bubble. If so, was it right, and necessary to end injustice?)
14. I know from my own experience that life would be meaningless without my family religion. (Have you, or has some-

one you personally know, "fallen away" from your family religion? If not, blacken the "0" bubble. But if so, was it your experience that life became meaningless without it?)

15. Whenever I did things my parents warned me against, it was usually a mistake and resulted in a bad experience. (Have you done things that your parents warned you against? If not, blacken the "0" bubble. If so, did it turn out to be a mistake resulting in a bad experience?)

    Remember, the question is not what have your parents taught you, or your teachers, or your church. It is not, what do your friends believe, or what seems to be true because of the news broadcasts and stories in the newspapers. It is, instead, what has YOUR OWN EXPERIENCE taught you.

16. I have been favorably impressed by people I know who continue to have rebellious ideas and a sharply critical outlook on life. (Do you, in fact, personally know people like this? If not, blacken the "0" bubble. If so, did they impress you favorably?)
17. The authorities and officials I have trusted in my life, at home, in school, et cetera have always treated me honestly and fairly. (Has that been your experience?)
18. It has been my experience that smoking marijuana is a big mistake. (Have you done this yourself or personally known others who did? If not, blacken the "0" bubble. But if you did, or know others who did, did it prove to be a big mistake?)
19. My contact with nontraditional families, in which everyone is more equal than usual, has convinced me that it is basically a bad idea. (Do you know any families like this, in which the mother and father and children are more equal than they are in the traditional family? If not, blacken the "0" bubble. If so, was it your experience that it was basically a bad idea?)
20. I have found that it's better to be unconventional than to be "normal." (Have you done unconventional things or known people who are unconventional? If not, blacken the "0" bubble. But if so, what was your experience? Was it better for you, or for your acquaintances, to be unconventional?)

Just one more reminder. The purpose of this survey is to see how you have been affected by the experiences you have had in life. It is not trying to find out what you think is true because of what you have learned from teachers, or parents, or priests, nuns, or ministers, or news accounts of other people's lives. But rather, what have you found out from your experiences?

21. The more I've thought about traditional religious beliefs, the more contradictory, irrational, and nonsensical they have seemed to me. (Have you thought critically about traditional religious beliefs, have you seriously wondered if they are true? If not, blacken the "0" bubble. If so, did they seem contradictory, irrational, and nonsensical?)
22. As I have gotten older, I have seen that the rebellious ideas I had earlier were really foolish. (Did you have rebellious ideas or periods earlier in your life? If not, blacken the "0" bubble. But if you did, do they now seem foolish to you?)
23. I have seen times when authorities used their power unjustly or excessively when punishing someone they did not like. (To what extent have you witnessed, or been involved in, situations in which authorities used their power this way?)
24. From what I have seen, the only way to handle troublemakers and people who break the law is to crack down hard on them. (Have you known such troublemakers or persons who break the law? If not, blacken the "0" bubble. If so, was it your experience that "cracking down on them" was the right thing to do?)

Note: The instructions between the brackets ([ ]) were both printed on the survey and read to the students (over a tape recorder) at the beginning of the session.

Appendix D: Letter Sent to Graduating Students in May 1986

THE UNIVERSITY OF MANITOBA DEPARTMENT OF PSYCHOLOGY Winnipeg, Manitoba Canada R3T 2N2

Dear "Potential Grad":

Four years ago, when you first arrived at the U. of Manitoba, you served in an experiment entitled "Survey" while taking 17.120. I doubt you recall anything about my study, but basically you gave your reaction to a series of statements concerning a variety of social issues. You signed your name to an attendance sheet then, which had your survey number on it. Those sheets, and the responses of the hundreds of students who served in that experiment, have spent the last four years "sleeping" peacefully in a filing cabinet.

An interesting question which arises is, have your opinions changed over time? They may have stayed essentially the same, or they may be different now. Would you mind completing the attached survey for me once again, and returning it in the enclosed envelope? It will only take about 15 minutes.

You will see that your old survey number from 1982 is written on the top of the questionnaire. If you leave it there, I shall be able to compare your two sets of answers. All answers will of course be kept as confidential as the last set. (Whatever has happened to you since 1982, I guarantee you the responses you made in Experiment Survey had nothing to do with it!)

If however you wish to answer anonymously, simply tear off the corner of the questionnaire which contains the survey number. I can still use anonymous answers for group analyses. (I expect answers from well over 100 potential graduates.)

Letter Sent to Graduating Students in May 1986, cont'd.

If you participate and wish to know the results of this study, simply phone the U. of M. Psychology Department (474-9338) and leave your name. I shall mail you a summary of the results in a month or so. (Would you please send me your answers in a week or so then?)

Yours sincerely,

P.S. You can see that I have enclosed a small sum to encourage your participation. (Last time you got an "experimental credit." Remember them?) If you choose not to fill out the survey, would you please send me the $1.00 back in the envelope.

Appendix E: The "Secret Survey" Administered in January 1985

Because this survey is completely anonymous, I would appreciate your answering *every* question, quite *truthfully*, for the scientific value of the study.

1. How unfair, how unreasonably hard, do you think my tests have been? (Circle one)
   Extremely unfair   Quite unfair   Moderately unfair
   Slightly unfair   Fair
2. Did you cheat on any of the tests by copying other students' answers?
   ____ No, not at all   ____On 1 or 2 questions
   ____ 3 or 4   ____ 5 or 6   ____7 or more
3. Most of the students in this class answered the Psychometric Survey at the beginning of the year. All who did were then eligible for additional credits by serving in the "fantasy study" and by having surveys sent home to parents.
   (a) If you were eligible for the fantasy study, but did *not* participate in it, why didn't you? It was an easy way to earn a credit.

   ____

(b) If you were eligible for the "parents' survey" but did *not* have booklets sent out, why didn't you? It was an easy way to earn another one or two credits.

____

4. You may recall the lecture on hypnosis dealing with Hilgard's research on the "Hidden Observer." Suppose there is a Hidden Observer in you, which knows your every thought and deed, but which only speaks when it is safe to do so, and when directly spoken to. This question is for your Hidden Observer: Does this person (that is, you) have doubts that (s)he was created by an Almighty God who will judge each person and take some into heaven for eternity while casting others into hell forever?

____ Yes, (s)he has secret doubts which (s)he has kept strictly to herself/himself that this is really true.

____ Yes, (s)he has such doubts, but others (such as parents or friends) know (s)he has these doubts.

____ No, (s)he totally believes this, and has *no doubts* whatsoever.

____ Yes, in fact (s)he openly says (s)he *does not believe* there is a God or an afterlife, but (s)he has some secret worries there might be.

____ Yes, in fact (s)he openly says (s)he *does not believe* there is a God or an afterlife, and (s)he has no doubts abot this whatsoever.

5. Again, this is another question for the Hidden Observer: Has the content of this course, 17.120, created any doubts about traditional religious teachings in his/her mind?

____ No, not at all.

____ Yes, it created some doubts that were not there before.

____ It reinforced doubts (s)he already had, but it has not created any new ones.

____ It reinforced some existing doubts and created some new ones.

6. What advice would you give me about making this a better course for you? How would you change my behavior, if you could?

____

____

7. Family violence has been in the news lately. What researchers usually mean by "domestic violence" is one member of a family trying to physically harm another member, through such things as striking, punching, kicking, or any of the other ways people have of physically hurting one another. An ordinary spanking for childish misbehavior would *not* count as domestic violence, but a "spanking" that was appreciably more severe and painful *would* count. Think back over the past year. How many times did acts of domestic violence occur in your family during 1984? (Write a zero if no such aggression occurred.) *What form did the aggression take?*
   (a) Father aggressing against child: ____ times.
   (b) Mother aggressing against child: ____ times.
   (c) Father aggressing against mother: ____ times.
   (d) Mother aggressing against father: ____ times.
   (e) Child (adolescent or older) aggressing against father or mother: ____ times.
   (f) Child (adolescent or older) aggressing against another child: ____ times.
8. Are you a virgin?
   ____ Yes, without qualification.
   ____ Yes, but I don't want to be.
   ____ Yes, but I have engaged in advanced sex acts (for example, oral-genital sex) as a way of having "sexual relations" without having intercourse.
   ____ No, but I'm married/was married.
   ____ No, but against my will.
   ____ No.
9. If you are *not* a virgin, (approximately) how many times have you engaged in sexual intercourse? ____ With how many different partners? ____
10. In general, how much have you enjoyed the sexual activity you have engaged in thus far in your life?
   0 ____ Not at all 1 ____ Slightly 2 ____ Moderately
   3 ____ Very much 4 ____ Greatly

11.* I have wondered at times how people react to me and thought this would be a good time to get some honest, anonymous answers. So would you use the scales below to rate me, on an overall basis, using all the information and all the impressions you have about me. (Place an "X" in the space on each line below which indicates your overall evaluation of me.)

	VERY NEUTRAL VERY	
Psychologically Unhealthy	___ ___ ___ ___ ___ ___ ___	Psychologically Healthy
Attractive as a Person	___ ___ ___ ___ ___ ___ ___	Unattractive as a Person
Disgusting	___ ___ ___ ___ ___ ___ ___	Admirable

12. Dave Martin (the prof who ran experiment "STEREO") would like your ratings of *homosexuals in general* on the scales below.

	VERY NEUTRAL VERY	
Psychologically Unhealthy	___ ___ ___ ___ ___ ___ ___	Psychologically Healthy
Attractive as a Person	___ ___ ___ ___ ___ ___ ___	Unattractive as a Person
Disgusting	___ ___ ___ ___ ___ ___ ___	Admirable

Thank you. Please fold this sheet several times, return to class, and place it in the sealed box in the front of the room. You will get your Experimental Card stamped then.

Dr. Altemeyer

* Control condition shown. See Chapter Six.

Appendix F: Example of Letter Sent to Legislators

THE UNIVERSITY OF MANITOBA DEPARTMENT OF PSYCHOLOGY Winnipeg, Manitoba Canada R3T 2N2

21 January, 1985

Dear Member of the British Columbia Legislature:

I am writing to ask your cooperation in a bit of research I am doing. Attached you will find a single sheet which asks your opinion on a variety of social issues, many of which you may find quite familiar. I am studying the opinion of Canadians from all walks of life on these matters, and as an elected official your attitudes are perhaps more significant than anyone else's. It will probably take you about ten minutes to answer the items. An addressed, stamped envelope is enclosed for your convenience.

The results of this survey will probably, someday, be published in an academic publication, along with many other findings. Though it is a meagre return, I shall share the results of the survey with you once all the responses are in. All reporting will be done in terms of group scores; everyone who participates in the study will be completely anonymous.

Finally, it is an important principle of psychological research such as this that persons only participate in it if they freely want to. If you feel this survey constitutes an infringement upon your privacy, or a frivolous use of your time, for example, I would not want you to participate, even though your participation would be quite valuable to me.

Thank you for your time in this matter.

Yours sincerely,

References

Adorno, T. W., Frenkel-Brunswik, E., Levinson, D. J., and Sanford, R. N. *The Authoritarian Personality*. New York: Harper & Row, 1950.

Allport, G. W. *The Nature of Prejudice*. Reading, Mass.: Addison-Wesley, 1954.

Allport, G. W., and Ross, J. M. "Personal Religious Orientations and Prejudice." *Journal of Personality and Social Psychology*, 1967, *5*, 432–443.

Altemeyer, B. *Right-Wing Authoritarianism*. Winnipeg: University of Manitoba Press, 1981.

Asch, S. E. "Studies of Independence and Conformity: A Minority of One Against a Unanimous Majority." *Psychological Monographs*, 1956, *70* (9, Whole No. 416).

"Balance or Bias? A Challenge to Class 'Monitors.'" *Time*, Dec. 23, 1985, p. 57.

Bandura, A. *Aggression: A Social Learning Analysis*. Englewood Cliffs, N.J.: Prentice-Hall, 1973.

Bandura, A. *Social Learning Theory*. Englewood Cliffs, N.J.: Prentice-Hall, 1977.

Bandura, A. "Psychological Mechanisms of Aggression." In M. von Cranach, K. Foppa, W. Lepeenies, and D. Ploog (eds.),

Human Ethology: Claims and Limits of a New Discipline. Cambridge: Cambridge University Press, 1979.

Bandura, A. "Mechanisms of Moral Disengagement." Paper presented at conference of the International Security Studies Program, Woodrow Wilson International Center for Scholars, Washington, D.C., Mar. 1987.

Bandura, A. "Social Cognitive Theory of Moral Thought and Action." In W. M. Kurtines and J. L. Gewirtz (eds.), *Moral Behavior and Development: Advances in Theory, Research and Applications.* Vol. 1. Hillsdale, N.J.: Erlbaum, 1988.

Bandura, A., Ross, D., and Ross, S. "A Comparative Test of the Status Envy, Social Power, and Secondary Reinforcement Theories of Identification Learning." *Journal of Abnormal and Social Psychology*, 1963, *67*, 527–534.

Bandura, A., and Walters, R. H. *Adolescent Aggression.* New York: Ronald Press, 1959.

Barker, E. N. "Authoritarianism of the Political Right, Center, and Left." *Journal of Social Issues*, 1963, *19*, 63–74.

Batson, C. D., and Ventis, W. L. *The Religious Experience.* New York: Oxford University Press, 1982.

Bendig, A. W. "Reliability and the Number of Rating Scale Categories." *Journal of Applied Psychology*, 1954, *38*, 38–40.

Berkowitz, L. *Aggression: A Social Psychological Analysis.* New York: McGraw-Hill, 1962.

Berkowitz, L. "The Concept of Aggressive Drive: Some Additional Considerations." In L. Berkowitz (ed.), *Advances in Experimental Social Psychology.* Vol. 2. Orlando, Fla.: Academic Press, 1965.

Berkowitz, L. "Whatever Happened to the Frustration-Aggression Hypothesis?" *American Behavioral Scientist*, 1978, *21*, 691–708.

Blishen, B. R., and McRoberts, H. A. "A Revised Socioeconomic Index for Occupations in Canada." *Canadian Review of Sociology and Anthropology*, 1976, *13*, 71–79.

Brown, R. W. *Social Psychology.* New York: Free Press, 1965.

Brown, R. W. *Social Psychology.* (2nd ed.) New York: Free Press, 1986.

Bryant, J., and Zillman, D. "Effect of Intensification of Annoyance Through Unrelated Residual Excitation on Substantially Delayed Hostile Behavior." *Journal of Experimental Social Psychology*, 1979, *15*, 470–480.

Carlsmith, J. M., Ellsworth, P. C., and Aronson, E. *Methods of Research in Social Psychology*. Reading, Mass.: Addison-Wesley, 1976.

Carlsmith, J. M., and Gross, A. E. "Some Effects of Guilt upon Compliance." *Journal of Personality and Social Psychology*, 1969, *11*, 232–239.

Christie, R., and Jahoda, M. (eds.). *Studies in the Scope and Method of "The Authoritarian Personality."* New York: Free Press, 1954.

Cook, S. W. "Interpersonal and Attitudinal Outcomes in Cooperating Interracial Groups." *Journal of Research and Development in Education*, 1978, *12*, 97–113.

Coulter, T. T. "An Experimental and Statistical Study of the Relationship of Prejudice and Certain Personality Variables." Unpublished doctoral dissertation, University of London, 1953.

Cronbach, L. J. *Essentials of Psychological Testing*. (3rd ed.) New York: Harper & Row, 1970.

Cronbach, L. J., and Gleser, G. C. "The Signal/Noise Ratio in the Comparison of Reliability Coefficients." *Educational and Psychological Measurement*, 1964, *24*, 467–480.

Deutsch, M., and Collins, M. E. *Interracial Housing: A Psychological Evaluation of a Social Experiment*. Minneapolis: University of Minnesota Press, 1951.

DiRenzo, G. J. *Personality, Power, and Politics*. Notre Dame, Ind.: University of Notre Dame Press, 1967.

Dollard, J., and others. *Frustration and Aggression*. New Haven, Conn.: Yale University Press, 1939.

Duckitt, J. H. "Directiveness and Authoritarianism: Some Research Findings and a Critical Reappraisal. *South African Journal of Psychology*, 1983, *13*, 10–12.

Duckitt, J. H. "Reply to Ray's 'Directiveness and Authoritarianism: a Rejoinder to Duckitt.'" *South African Journal of Psychology*, 1984, *14*, 65–66.

Eysenck, H. J. *The Psychology of Politics*. London: Routledge & Kegan Paul, 1954.

Eysenck, H. J. "Left-Wing Authoritarianism: Myth or Reality?" *Political Psychology*, 1981, *3* (1), 234–238.

Eysenck, H. J. Review of *Right-Wing Authoritarianism. Personality and Individual Differences*, 1982, *3*, 352–353.

Eysenck, H. J., and Coulter, T. T. "The Personality and Attitudes of Working-Class British Communists and Fascists." *Journal of Social Psychology*, 1972, *87*, 59–73.

Feldt, L. S. "A Test of the Hypothesis That Cronbach's Alpha or Kuder-Richardson Coefficient Twenty Is the Same for Two Tests." *Psychometrika*, 1969, *34*, 363–373.

Feldt, L. S. "A Test of the Hypothesis That Cronbach's Alpha Reliability Coefficient Is the Same for Two Tests Administered to the Same Sample." *Psychometrika*, 1980, *45*, 99–105.

Fest, J. C. *Hitler*. San Diego, Calif.: Harcourt Brace Jovanovich, 1973.

Festinger, L. "A Theory of Social Comparison Processes." *Human Relations*, 1954, 7, 117-140.

Fishbein, M., and Ajzen, I. *Belief, Attitude, Intention, and Behavior: An Introduction to Theory and Research*. Reading, Mass.: Addison-Wesley, 1975.

Fisher, S., and Greenberg, R. P. *The Scientific Credibility of Freud's Theories and Therapy*. New York: Basic Books, 1977.

Fullerton, J. T., and Hunsberger, B. E. "A Unidimensional Measure of Christian Orthodoxy." *Journal for the Scientific Study of Religion*, 1982, *21*, 317–326.

Galin, D. "Implications for Psychiatry of Left and Right Cerebral Specialization." *Archives of General Psychiatry*, 1974, *31*, 572–583.

Garner, W. R. "Rating Scales, Discriminability and Information Transmission." *Psychological Bulletin*, 1960, *67*, 343–352.

Gazzaniga, M. S. *The Bisected Brain*. East Norwalk, Conn.: Appleton-Century-Crofts, 1970.

Gerbner, G., Gross, L, Signorielli, N., and Morgan, M. "Television, Violence, Victimization, and Power." *American Behavioral Scientist*, 1980, *23*, 705–716.

Gerbner, G., and others. "The Demonstration of Power: Violence Profile No. 10." *Journal of Communication*, 1979, *29*, 177–196.

Gibbons, R., and Nevitte, N. "Canadian Political Ideology: A

Comparative Analysis." *Canadian Journal of Political Science*, 1985, *18*, 557–598.

Guilford, J. P. *Psychometric Methods*. New York: McGraw-Hill, 1954.

Hamilton, D. L., and Bishop, G. D. "Attitudinal and Behavioral Effects of Initial Integration of White Suburban Neighborhoods." *Journal of Social Issues*, 1976, *32*, 47–67.

Heaven, P. C. L. "Predicting Authoritarian Behaviour: Analysis of Three Measures." *Personality and Individual Differences*, 1984, *5*, 251–253.

Hilgard, E. R. "A Neodissociation Interpretation of Pain Reduction in Hypnosis." *Psychological Review*, 1973, *80*, 396–411.

Hilgard, E. R. *Divided Consciousness: Multiple Controls in Human Thought and Action*. New York: Wiley, 1977.

Hunsberger, B. E. "Religious Denomination, Education, and University Students' Reported Agreement with Parents' Religious Beliefs." Unpublished doctoral dissertation, University of Manitoba, 1973.

Hyman, H. H., and Sheatsley, P. B. "'The Authoritarian Personality': A Methodological Critique." In R. Christie and M. Jahoda (eds.), *Studies in the Scope and Method of "The Authoritarian Personality."* New York: Free Press, 1954.

Josephson, W. L. "Television Violence and Children's Aggression: Testing the Priming, Social Script, and Disinhibition Predictions." *Journal of Personality and Social Psychology*, 1987, *53*, 882–890.

Kleiman, D. "Influential Couple Scrutinize Books for 'Anti-Americanism.'" *New York Times*, July 14, 1981, pp. C1, C4.

Knutson, J. N. "Psychological Variables in Political Recruitment." Mimeo. Berkeley, Calif.: Wright Institute, 1974.

Kohlberg, L. "The Development of Children's Orientations Toward a Moral Order: I. Sequence in the Development of Moral Thought." *Vita Humana*, 1963, *6*, 11–33.

Kohlberg, L. "The Child as a Moral Philosopher." *Psychology Today*, Sept. 1968, pp. 24–30.

Kohn, P. M. "The Authoritarianism-Rebellion Scale: A Balanced F Scale with Left-Wing Reversals." *Sociometry*, 1972, *35*, 176–189.

Komorita, S. S. "Attitude Content, Intensity, and the Neutral

Point on a Likert Scale." *Journal of Social Psychology*, 1963, *61*, 327–334.

Komorita, S. S., and Graham, W. K. "Number of Scale Points and the Reliability of Scales. *Educational and Psychological Measurement*, 1965, *25*, 987–995.

Lee, R. E., and Warr, P. B. "The Development and Standardization of a Balanced F Scale." *Journal of General Psychology*, 1969, *81*, 109–129.

Levinson, D. J., and Sanford, N. "A Scale for the Measurement of Anti-Semitism." *Journal of Psychology*, 1944, *17*, 339–370.

Lieberman, S. "The Effects of Changes in Roles on the Attitudes of Role Occupants." *Human Relations*, 1956, *9*, 385–402.

Likert, R. "A Technique for the Measurement of Attitudes." *Archives of Psychology*, 1932, No. 140.

Lorenz, K. *On Aggression*. San Diego, Calif.: Harcourt Brace Jovanovich, 1966.

McGuire, W. J. "Inducing Resistance to Persuasion." In L. Berkowitz (ed.) *Advances in Experimental Social Psychology*, Vol. 1. Orlando, Fla.: Academic Press, 1964.

McKelvie, S. J. "Graphic Rating Scales—How Many Categories?" *British Journal of Psychology*, 1978, *69*, 185–202.

McMillan, D. L., and Austin, J. B. "Effect of Positive Feedback on Compliance Following Transgression." *Psychonomic Science*, 1971, *24*, 59–61.

Manchester, W. *The Glory and the Dream*. Boston: Little, Brown, 1974.

Martin, D. G., Hawryluk, G. A., Berish, C., and Dushenko, T. "Selective Forgetting of Aversive Memories Cued in the Right Hemisphere." *International Journal of Neuroscience*, 1984, *23*, 169–176.

Masters, J. R. "The Relationship Between Number of Response Categories and Reliability of Likert-Type Questionnaires." *Journal of Educational Measurement*, 1974, *11*, 49–53.

Milgram, S. *Obedience to Authority*. New York: Harper & Row, 1974.

Miller, A. G. *The Obedience Experiments: A Case Study of Controversy in Social Science*. New York: Praeger, 1986.

Morokoff, P. J. "Effects of Sex Guilt." *Journal of Personality and Social Psychology*, 1985, *49*, 177–187.

Myers, D. G. *Social Psychology*. New York: McGraw-Hill, 1983.

Newcomb, T. M. *The Acquaintance Process*. New York: Holt, Rinehart & Winston, 1961.

Newcomb, T. M. "The Persistence and Regression of Changed Attitudes." *Journal of Social Issues*, 1963, *19*, 3–14.

Osgood, C. E., and Stagner, R. "Ease of Individual Judgment-Processes in Relation to Polarization of Attitudes in the Culture." *Journal of Social Psychology*, 1941, *14*, 403–418.

Osgood, C. E., Suci, G. J., and Tannenbaum, P. H. *The Measurement of Meaning*. Urbana: University of Illinois Press, 1957.

Payne, R. *The Life and Death of Adolf Hitler*. New York: Praeger, 1973.

Pettigrew, T. F. "Personality and Sociocultural Factors in Intergroup Attitudes: A Cross-National Comparison." *Journal of Conflict Resolution*, 1958, *2*, 29–42.

Piaget, J. *The Moral Judgment of the Child*. New York: Free Press, 1965.

Ray, J. J. "Do Authoritarians Hold Authoritarian Attitudes?" *Human Relations*, 1976, *29*, 307–325.

Ray, J. J. "Half of All Authoritarians are Left Wing: A Reply to Eysenck and Stone." *Political Psychology*, 1983, *4*, 139–143.

Ray, J. J. "Defective Validity in the Altemeyer Authoritarianism Scale." *Journal of Social Psychology*, 1985, *125*, 271–272.

Regan, D. T., Williams, M., and Sparling, S. "Voluntary Expiation of Guilt: A Field Experiment." *Journal of Personality and Social Psychology*, 1972, *24*, 42–45.

Remmers, H. H., and Ewart, E. "Reliability of Multiple-Choice Measuring Instruments as a Function of the Spearman-Brown Prophecy Formula, III." *Journal of Educational Psychology*, 1941, *32*, 61–66.

Rokeach, M. *The Open and Closed Mind*. New York: Basic Books, 1960.

Sears, D. O. "Life Stage Effects upon Attitude Change, Especially Among the Elderly." Paper presented at the Workshop on the Elderly of the Future, Committee on Aging, National Research Council, May 3–5, 1979, Annapolis, Md.

Shaw, M. E., and Costanzo, P. R. *Theories of Social Psychology*. (2nd ed.) New York: McGraw-Hill, 1982.

Sherif, C. W., Sherif, M., and Nebergall, R. E. *Attitude and Attitude Change: The Social Judgment Approach*. Philadelphia: Saunders, 1965.

Sherif, M. *In Common Predicament: Social Psychology of Intergroup Conflict and Cooperation.* Boston: Houghton Mifflin, 1966.

Sherif, M., and Hovland, C. *Social Judgment*. New Haven, Conn.: Yale University Press, 1961.

Shils, E. A. "Authoritarianism: Right and Left." In R. Christie and M. Jahoda (eds.), *Studies in the Scope and Method of "The Authoritarian Personality."* New York: Free Press, 1954.

Shirer, W. L. *The Rise and Fall of the Third Reich*. New York: Simon & Schuster, 1960.

"The Sins of Billy James." *Time*, Feb. 16, 1976, p. 52.

Smith, M. B. "McCarthyism: A Personal Account." *Journal of Social Issues*, 1986, *42*, 71–79.

Snyder, C. R., Shenkel, R. J., and Lowery, C. R. "Acceptance of Personality Interpretations: The 'Barnum Effect' and Beyond." *Journal of Consulting and Clinical Psychology*, 1977, *45*, 104–114.

Statistical Package for the Social Sciences: SPSSX User's Guide. New York: McGraw-Hill, 1983.

Stone, W. F. "The Myth of Left-Wing Authoritarianism." *Political Psychology*, 1980, *2*, 3–19.

Thurstone, L. L., and Chave, E. J. *The Measurement of Attitude*. Chicago: University of Chicago Press, 1929.

Twain, M. "Corn-Pone Opinions." In *The Family Mark Twain*. New York: Harper, n.d. (Originally published 1900.)

Wilson, G. D. (ed.). *The Psychology of Conservatism*. Orlando, Fla.: Academic Press, 1973.

Wilson, G. D., and Patterson, J. R. "A New Measure of Conservatism." *British Journal of Social and Clinical Psychology*, 1968, *7*, 264–269.

Zillman, D., and Bryant, J. "Effect of Residual Excitation on the Emotional Response to Provocation and Delayed Aggressive Behavior." *Journal of Personality and Social Psychology*, 1974, *30*, 782–791.

Zwillenberg, D. F. "Predicting Biases in the Punishment of Criminals as a Function of Authoritarianism: The Effects of Severity of the Crime, Degree of Mitigating Circumstances, and Status of the Offender." Unpublished doctoral dissertation, Columbia University, 1983. (University Microfilms No. 8311876.)

Index

A

D

E

L

M

Q

R

S

T